THE WYN

THE
WYNNE DIARIES
1789-1820

PASSAGES
SELECTED AND EDITED BY
ANNE FREMANTLE

WITH AN INTRODUCTION BY
CHRISTOPHER HIBBETT

Oxford New York Toronto Melbourne
OXFORD UNIVERSITY PRESS
1982

Oxford University Press, Walton Street, Oxford OX2 6DP
London Glasgow New York Toronto
Delhi Bombay Calcutta Madras Karachi
Kuala Lumpur Singapore Hong Kong Tokyo
Nairobi Dar es Salaam Cape Town
Melbourne Auckland
and associate companies in
Beirut Berlin Ibadan Mexico City

The Wynne Diaries *first published in three volumes 1935, 1937, and 1940*
This selection first published 1952
First issued as an Oxford University Press paperback 1982

British Library Cataloguing in Publication Data
Wynne, Elizabeth
The Wynne diaries 1789–1820. – (Oxford paperbacks)
1. Wynne (Family) *2. Europe – Social life and customs 3. Europe – Description and travel*
4. Europe – History – 1789–1900
I. Title II. Fremantle, Anne
940.2'7'0924 D360.F72
ISBN 0-19-281304-8

Printed in Great Britain by
Richard Clay (The Chaucer Press) Ltd.
Bungay, Suffolk

CONTENTS

INTRODUCTION

One day in 1928, while staying at the Buckinghamshire home of the Fremantle family into which she was soon to marry, the editor of these diaries was shown the twenty-five volumes in which 'great grandmamma' Wynne had made a daily record of her eventful life. They were of 'all shapes and many sizes' from small brightly coloured paper-bound exercise books, whose pages were filled with the writing of a little girl's hand, to heavy red morocco volumes stamped with gold lettering in which the writing had become more mature, more confident and far less easily decipherable. The first exercise book began with the date 17 August 1789; it was headed 'Handleau, Stotzheim'; and was written in French. Later volumes, written in rather fractured, ill-spelled and badly punctuated English, with brief interpolations in French, Italian and German, were headed with the names of a variety of towns from Venice to Ratisbon, Treviso to Zurich and of various ships in His Majesty's Navy. Later other diaries came to light, a further sixteen volumes compiled by Elizabeth Wynne, usually known as Betsey, and some twenty volumes written by her younger sister, Eugenia. Passages from these voluminous diaries, supplemented by letters from Betsey's husband, were prepared for publication by Anne Fremantle in the early 1930s and were published in three volumes in 1935, 1937 and 1940, then, in a shortened version, in one volume in *The World's Classics* series in 1952. The pages that follow are those selected and edited by Mrs Fremantle for the abbreviated version.

Betsey and Eugenia began keeping their diaries on the same day in exercise books purchased for them by a member of their household, Monsieur Benincasa, who occasionally gave them lessons and was the lover of their aunt, Justiniana Wynne, Countess von Rosenberg. Betsey was then ten years old, Eugenia nine. It becomes immediately clear that their family is rich, well-connected and Roman Catholic. Their parents, though, are rather shadowy figures, particularly their mother, a French lady of nervous temperament and hypochondriac tendencies. Papa appears as a man of unpredictable moods, suffering from gout, piles and rheumatism, and much given to practical jokes such as the placing of a bat on the dancing-master's mirror. Richard Wynne was, in fact, a man of great charm as well as irresponsible behaviour. His mother was Venetian; his father, a gentleman of Welsh extraction, had owned property at Falkingham, Lincolnshire, which Richard had inherited and sold after the birth of his last child in 1786. With the proceeds of the sale he had left with his family for the Continent where with an enormous suite, which on occasions numbered almost twenty people, not to mention numerous horses and dogs, he moved about wherever fancy drew him, his wife and children following him, not always complaisantly. There were five children, all girls. Mary, the eldest, married an Italian count with whom she was to be very unhappy. After Betsey and Eugenia came Harriet, aged five when the diaries begin, then the baby whose name was Justina.

Their father does not seem to have been unduly concerned as to whether or not his children spoke or wrote good English; indeed, he and his wife evidently allowed them far more latitude in their behaviour than was usual for girls of their class and age in England. It was not unusual, for instance, for Betsey and Eugenia to go to balls where they remained until three o'clock in the morning. One of these balls was described by Betsey as 'the loveliest and maddest of balls' with 'mascarades, changing of sex, tumbling of women and men on the floor'. There was a great deal of drinking in the house, and frequently both men and women of the household and their servants got drunk, occasionally so much so that they could not stand up, a state of affairs which the girls usually regarded with tolerant amusement rather than distaste. 'Mary was dressed as a man', Betsey recorded of one of the evening entertainments which were a common feature of life at Stotzheim. 'Papa as a woman and Mons. Jaegle [the tutor] also as a woman. Charles [the groom] dressed up as a girl . . . I danced a minuet with the curé's nephew who is a very bad dancer. Mons. Granger [the dancing-master] danced one with Mons. Jaegle who took a toss, they amused us vastly. The kitchenmaid dressed up as a man. Odile [the cook] also dressed as a man. She has very fine legs. All these people stank terribly . . . they were . . . all a trifle tipsy.' Sometimes the girls encouraged visitors to the house to drink too much; and on one occasion a monk to whom they had acted as precociously liberal hostesses fell over on his way out. 'If you give to drink in order to make drunk,' the tutor wrote in the margin of the page in which this episode is recorded, 'you are very naughty.'

The girls, however, seem rarely to have been rebuked, and the days passed in never too demanding lessons, in games and parties, walks 'to ketch butterflies', visits to castles, singing and playing the harpsichord, catching bats and tormenting their father's ugly secretary, who annoyed Betsey with the kisses he planted upon her cheeks, by putting nettles in his bed. Hedgehogs were placed in Monsieur Jaegle's bed.

At the end of October 1789 the family left for Italy on one of those frequent peregrinations which Richard

Wynne's restlessness or the upheavals of the revolutionary wars were to impose upon them. And Betsey artlessly provides a telling evocation of the hazards and discomforts of eighteenth-century continental travel. Carriages break down; wheels fall off; favourite dogs are run over; badly paved streets of cobble stones cause Papa 'to suffer greatly and to swear'; 'frightful' inns kept by overcharging rogues are noted for their bad food and worse service; the groom loses his temper when an accident hurls him from the box into a ditch and he draws a knife on the postilions, who threaten him with theirs and would have killed him but for the intervention of his wife; negotiations for the renting of villas fall through 'which puts us all in a very bad humour'.

Both Betsey and Eugenia recount such events with far more verve than they can summon up for descriptions of the places through which they pass and the people who inhabit them. One feels that many of these descriptions are inserted out of a sense of duty: 'We parted today for Vicenza', writes Eugenia on 16 September 1790, and one can picture her yawning as she dutifully sets down the words, 'and at last we arrived in that town which gave birth to a very famous architect Palladium. We saw there several fine houses of his building and an Olympic theater wich is very fine . . . I went with an English lady wich is very ugly.' Betsey, too, is little interested in such things. She wishes, she says, on 12 October 1791, to give a small description of the Tyrolese, but when she has provided it nothing very remarkable has been observed. When Monsieur Jaegle makes them read an English book, *The Vicar of Wakefield*, she can find no more to say of it than that it is 'very pretty, interesting, well wrote and where there are some very good characters'. But once their interest and curiosity are aroused both girls are irresistible. We share their laughter when Monsieur Jaegle wants 'to show how brave he is when sliding on the ice' and finds it 'not strong enough to support a weight so tremendous'; we share, too, their excitement when, in Venice, a man 'comes down from the top of the Campinil on St. Marc on a rope and gieves a nosguay' to the Doge, as also we share their fascinated pity at the sight of a little female freak with two faces and two legs growing out of her breast. And we join in Betsey's revulsion when her father takes a box to watch the animal baiting at Padua, where she sees the head of a 'poor oxen' cut open 'very badly indeed' by dogs, and the dogs in turn killed by a bull. 'All this is very cruel', she decides; but it does not prevent her from enjoying a 'very good dinner' as soon as she gets home.

Betsey was nearly thirteen by then, already a very self-possesed young girl, bright and occasionally rather pert, witty and intelligent. She was also, in the opinion of the more susceptible, kinder and introspective Eugenia, obstinate and inclined to be quarrelsome. She was certainly increasingly tart and outspoken in her criticism of her parents' friends and acquaintances. When presented to the Grand Duchess of Tuscany she deems her 'quite stupid, the most insupportable creature in the world'; when introduced to the sister of one Mr Biadena, she describes her as 'rather ugly, has got rotted teeth and a large mouth what is horrid'. Mrs Bosso 'sings very bad, and in a very rediculous manner'; Mr Poar's cousin is 'monstrously ugly and seems to have very little wit'; Mlle Fouchemoulin sings 'horrid bad in a voice like a cat that one kills, and she pronounces french like a pig'; Italian puppet shows are 'very great nonsense' by which one could see 'the Stupid cruel and piggish amusements of the Italians'.

Events in the outside world do not yet have much influence upon the children's life or vision. The French Revolution is an eruption which is scarcely noticed. Mamma comes home with a story, which the French Ambassador has told her, of the mob making brocades from the skins of the people they massacre and of their tearing out the heart of a poor gentleman, and cutting it into bits which they sell off 'very dear'. Other stories, equally lurid and usually untrue, are overheard at table. But events in France seemed far away to both girls, unlikely to trouble the rest of Europe. Betsey watched a party of Jacobin emissaries on their way to Venice and she and her companions could not help laughing derisively at their 'foolish, poor, pale faces'.

Less than three years later, however, the 'duced French' were no longer a laughing matter. On 9 May 1796 Betsey recorded that their armies were making such progress 'that we fear to have their visit here [in Florence] and though this is a neutral country and we have nothing to fear it would be vastly disagreeable to find ourselves where those dirty creatures are'. The next week she learned that the French had defeated the Austrians, crossed the Po and taken Milan. They are 'masters of all Italy now', she writes, 'they may go wherever they please. Papa wants to leave this country and all is packing up, but where shall we go? To Venice we may meet the french of the road. He talks of going to Corsica to Spain etc.'. As the summer weeks passed he grew increasingly anxious and, to Betsey's annoyance, talked of returning to 'his beloved Germany', to take a country house there and lead a quiet life—'fine projects for him', his daughter comments sardonically, 'that cannot be a moment without any society. All this vexes me dreadfully . . . I cannot describe how sorry I am to quit Florence.'

But although everybody laughed at 'his being such a coward', Mr Wynne was determined to leave Italy; and, on the night of 23 June, he fled with his family to Leghorn to seek the protection of the English fleet. Betsey was 'very much tormented' by this hurried flight. She 'was not by far as frightened as the rest' and had 'not the least wish of going a sea voyage'. Once aboard the frigate, the *Inconstant*, however, she immediately changed her mind. It was 'a most beautiful ship . . . so fine so clean so comfortable'. The officers and crew were so civil that she was 'quite delighted' and regretted no more that she had been obliged to run away. She was entranced above all by the captain. He was not handsome, but there was something in his countenance and his 'fiery black eyes' that she found 'quite captivating'. He was 'good natured, kind, and amicable, gay and lively'. He pleased her more than any man she had yet seen. He was, in fact, to transform her life.

Thomas Fremantle, who now assumes so prominent a part in the diaries, was then thirty years old and had been in the Navy since the age of twelve. He had served in several different ships on the Jamaica station, and in 1791 had been promoted to the command of the sloop, the *Spitfire*. Soon after war had broken out in 1793 he had been promoted to be captain of the *Tartar* and had sailed for the Mediterranean where he had gained the regard and friendship of Nelson, seven years his senior. To gain Fremantle's regard was now the principal object of Betsey's life. She was thrilled when, waiting for an opportunity to put the family aboard a ship sailing for England, an urgent order obliged him to take them with him to Elba. So long as they could stay on board the *Inconstant* with 'this excellent man' she did not care what part of the world they went to. Yet, while he regarded her with affection, the passion she felt for him was not returned. When the time came for them to part he gave her a ring for her to keep until they met again, but he 'did not say much' to her. She had set her young heart on marriage but he had not: an imprudent match, he thought, 'would be his ruin and make him lose the fruits of eighteen years service and pain'. Indeed, it is clear from the laconic entries in his own journal that he did not think much about her when they were apart and that he continued to make love to other women as he had done before he met her. On seeing her once more after a prolonged absence he found himself 'amazingly attached' to her but he still could not make up his mind to marry her. 'I can't say', he concluded, 'I have on the whole behaved very well.'

During their separation Betsey was 'always tormented by the fear of never meeting him again' and dismayed by her father's refusal to permit the marriage unless Fremantle got 'a pretty good fortune' from prize money. In the meantime she was plagued by the attentions of his fellow-officers, particularly by Captain Foley, an 'old Gentleman' of thirty-nine, whose pursuit of her was encouraged by her parents.

We do not know how Betsey felt upon Fremantle's return, for her diary from the end of September 1796 until January 1797 was lost on board the *Inconstant*. But the entries in Eugenia's diary suggest that she cannot have been encouraged: 'One thing which I am sorry to discover in him is that he seems to be perfectly cool on a *certain point* and I believe that *indifference* has taken the place of what he felt *at first*.' A month later Fremantle 'is a riddle' to Eugenia. She 'cannot doubt but he is in love, all shows it, the most trifling incident a new proof of it, and yet he does not talk of marriage and if he does he contradicts himself the next moment'. But then on 11 January 1797 at Naples, on a cold morning when the top of Vesuvius was covered with snow, Eugenia's diary contains the entry which makes her smile with pleasure at Betsey's happiness, then cry at her own distress in having to say goodbye to her: 'Fremantle was here both in the morning and evening, he spoke to Papa who behaved very handsomely in granting him my sister and 8000 pounds.'

The wedding was held at the house of Lady Hamilton, Nelson's 'dolly' as Fremantle described her. He did not like her and thought Nelson made 'himself ridiculous' with the woman. Betsey agreed that the affair was ridiculous for 'a man at his age and such a cripple', but she was fond of Lady Hamilton, 'a charming woman, beautiful and exceedingly good humoured and amiable'.

Although she was only eighteen years old at the time of her marriage, Betsey was now expected to behave and largely succeeded in behaving—as a mature woman. She sailed with her husband aboard his ship and was deeply distressed to hear distinctly from her cabin his men's cries for mercy as they were flogged for drunkenness; she was still aboard when the disastrous attack was made on the port of Santa Cruz in which Nelson lost his right arm and Fremantle was so badly wounded in his that he never fully recovered his health; she nursed them both in the *Seahorse* on their way back to England, the ship being 'worse than a hospital' with men groaning in agony throughout the night, Nelson fretful and 'a very bad patient', her husband 'very unwell' and in constant pain, she herself sick in the mornings as the *Seahorse* rolled in the heavy seas.

She arrived home on 3 September 1797 at Portsmouth, her first sight of England in almost ten years; and from then on she settled down to a country life at

Swanbourne in Buckinghamshire which she recorded as faithfully as she had done her continental journeys. We are given fascinating accounts of house parties and garden fêtes, of visits to London, to the opera and to her husband's grand patrons, the Buckinghams at Stowe. We catch glimpses of the Prince of Wales drinking six glasses of cherry brandy at luncheon with a bottle of mulled port, of Lord Lowther in misery at the death of his friend, Pitt, whose 'Stomach was quite destroyed from great application to business and the quantity of cordials he had taken to keep off the gout', of Louis XVIII, on a visit to Stowe, eating immense meals with apparently limitless appetite. We are invited to share Betsey's exasperation at her servants who are 'great torments' and her pride when her husband gives her an account of the victory at Trafalgar in which he distinguished himself in command of the *Neptune*.

Eugenia's diary takes us to Scotland where, after a tempestuous love affair, she was married to Robert Campbell, one of whose tenants on being introduced to her remarked to the laird that she might be good but that she was 'very wee'.

With the help of Lord Buckingham, Fremantle's career prospered. He was brought into Parliament and appointed a Lord of the Admiralty, though not without some heart-searching by his patron's family who knew that, efficient as he was at sea, his essential laziness might impair his proper conduct of the office. Betsey voiced no such doubts. She was as proud of him as ever. She bore him ten children, 'the brattery' she called them, and was proud, too, that they promised to do as well in life as their father. In most cases the promise was fulfiled: the eldest son became the first Lord Cottesloe, another Admiral Sir Charles Howe Fremantle. Their father died at Naples in 1819 as commander-in-chief in the Mediterranean. Their mother was overwhelmed with grief, and for the first time since she had begun it thirty years before felt unable to make the daily record in her diary. But, on New Year's Day 1820 she forced herself to take up her pen again and wrote the last of her published entries.

The diary continued, however, throughout the reign of George IV which began that year, throughout that of his brother, William IV, and well into the reign of their niece, Victoria. When Lady Fremantle died in 1857 in her eightieth year she could claim to be not only one of the most conscientious but also one of the most amusing 'and illuminating' diarists of her age.

CHRISTOPHER HIBBERT

THESE JOURNALS

OF

ELIZABETH FREMANTLE

NÉE WYNNE

HAVE BEEN EDITED FOR

JOHN TAPLING FREMANTLE

AND

ADAM FREMANTLE

HER

GREAT GREAT GREAT

GRANDSONS

PREFACE

MY first introduction to the journals of Elizabeth Wynne was early in 1928 when, just eighteen and newly engaged, I went to stay for the first time at Swanbourne, in Buckinghamshire, with my future in-laws. There one evening Christopher Fremantle (who married me in 1930) took out of an old chest full of manuscripts the first volumes of what was known in the family as 'great grandmamma's Diary'. There were twenty-five volumes of all shapes and many sizes, varying from small gay paper-bound exercise books written in a very childish hand, and illustrated by the author, to pompous red morocco and gold-lettered tomes filled with almost indecipherable and very domineering Mid-Victorian script.

The first volume was dated 1789; the last 1857. The first two were written in French as well as extracts in many of the later ones; extracts there were too in German, Italian, and in a 'disguised' hand used by the diarist only for writing secrets.

Such was my first meeting with Elizabeth Wynne and her Journal. At first it was difficult to discover further. No one remembered her, and from the family I could find out very little about her. No one had ever read all through the journals and although certain phrases such as 'papa came home drunk by my advice' and 'the rascally Neapolitans always make papa a fool' had passed into family parlance, yet no one could tell me who the Wynnes were or why Elizabeth left so voluminous a diary, and in so many languages. Some information there was, however, and some clues. Elizabeth was the wife, I learnt, of the first Admiral Fremantle, and Burke gave her father as 'Richard Wynne Esquire'. At Swanbourne there were miniatures of her, of her father, her mother, her sisters, and a mysterious, and strangely plain, Countess of Rosenberg. There were 'Aunt Emmy's Memoirs', a charming handful of typescript reminiscences acquired by my father-in-law from his great-aunt, Elizabeth's granddaughter. There was a pair of bellows given to Lady Fremantle, *née* Wynne, by Nelson's Lady Hamilton; various medals and orders of her husband's, exercise books of her children, numberless letters from her husband, and above all, the house itself, her house, small, and, as she would have called it, 'snug': still exactly like the drawing she made of it on the first page of the tenth volume of her diary.

Then in 1929 I went to Glasgow to stay with the Hon. Mrs. Campbell, widow of the sometime Bishop of Glasgow and Galloway. She had married a descendant of Eugenia's (Elizabeth's younger sister, who in 1806 married Robert Campbell), and had in her possession some twenty volumes of Eugenia's diary, the earliest covering the same period as Elizabeth's and relating to the same episodes (as for example from the years 1789 to 1795, when the two small sisters grew up together), others describing later and very different scenes and life: the Court at Naples under 'Il Re Lazarone'; the London 'Routs'; and the Highlands and Islands of Scotland in the early nineteenth century: but all as vividly and with as much intimate and original detail as in Elizabeth's own diary.

In the same year Bruno Brunelli's *Casanova Loved Her* was published in an English translation. The heroine, Giustiniana Wynne, proved to be none other than the mysterious Countess of Rosenberg, and 'Riccardo', credited by Brunelli with a baronetcy which he never claimed, and to which indeed he had no pretensions, was Elizabeth's own father. A cousin of my husband's, Sir Francis Fremantle, by a curious coincidence the present owner of Bedwell Park, Hertfordshire, which was one of Richard Wynne's estates, wrote to me soon after the publication of Brunelli's book, giving texts of the Wynne memorials in the Essendon Church, and of the Bedwell title-deeds.

In 1933 my father-in-law discovered sixteen more volumes of Elizabeth Wynne's diary which had been lost in the general family upheaval on the death of the second Lord Cottesloe in 1918. The continuity of the now reassembled forty-one volumes is unbroken, except for a part of 1796 when one slim exercise book was lost by the diarist on board the *Inconstant* (she notes the loss herself and it is to be wondered whether it was entirely accidental!). Elizabeth—or Betsy, Betzi, or Betsey, as she always called herself and was called by her contemporaries—was ten and Eugenia nine when the little sisters sent M. Benincasa to buy the books for the diary, as is recorded in their first entry. But while Betsey never failed, from August 17th 1789, until she lay dying in the last days of March 1857, daily to confide to her journal, her sister, from ill health, laziness, or 'being too much occupied' left numerous lacunae often of months and sometimes of years, and cannot be relied upon to carry on a continuous narrative for very long.

[I have made no attempt to correct misdated entries, or to correlate spellings.]

1935 A. F.

PUBLISHER'S NOTE

While selecting passages from the Wynne Diaries for the 1952 edition Anne Fremantle took the opportunity to add Fremantle's own brief account of his engagement and marriage to Betsey (see pp. 251–61).

TABLE I. WYNNES OF GWYDIR

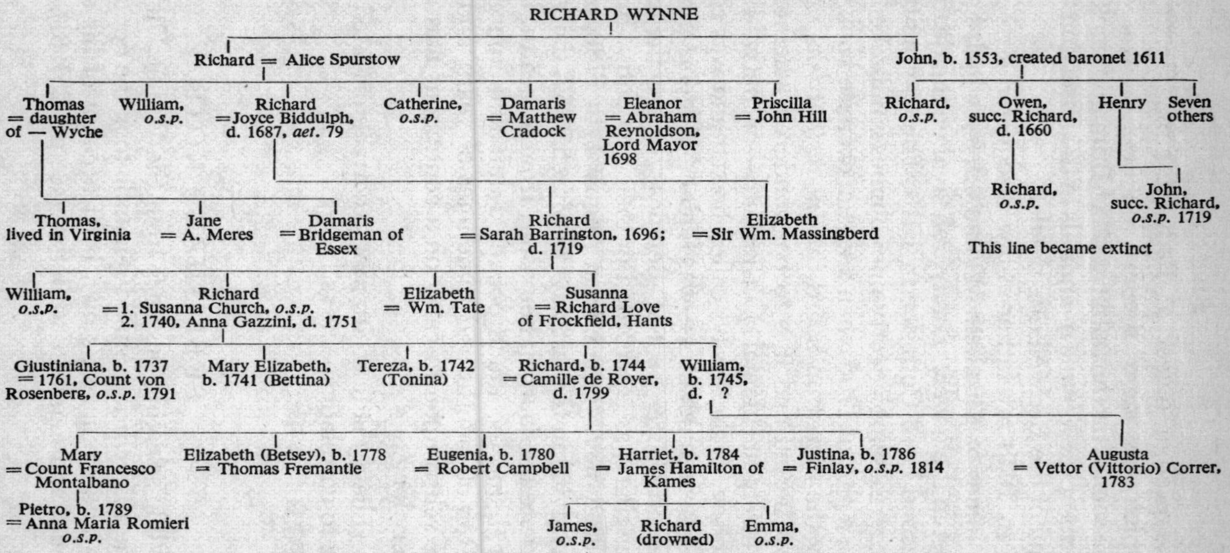

TABLE II

CORRER FAMILY

GIACOMO CORRER

- Theodoro Maria, founder of Corror Museum, d. 1830
- Vettor (Vittorio) = Maria Augusta Wynne 1783, b. June 23, 1753
  - Giacomo = Maria Baldassare
    - 2 daughters

TABLE III

MONTALBANO FAMILY

PIETRO, CONTE MONTALBANO

- Ernesto
  - Francesco
    - Riccardo
- Francesco = Mary Wynne, 1789
  - Pietro = Anna Maria Romieri, June 3, 1818, *o.s.p.*, b. Oct. 15, 1789
- Silvestro

PRINCIPAL PERSONS IN THE DIARIES

WHO WERE MEMBERS OF THE WYNNES' ESTABLISHMENT

RICCARDO GULIELMO CASPARO MELCHIOR BALTHAZARO WYNNE, ESQ. (otherwise Richard Wynne): the diarist's father.

AGATHE CAMILLE DE ROYER: the diarist's mother, wife of Richard.

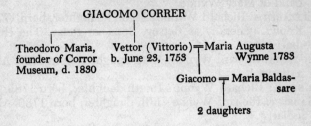

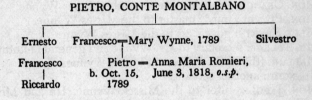

PRINCIPAL PERSONS

MARY (generally called 'Mary my sister' or 'Mary Montalbano'), born 1771: Richard's eldest daughter who married in 1789.

FRANCESCO MONTALBANO, generally known as 'Mont': husband of Mary Wynne.

ELIZABETH: Richard Wynne's second daughter, born 1779. Known generally as Betsey, Betzi, or Betsy. The chief diarist.

EUGENIA: Richard Wynne's third daughter, born 1780. Also a diarist.

JUSTINA: Richard Wynne's fourth daughter, born 1785.

HARRIET: Richard Wynne's fifth daughter, born 1786. Also a diarist.

COUNTESS VON ROSENBERG: Justiniana, born 1737, sister of Richard Wynne. Married in 1761 Count von Rosenberg. Known as 'the Countess' or 'my aunt'.

BENINCASA: ex-Jesuit. Sometimes given the title of 'Count'. Countess von Rosenberg's last and most faithful lover.

MON. FRIES: tutor to Elizabeth and Eugenia Wynne.

MON. GRANGER: dancing master to the Misses Wynne.

MON. PLEYEL: music master to the Misses Wynne.

MLLE EBERTS: governess to the Misses Wynne.

MR. BULLER: secretary to Mr. Wynne and general factotum.

MARIANE (the wicked): servant to the Wynnes.

BLANCHE: another servant.

MON. JAEGLE: tutor to the Misses Wynne. He and Mon. Fries seem to have done duty alternately.

MLLE CATICHE, MLLE ADELAIDE, ALEXANDRE: children to Granger.

CHAPPUI: music master, a French refugee.

MARY EDMONDS: nurse to the 'little sisters' Harriet and Justina.

FRANCIS: footman to the Wynnes.

CHARLES: groom to the Wynnes.

MON. BARTOLOZZI: drawing master to the Misses Wynne.

MON. CIMADOR: music tutor to the Misses Wynne.

GEORGE: groom.

ODYLLE: cook.

CHAPTER 1

AUGUST 17TH, 1789. HANDLEAU, STOTZHEIM. MONDAY.

Betsey: 'We danced, and after that Mons. Scotty, Mons. Fries and Mons. Grangé went as far as Strasburg my sister and I went with them to Benfelt, where there was a big fair. After dinner Papa and Mama went to the Marclesys'. Mons. Pleyel came to the house, I began to accompany him, but it did not go well, so that we played a few Sonatas.'

Eugenia notes that just as she was about to begin an interesting book, the noise made by her little sisters prevented her from enjoying it. She adds, in a flowery-margined note, 'Mon cher journal, je t'ai barbouillé, me le pardonnes tu? Dis oui, je te pardonnes.' Then, in a further marginal note, is 'J'ai neuf ans'.

AUGUST 18TH TUESDAY. STOTZHEIM. My aunt went with my two little sisters to meet Mons. Benincasa at Benfelt. He brought me ['us' scratched out] the book for the ['our' deleted] diary which I ['we' erased] began as Monday's journal describes. Mademoiselle Eberts gave us our dictation as Mons. Fries is away for a few days. After dinner Mama went to Bar to do a little shopping and paid a visit to the Curé of Berkheim. Whilst she was out I practised the harpsichord. The Baroness de Vrintz came with Mrs. Kinn and they drank tea. My aunt played cards with the Curé from three o'clock until after supper without ever getting up. [In the margin, in English, writ large, is 'What I should stay'.]

Eugenia says the Baroness was amiable, but Madame Kinns an ass. She added that 'Mr. Buller gave me great pleasure, he kissed me tenderly', but then modestly scratched it through.

August 19th Wednesday. Mons. Benincasa went with the Curé of Stotzheim to dine with the Curé of Berkheim. My aunt, my sister and I we went to fetch them. We found there a Capucin, brother to the Curé of Berkheim, just back from Rome. I asked him for a rosary and he gave me a very pretty one from the holy house of Loretto which had touched the Holy Stoop. The Curé of Berkheim's house is very pretty. There is in it a sofa and net curtains which he himself has made. We went to take a short walk in the village but there was nothing pretty in it so we retraced our steps. Coming back home we stopped at Madame de Vrintz's house, where we found Madame Künne, Mons. le Curé of Stotzheim stayed there and we came quietly home. Papa had been to the Marclesy and he said she was very ill and that the poor blind creature had tears in her eyes.

Eugenia commends the 'industrious Curé of Berkheim' and also his 'superb bed and fine library'.

20. Stotzheim. August. Thursday. Mons. Benincasa dressed up as a woman, and my aunt as a man. I came downstairs without recognising them [in the margin, a grown-up hand has written 'et je ne les ai pas reconnus']. But at last Mons. Benincasa made such an absurd curtsey that I knew him and my aunt also from her voice. After dinner Mde. Marclesy wished for company, everyone from the castle went except my sister and I. In the evening I practised accompaniments with Mons. Pleyel.

Eugenia is not kind about Mde. Marclesy: 'she sent for mama to come and sit with her, as she has had a terrible night, but when the doctor came he said it was nothing but an indigestion.'

21. Friday. This morning a terrible accident occurred. A poor boy who had gone to pick wild apples in

the wood, a peasant mistook him for a deer, and, as the shooting season is now open, shot him with his gun. Hardly had he seen what he had done when he was terrified and fled. After dinner Mademoiselle Vandœuvre and the Baron and Baroness de Vrintz came to drink tea. The doctor, Mr. la Chose, came from Strasburg, a very intelligent man. The Curé came to play cards with my aunt and told us that everything had been settled about the little boy that had been killed.

Eugenia gives a more detailed description of the accident. 'A peasant here that was gone hunting, heard a rustling in the bushes, and, thinking it was a deer, took aim. When the hunter came to gather up his quarry, alas!, what a horrid spectacle! A child lay stretched before him, with two bullets in his temples, two in his cheeks and one in his throat. The miserable peasant, overcome with remorse, fled from the scene. The Baron de Vrintz came for to drink tea and spoke with great fervour of the oath of fidelity made by the French troops to their King. For my part this did not make the slightest impression on me.'

[Fries, and the two Grangers, father and son, returned from Strasburg on the 22nd. On Sunday, the 23rd, after Mass, *Eugenia* writes: 'the de Vrintz's came and four canonesses from Handleau. We danced for them and were much applauded, "mais ce n'était que des flatteries".']

SEPTEMBER 1ST 1789. [Still the painfully correct writing and sentiments.] To-day there was an arithmetic session with Mons. Benincasa, that was a trifle muddled. After dinner the whole Marclesy family, as well as a sister of his, an old maid, the Vrints, Kien, and the Curé, etc. A long piquet innings, and also at the harpsichord. It was said that I distinguished myself. In our family providence has more to do than elsewhere, as it alone is responsible for the future.

SEPTEMBER 2ND. STOTZHEIM. The morning was fine, but we paid for it heavily after dinner. All my relations went to the Marclesy. I was made to study accompaniments at the harpsichord. After supper mama retired to bed with a terrible attack of convulsions accompanied by colics. The doctor from Obernheim was sent for. He arrived when the indisposition was over—a thing which often happens in the country. I was wakened by her cries, but I had neither the heart nor the courage to get up.

Eugenia adds that she had the good fortune not to be woken by her mother's screams.

6TH SEPTEMBER. SUNDAY. Mass, and funeral, at church, of the village midwife. All the women were in tears, for the deceased had been very useful to them. Mama is still very ill. The trunks of the housemaid (the wicked Mariane) have been sent for from Strasburg which delighted everyone. We played at *mouche* with Grangé father and son, and at Lotto with the above named and the Lieutenant of Mons. Fries, because the weather was so bad that we could not go out.

[On the 7th, a Monday, *Eugenia* has 'mama to our great pleasure got up to-day out of her bed, but she made herself very furious sending Mariane away. Mariane cried a great deal, but too late; Blanche also cried from friendship for her. Mary also, but she does not know why, everyone else laughs. How wicked we are! May God pardon us!']

SEPTEMBER 8TH. TUESDAY. After we had missed Mass we went with our Aunt and the Pleyels to meet Benincasa who was accompanied by Chappuis. An unexpected gathering at dinner: the Massenets,

Vogt. A noisy table, and varied expressions on the faces of the diners. Mademoiselle Eberts seemed annoyed by the trick papa played her in dirtying her dog over whose toilet she has taken great trouble. The court of Andlau came in semi-gala. That is to say, the Princess and three ladies. As a result, we were given plenty to do, but were rewarded by the pleasure we gave. We were gone to bed, when all of a sudden there was a musketry discharge, and shouts of joy in the court-yard startled us, and made us leap out of our beds. We found the whole house in the drawing room, servants and masters, Grangé masked as a gardener. Then followed the loveliest and maddest of balls, mascarades, changing of sex, tumbling of women and men on to the floor—in short, we stayed up, all of us, still dancing, until after midnight.

24TH, THURSDAY. There was a grand dinner party at the Princess of Andlau's. All of our company were at it, and the Vrints and Mde. Marclesy also. My aunt as she went in fell down flat (the fault of the floor which was slippery). All the ladies were very agreeable, there are only two that are tolerably pretty. After dinner we were shewn the church and the cellar, there is a cask that holds thirteen hundred measures of wine. The church is not bad. Papa played a trick upon Mr. Granger, he put a bat upon his mirror.

Eugenia says: 'the canonesses were very kind and did their utmost to amuse us'.

On the 25th she notes: 'O wonder! My aunt went on foot with Benincasa as far as the Baroness de Vrintz.'

SATURDAY, 26TH. Mons. Granger and Mons. Fries came back from Strasbourg. The latter's breast is now better, but he is still not well enough to stay with us: he brought us the answer to our letter. After dinner Mons. and Mde. Kuën and the Curé of Stotzheim came, there was the usual meeting of the States General, our game of *mouche* with Mons. Granger and Mons. Jaegle, papa played Trictrac with Mons. Benincasa. The weather begins again to be fine. All the better for our walks. Mde. Chappui laid in yesterday evening of a little daughter at Strasbourg.

Eugenia says: 'the States General played their customary game and played the whole evening, yet the vicious creatures complained they had hardly played at all'.

STOTZHEIM, SUNDAY, 27TH SEPTEMBER. Mass. My aunt and Mons. Benincasa paid a visit to the Marclesy's. Preparations for this evening's masquerade. Mons. and Mde. Masnet came to dinner: after, there was a big ball: all the peasants were at it. It began at 4 o'clock. I will now tell about the masquerade. We dressed Granger as a woman, Eugenia as a Turk, Mary as a shepherdess. The little groom, Charles, became a nobleman, Francois carried a lantern to light him his way, and the gardener walked behind him as his servant: he was not recognised, although he wore no mask. The other groom, Robert, had a horse cloth on, the coachman was a chef and I a pierrot. The Vrints were there. I was also dressed as a peasant. We kept many peasants and their womenfolk to supper. Mons. le Curé and his nephew came to supper. After we danced, Mary was dressed as a man, papa as a woman and Ms. Jaegle also as a woman. Charles dressed up as a girl. Everyone danced in their disguises until eleven o'clock. I danced a minuet with the Curé's nephew who is a very bad dancer. Mons. Granger danced one with Mons. Jaegle who took a toss, they amused us vastly. The kitchenmaid dressed up as a man.

Odile also dressed up as a man. She has very fine legs. All these people stank terribly, they had drunk a measure of wine and were all a trifle tipsy.

OCTOBER 2ND. A great day's shooting. Mons. Kuën, the Curé, Mons. Benincasa, papa and several huntsmen. Two buck were killed. The coachman broke a vessel containing six bottles through wishing to carry it on his shoulder stuck into his knapsack. He atoned his fault however, by the good omelettes he made for the hunters. On our return a sit-down supper.

SUNDAY, OCTOBER 4TH. We arrived too early at Mass, so mama and my aunt went and paid a visit to the Curé and left us in church with little Adelaïde. Mde. Massenet and her husband came here for this evening's ball which was vastly pretty. After dinner we went into the garden with Alexander, who made a head out of a pumpkin, after that the musicians came and the peasants were set to dance in the courtyard. On a sudden Eugenia comes down masqued—half as a genii, half as a negro, so I went and masqued myself too. I was dressed as a shepherdess, the Baroness de Vrintz, Mrs. Kuën and another lady came when I went downstairs. Mons. Kuën danced with me. Mde. Massenet was dressed as a peasant, Mons. Granger was masqued I don't know quite as what. A little later several of the canonesses of Andlau came, they wished to see us dance and we danced the Court minuet, and the Cosacke. After I dressed myself again in my clothes, and we danced till 8 o'clock. I forgot to say that before supper papa dressed as a pierrot with M. Granger. Papa supped in his travesti. After supper we put a wig on the marrow and a candle inside. Mary and I dressed ourselves as Sultan and Sultana, and we amused ourselves greatly until eleven o'clock. Mde. de Vrints stayed with us all the time.

Eugenia's contribution is in verse:

Comment j'ai passé toute ma journée
À faire des poèmes
Oui, c'etait ma chême
Sur M. de Saint Martin
Et sur sa main
Oui, je le fis et nous allâmes chez Mde de Crock
J'achetois un cordon de montre sans barlocks
J'achetois des gants
Et des eventails pour des presents
Nous goutâmes chez Granger
Notre bon maitre à danser
Nous jouâmes au lotto
Et la petite Lily chanta toto
À notre retour au logis
Petit souper sans soucis
M. Martin y assista
Ce qui fort nous amusa.

FRIDAY 9TH. I went walking with Mademoiselle Eberts and my sister. We went to Mons. De Billard who has been in bed for six weeks in Made. de Saint Felix's house and Mons. Fries who has had a second operation to his breast. We danced this morning. Mons. de Vrints to dinner. After dinner we saw the horses exercising in the royal stables which entertained us greatly. We had supper with Granger. Mons. Buller came he went to pay a visit to my aunt but she would not receive him he sent her two bottles of Porter.

SUNDAY, 18TH. Burial at Mass of a shoemaker. The Curé's nephew said mass and took the funeral. It is lovely weather. The Vrints, the Kuëns and Mons. le Curé and his nephew came to see us also M. Kinser. I played a trick on Buller. [*Eugenia* was very outraged because the Curé asked her 'if she were frightened at Mass because of the dead person in church': 'I must admit this question shocked me as I do not like to be thought a coward.']

MONDAY 19TH. I forgot to say yesterday in my journal that the Massenets came here to sleep. Mons. Granger left to-day for Strasburg with his wife and Lyly. Papa went shooting with Mons. Kuën Mons. le Curé and his nephew they killed two bucks all the guns supped with us. Mr. Buller did not suffer much from the nettles we put in his bed.

Eugenia says: 'Mon. Jaegle went to Baar to buy nuts. The tailor brought us our Greek dresses which are very well made only the bodices are an ugly black which makes them look like peasants clothes.'

MONDAY 26TH. I forgot to say yesterday that the grooms, coachman, horses and dogs were gone to Italy which makes me certain that we shall go also. Mons. Granger, the Baron de Vrints, the Curé's nephew who I have already explained was the Curé of Molzheim, and Alexander all went to Strasburg. The Baron de Vrints came to play tric-trac with the wicked Buller who has done nothing at all since he came but torment us. He is only going to Strasbourg on Friday with us. The doctor dined with us. The Massenets left in the afternoon.

TUESDAY. Mons. and Mde. Marclesy came and dined together with Mde. Vendœuvre after the meal I played a sonata of Kozeluch on the little harpsichord. Papa saw the ladies home and played Dame Trou with Mad. Vendœuvre he came home at 8 o'clock. Whilst he was out I played a game of Trictrac with Buller who after that teased me until supper time I did a lot of ironing.

[On Wednesday the 28th *Eugenia* finds Buller intolerable. 'Papa dined with the Marclesy's so we had a solitary meal with Mama and Buller. After being much tormented by the ugly Buller and after having received many of his importunate kisses I had supper and went to bed. I wrote a letter four times and was never successful, because I write like a pig.' *Betsey's* only record is that they confessed to a Capuchin who came on purpose from Stotzheim.]

FRIDAY, OCTOBER 30TH. We left Stotzheim at 8 o'clock for Strasburg with Papa, Mary who was sick in the carriage, Buller and Harriet, who was very good. George brought Juno a bitch that is in pup and a little dog. At the Hotel de Lyon where we are lodging we found Mon. Eberts and Andrew who were waiting for us to go and dine with Made. Eberts.

Eugenia adds: 'After dinner we played a hand of Wisk. Then we went to the comedy they gave *Merope* a superb tragedy by Mr. Voltaire and a little comic piece in one act, *Les Fausses Consultations.*'

SATURDAY OCTOBER 31ST. Papa has rheumatism in his left arm which prevents him from getting up and going to breakfast with Buller, so that I went with Mary, Eugenia and Justina. On our way we stopped at the house of a hump-backed old cook we had last winter they gave us some cakes then we went to Buller who gave us a very good breakfast. There were Mons. Granger and Mon. Chappuis Mon. Buller and Mon. Chappuis came with us to Mr. Fries who is much better we saw there Mr. Jaegle who is no longer bonneted as a priest but like a Nobleman with a pigtail this headdress does not become him well. Mon. Fries gave me two little volumes of La Fontaine's *Fables* and to Eugenia two little books that I did not see excellent dinner at the end at the comedy they gave *Fellomar* or the continuation of *Tom Jones* this piece is very pretty they gave also the *mariage of Antonio* very pretty opera the music by Gretris. At home Mad.

Eberts supped with us with her father and M. Buller papa is better. [*Eugenia* says the little books were a *Recueil de Poesies Choisies.*]

MONDAY NOVEMBER 2ND 1789. We left Strasbourg at 8 o'clock before leaving we saw Chappui, Buller, Madame Eberts and her father, they were all very sorry to see us go. We passed Kehl, Bishoffsheim, Stotzofen, and Rastadt, where we slept it is a very pretty town. Papa endured the journey fairly well, but he suffered greatly from the jolting for the roads at present are very bad. Mary is very ill from her teeth. We went with Mons. Jaegle to see the castle the ancient residence of the Molgraffe of Bahd it is a very fine palace with all sorts of antiques in it especially Turkish Costumes. A very bad supper at the Inn which we awaited with great impatience—and it wasn't good.

TUESDAY 3RD.

Eugenia says: 'We were obliged to stay all day in Rastadt on account of Juno, Papa's excellent sporting dog, which whelped today. She had a litter of puppies, all bastards and George says he will throw them "zur la l'eau". Papa put a *vissigatoir* on his arm and Mary had such bad tootheak that she went to bed.'

Eugenia has for November 4th Wednesday: 'We left Rastadt at 8 o'clock and went through Ettlingen and Durlach where we were obliged to stop as there were no post horses to go on further we sent for some peasants' horses and when waiting ate a good soup. After waiting for 3 hours we got 4 horses but there were so many mountains that we only got to Pfortzheim at 7 o'clock. It seems a pretty little town and has a steel and ivory manufacture. We heard that Marianne passed here and also our horses, dogs, postillions and grooms and that all are well.'

Saturday 7. We bought some more things from the women. Papa was able to get up and we left at last at half past ten. The roads were very bad which caused papa to suffer greatly. Ulm is a badly paved Imperial city [*Eugenia* says 'whose cobbles caused Papa to suffer greatly and to swear'] the Danube flows through it. We lodged at the Black Bull. A good enough supper but they are very slow. Papa feels very unwell and will stay here three or four days.

Sunday 8th. No mass there is but one Catholic church. Took a lesson with mons. Jaegle. After dinner to Vespers with the cook, little Justina and Andrés. The church is pretty. We went up the belfry with Mon. Jaegle there is a stone balustrade there is always a watcher to see if there is a fire in the town he puts up a lantern on the side where there is the fire. One has to go up 340 steps which fatigued us greatly. We were told that Maximilien 1st father of Charles V dared to stand on the Balustrade with one leg in the air and made several pirouettes. Justina went to bed without any supper because she gave the cook such a smack that for two hours she could not open her eye. I slept with mama. Papa has a fever this evening. A geography lesson with Mons. Jaegle. [*Eugenia* says they went to meet M. Jaegle at the Lutheran Cathedral where they saw such funny costumes they almost laughed.]

Monday 9th November. Ulm. We were told that yesterday evening at the inn two officers wished to fight but Odile put herself between them and separated them. They were frightened of one another. Papa's rheumatism is much better which gave us great pleasure. A little walk in the afternoon with Mons. Jaegle we went into a bookshop where there were several German, French and English books. Eugenia went to bed with a heavy cold and a slight fever. Odile slept with her husband.

10TH TUESDAY. Eugenia stayed in bed all day and we had the pleasure of seeing papa out of his bed and dining at table. After the meal I went walking with Harriet, Justina, the cook and Andrés we saw several big ships which are being built to send to Vienna with corn (oats) for the Emperor's troops they are sold there it being too expensive to bring them back. A lesson with Mons. Jaegle.

[On the 11th both invalids are better.]

12TH THURSDAY. Spent the day rather sadly preparing to set off on our journey to-morrow. I went with Jaegle to do a little shopping and we heard there was a concert. We asked papa's permission to go to it which he accorded us. It was really quite passable they played a Sonata not badly.

13TH FRIDAY. We left Ulm and passed Gruisberg, Zusmershausen and Augsburg we arrived at the latter as night was falling and stayed at the Three Moons, a good inn. We had wretched weather and poor Juno fell from the box under the carriage which passed over her belly which made papa very cross which is a sad change as he had been very gay all the journey. A very bad supper.

Eugenia is more explicit about the sad accident: 'As we were going quietly along, suddenly we heard cries and barking from the dogs. Mama looked out of the window. What a spectacle for Papa! His best bitch, Juno, stretched out in the middle of the road. The wheels had gone over her belly. She fell out having bitten through her chain. George nursed her tenderly, but her life is despaired of.'

SATURDAY 14TH. We had to pay heavily for last night's bad supper. Mons. Emmerich paid us a visit. Went with mama to buy crockery and changed our money.

We only left at noon and passed but Schwabmünchen where we waited two hours for horses at last we arrived at Buchloe a very ugly place but to make up for it we had a very good supper and excellent beds. Juno wags her tail a little but cannot stand upright. [*Eugenia* says she was bled by Georges and is a little better.]

15TH SUNDAY. We came well and the three posts Kaufbeuem, Stetten and Fuessen, unfortunately something broke in the wheel which prevented us going further. Now we are beginning to get into the Tyrol already one sees the mountains covered with snow, and the waterfalls make themselves heard. This inn seems very bad. What pleases me is that Papa suffers much less from his rheumatism.

Eugenia says that before they started 'mama bought a coffee set in silver, for 26 louis, and also a sugar basin, a teapot and candlestick, a milk jug and a lamp all in the same metal.'

[On the 16th they arrive at Reiti, where they dine, and Parwis, where they sleep. *Eugenia* is very poetical: 'The lovely view one enjoys seeing there beautiful mountains whose frowning crests all silvered are lifted audaciously towards the skies. In spite of the snow the pine forests of everlasting green offer a smiling landscape to our eyes. We are certain the Postillion that brought us is not German, because he is witty and conducted us well.']

TUESDAY 17TH. Again we started at half past five. The post from Parwis to Dirchenbach is very long. From here we passed Innsbruck. The wicked Marianne stopped the old carriage after we were gone as she was afraid to show herself before Mama and Papa. She talked a lot to Mary. We arrived at Brenner only at 8 o'clock the rooms had already been warmed for us. It is very cold just now. The Brenner is the highest mountain in the Tyrol.

Eugenia says: 'The wicked Marianne . . . was weeping her tears were certainly hippocritical she told Mary my aunt had obtained a place for her for my part I am sorry for it' but adds in the margin, in 1792, 'I say that it is proof of a very bad heart to be sorry that this girl should have a place, even though we could not exactly praise her conduct'.

THURSDAY 19TH. TRENT. We had to wait more than three hours in Bolzano as the wheel of our carriage was again broken. Francis rode ahead to each post so that we always found the horses ready which helped us greatly. From Bolzano which is only one post from Deutschend we went through Branzol, Neumark, Salem, Lavis and Trent we only arrived here at nightfall and we are lodged at the Rose a frightful Inn. We found two letters from Montalbano who tells us he has not taken the house we wished for, and that negotiations could not be entered upon until papa arrived which put us all in a very bad humour.

Eugenia is more dramatic: 'We found two letters from my brother-in-law Montalbano who wrote things that took away our appetite. He said he had not got the fine house we flattered ourselves would be ready for us, as the proprietors would wait till Papa came in before making a price as they were in need of money, and wished Papa to pay five years rent in advance. This made me so sad I went to bed after eating hardly anything and even so it was a bad supper.'

FRIDAY 20TH. The weather very bad which prevented our leaving as soon as we would have wished every one slept badly as the beds were so bad. The rogues in the hotel made us pay 25 florins for our bad supper and apartments without including breakfast. We only passed Pergine which meant we had to stay in Borgo di Valsugaro as on our way driving over a hole which had a little stream running through it we broke away entirely the front of the carriage. By great fortune we were only half a mile from the post. Here they gave us *poulante* which was excellent.

SATURDAY 21ST. We left Borgo di Valsugaro very early after the carriage had been successfully mended. We passed Brinolano and from thence went on to Bassano the roads were quite terrible: on one side is the Brenta on the other mountains from which fall great rocks. At Bassano we saw Mons. Ferrari and a man who had been sent by Montalbano this fellow told us he was waiting for us at Castelfranco and that we should sleep there which is what we did but we did not arrive as soon as we hoped as the postillions were drunk. I think they hatched a plot together to upset us when we were five miles from the post it was the new carriage which papa, mama, Mons. Jaegle, Eugenia and I were in luckily it overturned in a ditch where there was no water and no one was hurt except George who was on the box he fell against a big tree and in a fury with the postillions went for them with his knife whose point he broke. All the ruffians that is to say the postillions drew their knives and were going to kill him, but his wife got between them and carried him off to the old carriage at last we can continue our journey. We met Mary my sister and her husband on our way they had come to meet us. At last we got there two gentlemen came one went to see the Podesta and we could have put the postillions in prison but papa did not wish it.

Eugenia says: 'We had very bad roads and were

often but a hair's breadth from the precipice. At last, praise be to God, we arrived safe and sound at Bassano, where we only halted a few moments for dinner.'

SUNDAY 22ND. We only left in the afternoon before leaving we saw the theatre which is very pretty we also saw the children of one of yesterday evening's gentlemen. After the postillions had stopped on the way three times to drink we arrived at Treviso at one o'clock in the night we saw here many of our acquaintance Count Turrian with his wife the Countess Polla with her son Volpato and others we went to bed rather late.

MONDAY 23. At last we left and arrived at Conegliano we went to Rosseti's house where we must stay until we have another. Mary and her husband dined with us and also Momolo Judico. Everyone is very glad to see us again.

TUESDAY 24TH. Mary my sister, Papa, Checo, Montalbano, Eugenia, Justina and we all went to the Montalbano's country estate which is called Marin. We saw my little nephew who is pretty and fat. Papa went shooting. Mary my sister's mother in law is always dressed like a servant. We were given a good dinner very late after which we danced with the countesses and peasant women of this village. I slept with Mary my sister we have a very cold room.

[On Wednesday they come back to Conegliano and find Mama 'cutting out dusters by the fire half frozen as we all are'.]

THURSDAY 26TH. I went early to the baker's. After dinner we took a walk and went to see Leon Cavazza's house when we returned I saw with great annoyance that the Count Benincasa was come from Venice.

CONEGLIANO, FRIDAY 27TH. Mon Benincasa went back to Venice which gave me pleasure. We came to do our lessons to a room in Mrs. Momola's house where there is a good fire. Mon. Brandolin and other gentlemen paid us a visit in our new house. Justina worked passably well. Before dinner we went to Boca di Strada to see a house which is for sale it is big but needs putting in order. In the evening we went and danced at the Malvoltis' house.

THURSDAY DECEMBER 3RD. I had a letter from Mademoiselle Eberts who tells us that the coachman's wife has died in the greatest misery, no one wanted to take charge of the two children of whom the eldest is a little girl of ten years old quite crippled, she cannot use any of her limbs the other a little boy of three. Now a woman will take them and will be given 20 francs a month. I gave my pink and white hat to my sister Mary. I spent to evening with Count Bepo Montalbano. We worked.

Eugenia adds: 'We took no lessons with Mons. Jaegle as he was occupied from three o'clock to 6 writing a letter of *one page*. I learnt how to mend holes in silk shifts. After supper we danced and made dusters.'

[On the 4TH *Eugenia* wrote: 'After dinner we saw the bull hunt: that is to say they make the bulls run and dogs after before killing them a barbarous habit they have in this country.]

SATURDAY 12TH. We dined with the Montalbanos. And took possession of Leon Cavazza's house where we sleep and shall live. To-morrow stoves will come from Venice for the rooms which are cold.

SUNDAY 13TH. We went to St. Lucy's fair which is very ugly. There is nothing to buy but linen, cotton, oxen, pigs and all kinds of animals. Mons. Jaegle went on foot. We dined late but with good appetites. I played in the evening with Mons. Jaegle who lost a sou but won it back at backgammon.

MONDAY 14TH. Through the hole of Mons. Jaegle's window we caught more than 100 bats and they still make a dreadful row. Mary and her husband slept in the house.

TUESDAY 15TH. The crate of books, the harpsichord, and Mons. Jaegle's two trunks arrived at last the harpsichord is a very good one specially made in Ratisbon. Juno died this evening. Mary is still with us and sleeps here. There was an old priest who last Sunday at the fair was very drunk and he insulted Papa and Montalbano. They met him to-day on the bridge Montalbano took his wig and threw it in the water it is the only one he has and he is very angry indeed that his false hair has been touched.

SUNDAY 20TH. Just as we were going to Conegliano here comes the ugly Catterini to make us dance, but we went after with Mary Edmonds, Correr, Mons. Jaegle my three sisters and Charles. Mon. Correr treated us to coffee we paid a visit to Mary on our way back Mons. Jaegle wanted to show us how brave he was by sliding on the ice but it was not as successful a gesture as he hoped. The ice was not strong enough to support a weight so tremendous as that of Mons. Jaegle, he fell into the water with one leg and his stick up to the knee. The Colletis dined here. Played the harpsichord a little.

WEDNESDAY 23RD. We went to dine in Treviso with mama, papa, Justina, Mary and her husband. The horses made many faces and fusses before they would go into the Piave boat which frightened me. At Treviso at the Polla's we waited a long time for Justina Michaeli who came from Venice with Correr. After dinner we went to the convent to visit the

Polla's and Colleti's children. In the evening we went for a little while to the café where I was very bored. We played a little Panfile. Justina has a small beginning of a rupture.

THURSDAY 24TH. Bought gloves for Mary Edmonds. Mary Montalbano is not well. Correr is going to accompany Justina Michaeli to Mestre and then he will come back and dine with us. Hardly did we think ourselves safely at home and we were but 30 paces from the stables going up the hill the horses began to go backwards the coachman was terrified and jumped off the box and let the horses go where they would one of the wheels bounced six feet in the air and the carriage upset completely Papa, Mama, Justina Eugenia and me were in the carriage. Very late dinner. Won 2½ at Panfil—Eugenia lost 5.

25 FRIDAY. CHRISTMAS DAY. We heard the three Masses at the Munighe Vechie the Capucin was very slow. ['so slow', *Eugenia* says, 'that my knees hurt me'.] Afterwards to the Café Marige to eat cakes. Mama has a bad headache and went to bed before evening. Mary Montalbano was bled. Mary Edmonds has toothache. I rode a little. A few visitors came in the evening.

Eugenia says they went to watch birds being snared and that Betsey caught one. 'I rode and the horse jumped with me but Charles was holding it so I did not fall off.'

THURSDAY 31ST. Correr is going to-morrow to get money for Papa in Venice. He is to come back to-morrow. The coachman and our horses will take him to Mestre. Robert cuts the tail of Correr's mare and is riding her. A little music. A stove was put in our room which gave me great pleasure. Preparations for the Roast Beef and Plum Pudding which Mary Edmonds is going to make to-morrow.

1790 FRIDAY, JANUARY 1ST. Mama gave us money to buy our shoes and gloves. Very bad weather. We did not think Correr would come back to-day but whilst I played my harpsichord he made a noise and came in with Justina Michieli. I played him two sonatas. I eat a great deal of Roast Beef and Plum Pudding.

SATURDAY 2ND. *Eugenia* writes they had a half holiday and Mary Montalbano and many gentlemen to dinner: 'nous avons tous joué Blindmans Buff, Quatre Coins, Frog-in-the-Middle, Slippers, et d'autres jeux'. On the 3rd she gave 30 sous to an 'ugly woman who pretended to be mad, I am very sorry I did so'. Two pigs were killed.

THURSDAY 7TH. Dined very early. Mama went to meet papa on horseback in the English fashion. Mary went too on her little horse. Whilst she was out the Father *Guardien* and another Capucin came here and we made them drunk. [*Eugenia* adds: 'so that as they went away one of them fell down' and in her margin, in Mons. Jaegle's hand, is the rebuke, 'if you give to drink in order to make drunk you are very naughty'. However, next day she mended his stockings and he was very pleased.] Papa came in the evening with Bartolozzi who told us that it was not the same Pattyson who was dead and who came with him to Strasburg that the name of that one was William and that it was his brother. I am very glad of it as he was a good fellow. I played two of Pleyel's Sonatas but as I was sleepy I did not play well.

MONDAY 11TH. Gera's uncle came he is an idiot or fool he has a great veneration for the stars I even think he worships them. Mama went to Conegliano. I played the harpsichord morning and evening.

Eugenia adds: 'he is dressed like an Italian that is to say very dirty.'

Tuesday 12th. Papa killed a hare and the gentlemen another hare and a fox. Mary came after dinner in the evening quartets were played and I played two Sonatas. I won an apple from Miani.

Eugenia received 'a little bird from papa wich he had caught but it dies'.

13th Wednesday. I was told to-day that this house where we have been living for a month that is the house of Leon Cavazza is called Monteselle which I now put in my journal, for Conegliano is an Italian mile away from here. Mama went to Conegliano with Papa, Bartolozzi and brought back Mary, and Vallegio a violin player who was with us when we were at Pordenon and who married a housemaid of ours. I went to the stables with mons. Jaegle. We saw there Correr's mare which Robert was bringing. He told us that she had thrown herself down three times. Miani went shooting with George when he had come back and was tired Mons. Jaegle gave him so much to drink that he was very drunk. After dinner Papa Bartolozzi and Mary and the Colletis played Tresette Papa won 6 Lire and 10 Soldi which he gave me. We had a half holiday in the afternoon I don't really know why but to tell the truth I am extremely glad of it. The cook has very bad toothache which makes her look ten times older than she is. Miani didn't want any supper I don't know why.

Eugenia describes a quarrel 'between two obstinate people that is to say Betsey and Jaegle. First one gets angry and then the other for first one and then the other wants to read. I let them quarrel as they like and say nothing but go on working the while.'

15th Thursday [*sic*]. *Eugenia*: Bartollozzi went back to Venice. I am sorry for it for although he is an

Italian he was brought up in England and has all the virtues and qualities of a good Englishman. Miani only drinks water now. Papa went shouting. George wounded a Hair.

CHAPTER 2

JANUARY 17, 1790. MONTEZEL. DIMANCHE. SAINT ANTOINE.

Eugenia has: 'We were exceeding lazy creatures this morning for we breakfasted into bed in the Italian fashion. Betzy bought Mary Edmonds a handkerchief pin, but I could buy her nothing because the things that were pretty the Jews had them, they wanted so much money for the things I was not able to buy anything, and Mama bid me to buy a pin for Odyle (the cook) that's what I did but not very willingly. Papa and Checo brought with them home a singer that sung some Funny songs.'

FRIDAY 22ND. Came home with Miani's Brothers that we met on the rode Ceco made me a present of a very pretty Canary Bird that sings very well. Papa played quartets with some gentlemen.

Eugenia is bored: 'This day is not a day for Journells because I have got nothing almost to say on it only that in the evening we made music and took our lessons. I don't know what to put in here for one has got almost nothing to say upon the days they are all so dull.'

SAT. 23RD JANUARY. Passed a very dull day nothing remarquable for the journal.

JANUARY 24TH. *Eugenia* writes: 'The countess Gera comes here with her great bakside krushed tail and little humped back and her nasty dirty handkerchief. She talks all the wile one makes musick like a Mackpie for she can't bear it, a parcel of gentlemen came tonight.'

JANUARY 28TH THURSDAY. Mama received a letter from Miss Eberts. Mr. Jaegle fought with Miani with snowballs.

Eugenia describes how they 'went to see a stone which was some shades which represented Europe, Asia, Africa and America some Kings etc. then we saw the Assault of Belgrade with Puppetts. We dined after all that with Mary.'

FRIDAY 29TH JANUARY. Great preparatifs for to go to Venice. Ran very much this afternoon for to throw snowballs at Miani. Took our lessons.

SUNDAY JANUARY 31ST. VENICE. Left Montezel at 7 o'clock. Our horses conducted us very well to Treviso were we stoped to have some victuals. As soon as we left the Inn the horses made the fools but we continued our journey to Mestre very well. We found the Terralio pretty good. Drank coffee at our Aunt's. Had many visits. The appartment we got is very nasty. Went to the Opera at St. Beneto they gave *Zenobia* very handsome Drama. Suped at home. The beds and Rooms are very cold.

MONDAY FEBRUARY 1ST. VENICE. At 5 o'clock we went at the Embassador of Vienna the Count Breunner. There we met My Lady St. George an Old English Lady who is maryed to a frenchman. Went with her to a theater of Gentlemen our cousin Augusta acts very well they gave *Olimpia*.

Eugenia: 'The old Uncle Nicholeto comes here and our aunts. Mrs Bartolozzi comes to with her son she is an amiable and handsome woman. This evening we go to a play house where they gave *Olympia* a very pretty tragedy of Voltaire translated in Italian.'

TUESDAY FEBRUARY 2ND. Had music in the morning. We were in the evening at the Embassador's of Spain and France very good sort of people passed the evening to the last.

WENESDAY FEBRUARY 3RD. Took a lesson of tuning the Harpsichord. We went to see some men and a little girl of seven years old danze on the horses they do it pretty well. Correr came for us at 11 o'clock we walked very long on the place of St. Marc. Mama goes tonight to pay visits and saw to the Michaeli and Mrs. Spinola, a nasty Italian pig that always drinks very much. we staid at home and played danced acted tragedies of our own heads.

THURSDAY FEBRUARY 4TH. Our Aunts Tonina and Bettina came to see us. Took a lesson of tuning the Harpsichord Cimador made me Accompany and play some sonatas and songs of his own composition. Mr Bartolozzi dined hear he begins to make us Draw. Went to the play at St. Angelo they acted the *Illusion of Virtue* the players not very good the decorations very Handsome. Mrs. Virtue disgusted one with her languishing tone I am sure it is enough to make one hait virtue.

FRIDAY FEBRUARY 5TH. Took my lessons as usual. Our Aunt the Countess dined with us. Went to the Opera they gave *Aspasia* and a danze called the Scotch Robbers. At twelf o'clock after the play went to a ball were we stayed till three o'clock in the morning danzed very little.

FEBRUARY 7TH. SUNDAY. Had music in the morning. Dined at the Embassador of france we had a very good dinner. Jeny[1] and me dansed and I played the Harpsichord. Went to the Opera at St. Samuel they gave the *Conquest of the Golden flies* and a danse called Rinaldo and Armida. We went with the children of the Embassador of france. Then we go to the Ball were we see Augusta Correr we danse several contredances and go home at 3 a clock in the morning.

Eugenia: 'We go to dine to the Ambassador of France and their children did everything in their

[1] Jenny: Justina Wynne.

power to amuse us and they begged mama to let us go to the opera of St. Samuel it is very pretty it is called *Jason or the Conquest of the Golden Fleece* I had the misfortune to lose my wach for when I wanted to take it, I found it no more.'

MONDAY 8TH FEBRUARY. *Eugenia*: 'I had the happiness to find my wach wich the waterman of the Ambassadrice of France brought me back but I gave him a ducat for his honesty in bringing it back. We go to walk at the place of St. Marck and see a little girl with to faces and behind she is as well formed as any child can be she hath got to legs a coming out from her breast for the rest she is very well shaped. She received christening and lived 32 hours.'

TUESDAY FEBRUARY 9TH. Took my lessons after, went to see people danse on the rope what they do very well. To the Embassador of Vienna till Opera time there was *Andromeda* and Rinaldo and Armida again and the End of it What would be to long to discribe in our Journals.

VENICE, FEBRUARY 10TH. I have been to Mr Bartollozi were there was a concert. Went to the Cavaliera Monzeniga were we dine I dansed and played the Harpsichord. Had an axceeding good dinner at five o'clock there were 80 candles in the dining room. Went to bed with a very bad cold.

THURSDAY, FEB 11TH. Took my lessons after which we went with Mary Edmonds and Mr Jaegle to see the feasts. There was a great quantity of people. There is a man that comes down from the top of the Campinil on St. Marc on a rope and gieves a nosguay to the Doge and then they made the forces of Hercules and some very good fireworks. Went to bed very soon because I had got a very bad cold.

FEBRUARY 13TH. SATURDAY. I went out all day long for to bye cloth for the mascarade that we will make

Monday for the Sons of the embassador of france. Mama went to the Play.

SUNDAY. FEBRUARY 14TH. Little music here this morning, walked a little in the place St. Marc with Mr. Jaegle.

MONDAY FEBRUARY 15TH. Dressed very soon in a Shepherdess. Stoped very long for our *Cavalier Servants* which are the sons of the Embassador of france. Walked in the Place St. Marc everybody knew us Payed a visit. Papa was dressed in weomen's clothes. To St. Benete. Went in a great many Boxes were they knew us but they took Papa for a Woman went to bed at twelf o'clock.

Eugenia: 'Went to the opera of St. Benetto and run about the boxes always masked in the Italian fashion. They made a great furore for Mrs Banti they throwed verses in her Prayse, Peacocks, Pols, Pigeons and golden rain was thrown to. They made us a present of 3 pigeons. I like a great deal more Mrs Mara than Mrs Banti, for she sings exceeding well.'

FEBRUARY 16TH TUESDAY. Took one lesson and then we went to the Opera in the daytime and one at night because they give two to-day as it is the last day of Carnival. Met there Messieurs Bonbels that are the Sons of the Embassador of France they were masked so I put a mask on my face and hardly nobody knew me. To bed very soon.

FEBRUARY 19TH. FRIDAY. At 5 o'clock I went with my Aunt to Lady St. George. she has got a very pretty Parrot that she bought in Portogal it is 15 years she as got it. We went to the Embassador of France. Bitch and Charles were gone to bed.

SUNDAY FEB. 21ST. Studayed a good deal. Dined at our Aunt's. Great concert for the Embassador more than 50 people. I played a Concert and Sonata. It finished at 12 o'clock there was the children of Mr de Bonbelle the concert very good. Mama goes to-night to the assembly of Mr Molsenigo and coming home she falled in the water with her two legs in the water but did not hurt herself at all.

Eugenia: 'Preparatives all the morning for the concert of this evening so much wished by me. We dined at our Aunts for not to dirty the rooms or make such a mess in them. At 6 o'clock came about 50 people and as it was all for the Ambassadors we went to play with the children of France in another there was tea coffee and ices served about we went to bed at one o'clock after midnight.'

FEBRUARY 23RD, 1790. TUESDAY. Got up pretty late. Payde a good many visits especially to the sister of Papa's mother she is a greec and is 80 years old. Our Aunt Anthony and Justina Michaeli dined with us. To bed at six.

FEBRUARY 27TH. There arrived 3 very great accidents last night. The man that comes with the letters from Conegliano was in a boat to come over the Laguna the boatmen with another boat begun a-quarrelling and they took out their knifs, The postmen only told them to be done or els he would never arrive to Venice and so they put him in the Water he was obliged to stay their till a boat went past and they pulled him out of the Water. There was too a thief that brock the window of a Shop and stold 2 gold snufboxes and a repetition watch. The third accident was that their was a man that owed the other a zechin. And he told him in the street when will you give me back my zechin the other told him pray don't insult me before all these people. They began quarrelling and the other killd him. Papa went out a-fishing at Muron and Mama went to dine with them. Went out a-walking while they were out. To bed very soon. Papa is much better of his gout.

SUNDAY FEBRUARY 28TH. Studied all the morning until twelf o'clock nothing els remarquable little walk with the children.

Eugenia: 'Went to the sermon that they make in the place of St. Mark which made me laugh very much instead of making me grow good.'

WENESDAY MARCH 3RD. Music. Out with Mr Jaegle went on top of the Campanile of St. Marc there is a beautiful vew. Had the Musicians to diner. Papa goes to learn to print. We invite the boys of france to come Saturday to stay all the evening with us.

SATURDAY MARCH 6TH. This evening the children of france came and passed the evening with us as well as Miss Moro. I am very glad that Bitche is Jealous of his brother so he took me for his Lady. Mama was obliged to go to bed this afternoon.

MONDAY MARCH 8TH. *Eugenia*: 'The proud and ugly Mrs Vendramin and her amiable daughter called. We went to see Mr Orsoni's children which are in the convent and there is a nun that is 84 years old and that fasts all the Lent as would do a young woman of 20 years old she was never sick in her life and never took physick.'

MARCH 9TH. Mama could not go to the Embassador of france with us but we went with our Aunt they made a ball on purpose for us we stayed there till very near 2 o clock we are invited to go and pass the evening there next Friday.

MARCH 11TH. Went to see the Palace of the Doge which is handsome. There is some beautiful pictures. Mama came back from Padua. At the embassador of Spain's mama would not come because she was tired of the journey. To bed very late. My Aunt winned 80 livers in playing at twentyone.

FRIDAY MARCH 12TH. Walked a little in the morning. Mama had a violent Assault of feets after diner so that Mary Edmonds came with us to the Ambassador of France where we played all the evening.

Eugenia: 'Went with Odyle and George to see the Arsenal wich is very pretty we saw several ships and several rooms full of curios I found everything very pretty and was very fatigued for we walked nearly 4 miles and I think that this is the most interesting day we passed all the while we have been here. Mama was very sick so she went to bed at 4 or 5 o'clock.'

SUNDAY MARCH 14TH. MONTEZEL. Many people came to see us before we left Venice. Mr Bartollozzi came to accompany us till Treviso. And Cimador till Mestre. Mary Montalbano came to meet us at La Campagna went to bed very soon.

MONTEZEL. MARCH 15TH, MONDAY. Got up very soon the weather not very fine. Took our lessons with Mr Jaegle. I have got 2 female Canary Birds and one male. Not many people here tonight. Mary Montalbano slept here.

WEDSDAY 17TH MARCH. *Eugenia*: 'Montalbano gave me a little bird called a *Lugarsin* that if you put a little bit of almond in your hand will come out of the cage and fetch it and go in again.'

FRIDAY MARCH 19TH. The day very fine only a little winday. Played at Blind Man's Buf. Put in Miani's face some glue. Little persons in the evening.

Eugenia: 'Not a remarquable day but we mayd this afternoon Miani play at Blind Man's Puff and as he was it Montalbano took a stick and put it on his mouth he was very mad of it but soon forgot it.'

MARCH 20TH SATURDAY. Got up very soon danzed before breakfast. Played another trick to Miani in putting some Glue all over his face and his Hare he was very angry. Nothing remarquable.

Eugenia: 'This day there was a great wind and a little rain with it we put a paper all full of glue to catch birds in Miani's face he was more in a passion than he was yesterday but forgot it before evening came.'

MARCH 21ST SUNDAY. *Eugenia*: 'A very winday day after having heard mass we went to the fair which was very ugly I only bought a yard and a half of corse muslin and gave it to Odile our cook.'

THURSDAY MARCH 25TH. To Conegliano. Payed a visit to Mrs Momola. To a fair where there was nothing at all but apples. Went to see the Parson of this Place that Weights 400 livers, he is monstrous. Walked all the way at home which is 2 miles. At my return home Mr Buller was so drunk that he could not stand up and he was very knaughty with Jenny. But in the evening he recovered a little his senses and he begd Jenny a thousand excuses had a very good company in the evening I played the Harpsichord.

Eugenia: 'After having heard mass we went to Mary Montalbano where we dined and to the fair where there was nothing to buy and to see but rotten chesnuts and peasants drinking wine therefore we went to see the Archpriest of that village he is fat enough to weigh 500 pounds and of him one might make 40 little girls like me. We came home with Mary and found Buller tipsy he made a good many follies in the loss of his mind which are not remarquable enough to be put in my journell made it up with Buller when he had recovered his mind because I had not been the object of his past follies.'

PADUA. APRIL 9TH, FRIDAY. Got up very soon and

arrived at Noale at 12 o'clock. Stoped and dined here. Met Papa in Padoua. We don't goe to Albano which is 6 miles from here, we have got a house for 6 months, but it is not furnished; the Waters will come from Albano. Very great confusion. To bed very soon.

APRIL 18TH, SUNDAY. Mad. Calverini with her children dined here they are very aimiable, the little one that is only 7 dances exceeding well her dancing master will come for to make us dance to-morrow for the first time. Went to see a little room full of birds and animals dead. To the Botanic garden. They gave us a branch of an Egipt tree. There is a Wood of No other Trees but American and African. Papa went to the play.

MONDAY APRIL 19TH. My birth day. The dancing master came at twelf o'clock. Mr Santanini dined with us. It was celebrated in no maner.

THURSDAY APRIL 22ND. I am very well contented with my Danzing Master. Mr Buller as took a dancing master. Took our lessons with Mr Jaegle. Walked out a little we saw nothing remarquable.

FRIDAY, APRIL 23RD. Came very well with our own horses to Padua.

SATURDAY APRIL 24TH. I went with Mary Edmonds Odyle Jenny and Mr Buller to St. Angelo to see the treasury. there was very handsome Calices with diamonds and Rubis and Amerols. We saw St. Anthony's tongue and chin which were surrounded with very precious stones. We went again in the Cabinet of the Natural History there is many fine animals. Up the tour and as it is a very fine day we had a very fine vew. Going home we went into a Coffy House and Mr Buller gave us some Chocolate and cakes. Madam Michaeli passed the evening with us as usual.

Eugenia has: 'Went to see the treasure of St. Anthony we saw there very riche a great golden cup with cameos another one of gold with figures on it and another with very pretty pictures and a pretty little gold temple of St. Anthony's tongue and several other very rich and agreable things.'

April 25th, Sunday. It rained very hard in the morning but the sun appeared in the afternoon. After dinner we went out walking with Jaegle and Buller to see the famous picture of St. John Baptista by Guido wich is very fine it is a pity it to be in the ugly church of the Hermiti. To the church of the Carmeniti which is not pretty. To the Cathedral which is a fine building and as some pretty pictures in it.

Wensday, April 29th. *Eugenia*: 'Went to here a great mass for the day at St. Justina and the monks made us go in and gave us some very good chocolate some dainties and flowers a very fine day went a walking on the ramparts and found a snake that we brought home.'

Thursday April 30th. Walked in the morning. Mama as got the Head eack very bad, she got up very late. There was a man burryd to-day. He had been assassinated yesterday coming out of an inn. Two men playing cards quarrelled he meddled himself about it and one of them killed him he was but twenty two years and was marryd and had children.

CHAPTER 3

[Betsey's English was becoming, she must have felt, too much of a strain, and she relapses into French with an almost audible sigh of relief, but Eugenia, younger, sturdier, less easily daunted, and with perhaps *la langue plus facile*, continued gallantly, doubtless to please Mary Edmonds, for mama and papa worried little whether their daughters were proficient in the paternal tongue. The following extracts from Eugenia's diary are supplemented by very occasional efforts in English from Betsey's pen.]

FRIDAY, MAY 7TH. We went to Mr Querini's Palace with the Countess and Mary. It is a very fine house where there was very fine pieces of sculpture and antiquities, he has a beautiful garden with a little labyrinth and several other fine things little temples with statues of gods and some ancient sepulchral urns and a ring of the great Cato and one of a Roman soldier little statues of transparent marble etc. etc. that is what he has got upstairs and little Egyptian Gods besides several utensils of the ancient Romans. It was very bad weather. We went to a Chimyst that could show us nothing but a bottle that when he opened it threw a little of the matter that was in it out it smoaked very much and burnt a bit of Cloath that he threw near it. A Milanese Gentleman came to hear Betzy play he seems rather an amiable gentleman.

SUNDAY 9TH. We went to the Brentelles with Mary and Buller and the children and in the afternoon to the Specula where they make the astronomical obversations the professor maded us see by the telescope a castle that is 10 miles off and the Place of St. Mark. It was nice weather today.

MONDAY 10TH. Received a letter from the French Ambassador that Begs Mama to let us go there to For a Ball that they Have it is established that Jaegle and Buller will go tonight in a Boat to Venice and that we will go tomorrow with Mama and Papa I am very much satisfied of it.

TUESDAY 11TH MAY. We parted from here about 7 o'clock and stoped at Taglio to eat something we arrived at Venice at dinnertime and went to the French Ambassadors were there was a ball there was a parcel of Frenche men and Women very amiable.

THURSDAY MAY 13TH. As it was very bad weather we did not go to see the Function For they did not do it But went to breakfast at France's house and went to walk about the fair of the Ascension with them and to see the Horses what they call here *Casotto* they are better than those at the Carneval. After it we came home dressed and dined at the Chevalier Molsenigo.

THURSDAY MAY 20TH. We arrived at Padua after a very Happy journey Mary Jaegle us too and the servant of Mr Buller and found Mama in a rather good state of health.

SATURDAY MAY 22ND. Went to the Countess and to Mrs Molsenigo and to the French Ambassadrice. This morning we found ourselves all covered with Buts and we did not know what it was till the Phisician came and told us it was the warmth of the blood.

TUESDAY, MAY 25TH. Buller goes away it is indifferent to me.

MONDAY 31ST. Betzy has a little fever and is obliged to stay to bed for it. Papa came home. I went this morning to Mr Bartolozzis. Odylle and George comes back. I go out a walking with Mr Jaegle and Mama.

Wensday, June 2nd. Went to confess writ a letter to the Countess. I am not at all contented with my confessor.

Friday 4th June. Betzy is a little better nothing else remarquable Papa went in the country.

Saturday, June 5th. Finished the Scotch Real. Betzy is so so, but little Giustina has some fever and was obliged to stay to bed for it.

Sunday, 12th June. The ambassadrice and her children dined here again today we went to see the procession at her house it is the day of St. Anthony or *Il Santo* the great and revered St. of Padua the Procession was not very pretty.

Wensday, 15th. Went at Attiechiero with the French Ambassador his wife and three children and the countess they dined here certainly attechiero is a very fine place and seeing that garden one would say that Mr Querini is a *Dolatre* for he has in it the temples of Apollo Venus the Eumenides, Hercules, Isis, Egyptian God and of the Folly. On the door of that Temple there is writ this inscription '*de la sagesse à la folie il y a qu'un tour de cheville*' this is writ because the statue of Marcus Aurelius is jest neer the door he was a very wise man venuses temple is in the form of a china house the inscription is very fine that one of Apollo is in the form of a Roman temple that of the Eumenides is not very pretty but that of Hercules is fine enough for it is a high column of a certain marble called yranive and at the top of it there is Hercules statue that of Isis is not a great thing there is a labyrinth that I have already mentioned but I could not find my way out for that I run a good deal and was fatigued enough when I came home as I was with the children.

SATURDAY, JULY 8TH. Dined to the Countess and saw a giant he is so tall that Benincasa passes under his arm went to the horses and saw the races of the horses by themselves by which is very ugly.

MONDAY, 17TH JULY. Had my picture begun for the curé of Stotzheim.

TUESDAY. Contineued the picture.

SUNDAY, 23RD JULY. Went at the Ponte di Brenta and the wife of the master of the coffee house layed in all at once of a boy an girl.

MONDAY 24TH. Nothing remarquable only that we would have gone to the Brentelles if the coach man that was tipsy had not prevented us from it.

Betsey: 'Papa is still at Strasbourg. We went to Abano with the little Calderini, we saw the spring that feeds the baths, it is boiling in some places and the poors that live near boil their eggs in it. Mde. Calderini and Mons. Jaegle made us a long walk on the Mont. St. Daniel there is a fine view and a strong odour of Musk it is thought that that comes from the vipers of which there are a great number.'

AUGUST 7TH, SATURDAY. *Betsey* tells how 'Mr Jaegle took a purge today and gave us no lessons. It is extremely hot. We went into the town to buy some vests [waistcoats] for Mr Jaegle.'

MONDAY, 16TH. Mde. Spinola came here and she took us three Harriet Betzy and me and brought us in the coach to her country house where we stayed til about 7 o'clock and then came home I forgot to put in Sundays journal that in the morning an old man came he is an englishman and aged 60 years he says it is 40 years he is in the service of King George and that he has been taken twice prisoner and that he had by many misfortunes lost his memory he asked assistance and it was given him by everybody in the house.

FRIDAY 20TH. Went out a walking with Mr Jaegle and my sister I saw a church all full of women dressed in white we entered in the church and asked who they were they said they were orphans that was like in a sort of hospital and that they were going to fetch a dead child for to bury him. We stayed to see the burial of this child it is the custom to bury here in the churches in great caves and without coffins the dead are brought in the churches very well dressed and with a discovered face.

AUGUST 23RD, MONDAY. *Betsey*: 'After dinner we went to the Brenta Bridge in a carriage. We carried a water melon with us that the cook cut and gave pieces to all the poors that surrounded us.'

TUESDAY 24TH. Great quarrels this morning between the footmen. As we were at our lesson with Mr Jaegle we heard a great noise we run therefore to the kitchen to see there we found for the first thing Harriet brawling François and Robert were fighting together nothing else happened.

SATURDAY, 28TH AUGUST. We departed this morning for Conegliano at 3 o'clock after midnight and arrived at Conegliano at 6 o'clock after having let our horses repose at Treviso where we paid a visit to Mrs Colleti that grows old and ugly.

MONDAY, 30TH. We rode out on jackasses today betzy tumbled twice for her jackass tumbled but I did not but was very near it having no stirrups.

Betsey adds: 'the ambassadrice could not come to stay with us for that she embroiders a vest [waistcoat] to the Ambassador for the wedding of the young Polignac.'

TUESDAY. Dined here but after diner went to Treviso where we slep.

SEPTEMBER THE 1ST, 1790. WENSDAY. Parted this morning from Treviso very soon and stoped at Noal breakfasted there and arrived at Padua soon enough to dine we found Papa with the gout.

THURSDAY, 16TH. We parted today for Vicenza and at last we arrived in that town wich gave birth to a very famous architect Palladium. We saw there several fine houses of his building and an Olympic theater wich is very fine This afternoon we went to see the race I went with an English lady wich is very ugly but amiable the races were a good deal finer than them of Padua. I went this evening to hear the *Pigmalion* wich is very pretty.

FRIDAY 17TH. Went at the Madona del Monte one goes up there under an arcade and there is a very fine picture of Paul Veronese a famous painter. After that we went to see a house wich is remarquable for its good pictures and to the Rotunda wich is builded by Palladium.

SUNDAY, 19TH SEPTEMBER. This is my birthday. I am eleven years old. Today I did not go out but this evening for to celebrate my birthday we made a funny and ridiculous mascarade.

WEDNESDAY 22ND. Went out for to buy a pair of stockings à piece to the grooms.

MAY 11 TO AUGUST 1790 IN BETSEY'S DIARIES

We went to Venice, where I made the acquaintance of a number of very charming French men and women, and was delighted to see the Ascension ceremonies which were magnificent. The weather was superb, and a large number of gondolas and barques carrying bands accompanied the Bucentor. We heard Mass on the Lido. We were a week at Venice and then returned to Padua where I remained until I began again to write my Journal. Mde. de Bombelles was a month at Padua whilst we were there which procured me some amusements, and we had several Balls in our house in short my time passed quickly and agreably. I also learnt to ride whilst at Padua.

A SHORT DESCRIPTION OF MONTIZELLA, NEAR CONEGLIANO

Our house is on a hill just about half a league from the little town of Conegliano. On one side the hills rise in a sort of amphitheatre, on the other a large, far-extending plain unrolls itself before our eyes. Sometimes when it is fine we can see the belfry of St. Marks with the help of opera-glasses. The Friuli mountains, which are a few miles away make a charming vista, and various fine country houses which surround us on all sides make a most pleasing spectacle. In short I can say that I have never until now seen a lovelier place, nor one that in the least resembles this.

1790. SUNDAY, SEPTEMBER 26TH. The dentist cleaned my teeth and stoped a large one. He cut a great piece off but did not hurt me. I had to go back to the house directly after dinner to accompany a De Profundis composed by Papa. It is for eight voices. A great lot of people came here it was very badly sung. Eugenia sang too and I played on the harpsichord.

WEDNESDAY SEPTEMBER 29TH. Cimador told us that yesterday at the Opera Mad. Spinola, Mde. Correr and Mr Contarini had supper together at the Inn and they all became drunk. He said Contarini was so tipsy that he was like dead and was sick without remarking it. Mde. Correr thinking he was dead had convulsions and quarrelled with Mde. Spinola They all stayed till the morning as drunk as pigs. Mamma visited Mde. Spinola today she was in bed a little indisposed. Eugenia rode and I went for a long walk.

OCTOBER 1ST. Today the whole household, the cook, Harriet, Justina, Mary, Odile, George the dogs and the coachman and horses went to Conegliano at three in the morning and got the house ready for us. Papa is better of his gout.

OCTOBER 4TH, MONDAY. Papa is quite recovered and we left Padua at 10.30 and arrived at sunset at Conegliano. We found the little girls very well.

OCTOBER 7TH. This evening a parcel arrived which was some sonatas which Mr. Pleyel had composed and dedicated to me. They are very pretty but very difficult.

OCTOBER 8TH. This morning some music came from Strasburg, some shoes and two little books sent us from Mr. Fries.

OCTOBER 10TH. *Eugenia*: 'We heard Mass in our little chapel. Montalbano came to tell us his wife and little boy were unwell. This morning Mr. Brandolini his wife, another lady and a lot of gentlemen came on horse back, all on ugly horses, it was like a caravan.'

Betsey: 'We played at l'égard with Mr. Jaegle, and read this evening with mama a comedy of Goldoni.'

THURSDAY OCTOBER 14TH. Vindamated in the morning. It was not very agreeable as there was nothing but old women. Montalbano dined with us and brought a live hare and tried out our dogs but it could not run fast and was soon caught and the dogs ate it up. Betsy was thrown by the jackass that started to kick and cut her lip a little but did not hurt herself. Papa was not lucky with his chace, did not catch many birds which made him in a bad humour. I wrote in German to thank Mr Pleyel.

Eugenia read a comedy she had translated from the German which is very fine.

MONDAY OCTOBER 18TH. *Eugenia*: 'We went to confession, were examined by our confessor and judged worthy to be confirmed, on Wednesday when the Bishop will come. Betsy wrote to the Ambasadress of France and sent her some grapes and chestnuts. She wrote to Pleyel to thank him for his Sonates.'

WEDNESDAY OCTOBER 20TH. After dinner we went with the Countess Cesare who is our godmother and who dined with us, to the Cathedral where we waited a long time for the Bishop. When he came we went first into the sachristy where we were confirmed with other little girls. Afterwards he sat on a kind of throne which was put up in the middle of the Church, then two children of about six years old dressed as angels, each said a sonnet to him of which they did not understand one word and after kissing his hand gave him a bouquet which was rather pretty worked with silver threads. After that a large quantity of girls and children set up a sort of platform in front of the Bishop and with their hands on their sides made a very awkward curtsey and each said a sonnet with such jestures that the poor Bishop has great difficulty not to laugh. After this we went to a coffee house. Just as we were going the Bishop sent a man to us with the bouquet begging us to accept it which we did with great pleasure.

THURSDAY OCTOBER 21ST. The English Gazettes came today, there is nothing in them to remark except the death of the Duke of Cumberland. We began to clean and prepare the rice for Sunday, we need 20 pounds of rice. A sheep was killed that is destinated for the peasants also.

SUNDAY OCTOBER 24TH. Today is the end of the vindamating we worked very hard all morning to prepare the dinner for our peasants. At midday there came 50 peasants, men and women, girls, children, old men and our servants, all sat down at a table prepared in the courtyard. They all ate as if they were starved. We dined after with Mary Montalbano, her husband and Silvester and all the peasants danced in front of us whilst in a corner the old ones roasted chestnuts. When our dinner finished I went to dance. We soon had to come into the house because it began to rain. We danced in doors till midnight. We danced many waltzes with the servants. The peasants in order to be lighter took their shoes off and danced bare footed. There was one peasant who was drunk and one of the girls danced with him and turned him well round and then left him. He fell down at once and gave himself a horrid blow. At the end of the evening all the women were tipsy. Eugenia and Mr. Jaegle masked themselves. I danced a minuet with the coachman who pretended to be a great dancer. I amused myself very much.

NOVEMBER 4TH. My sister rode on horseback. She was pricked by a wasp. I cannot fail to mention it because although it is a little thing because when there is nothing else to put in ones journal one must put in such little things. I walked out with the *Heretic* and it began to rain.

NOVEMBER 9TH. What wind! what rain! I said as I woke for it has been raining now for a week; I could not make up my mind to get up and when I did so went down to the kitchen as there was no one up the dogs rushed at me and I ran very fast to get away from them but they made such a noise that they woke everyone up.

NOVEMBER 18TH. I heard this morning news which gave me much sorrow which was the death of the little Momo Montalbano, Countess Bettina's son, a lovely child of six years with an excellent heart. He died this morning of smallpox and his Father and Mother are ill with sorrow. I cannot help giving an example of this childs goodness. Last winter when it was very cold he saw a poor child asking charity on the door of his house and he gave his own coat to that little child who had none. His mother must have a double pain because he was so good. But we must all die.

TUESDAY NOVEMBER 23RD. We spent almost all day painting our little paper lanterns for the fireworks and the illumination this evening. The fireworks were not fine because it rained but in spite of that we hung all the house with lanterns which amused us and we dug a hole and put a candle in it, also we caught a hedgehog and put it in Mr. Jaegles bed. He went to bed but we had put it too low and he did not find it until the middle of the night when it frightened him and he took it out and put it in a drawer where it made such a lot of noise he could not sleep so he put it outside the window and it ran away.

DECEMBER 2ND. Mary Montalbano and her husband came here. Mamma told him a story the Ambassadress of France told her. They make brocades there of the skins of the people they massacre, and they tore the heart out of a poor gentleman they killed and cut it in bits and sold it very dear. It was considered honourable to eat of it.

SUNDAY DECEMBER 6TH. We went with Mamma to make our first communion, we were all dressed in white. We had dinner with the Montalbano's. Montalbano sent us this morning his little mare for Robert to ride which he did.

DECEMBER 9TH. But for Mamas prudence we should

all have been roasted alive, for they put such a quantity of wood in the chimney that the fire caught the rafters and the chimney went on fire which was only put out with a lot of water. I was in bed and did not hear anything of it.

DECEMBER 13TH. We left this morning before day light our dear hill not without regret. We went in the old carriage with Mary and the cook. We arrived at three o'clock at this place (Mestre) which is full of rogues. We sleep here.

DECEMBER 14TH. We arrived at Padua having got up at two o'clock in the morning. Mamma was very sick and went to bed as soon as we arrived.

DECEMBER 16TH, THURSDAY. My throat is always sore. I gargled myself with vinegar and water. The Countess arrived consulted Bognolo this morning and as got a very bad illness of what he wont have the cure, because it will be impossible to make her well.

DECEMBER 25TH. CHRISTMAS DAY. Harriet is a little better of her fever.

DECEMBER 26TH. We went this evening to the opera with Mamma. The music which was Paesiello was very pretty but it was badly sung. It was called *Li Zingari à la fiera,* that is to say the Gypsies at the Market.

DECEMBER 30TH. Mamma received a letter today from Penin who tells her that they sent to the Ambassador of France to order him the taking of the Civil Oath. For all answer he sent in his resignation. This evening we made verses to say to Mamma on Saturday.

CHAPTER 4

1791. JANUARY 1ST. After having been this morning to confess and to comūn we went to wish Papa a happy new year. He gave me six ducats but Mamma more generous gave me a gold piece worth 4 sequins. It was my wit that gained me this money for I wrote verses to them both.

THURSDAY, JANUARY 13TH. Papa has ordered a Marionette theatre and we are going to make plays for it.

SATURDAY JANUARY 15. The theatre came today. I walked out and bought a piece of stuff to make a curtain for the theatre which was pretty. I went also with Eugenia to see Bognolli where I saw two skeletons and a great number of medical instruments. Mama had a charming letter from the Ambassadrice which decides her entirely to go to Venice.

JANUARY 18TH. We have decided to go to Venice Friday week. We tried to play a comedy on our Marionette Theatre but it was not successful.

JANUARY 22ND. Comte Corbelli's nephew dined here. He is an ugly little animal and eats like a pig. We went to the convent of St. Lawrence to see his sister who is a little fool and as ugly as her brother.

MONDAY, JANUARY 23RD. Went to the Comedy. *La Poverta di Rinaldo*, I was much amused.

TUESDAY JANUARY 24TH. This evening we went again to the Comedy they gave a piece by Rinaldo which was called *Nina*. It was very well played but I did not cry. Jaegle cryed. He made some verses about it.

JAN. 26TH. Mama and I went to the Comedie they gave *Semiramis* which was not badly played. I went a walking today and bought a pair of gloves and a ribbon, then with papa that was on horse back we met Mde Trou who is come especially for the comic opera.

JANUARY 27TH. *Betsey*: 'Tomorrow when we get to Venice we will find the Comte d'Artois will still be there that I want very much to know as they say he is adorable, beautiful and witty. Eugenia has a bad cold. She went to bed and did not get up all day. I went out with M. Jaegle but did not stay out long. Mama gave me 10 Livres quite new.'

JANUARY 28TH. We left Padua in the rain and had a wet journey. The Ambassadress of France with whom we stayed was very polite to us and sent us this evening to the stupid Comedy. Madame Michieli gave us each two little gold rings. We went after to the Countess who is very thin and seems ill.

SUNDAY JANUARY 30TH. *Betsey*: 'We went to see the rope dancers and after we went to the Polignacs. The children are pretty and amiable; they are Jules, Melchior and Edmund. The Comte d'Artois was there he is very amiable. When the ambassadress says her prince is beautiful she is right. After dinner we went to see *Harlequin King of Thebes* wich is very amusing. In order not to forget I will say that Eugenia's two *chevaliers servants* (these are the fashion in Venice) are Louis de Bombelles and Jules Polignac.'

Eugenia: 'This evening we went to the Polignacs there was M. le Comte d'Artois, Mad. de Polastron 'qui est sa favorite c'est une belle femme, la duchesse de Polignac qui est la plus jolie femme qu'on puisse voir aimable et bonne aussi que la Duchesse de Guiche'.

FEBRUARY 1ST. *Betsey*: 'We dined today at the Ambassadress of Spain where we had an excellent diner we had to return early to the Ambassadress of France for the Musick and the Ball she gave for the Count d'Artois. He came, as also all the Polignac family except the children, all the French and a quantity of ladies that I don't know. The Countess of Rosenberg was there, I played 2 sonatas. Eugenia sang, the Dutchess of Guiche sang also a duet with Miss Idalie this last executed a piece for the harpsichord by Clementi that was very difficult perfectly well. After we dansed Miss Idalie dansed the minuet perfectly she has had Vestris for master, I dansed several country danses, and the Russian and the Cossacke these two were infinitely admired, the Count d'Artois kissed Eugenia wich I think was very flattered although she says that it did not please her. I went to bed before all the persons were gone I was told they dansed yet more valses I was tired. M. de Challanton the tutor of the de Polignac children is a man that is very good and wise with the children and very honest towards all the world.

FEBRUARY 2ND. *Betsey*: 'The Comte d'Artois teasingly asked pardon of Eugenia for having kissed her. He was very funny. The Ambassadress is ill and unhappy because of the bad news she has had from France.'

FEBRUARY 4TH. We left at last covered with caresses, kindnesses and compliments. It was lovely weather and we arrived at Padua by night fall. The children are very well and very pleased to see us. I amused myself very well at Venice but I am glad to get back to Padua.

PADUA. FEBRUARY 5TH. I am glad to be home. We went this evening to the Comedy to see *Nina*.

FEBRUARY 9TH. Mamma received today a letter which worried her to say that Mary Montalbano is dangerously ill. She layed in for 41 hours and one does not know yet that she is out of danger.

FEBRUARY 10TH. We went to see the monks of St. Justina. They gave us excellent chocolate. They are very rich. Papa and Mamma went to Conegliano for Mary Montalbano is worse. I am afraid this journey will do Mamma no good.

FEBRUARY 14TH. Robert came back this evening with a letter to tell us that Mary is better but the child is dead. Papa and Mamma will be back tomorrow.

FEBRUARY 15TH. I went to the Zorzi Palace which has been lent to the Countess of Rosenburg for next summer, it is very beautiful and the garden is superb. Papa and Mamma came back after dinner and we went and ate ices and watched the masques, after we went to the Comedy where they gave a farce. Mary my sister is better.

FEBRUARY 16TH. Today we had an example of poverty and misery which are at Padua. Whilst at our lessons we heard a lamentable voice, we ran to the window and saw a little boy who was naked but for a little petticoat. He cried for the cold. We gave him some clothes.

FEBRUARY 18TH. *Eugenia* says: 'We went to the Comedy they gave *Teresa and Claudio* a pretty piece with a good moral.'

FEB. 19TH SATURDAY. The monks of St. Justina made a great mascarade 24 of them drest in womens cloaths they made much music most of them can sing well.

FEBRUARY 20TH. We went to the Comedy, they gave *Romeo and Juliet* which is translated from *Shakes Pear* but it did not please me.

FEBRUARY 21ST. The first actress of the Comedy came here and dined with her father and Mother and sister. They have all quite good manners for theatre people. Papa went to Conegliano and coming home a man on horse back waiting for the carriage fired a pistol into it. This frightened Papa and today he went on horse back to the Governor to discover who it is that shot at him.

PADOUA—MARCH 3, 1791. THURSDAY—Papa had bought a window for to go to see the Bull fighting, I went their was about ten oxen for wich they send the dogs after than they cut the head of a poor Oxen very badly indeed, however after come a Bull wich killed two dogs on the spot and all the others were slew, all this was very cruel we dined here and had a very good dinner, as soon as I was home I went to bed as I was very tired of this nasty amusement. The Count d'Artois passed at two a clock in the morning and is going to Turin.

VENICE—MARCH 24—1791. THURSDAY—We arrived at Venice a little before the Arrival of the Princes and Princesses This was beautiful We found the Countess not well there came many people to see this arrival There is of these Sovereigns The Emperor, King and Queen of Naples Grand Duchess and Duc of Toscany the Archduc and Duchess of Milan and two Sons of the Emperor, they were accompanied by all most all of the Venecians that went to meet them at Mestre they had twelf Bisones that went before them and all the little boats of the Regata that there is going to be after having seen all this I went to the Ambassadrice of France she can treat with the Venecians now She lodges at Mad. Spinolas from thence I went at Battagas They were all very glad to see us we dined at the Countess of Rosenberg were we lodge Their is fresco every day I went to it with Mama and Papa the Bissons are very fine they are all made with Satin and Silk and there is a boatman to each very finely dressed. We payed many visits but no body was at home so we came home and Went to Bed very soon.

MARCH 25—91 VENICE. FRIDAY We breakfasted at the Embassadrice of France and Dined at Battajas the Bride took us to the place of Saint Mary in the Church for to see it and to see the rooms of the *Filarmonicis* their is 10 Rooms beautifully furnished were their is every evening two rooms of Music and One of Ball and all the other rooms of Company Mama went this evening to the Filarmonicis, for my part lodged at Battagas till night then kept company to the Countess but soon wished her a good night.

VENICE MARCH 27—1791. SUNDAY—We breakfasted again at the Marquis of Bombelles and stayed there a part of the morning Then came home to dinner and dress for this evening we went at Brunners they gave a little opera for the Sovereigns were Mad. Adilind Piombelli sung the Theatre was very fine very prettily furnished all with flowers and Glasses. We was presented to the King and Queen of Naples the King is a very drole man but very good the Grand Duchess of Toscany is daughter is quite stupid she is the most insupportable creature in the world. From here Mama went the Filarmonicis and I come home to the Countess.

VENICE MARCH 28—1791. MONDAY. The boys of France and Jules and Louis of Polignac breakfasted here. I had never seen Louis of Polignac before he is a pretty boy and talks English not very bad. Melchior stayed at home to keep company to Edmond that is sick the boys of France stayed till the afternoon then we dressed to go to the Filarmonicis so we sent them away. Their was a Cantata at the Filarmonicis which was very ugly after I dansed but it was so hot that I soon came home.

WEDNESDAY, MARCH 30TH. We was to go today but

did not. We dined at the Embassadrice of France in the afternoon but was not well all day long. We wished to make some Chinese shadows with the boys of France but they were not successful so we played at other games. We sent for the boys Polignac but they was a-bed when we sent for them.

Thursday, 31st. As the Emperor has granted my aunt[1] a pension Papa will stay here today to thank him for it and promises to stay also tomorrow for the regatta if it is fine. All the boys promised to write to me.

1st April. As the weather was bad we left Venice this morning and came to Padua thinking there would be no regatta indeed it did not take place and we arrived very happily at Padua: the children were very glad to see us.

Sunday, April 3rd. There was an eclipse of the sun but not very strong. We sent yesterday away our kitchen utensils and our silver we dined at the Inn.

Mon: 4th. We dined again at the Inn. The King of Naples arrived today and they prepare a Pallio for him. This afternoon we went to the Botanic garden to see the fountains. We returned home and found Mde. Bonaldi at whose house was the King of Naples who came to see the manufactures.

Conegliano—April 5, 1791. Tuesday—Left Padoua very soon and come very well to Conegliano. We left all the Servants at Padoua there being no post horses to take them here but we came with our own horses and papa went on horseback The roads till Treviso were very bad but after very good Mary Montalbano came to meet us at *bocca di strada* and got in our carriage till up at our house Montezella.

[1] It had taken her some fifteen years' pleading to obtain it.

I had Harriot to sleep with me I have got a little room all to myself.

April 6th. *Eugenia*: 'I got up very soon and went for to run in the fields after I went to Conegliano with Papa to visit Mary Montalbano their I dug in the garden until dinner time then I gardened again and went for to catch Birds with Papa.'

Montezel. April 9, 1791. Saturday. I went in the afternoon to ketch birds and after a little to Conegliano, and came up again I was rather tired. Usual gentlemen up here. Mary did not come up to day. We made machines to ketch butterflyes and we ketched a great many.

Friday, April 15th. We dansed in the morning very soon. Justina as got a sore finger and did not sleep all night. There came this evening a great quantity of people to hear me play the harpsichord.

Eugenia: 'The cow has dropped a calf which is pretty enough I went to pay it a little visit. One of the children of Tita our bird ketcher of 3 years of age having a rupture since 18 months mama called a Surgeon what said the child could be cured by wearing a bandage.'

Montezel. April 19, 1791. It was my birthday I am 13 years of age. Mama gave me a Louis. The governor of the town and his wife came to pay us a visit this morning we invited them to come this evening to hear a little music we sent them our carriage and they came with Mrs Basilico, Mary Mont. and many Gentlemen I played the harpsichord pretty well. Our gentlemen made a deal of music. Eugenia sung but not so well as last night.

April 20th. *Eugenia*: 'Mlle. Eberts sends us a new that gave me much pain, that the child of Odylle since it had smallpox has a fever and cough and despite the care of its aunt is dead. Mama does not know how to break the new to her.'

21st. *Eugenia*: 'The stupid Andrews to console George that cryed because he thought his child ill (what mama told him) said it was dead George and his wife have done nothing but cry all day.'

April 24th. *Eugenia*: 'This being Easter Sunday the Mass cannot be said here at our house we were therefore obliged to go to Conegliano for to hear one.'

Monday 25th. We went today again to Mass and Mary Mont. dined here with her little boy. We amused ourselves very much to break eggs at dinner.

Treviso, April 26, 1791. Tuesday. Our musicians went to Treviso and are going away to Venice I went with Mama, Mary Mont. and my three Sisters at Treviso in the after noon to see Mrs de Bombelle that is going at Houcart she came from Venice but at 3' a clock she is not very well Mr. de Bombelle is not going with his family. The Queen of Naples has given them a Pension of 12,000 *francs* in a very noble manner. Did not stay up very late. Mrs. de Bo. went to bed Without supper and very Soon.

April 28th, Thursday. The Embassadrice and her family went away and continued her journey into Germany. We came back to Montizella and I came in Montalbano's carriage. Mr. Cimador did not go to Venice till to-day. We are now allone and our dog *Hero* having beaten Don Gaetano[1] everyone of Conegliano is affraid to come up in the evening for our dogs.

Montezel, May 1, 1791. Sunday. Papa's banquer and his brother that has been a Jesuite came from Treviso this morning and will stay with us till to-morrow

[1] Don Gaetano = Bartolozzi.

after noon their name is *Vanant garden* they are both very old, rich and avaricious. Not beeing very well to day I took some Physic. We went with our strangers in the morning to Conegliano on foot but came back in the Carriage. My brother in Law is Sick did not get up all the day. There is a play to night, it is all the young Gentlemen of Conegliano that makes it. We went and they did not act very bad it amused me.

MONTEZEL, MAY 2, 1791. MONDAY. Mr. Vanant garden and his brother went away this Afternoon we were very tired of them. I had a drole walk this after noon for to go to Conegliano I could not Jump over an Edge and would not have been able if a peasant that come past did not help me, it tired me very much I was with Jaegle. Few gentlemen this evening. I played the harpsichord by what every body said, well. Checo mont: was up and is better. Eugenia went to bed with a headack.

MONDAY, MAY 9TH. I wrote this morning to Fries and Mr. Battaga. The man is come that is to put the Conductor but cannot stay himself to do it he'll tell how it is to be done to the brother of Veneranda, and he will place it. I went to the sermon which was not bad for this country it treated on our *Soul*. I went on horseback this afternoon and this evening I played at cards and wan / winned 3 livers.

MAY 11TH WED. *Eugenia*: 'I went on horse back today and Betsy and Jaegle came in the little carriage. I was much laughed at by them for my manner of riding. Piero Gera made my picture he never learnt to draw.'

MONTEZEL, MAY 12, 1791. THURSDAY. I went with papa mary Mont: and her husband to the Lac that belongs to Justinian papa asked this Gentleman's leave to fish there so he put something for to ketch the Eels. Mary had her little boy sleep up here with her. It was very dusty for to go to the *Lac* and we came back round the *Alperos*.

MONTEZEL, MAY 13, 1791. FRIDAY. Mary went away very soon Mama went to conegliano with her but soon came back I went with mama this afternoon to Justinian's house 2 ugly he-goats that were in a field chased us then it begun raining so we stopped at a peasants house, there was an old woman and we asked her how old she was she said I do not know I am 60 and 21 I married at one and twenty and it is sixty years I am married my husband is dead 16 years a go and the old woman did not know she was 81 it made me laugh very much we went two to another peasants house there was but one woman at home with her child she is a pretty girl.—I playd this evening.

SATURDAY 14TH. *Eugenia*: 'No eels! Pierin Gera brought me my portrait that is not at all like me but that of Betsi that he has done is really not at all bad for he has never learnt and it is a good likeness.'

MONTEZEL, MAY 20, 1791. FRIDAY. In the afternoon Papa went to Conegliano for to invite some people and Mrs. Biodene to come and Sup with him to morrow. We had the *popet Show* up here this evening it was a very great nonsense one can see by it the Stupid cruel and piggish amusements of the Italians. I will never go again to see that ugly play.

Eugenia: 'Papa went to Conegliano for to order the man of the *Poppet show* to come up. He came this was very ugly indeed it was as stupid as indecent and it wearied me very much.'

TUESDAY, MAY 24TH. It was today the fair of St. Urbon. Papa went in the morning and dined there with the Montalbanos I went in the afternoon with mama, Mary Mont, Jenny and Jaegle in the carriage it is about 5 or 6 miles from here it is more a fair for cattle than for anything else though there is many shops, but what is there to buy of good? There was a great abundance of Oxen, Cows, Horses, Asses, pigs, lambs however of all sorts of animals. Papa wants to buy a very little horse they will not give it him for 1100 livers he hopes of having it tomorrow for that price. There was many coffee houses as soon as we arrived we went to the best, there was no good company. The gentlemen with their long pipes in the hand, a Labble at their sides a long whip in the other hand is a sight that shocked me, the ladies are drest in a manner that they seem Witches however I could not compare this fair (though it is the best of the country) with an English one. Papa came back with us stopped at Conegliano and did not come up till 10 o'clock. I played a little afterwards with the 2 boys Gera. Mama was not well this evening.

MAY 25TH. I think Mrs. Biadena is one of the most disagreable creatures of the world. Her husband is very much punished for having married such a stupid and ugly woman he took for interest. Captain Shalk visited us today, he was at the siege of Belgrade.

MONTEZEL—JUNE 11, 1791. SATURDAY. Though it rained this afternoon we went to Conegliano and saw the Young Ladies Gera that are in the Convent of St. Rocco as likewise, little augusta Mont: and Miss Biadena this last is a little monster exactly like her mother she makes all her grimaces. After paid a visit to Mrs Momola Christopholi and Mrs Buffonelli. Papa came with us to Conegliano and stayed at the Coffy house whilst we payed our visits it rained all the while. Took home with us Mr. Peter

Gera and that priest of Mell. Papa lost today a dog that he had bought from Bellan he was in a great passion for it and sent two men for it. The sister of Mr Biadena came this evening she is rather ugly has got rotted teeth and a large mouth what is horrid.

MONTEZEL, JUNE 17, 1791. FRIDAY. Mary Mont: came on horseback and dined here with her husband. This after noon received from Padoua a letter from Mr Benincasa which tells us that the Countess Rosenberg had been very bad in the night and that while he wrote they did not know whether she was a sleep or in a Lethargy, but says she has but few hours to live, Papa and Mont: set off directly for Padoua but as the courrier was 5 hours a coming they fear of finding her dead. This new did not surprise much because Bognoli had sayed she could not get rid of her sickness. I am very sorry it will be a great loss to the society of Venice. Mrs. Biadena came we played at *Pamfile* I lost 4 Livers. Mary Mont: slept here with me being afraid to sleep with mama.

MONTEZEL—JULY 4, 1791. MONDAY. Mama and pappa went to diner at the Vazzola it is a very fine country house a few miles from here, they had a very handsome dinner the governor his wife all the Mont: of the two families and many people were of the party, Miss Biadene came this afternoon and stayed all the evening here. I went to see my peasant this afternoon, the little boy grows always fatter, prettier and healthier. Had news Yesterday that the king of franse took flight with his family but was taken at Nemours. While they were bringing him back at Paris with an escort of six hundred men, 8,000 men of the Emperors took him and brought him at Luxembourg where he is in safety with the Queen and the Dauphin. The Emperor, that was at Padoua, quitted that town and took the way at Luxembourg. I do not know whether all these news are true I know of certain that he is escaped. I hope all is true.

WENESDAY, JULY 6TH. Mary Montalbano came on horseback this afternoon with her husband. We made again the proof of papa's tragedy. I went this after noon out a walking to ketch butterflies the other side of the river. Jenny was sick today she has got the headack, nothing else.

MONTEZEL—JULY 10, 1791. SUNDAY—I fainted allmost at Mass and was obliged to go to bed as soon as it was finished. I stayed in bed till twelf a clock, then got up. Montalban his wife, Mr. Diadene Amigoni and Jiudice dined all here. One does not know any thing of the king of fronce, the frontiers of that kingdom are so much garded that one can not have any news, all the letters are opened—I went to see the game of Ballon, Mr. Diadene played he playd very bad. Mrs. Morozini came at the Mont: with another Lady.

TUES. JULY 12TH. Papa went at Conegliano with Mr. Jaegle. There is a priest named Tofoli that came this evening he has got a myceroscope and a machine which we'll go to see tomorrow.

MONTEZEL—JULY 13, 1791. WENESDAY. We went to the Gera's where is Mr. Tofoli, he showed us that machine that shows in the best manner the movements of the planets Round the Sun, he made it himself it is very instructive and fine. I saw by the mycroscope the worm which produces the itch, some hair, a louse of a flye, a flee, a louse, and many other things, which amused me very much—From here I went to Mrs. Amigoni then to see a little of the game (Ballon) They played terribly bad. Mr. Diadene can never git the ball just, he is very drole in that dress they got to play, its white with a black Sash, rather ugly.

AUGUST 2ND. TUESDAY. Music continually, I sing play the harpsichord accompany and do every thing.

AUGUST 13TH, SATURDAY. Mary came up with her husband I went with him in the night to Catch nocturn butterflies with a lantern. We took nothing. I amused Myself the evening being so fine. After, I stayed up to hear the Music late.

AUGUST 17TH, WEDNESDAY. Papa could not play the Violin for his finger which gives him great pains.

AUGUST 23RD, TUESDAY. Papa could play the fiddle sign that he is well of his hand. Today we received the fatal new of the death of the poor Countess Rosenberg which died the 22 of this month: new very afflicting for this family.

AUGUST 29TH, SATURDAY. Mrs. Betsy Montalbano layed in of a little girl this evening, Mamma is to be its god mother.

[Here Betsey's second volume ends, and the next volume, number three, follows after an interval of only two days, during which time it is to be presumed Mr. Jaegle or Papa, since Mr. Benincasa was now happily absent, went and bought 'the book for the journal'.]

CHAPTER 5

SATURDAY, 8TH SEPTEMBER. The Governor and his wife came to pay us a visit this afternoon. This evening there was not much music. We were none much in a mind to make some. There were many people here. They all seemed dull for our departure. Mr. Bosso dined here, this seems to be a very great fool, without education. These sorts of persons are generally in the company of His Excellence.

FRIDAY, 9TH SEPTEMBER. The musicians all went away except Cimador, that is coming to Constance and Mano with us. I am glad for some reasons, and sorry for others. It is not properly at Constance that we are going, but at Roschach that is more near St. Gall (to which it belongs) I rather it, because it is a more industrious place than Constance, that's very dull. The Situation is very agreeable upon the lac. The Montalbanos dined with us. I could not play the harpsichord to-day, because it was packed up.

SATURDAY. 10TH SEPTEMBER. My sister Mary did nothing hardly but cry till we went away, what was at about 4 o'clock in the afternoon. We stopped at the Ambassador of Vienna; there were many gentlemen of Treviso which I did not know. We staid a little there, then continued to Treviso. We went to Mrs. Polo to pass the evening. I played the harpsichord, and heard Mrs. Bosso sing. She is the wife of that foolish fellow that dined with us Thursday. She is rather pretty, but sings very bad, and in a very rediculous manner. The Ambassador of Vienna passed there the evening with us; went home late. I was very tired when I went to bed.

SUNDAY, 11TH SEPTEMBER. Left Treviso very soon this

morning, and did not stop till Padoua. I went to the Battajas. They are all very well, and the little Louisa grows charming. I was very glad to see this family that was very kind to us indeed. We dined at the Golden Eagle with Mr. Poar. He is got very fat. This afternoon I saw his cousin, he is monstrously ugly and seems to have very little wit. Mamma and Papa went to Abano before us. We all soon went too. I am afraid I shall weary myself very much here. I was in bed before it was quite night, I was so sleepy and tired.

FRIDAY, 30TH SEPTEMBER. Papa and Mamma went to Padoua this morning, for to see whether they can make an agreement with some Veturins for to take us to Trento by Verona, the road being so narrow and bad by Bassano, that we do not think it would be possible for our carriages to pass that way. I should be very glad to go that road, Verona being certainly the finest town of Venetian estate, so I am very desirous to see it.

SATURDAY, 1ST OCTOBER. After we had took our lessons we went this morning at Monte Grotto it is more than two miles distant from here and as we went on foot I found myself extremely tired. There is there ruins of baths of the ancient Romans. I saw two they are very large, the water is cold. They were once all of beautiful marbles but Mr the Chev. Orologio had it all taken away for to make the baths here it is a very great pity and shame. His house is all full of these fine marbles I wanted to see it but it was shut I was very sorry for it after I had made such a very long way not to be able to see the finest things that is there. In coming back we took yet a longer way it was though very agreeable. Papa and Mama came back this morning from Padua, they had found so much to do that they could not come back yesterday. They have not made an agreement with the Veturins so we'll go with the post through Verona.

SUNDAY, 2ND OCTOBER. This afternoon we went to boil some Eggs to the hot waters of Abano with our company. I ate one.

TUESDAY, OCTOBER 4TH. Left Abano this morning and all arrived safe to Padua. We dined with the Battajas where I amused myself very much; they took us home and there was a great many people at the Eagle our Inn. In the evening we went to Mde. Michaeli where I played the harpsichord and Jenny sung. Our aunt Catherini that came from Venice on purpose for to see us with her husband stayed all day here with Mama. I went to bed late. The same Veturin that came the first, made an agreement with Papa to take us to Verona and stopping one day there for 85 Livres paying for everything except the corn of our horses. He had asked before Louis 150 and now agrees for 85. We shall begin our journey tomorrow at 10 o'clock.

OCTOBER 6TH, THURSDAY. VERONA. We left soon the pretty little town of Vicenza passed by Montebello and Caldiero. This road is dangerous for the robbers and generally one takes an escort, but we did not need any as we were so many people. We arrived in Verona quite early. It seems to be a pretty town, and there is a fine view from the new bridge over the Adige. That is all we saw today we had a very good supper we stay at an excellent inn the *two towers*.

VERONA. FRIDAY, OCTOBER 7TH. We hired a carriage this morning in order to see the different sights in the town. We went to the Cathedral the Churches of St. Stephen St. George and St. Paul. There are very fine pictures in all of them. Above all in the last two there are some by Paul Veronese that are superb. We also saw the garden of the Ct. Justi which is very beautiful, there is a grotto a couple of fountains and statues. The garden is upon a little hill from which one has a superb view of the town, and the surroundings. Papa and Eugenia saw the towers of Mantua but my eyes were not good enough to see such a long way. After leaving the garden we went to the Labyrinth then to the fair and the amphitheatre called the arena by the Veronese. It is a really magnificent place where 22 thousand people could sit. In the old days there were gladiator combats there and when some Princes come by they give bull fights in the arena. We met our little sisters there and took them in the carriage and came back together, and after a very good dinner of fish from Lake Garda we got into the carriage again to see the pictures of Mr. Girardini which are very fine. A Susan of Guido's is to be remarked. Then we went to the Military College and the theatre. The thing that interested me most was the geological museum. It is a collection of inscriptions, urns, statues and heads mostly found in the amphitheatre in a ditch. The most beautiful are a head of Livia, two masks, 4 of Phaedon, a race, a hare and others which I cannot remember. It is a pity that we did not have time to read the book which explained all these inscriptions which are in Greek Hebrew and Latin. But if ever I come again to Verona I will arrange to understand well the explanations of all these. After having seen all there was to be seen we went out at one gate of the town and came in by another. I found Verona a very pretty town on almost every bridge over the Adige there is a superb view and the roads are clean and well paved. Pisani is the Podesta. We would have gone to see him as we know him but he would have wanted us to stay longer and we could not therefore we did not go. Papa paid for the dinner today as we had agreed with the veturin. I forgot to say that in the garden of Justi there is a statue that is of stone but which resounds when struck with another stone like bronze. One finds in this country very fine marble with which all the churches are ornamented. We only had some punch for supper.

SATURDAY OCTOBER 8TH. We left this morning very early. Cimador could not ride as the little mare kicked the old mare and the grey mare so badly yesterday evening that she has made them both in a very sorry state.

Ala. We went all the way today between two chains of mountains along the edge of the Adige, after having walked a little we stopped at Dolce, a miserable village and the dinner we had was smelling of soot. We came next to Borgetto where is a customs. We were afraid they would open our cases but for half a ducat we bought a *bolletin* which made us pass freely through all Tyrol. We arrived late at Ala which is rather pretty but one is in a hole one can only see the rocks and water which makes me sad. We stopped at the Crown a passable Inn where we had quite a good supper.

SUNDAY OCTOBER 9TH. Heard a very early Mass at Ala before it was even day light and after leaving this place passed Roveredo where I began to see the hand of *industry* and not of *idleness* for we are in the states of the Emperor. We came straight to Trent at the *Europe*. The inhabitants all speak a German or Italian patois. We went to see the Cathedral which is very ugly. What is best is the fountain in the square.

BOLZANO. MONDAY, OCTOBER 10TH. We got up very early again. I was very sleepy but woke up at the sight of such well cared for vines and such nicely ploughed fields, and such fine lovely mountains whose crown seems to touch the skies and which make we want so much to climb them. We stopped for dinner at Vigna after which we came all the journey to Bautsen where we had a good supper. They only talk German here. I could not see much of the town for it was dark.

TUESDAY, OCTOBER 11TH. We left at 6 o'clock and we quit the Adige to follow the course of the stream Eissah. I would need the pen of Gessner to describe the lovely views which I saw today, waterfalls tumbling from the tops of mountains, which are covered with vines and fields. These arid rocks are changed by the industrious peasants into fertile fields. The Tyrolese are indeed a good people, they all look robust and well. We stopped for dinner at Colman, we could not walk as it was raining. The dinner was good but the linen dirty. We arrived at last at Brixen and stayed at the *Elephant* a large Inn.

WEDNESDAY OCTOBER 12TH. The weather was bad almost all day the clouds prevented us from admiring the beauties of nature. We dined at Stersingen where we had an excellent dinner which we ate with a good appetite. After dinner we climbed the highest mountain in the Tyrol, the Brenner, and arrived late at Stenach. I wish to give a small description of the Tyrolese. They are handsome generally, above all the children and women, an air of health and contentment spreads over all their faces. The costume of the Tyrolese is pretty but I dont like the bonnets they wear on their heads which are made like night caps in many colours of thick cotton and are very hot but they wear them even in summer. The Tyrolese are honest, industrious and affable, to conclude, I like them very well. We left Stenach early. The weather was very fine. I walked for some time and went in the little carriage. We arrived for dinner at Innsbruck a fine town watered by the Inn. We saw there Count Schalk who has visited us at Conegliano and who dined with us. After dinner I wrote to Mary Montalbano and then we set out again and arrived at *Zuil* at the Crown a decent Inn. We came down a very dangerous hill before Innsbruck and saw many precipices. We are all a little tired of always being in the mountains I hope we soon will come out. Here in the Inn one is served by young girls and not by men as is usual in other countries.

FRIDAY OCTOBER 14TH. We left this morning rather late and arrived at Nazaraiten. It is only a small place at the foot of the mountains. We drank much small beer which I found good. Nearly all the Tyrolese have got goiters but these dont show as they hide them with a black cravat. The women are beautiful and healthy looking and even those who are not themselves pretty are fresh coloured and preferable to the most lovely Italians who are always so dirty.

SATURDAY OCTOBER 15TH. We left by moonlight and had a terrible mountain to climb. In spite of the cold I walked right up to the top. I was bitterly cold and there was a great wind so that I was delighted to climb back into the carriage. The Inn where we dined was quite new. we had venison for dinner. Fortuna having been lost yesterday when we found her again Papa was so afraid to lose her once more that we were obliged to take her in the carriage. She is quite *quiet* poor beast. I had the pleasure of seeing the sunset that was one of the most beautiful sights I have ever seen. We slept at Issini a bad Inn that also was dear. The costume of the women is rich but tasteless. They all wear a little bonnet of gold cloth or silver and lace their corsets with a silver chain to which they tie small buttons of the same metal and often a medal quite nicely worked also in the same metal. They wear also round their necks huge collars to hide their goiters.

MONDAY OCTOBER 17TH. Today we arrived to dine at Lindau. We found at the Crown Baron de Loeben a German who is here on business and who will pass the winter with us at Wardeck. He sent a messenger at once to the Marquis de Bombelles to tell them of our arrival. He dined with us and after dinner he took us for a walk and we took a boat to make a tour of the town but as Mamma is always ill on the water we were obliged to return home. I have never seen anything as beautiful as the Lake of Constance. It is very long and one can hardly see the end, but it is so wide that one can hardly see across. We have arranged to go tomorrow to Wardeck so we went to bed early. We dismissed André today having no need of him, and Louis the coachman also as he is not honest.

TUESDAY. We left early this morning to give a surprise to the amiable family which lives at Wardeck. The road was superb. We changed horses at Breganz and arrived at Wardeck where we surprised the inhabitants by our arrival and I was charmed to see that the children have grown, especially Charles. They gave us a good dinner and after we went in a boat on the lake with the children and a maid servant. I was much amused and we had a favourable wind only the maid servant who was with us was very sick all the time. We spent all the rest of the day with Madame de Bombelles and the children who will stay with us until the Castle at Wardeck is ready to receive us. So we came back to Lindau which took two and a half hours and we dined very late and went to bed. The Castle of Wardeck is on a little hill well cultivated and surrounded with fruit trees, the view over the lake is superb and near Wardeck at the bottom of the hill is the village *Stadt* and a quarter of a league away the town of *Roschach.* I think we shall be very well here. The country is beautiful and the society which we shall enjoy will be delightful.

WEDNESDAY. Poor Fredericka the servant of the Bombelles children was ill in the night and had terrible convulsions and the coachman cried all yesterday because he did not want to leave us and made me so sorry for him that I and the good Marquis have arranged for Papa and Mamma that the poor man will stay with us since he is very sorry that he deceived us. But instead of him the Impudent Mde. Odile Buchols who will not deign for her husband who she says is a *grand seigneur* to clean the shoes of Messrs Jaegle and Cimador, is dismissed together with her husband and they will go tomorrow. One can never believe how far impudence will go and the vanity of this woman is incomprehensible to me. I am delighted she is going though I am sorry for George who is an honest man and had it not been for the *petticoat government* would have remained with us. We could not go out today as it was raining so we played all day. Madame de Bombelles will stay with us till Sunday when we shall all go to Wardeck.

TUESDAY OCTOBER 20TH. We walked this morning to do a little shopping. We also saw two little horses that Papa very much wanted to buy but happily he noticed that the handsomest of them was blind in one eye and lame and the ugliest of them would be soon so also. In the afternoon we went to see M. and Mde. Braun. He is adviser to the Princess of Lindau who is at the head of a Chapter like the Princess of Andlau. She is only twenty and if she had not a most hideous hump would be very pretty. Mr. Braun has a very large family. He has thirteen children. He is very respectable. From there we went to see the garden of the Mayor's house. In the evening Eugenia sang and Cimador played on the little harpsichord.

FRIDAY, OCTOBER 21ST. This evening we went to see the German Comedy which is very well played, and which is very interesting. It is called *the Good Father* We saw the Princess, she was very civil but I do not like her because she is a little mad.

SATURDAY, OCTOBER 22ND. Odile and George having been sent away because they would not do any work a new servant came today called Martin Cribler to whom we are to give 22 French francs and wine also and dinner. This man is tall handsome and strong. This afternoon a painter began to make our two portraits in miniature to put on a tobacco box as the Baron de Loeben asked for them. The Brauns were here all day, these children and their mother were expressly created to weary every body.

SUNDAY OCTOBER 23RD. After a very happy journey we arrived at Wardeck where we found Mde. de Louvois with her son and the Abbé Robert her son's tutor. She is a sister of the Marquis de Bombelles. The Baron de Loeben will come only tomorrow and then all the inhabitants of Wardeck will be complete.

TUESDAY, OCT: 25TH. Mde. de Bombelles, her husband, Papa, Mama and Eugenia went to St. Galles, I stayed at Home with the others, they came home late this evening and I will now give an account of their unfortunes, before I speak of my own. When they had come to St. Gall the coachman of the Prince came to tell them the Prince was not at home, but that his Grand Master would give them dinner at his country house, if they would be content with a little family dinner. After having gone a little way the same coachman came to tell them that they were mistaken and the Grand Master would give them dinner at the Convent (the Prince's palace) and that it was there that they would be given dinner. They did not hardly believe him, but they went where they were told and a fat monk very dirty brought them into a very cold corridor, and when they complained and asked if they might not have a fire, he said 'Dance, if you are cold'. At last the Grand Master came down and they had dinner: they were only seven dishes for twenty persons, and they were sitting two hours over it. Then they had coffee in the Grand Masters room which was warm, and went to the fair where Mrs Miller was. The palace is fine, and the fair pretty enough. Now for my turn I wished for to walk to Rorshach after my lessons but my shoes and stockings were not made for such terrible dirt and I had to come home I was muddy up to my ears and I had got my feet terribly wet.

THURSDAY, OCTOBER 27TH. We spent the morning in study and at dinner time we remarked how agreeable it was to be reunited after being alone and to find thus a pleasant society at such a hour really it is true. We went to walk at St. Gall and saw the manufactures of Muslin, Cotton, and embroidery that are there in great number the Muslin above all is superb. The way back seemed to me much shorter than when going for that town is so high that all the way home is downhill.

FRIDAY, OCTOBER 28TH. It is a feast day today there are many in this country. We went to Mass and the chaplain dined with us. It snowed and sleeted all day. We passed a very agreeable evening Mde.

Bombelles, my sister and I worked and Mama read to us three stories of Mde De Genlis (*La lingère*, *Le rosaire*, and *Le vrai Sage*) which the gentlemen and us heard with the greatest pleasure.

SATURDAY, OCTOBER 29TH. What a pretty view I had on waking! When I looked out of the window all was covered by snow; by noon this white carpet was changed into a fine green and a great wind got up and chased away all the clouds. Today the Baron de Loeben arrived at last, and now all the inhabitants of Wardeck are reunited. He is a very kind and a good man. What would we have done without him at Lindau? he took charge of all our affairs and bought all the things that we needed, coffee, sugar, candles, etc, *enfin je l'aime beaucoup*. Mr. de Regis also is both amiable and good it is he that will pass the winter with us.

SUNDAY, OCTOBER 30TH. Today we had the honour of having the two Princes to dine here, the Prince of St. Gall and him of Dissendis. This last is amiable, speaks well French and Italian but the first is very stupid and indeed his face does not reflect great intelligence. Since he is a monk he wears for only ornament an emerald cross. He did us a great favour to dine with us for since he is prince he has never dined once outside his own house. Several other persons were here too we were 22 at table without counting the two little girls and Charles. After dinner we sang dansed and played the harpsichord, and I think he was much amused although he did not understand anything. Happily they went away soon so that we had time to go to Horn to see Mde. de Louvois. Mama read the beginning of *Wateck* to us I went to sleep.

MONDAY, NOV. 7TH. I dined with Papa in his room because he could not go downstairs on account of the gout. Directly after dinner I went out a walking with the Abbé Brosse the two eldest boys Bombelles and my sister. We went farther than the Wartensee everything was covered with snow, but we amused ourselves exceedingly as the weather was clear we had a beautiful view over all the lac and its neighbour town and villages. It was very drole to see all the laboured ground covered with old rags, in one place a shoe in another a glove and old nasty stockings, it was pretty too for all the different colours they make dung of them rags. Tonight Mr. de Regis read us of a letter which he has received from Avignon, all the cruelties, massacres and dreadful things which as happened there. A man named Ecuyer who snatched the Calice out of a priest's hands while he was saying Mass was killd at the foot of the altar. The son of that monster yet a child was forced by one of which I do not know the name to kill twelve persons and he killed I do not know how many himself. A woman which would not walk upon the dead body of her son was torn to pieces however it is dreadful it is almost incredible. Papa suffers exceedingly with the gout.

Nov. 17th, Thursday. Mr Bombelles returned from St. Gall. His servant told us that since Mr Barthese quarelled with his negro (servant) he last night stole his masters purse where there were only four ecus and some rings in fact all he could find, and ran away with it, it's a great loss for poor Mr Bathese who is very needy and has children and a proud wife who makes him spend what little he has, on her. This afternoon came here one of the deserters of the army of Mirabeau, he spoke to Mr le Marquis, and told him he had killed three men and required a bath of blood to which Mr B. answered he hoped he would not take his bath in his house; and to get rid of him he gave him an ecu of six francs. Mr de Regis had seen him today at Mde. de Louvois, and feared he wished to hurt Mr le Marquis, as he asked him the way and said he must absolutely come to Wardeck, he was a man of twenty five years, very tall and strong and he had 14 wounds, truly this history frightened me a trifle, but my spirit was calmed when Capt Schalk arrived we were very happy to see him, gave him supper and offered him a bed which he accepted with pleasure I think, the wind was extremely strong and he would not have been pleased to sleep in Stadt at a bad inn. Mr Cimador gave him up his bed and his room. Papa is much better which makes us pleased and him gay. This afternoon we intended to make a walk the weather being fine, but all at once a great wind got up and we only went a little to the garden, and after dansed, played, etc, until the time for lessons, and when that came we studied. Mr. Jaegle makes us read an English book that is called *The Vicar of Wakefield* which is very pretty, interesting, well wrote and where there are some very good characters.

FRIDAY, NOV. 18TH. The new that Mad. Bomb. had today from the princess Elisabeth that if all the emigrés are not returned into France by the first of January all their goods will be confiscated and they will be condemned to death gave much affliction, but we hope that it will be of no consequence. I shall say nothing of it, if one day I read in that newspaper I will perhaps judge better of it myself.

SATURDAY, NOV. 19TH. The inestimable Mad. de Louvois came to us this morning she carried her brother with her. The new that she has had from the National Assembly do not force her to go back as women and children are exempted I am very contented of it as I should have been very sorry to lose her neighbourhood and society. As today it is the birthday of Mad. Elisabethe (sister to the King of France) to celebrate it we had tonight fireworks and drank some punch which was excellent.

SAT. NOV. 26TH. Mde. de Louvois her son and Braun dined here, in the afternoon we dansed Mad. L. also and made several games she is very kind and amiable when she was gone we made our lessons. Suddenly after supper we heard a horn of the post, we were all very surprised and could not think what it might be, we ran out and the coach boy gave Mr de Bomb. a letter from the Prince of Spire, crys of joy are made, and Mama reads to us that the King (of France) and Monseigneur the Dauphin are in the Low Countries the queen is on the sea with Viomenil and Mde. Elisabeth with the woman Mommorit. On hearing this good news tears came to our faces of joy, but Mde. B, anxious for the queen and for her princess wept bitterly. Now at last wil finish in a short while this revolution the king has 16000 austrian men with him, he is safe. Papa ordered some Punch we all stayed up late and we drank to the health of this prince. Mr de B. sent at once a copy of the new he received to Mad. L. Le Clergé when he came back said she went at once on her knees and thanked the good God. Many plans were made. Mr de B. fears he will have to depart he wants and does not want to go at any rate he will wait for new orders. How much blood there is that will be spared? All that have the courage will now run after their sovereign, all the cowards will submit themselves the last time the king ran away they were quiet like sheep but when he was arrested they were again enraged. Amongst all these reflections Bitche cried out could Papa not make to walk his regiment? The poor child is colonel of 1000 men at Bitche. It was very sweet of him and amused us all. We wished to hear more new and Mr de B. will go tomorrow to carry the new to the prince. Even the servants shared our joy they drank Punch. We went to bed at last fearful that we should not sleep for joy.

THURSDAY, DEC. 1ST. Mde. Louvois came here to dine. Mr de B. sent the Abbé La Brosse to St. Gal to have the letters from France as soon as might be and to find out as soon as he could whether the King had escaped. Mama and Eugenia were sick they went to bed in the afternoon. In the evening when we were all sitting together a letter was brought which a courrier had left in passing it was from the Bishop of Spire we feared it was excuses to say that the new he had sent us were not true but we were agreably surprised when we read that Valenciennes had surrendered its keys to the king and that he was in a castle named Rheimt, belonging to the Viscount de la Maucet that the queen had embarked at Dieppe to go to Ostende from where she will come to Brussels. Actually we had hardly any doubts But Mr de Loeben, who had been to Lindau to get new for us brought back the *Gazzettes* where it was said that it was all a false alarm. In spite of the Gazettes and of a letter from Stoucart where it was said that the escape was false we had a few hopes, as for me I had many. I went to bed very late because they stayed up a long time talking politics and this conversation interested me enormously. I also read something of *The Ami des Enfans* of Berquin.

FRIDAY, DEC. 2ND. I had only studied two hours with Mr Jaegle before Mde. Louvois came. M. de la Brosse was already back with the letters and the King's flight is all an invention. This new gave me extreme pain as to all here it is terrible to have been so mistaken. But Mr de B. is truly the best of men how he reasoned on this subject! What philosophy he showed! it is impossible not to respect and admire him always more. I accompanied Mde. de Louvois to her house and she read me some verses the Abbé Robert had made on the birth of her son (which is tomorrow) and which were charming. All the servants will sing a couplet to him. Mama and Eugenia are still in bed. We played this evening but I was not happy.

Eugenia: 'Je pris une purge ce matin qui me fit beaucoup de bien mais ce qui me fit bien de la peine c'est que les nouvelles apprenent qu'il n'y a rien de vrai pour l'evasion du roi.'

Wednesday, Dec. 7th. As there is not anything to say for my diary today I will write of the place that we are in and I will begin with some account of the peasants. These are of a really revolting vulgarity especially the little boys Mr Cimador can never go by on horseback without these nasty children making impertinences to the horse and everything that one does is very laughable to their eyes for they *cock snooks* at one on every occasion. Does one go a walking? one runs no risk of being bid goodday unless one says it first and that with the greatest deference and politeness. They are as poor as they are rude: I admire the uniformity of their Sunday best. The Castle is on a hill not too high at the foot of which is the little village of Villerqui which consists of three or four houses and of that of the Chaplain and of the Church. We are surrounded with lovely hills and I greatly wish we may be here in the summer to enjoy the beauties of Nature.

Sunday, Dec. 11th. I amused myself well in going to Mass for their was a great deal of snow and one could slide. This afternoon we went in the carriage to Mde. de Louvois as she did not come to dine with us as her son is ill. She chattered a great deal as usual and showed us tapesteries that she has made which really are charming. On our return we played cards. We begin now to think seriously of playing the Comedy and a theatre is to be made which will be a very little one. The piece *Nanine* has been chosen and I have been given the part of Nanine. More new from Paris. The National assembly has made now this unjust law that mass can only be celebrated by a priest who has taken the civic oath. Do they call that authorising religion? Do they call that the tolerance they pride themselves on so greatly? Catholics will now only be able to follow their religion a very little. Happily the King has not yet signed this infamous order.

CHAPTER 6

JANUARY 1ST, 1792. SUNDAY. WARDECK. Today is a fine day for me, I like greatly New Years Day for one is always so gay. Papa gave me a gold Louis for a present and Eugenia and I gave also presents to the servants. Mde. de Louvois came to pass the day with us we had a rehearsal of *Nanine*. Mde de B. who plays the part of the old Marquise d'Olban plays very well, Mde. de Louvois plays like an angel, Mr de Regis is very cold. In the evening we played at cards until half past eight. Mr de Regis who had made himself nicely drunk with Punch and Kirsch-water lost at our little game where the stake is never more than 4 or 5 kreutzer 15 francs of France Mr le Baron of Loeben won 12 and I won 42 kreutzer. The year was begun very merrily. I took some tea before going to bed and was much amused by watching our cook who was very drunk she certainly began the year well. I wrote a letter to Mlle. Battaja.

JAN. 5TH, THURSDAY. We did not dine today because of the supper that we will give this evening. The Grand Master of St. Gall, with the Baroness de Muller his wife and his daughter came this afternoon and for supper came also the Prince of Diessendis with Mde de Louvois her son the Colonel etc. We made music until it was time to sit down at table, we drew the kings the Grand Master got the bean and made mama his queen and amongst the children Bitche got it (there were two cakes) and Eugenia was his queen. The diner was very good with a great noise and gaity afterwards I played and we dansed and amused ourselves well until our company left us. The wine had heated several heads. I went to bed very tired and sleepy.

FRIDAY, JAN. 6TH. Eugenia's reign lasted also today. We went this afternoon to Vespers and saw at church the Crêche and the three Magi who come to adore *Jesus Christ* these images were quite prettily made and amused the children. Mr de Bayer the one that plays the Clavichord is going to compose a sonata for me it will be a *beautiful* thing!

TUESDAY, 10TH JAN. At dinner Mr de Regis announced that he had a letter from his friends in *Saalon* who told him that *Nostradamus* a prophet who lived in that town about two or three centuries ago prophesied (so they say) the revolution that would arrive in France and that it would finish and everything would be restored in the year 1792, they believe in him but I did not even pay attention to it. I had a letter from Mde Battaja where she gives the sad new that her father and mother are going to separate themselves from the young Mr Battaja new which made me very sad the parents and their daughter will leave in April and will retire on to one of their estates until next winter. Mde de Bombelles received the new that the Ambassadrice of Spain at Venice (Lascasas) has given birth to a little boy this gave her the greatest pleasure for she has no children and a considerable fortune. This evening the fine trajedy of Racine *Andromaque* was read I did not hear all the play but I have read it before.

SATURDAY, JAN. 20TH. As the weather was not too bad we went for a walk till Roschach there was such a frost that I fell twice going down as did also Eugenia Mr Jaegle and all the company what made me laugh heartily at last we decided to sit down on the earth and slide like that untill we were at the bottom of the hill this was most successful. We went to our good colonel who gave us some coffee and amused us very much with his paroquet that can speak a great manner of things then we went back and found our carriage half way to the castle and climbed in. This walk has done me all the good in the world and was a great amusement to me.

SUNDAY, JAN. 21ST. Mde de Louvois dined here: all the children Louis, Bitche, Charles, Auguste, Justina, Harriet, Henri, Gebhardt and Eugenia masked themselves, but I went for a fine walk with Mde de Bombelles we went to Stadt to visit a poor family where there is a child that she protects that is very ill. The poor little children in this country are kept in a room that is terribly hot and where there is never any fresh air in consequence they can never have a good health. I think it is very remarquable that in a country that is so cold the peasants that is to say the people should be so sensitive to the cold I imagine it is because they are so accustomed to their rooms where there is the most unsupportable heat. The evening was spent rather wearily.

MONDAY, 22ND JAN. This evening we had a most charming surprise. Imagine what it was? *Marionettes.* The player arranged them in our theater up in the attic but the trajedy they played made us laugh not weep. It was the prodigal son, after they played a little farce that was not so fuñy as the trajedy and then a *Lustiger Tanz* of all the marionettes that was comical enough although it was in german. Our little theatre is truly more suited to dolls than to grown-up people.

TUESDAY, JAN. 22ND. Papa dined at Horn with Mde de Louvois wich gave a great feast. We occupied the evening in well setting and curling our hair for the *Picnic* of Roschach that will be tomorrow and to which we are going.

WEDNESDAY, JAN. 24TH. *Betsey's account.* I slept late this morning in order not to be sleepy at the ball.

I spent all the afternoon until three o'clock at my toilet then all those of Wardeck except the Baron and Mr Labrosse climbed into the carriage, we called at Mrs Hoffmann's before going to the Pique-Nique but she was at Constance on account of the death of her mother we arrived at last at the Crown where there was yet no one. We waited for a long time. It was raining very hard and we were afraid that nobody would wish to come, but at last a carriage arrives, it was the MMs de Bayer very elegant, with the sad new that their mother and sister were not coming and that the weather was so bad that they were afraid no one would come. A gentleman from St. Gall the brother of Mr Mesmer told us that the company from St. Gall was not coming and a messenger from Rheineck told us that those lovely ladies did not either wish to come. The horses were already being harnessed when a Lady from Roschach, a cousin of Mrs Bayer came this poor young person was as tricked as us. As there were six or seven men I dansed a few valses out of politness but as I had a great pain in my stomach I was begging for us to go away when Mde de Louvois entered in the greatest elegance, with all her jewels etc we stayed yet another half hour but then we set off again and arrived at Wardeck it was not yet eight o'clock the gentlemen who had stayed at home made great fun of us I was so ill that I went to bed after having vomited a great deal. Mde de Bombelles had good news of her husband who was in very good health but who had been upset in his carriage and had spent a whole night freezing under the stars. He wrote to her from P . . .[1] in I . . . where he will not remain long. I think that the eldest Mr Bayer that is the ugliest but who seems to be very good

[1] Pavia, where the princes were.

was very ashamed that his mother had not been at the *Pique Nique* to keep us company which really was a nasty action.

Eugenia's account: 'At last the famous day arrived which I had imagined was to be such a glorious feast. . . . In the morning we did our lessons as usual. The afternoon was passed in dressing our hair and brushing it, in changing our shoes a hundred times and having them sewn on and imagining we should have to danse a great deal and such like occupations. At length the hour so impatiently awaited came we went very quickly in spite of the weather and arrived at Roschach at about three o'clock, there was there nor cat nor dog at last the musicians came. We heard the sound of wheels. Joy! Joy! "It is a livery unknown to me," said Mr. Jaegle. Good. It is a dung cart! After having been very wearied of waiting and very impatient we saw the MMs de Bayer arrive, desolated and ashamed to find only us at the Picnic. We grow yet more impatient, we sulk and they do everything in their power to amuse us. Some people come when we are on the point of leaving we were all together only about 11 persons a cousin of Mr de Bayer's that was pleasant enough and some gentlemen. What use was my fine bonnet? My rouge? and my fine Fur? These were our cries. We began to dance and when for the second time we were on the point of leaving Mde de Louvois arrived well jewelled and painted what made her beautiful as an angel. We began again to danse. At last Betsi having a pain in her stomach and as no persons more came we all went away. The Ball and all our misfortunes had given me a famous appetite wich made that I eat a gay and copious supper one can be happy in spite of many misfortunes.'

CHAPTER 7

TUESDAY, JANUARY 31ST, 1792. I was a little distracted at all my lessons because of the mascarade and this evenings ball. They have turned my head round a little. I was very sad to see that though we prayed and tormented Mde. de Bombelles to come that she had got it into her head that she must stay because Charles had cried out for fear that she should go, so that our prayers had no effect. I masked myself this evening. How long this hour (in which I was to make my toilette) has been coming! I masked myself in a peasant. My dress, although simple, was vastly pretty and light. Eugenia and Lewis were very well masked as negro and negress. Papa and Mamma, Jaegle and Barthèse, this last having come specially to that intent from St. Gall, set off. The roads did not seem to me so very bad as they had been said. We stopped at Arbonne at Mr Vlintz's house and I made the acquaintance of four of his daughters after having stayed an hour with him he took us to the Ball which was in the Inn. There were many people, amongst them the Albertis ladies who were most polite above all the eldest what had four charming little girls who were also at the pique-nique. This society is of all those in the town that should pay themselves. Strangers do not pay any-thing. I danced a great deal above all with Mr Martinione who danced very prettily. Mr de Bayer the eldest and the youngest came late very well masked. They took off their masks to dance. There was a very good supper and after one danced a little. We left early in order to have a full moon and we arrived happily at home where we found M. le Baron still up. I cannot say enough how much I amused myself at this feast, all the ladies were so charming and so good that I loved them all very much. What a difference to the society at Roshach, I think except the family Bayer and the Col. all the others are so proud they are insupportable. I was very glad to get to bed as I was very tired.

Eugenia's account: 'My gaity became almost madness. At last they dressed me and I looked more like an Asiatic princess in all her splendour than like Eugenia with so much gold spangled muslin and pearls and diamonds—(false ones)—Lewis also was a negro and Betsi a peasant. At the Ball we had an excellent supper and politenesses and kindnesses were heaped upon us. We left about eleven in order to have a full moon.'

Eugenia: 'There has been a dispute between Mr Jaegle and M. l'Abbé of priests marrying and the validity of the vow made to God. One of them is according to me right and the other wrong. The one that is wrong is . . . Though I have nothing against priests who take orders under the new constitution and who marry for they will not make the oath of chastity, but I always despise the man who violates the Oath he made God.'

SUNDAY FEBRUARY 5TH. 'At last good news of Marys marriage. It will be on Sunday in eight days. This makes me very contented. Mde. de Louvois is really good and kind although too talkative.'

TUESDAY, FEBRUARY 7TH [in English]. I took no lessons today not being well. I laid in bed till ten oclock and worked at my mask for tomorrow. I shall be dressed in a Spanish woman with a black gown and red mantle etc. All the people of Wardeck except the children Mr Jaegle and me dined at the Colonel Klebach. They had I hear an excellent dinner. I gargled myself and took great care of myself so was much better tonight. I played cards with the others and I won two florins. The intrigueing and wicked curé of Roshach has put so many scruples into the head of the Prince of St. Gall about the permission which this weak but always charming man had given that he now will not any longer consent to Marys marriage with François as they are not of the same religion and he does not even give them leave to live in this country after having been married in another. The Parson of Roshach is a very noted man which is a great hater of all of us. It has been resolved to write to Rome and ask the Pope for permission to celebrate such marriages. My God! what a lot of troubles one must endure in a country which is intolerant like this one. It is against Religion that this feeble man has let himself be persuaded by that faulse, knaughty, Intrigant.

SUNDAY FEBRUARY 19TH. We had yet another repitition this morning and the piece went better than yesterday. Madame de Louvois arrived this afternoon to dress herself as did all the other actors. The audience arrived without my being able to see them and I only showed myself after having played. It was dark when we began the comedy. It went very well. Madame de Louvois played like an angel, she is one of the best actresses that I have heard in my life. Madame de Bombelles with her funny old womans clothes and her chatter made everyone laugh. The theatre did not seem too small and it seemed to me that all the persons were pleased with our spectacle. Directly after *Nanine* we danced. There were many people. Mr Barthèse was come with his two daughters, his son and one of his nephews. The youngest daughter a Miss of twelve years that I saw for the first time is pretty enough and they say has much wit but I think that her wit consists in a great gabble for she does nothing but chatter. The refreshments were in great number and the Ball charming. We danced till ten oclock and then we had a grand supper. All the ladies were seated and the gentlemen were at other little tables and served their ladies. It seems they found the punch very good for after supper nearly all the dancers were drunk but that only made the dance more gay. I danced continually till three oclock in the morning and then as the dancers were all tired they stopped. All went away except Mde de Muller and her daughter who will stay with us till Wednesday. Madame de Louvois and her son also stayed here. I was excessively tired when I went to bed but I had passed a very pleasant evening.

Eugenia says: 'Betsi played her part well; better than I expected.'

ASH WEDNESDAY, FEBRUARY 22ND. I got up very late and went to Mass and took the cinders. After we made a little walk and saw a child that Madame de Bombelles looks after. I was charmed with the sight I had in that little room, the old father mending his coat, two young girls embroidering a music stool which every peasant does well in this country, the boy making thick ribbon and the mother nursing her baby. It was touching to see how occupied they all were. After that we went to see the shoemaker that had his leg bitten. After we came home and Mamma read us the sermon of Massillon before dinner. In the afternoon she went to pay a visit to the Prince of Diessentis and during her absence an Italian came to show us a strange animal it was a Beef which had three horns, 3 eyes and two noses. It was very fat and was six years old. [*Eugenia* says: 'It was very tame and I touched it several times on the horns.']

I went down into the courtyard to see it better. [*Eugenia* says: 'He also had a little monkey which he carried on his shoulder.'] Soon after some peasants came in masks to bury the Carnival. It is the custom in this country to bury the Carnival on Ash Wednesday. Papa came back from Constance with Mr de Regis and said that it was a town that was deserted and not pretty. He did not amuse himself much there for he went to balls and does not know how to dance. He made there many acquaintances. I played the harpsichord this evening and went to bed a little ill. Is it always like this when one finishes Carnival?

Eugenia: 'Mary received a letter from her mother in which she consents to her marriage and in which she asks pardon of her for having reproached her so severely in her last letter. Madame de Bombelles received some news from her husband. He is at last arrived safely in Russia. I think that our prayers were not useless to him.'

THURSDAY FEBRUARY 23RD. It made a terrible wind and weather all the day. We received a very drole letter from Mde de Louvois for a trick that Papa played her yesterday when he went to see her on coming back from Constance. He had searched very much in all the town for a *chamber* for Madame de Bombelles but it seems that this piece of furniture is as rare in that town, as are inhabitants, for in spite of his researches he could not find one to buy but when he came to Horn he saw a very fine *chamber* in the room of Augustus and took it, Madame de Louvois guessed this to be Papa or Mr de Regis because they told her they had searched in vain in Constance, and this lead to her letter which was charming. She condemns the two gentlemen to go and drink two bottles of Burgundy with her, Madame de Bombelles to go and kiss her and amend for the theft. These pleasantries amused us very much. I was delighted that Mr de Muller did not send for his daughter. She will stay till Saturday. I had a bad sore throat and cold on my chest and in my head. We played at *secretary* during the evening which is very amusing if you do not get angry, because one can write all that one likes about the people that play at it. I went to bed early again at my own wish that I might be better tomorrow. Madame de Louvois told us that it is almost certain that her brother Mr de Mackau will come here in fifteen days with his family. She praised much her little sister in law. I confess I shall be charmed to meet this family.

FRIDAY FEBRUARY 24TH. *Eugenia*: 'To day was Madame de Bombelles birthday and Mr de Regis made her some pretty verses on that subject. She is thirty years old. I cannot help relating a story that pleased me very much in the History of France. Louis resolved to poison his father the King in order that he might enjoy the throne. Charles VII that was his father discovered the plot of his unnatural son and let himself die of hunger rather than to allow his son to commit parricide. The son, Louis the XI, sullied his reign with a dozen crimes each more horrible than the last, and finished his life in the horrors of the fear of death and the anguish and remorse that such a life caused him.'

SATURDAY, FEBRUARY 25TH. I found Madame de Louvois indisposed. Everybody at Horn and at Wardeck has a cold. It is the leaving of Carnival. The Prince of Diessentis had the kindness to confess us in our Chapel. He is too good a confessor. I made music this evening with Papa. I played a quatuor by Pleyel that Cimador arranged for the harpsichord.

TUESDAY, FEBRUARY 28TH. Papa dined at Horn with

Mr de Regis. As thief he had a cord round his neck all through dinner and drank two bottles of Burgundy for penitence. I had three letters from Mlle. Battaja. In one she tells me that her sister in law was brought to bed the 9th of this month happily of a pretty little girl. I am sorry that it is not a boy for Madame Battaja the wife has already got four daughters of whom two are dead. Music in the evening.

TUESDAY MARCH 6TH. I stayed in bed all the day. The Baron de Wirtz dined here with his son and Mde de Louvois. Harriet is very ill. She has pain in her ear and much fever. I played this evening at Backgammon, dominoes and Ecarté with Lewis and Mr. Jaegle. I got up a little this evening and heard a sermon which was on '*Keeping up Appearances*'. It was very beautiful. Madame de Bombelles came up, she is afraid that Harriet has got small pox. Mamma and she talked of marriage and of the jealousy of husbands and of the miseries that one suffers when one is married. How queer and wicked men are.

MARCH 12TH. *Eugenia*: 'The snow and cold continue. Mamma suffers much and was obliged to go to bed after dinner so Mr. de Regis read the sermon which was on *the small number of elect* and one of the finest that we have read. It seems there is much difficulty in saving oneself the way to heaven is narrow they say and that to damnation is wide. What I learnt from this sermon was that one must not be content with what one says, "I do, as others do", for it is just then that we say "I damn myself". Happily in Wartegg we have not many occasions to sin, we must therefore hope (since we are obliged to believe in a merciful God) that we will not go to the Devils house but will partake in Heaven with the saints of their happiness. So be it. Amen. What does not please me in Massillon are the praises he gives in all his sermons on Louis XIV (that was king then), and certainly did not merit them. For it seems to me that a priest from the pulpit ought always to leave flattery aside and to say rather the truth to kings than to put on a smooth air and tell them what he does not think. But everybody has their faults! and Massillon must be excused because he is not the only one who has committed this fault. This evening I told stories to the little ones as did also Eugenia and Louis. *Mr Bitch* seems to be a great coward he cried and trembled with all his might because his elder brother began a story about robbers.'

WEDNESDAY MARCH 14TH. We received yesterday a reply from Cardinal Bernis to whom we had written to obtain the Popes permission for the Marriage of Mary and François. The Holy Father only permits this marriage to take place with the permission of the Bishop of Meaux and as he is Constitutional his permission would be worth nothing. What to do! Truly I do not know how this affair will end. Papa wrote us from Wagen and should arrive today at Ratisbon. The doctor is to come and innoculate the children. He has sent us a medicine for them that is called Peruvian Bark or Quinine in order to prepare them for the small pox. He will be here in a few days. Dear God, how impatient I am to see them innoculated and recovered.

FRIDAY MARCH 15TH. The snow has gone but it rained nearly all day. I did not hear much of the sermon today, it was on *Apathy* for whilst it was being read the children made such a noise and Made. de B. whilst embroidering her waistcoat never stopped talking to the Abbé and giving him good advice all the time that I was distracted and could not pay the least attention to the sermon. [*Eugenia*: 'It is impossible to do anything that demands attention when the children are so rowdy and it is of no use to bid them to be quiet for it is as if one spoke to the wind, they take no notice. One comes in with a chair as his carriage pulling it after him with a great noise, another escapes with cries from the blows of his brother, that really it is not to be born, it gives me the colic. If it was my children or my sisters I would certainly have shown them the door for it is unsupportable.'] There was an assembly at Mr Jaegle's after dinner to drink some beer which Papa has given him. These visits to him are so frequent that I fear there will soon be none left. We had a letter from M. Sharp, the doctor from Bischoffzell that is to innoculate the Small Pox to the children, he says that the bad weather prevents his coming but that he will come next Monday. How I wish this horrid Smallpox were already over!

MARCH 16TH. The Bailiff told us at the fair of Arbonne today that a person that was come from Constance yesterday gave them the sad new of the Queen of France's death, no one believes it, I hope it is not true. We were invited to dine at Horn where we found also the two Mlles. Albertis who wore round bonnets which made them look more pretty above all the youngest who made a little music to us. We found Mde. de Louvois very sad for she had just heard the sad new from her sister Mde. de Travanet from Paris to tell her that all the goods of the emigrés were going to be sequestrated but in spite of that she must not return to Paris for one is always near being killed, that continually persons are murdered and massacred there and never before have such horrors been committed as there are today; that the civil war is already begun in twelve or thirteen places. Mde. de Louvois has perhaps at this moment not a cent and it was really touching to hear her talking to her son, who said all sorts of sweet things to her. She cried a lot: how natural her sorrow and her grief! She shewed much strength and courage (if this new of the confiscation of property is true) how she is to be pitied! Young Mr de Muller came to Horn this afternoon to tell us the Archduke Francis, king of Bohemia and Hungary has been poisoned, another thing I don't believe. I came home early. Mde de Bombelles is very sad because of what is said about the Queen's death. Mde de Regis also is not gay because there is civil war at Avignon and her daughter is there. In short all Wardeck and all Horn (I think every Aristocrat) is sad. The Sermon was read this evening: very fine but the praises of the king are too strong.

Eugenia: 'Poor woman she is not sure of bread. We told her the new of the Queens death that we did not believe. She was desolated. That Queen was strength to the King, without her France is lost. Ah, how happy I am that I am not French. God is indeed too good and just to abandon and to throw down into an abyss that house of Innocence and to permit that crime should conquer. Surely he will never allow to be trampled down a king whose only fault was weakness and those peoples whose only fault was to be faithful to him and to forbid the changes that it is wished to make in our religion?'

Saturday March 17th. *Eugenia*: 'It was seen in the German Gazette that the new of the Queen of France is false which gave me great pleasure. We received a very good letter from Papa written the 13th in a village a few miles from Augsburg where they were stopped because the weight of the fat Baron had broken a wheel of the carriage. They hope to arrive the 14th at Ratisbon. I cannot prevent myself from telling the way in which the amiable Queen of Naples gave to the Bombelles 12000 francs of pension when they were at Venice. M. de Bombelles with his children including Henri went to pay her a visit. Henri cried and the Queen drew from her pocket a little purse and gave it to him, as if to make him quiet. Then she sent them away saying that she was going to dine. Madame de Bombelles wanted to give back the little purse but she refused in a very touching manner. "No, let him keep it, it is for him and for all of you." She accompanied them to the end of the stair case. Mde. de B. saw to her astonishment that the good Queen was smiling at her. When they got into their gondola Mde. de B. opened the portfolio and found in it a most charming letter in which this noble and charming Queen guaranteed them 12 thousand francs a year until their father had a place worthy of their noble ancestors. The afternoon she went to thank the Queen who had the delicateness not to wish that she should show her gratitude in front of the world and told her to go to the Duchesse of . . . her lady in waiting and that she would go there soon and receive with tears of joy the signs of gratitude for her kindness. All this Madame de Bombelles told us. We spent the evening very agreeably in listening to this charming story and we read afterwards a little comedy given to the Prince Royal of Denmark on his birthday which is charming. But I forgot to tell the amiable reply which the generous and good Queen of Naples made. M. de Bombelles asked her what he could have done to merit such goodness, that he had never had the happiness to serve in any way the king of Naples and she answered "that he who served so well his king serves all kings".'

SUNDAY MARCH 18TH [in English]. Never have I seen such lovely weather, or such blue skies in this country. We walked out before dinner and after dinner. Madame de Louvois was gay I think she is resolved to go to Bitche for truly her goods are in danger of being confiscated. She sang, what she does very bad, her voice trembles like an old woman of eighty years. She is I think only forty five.

MONDAY MARCH 19TH. The weather was very fine. In the afternoon we went to Roschach on foot with Madame de Bombelles and all the gentlemen to wait for the post which was not yet come. M. de Regis gave us some coffee at the *Crown*. At last the letters and the gazettes from France arrived. They were very interesting to the french. Coming home it rained very strong and I was wet through to the bones for we were all on foot without umbrellas. We found at home the doctor who is come to innoculate our poor little children. Henri was at once sent for and as Harriet was some time coming back from Arbonne where Mamma had been with her, he was innoculated without waiting for the little girl. I have never seen such a good way of innoculating a child. It feels nothing and as Henri was amused by it he wanted to be innoculated a second time. Harriet came home and was innoculated without crying once. The doctor has a little lancet which is in a case so that only the point is shown, he pricks with it the arm of the child and rubs the place with a little sponge on which there is some small pox. without there being any blood, it is an excellent way. This doctor is a man who is rich enough and follows the occupation of innoculator to amuse himself. Mary had a letter from Françoise. Papa has at last arrived at Ratisbon and fears to be attacked by gout. We shall have some news by the next post.

WEDNESDAY MARCH 21ST. The weather was lovely and as we had agreed Tuesday to go the Appenzel we left this morning after having received a visit from our doctor's daughter that is very beautiful, and after having waited a long time for M. de Regis. Mr. de Regis, Cimador, Eugenia, Lewis, and Bitch de Bombelles me and Nepomuck (who carried a leg of mutton and some bread in a sack) took about 11 oclock the road to Appenzell, we went two leagues always up a steep hill and in a lot of mud and always on beautiful roads with a fine view. I must admit I was a little tired when I arrived. Where we went there was the house of a weaver, the best person in the world and perfectly good. We drank some milk when we arrived and we had some excellent butter with our dinner. These good people took all the trouble in the world that we should be well served. After having eaten well we left this charming place and made a long détour and came down by a road in the middle of the forest. It was charming and the weather was always fine.

MARCH 26TH [English]. I had apples and bread for my breakfast and felt myself very well. Mamma is begun to give us some money for our breakfast in order to unacustom us to coffee, she will give us 3 florins a month. Mary had a letter from François that reassures us about Papa's health. He tells us that he has never been so well since fourteen years and hopes to come back towards the end of next week.

MARCH 27TH. Henri had a strong fever today and directly after dinner he had a convulsion that alarmed us all very much. Always when he sleeps he has terrible jumps. Harriet is still very well only her arm hurts her. The affairs of France are in a very bad state, a Decree against the unfortunate emigrés says that their goods will be taken if they cannot prove that they have been in France for six months, it does not suffice that they have been in France they must have been on one of their estates. Good God how unjust they are!

Good Friday, April 6th. We got up early and went to the Morning Services at Roschach everything was nearly over. The Holy Sepulchre is superb it could not have been better illuminated. The Blessed Sacrament is exposed there. Mde de Louvois was there with her son. We went after to see the good Colonel Keebach. She was in a very bad humour and very sad, she is angry to have to go back to France, having terrible fears of being massacred. She said to her son that she leads him to the butcher and that he will have his throat cut and in short said such things to the child as to make him mortally afraid. She makes the danger a thousand times worse than it is. She received a letter from her lawyer in Paris to tell her that she must go at once on her estates. She has such an exaggerated imagination that hardly had she read this letter that she was seized with a terrible trembling accompanied with convulsions, nor did she cease to repeat 'how I suffer, how much I suffer, how glad I shall be to die!' At this Augustus threw himself into her arms and besought her not to speak like that. She went red and repulsed him with very great anger. She remained some time dumb staring fixedly and then she cried, 'Oh yes, now they are strangling him'. (He had already left the room) She began to cry bitterly and threw herself at the knees of Mamma asking her with trembling hands clasped together, to give her back her son and asking whether they had already killed him. She had entirely lost her reason. I could not prevent myself from crying for this poor woman makes herself very miserable by this yielding to her dispair, I thought I was at a play, at the tragedy. When she was a little calmer she went away and we did the same. She should surely have some courage and firmness! Mde. de B. was ashamed of seeing this scene as Mrs. de Bayer was there for she was persuaded that all Roschach would laugh at her. In the afternoon Mamma and Mde. de Bombelles went to see Mde. de Louvois who asked pardon for all the insults she said to them this morning. She is now very calm and has decided to go to Bitche. We played several games (I learnt that of *Solitaire*) until it was time for Church. After Tenebrae and Laudes we came home. Harriet is well, she can walk and her small pox begins to dry up. Yesterday the Curé of Roschach was very polite to us and had the kindness to give us candles at church. I think that very amiable of him, more so that he cannot stand us.

APRIL 7TH. The weather was so bad that we could not go to Roschach. We learnt the news of the assassination of the King of Sweden. This Prince was at a masked Ball when a monster shot him with a pistol and wounded him in the thigh. His pistol was loaded with nails. It is said that the king is in great danger of death. The author of this atrocity was recognised by his knife which he let fall and it was recognised by the man who had made it precisely for him to commit this wicked action. [*Eugenia*: 'For me I do not believe all this though a *man* much *wiser* than myself believes it yet my *little head* thinks to have *reason* likewise his *big head* thinks that he has so that it must be that we *both* have reason. The sermon that we read was on the *Passion* and was even finer than the last.'] Papa writes that he hopes he will be here on Wednesday. I wish greatly to see him. I embroidered all the evening. I fear the waistcoat for Louis will not be ready for the day of his first communion which will be Low Sunday.

MONDAY, APRIL 9TH. The good Prince of Diessentis came to confess us and Made. de Bombelles gave us an excellent breakfast. She read to us a letter of the democrats to the King full of insults, amongst others 'the people is everything without you and you are nothing without the people' could one carry insolence further! The attempt made on the life of the king of Sweden is confirmed. He is not dead but his life is feared. After Mass we walked with Mary, Eugenia, Clergé and the elder children of Bombelles we went to the Wartensee where we had milk and cream and delicious cyder. We climbed up to Weinach and went round the forest that is in Rheinthal. We found many beautiful places one especially charmed me. There was a little cabin with a garden surrounded by beautiful trees through which one could see a superb plain. One could see the sunset between the trees which was magnificent. We walked more than three hours.

APRIL 10TH, TUESDAY. We went at six oclock in the morning to the communion in our Parish and we came back after having heard Mass. We read this morning before going for our walk a superb sermon of Massillon which is the last that we have to read. Then Mamma her four daughters and Mr, Jaegle went for a fine walk on the road to Rheineck. As we had permission to work I embroidered all evening.

WENESDAY, 11TH APRIL. I took all my lessons to-day, and after dinner I went on foot at Roschach to meet Papa, which was to come all the children were with us. We went at the Crown, but as he never came and as it was late we came home. Down the hill we heard a Coach coming, and it was Papa—We came home with him, and was very much pleased, to see Harriot perfectly well, he is in a very good health, and has amused himself very much, he brought us some fine presents especially to me a great deal of music. The Baron is always as fat as usual. They came by Anspach and Ulm, and had a very happy journey, I am very glad to see Papa, it's more than a month he was gone. We were very gay at Supper, and very contented to see him back.

APRIL 15TH, LOW SUNDAY. We all left early for Roschach and went to the great Mass. Madame de Bombelles, her four sons, we four and Mary went to the Colonel where we found Mde. de Louvois with her son and we went to the church. I went to the organ with my sister. An instant after arrived all the 140 children who come to make their first communion. The curé make them a charming sermon, during the ceremony a hymn was sung. All the little girls had behind their heads little garlands of Rosemary. After Mass all the children went in procession to the curé's house and he gave presents to the 140 children. Louis especially had very pretty presents. It was very touching to see all those children who seemed full of devotion. At last we went to the Colonel where we had breakfast. Mde. de Louvois gave Louis a gold Louis. After dinner we went to Vespers. After we all went to Horn with Mde. de Louvois and saw *Lamassa* or the *Widow of Malabar* which was acted there. I understood very well the comedy though it was in German, it was well played. The Theatre is in a small barn and was very full. The music and dress and the songs of the actors were ridiculous and the funeral pyre which was made of wood and hay was supposed to burn the widow nearly burnt us all for the boards of the theatre were set alight and the gentle Montalban was obliged to leave his dear *Lamassa* in order to put out the fire. The Brahminesses were very badly dressed, they looked like ghosts come out of a tomb. The orchestra was detestable yet I amused myself for I laughed a great deal. We came home to Wardeck and found Mamma ill.

MONDAY APRIL 16TH. We read the French papers where there was a letter of a soldier written to the King of France which is of the grossest insolence and which horrifies one. We hear that Jourdain (the famous brigand) and his companions have been set free for their infinite merits and their patriotism. This monster is unworthy even to sully his life with new crimes. He has been led in triomph to Arles. Meanwhile an assembly has decreed that all monks nuns etc, must no longer wear their habits, not even in the house. The soldiers' letter says 'We still have the mercy not to deliver to the earth the object that is its horror, you could have been its delight but you are only its plague'. It is thus that they speak to him. The king of Sweden is dead and he that assassinated him when he was caught said, 'Ah, that I could have done the same thing to all the sovereigns of Europe'. The unhappy Prince Gustavus Adolphus the Third died the 29th March, aged 46 years, the Duke of Sudermanie his brother is Regent and the hereditary prince aged fourteen years will attain his majority when he is 18. At table it was decided to go to Appenzell for the general assembly. It will be in that place Sunday week. There will be about three thousand people there. It is suggested we go to Alstäten in the carriage and then we shall have three leagues to walk. I shall be delighted to go for it is a thing that only happens every 36 years. Papa thinks he is ill although he is not. He drugs himself and I fear that he will make himself ill. The music he brought me from Ratisbon is pretty but extremely difficult.

TUESDAY, APRIL 17TH. Louis, Bitch, Eugenia and me with Clergé went to dine at Mde. de Albertis at Arbonne. Augustus was ill. Mde. de Louvois did not receive any new yesterday. The king has sanctioned a decree against the emigrés goods so she does not know yet if she should go. She read us some of the letter to the king. They said to him, 'If you want us to bear with you, send away Antoinette (the Queen) drive out from you this *Brunehaut* who follows so well her model, and who will probably have the same end as that monster'. (She was tied to the tail of an unbroken horse and was thus dragged over stones and thorns) They were terribly mad. The ladies Albertis were in their garden and we went at once to dinner. When we arrived at table they pressed us to go to the comedy at Horn. I did not wish to consent without telling Mamma but the eldest having the kindness to write to her I consented with pleasure. We went in the carriage to the comedy. We met on the way Mr Cimador and La Brosse on horseback. They came with us to the spectacle which was charming. We saw *Baldriau Klau*, or the *Superstitious Lover*; although nobody explained the comedy to me I understood everything. The piece was long and the weather was not fine when we went back to Wardeck.

APRIL 19TH. I accomplish today 14 years at midday. How old I am! There was a very bad storm directly after dinner. I was afraid it would prevent us from going to Rheineck but hardly was it over we went with all the children and Mde. de Bombelles to M. de Lombach who was not there yet, he came soon and took us to the Ball room. I thought there would be a superb Ball and how surprised I was to see only five or six little boys and girls of peasants who were all that composed this big dance which was a little Ball of Bourgeois. I amused myself however quite well dancing like the others. They gave us tea. I made the acquaintance of a young lady of Stoucart that is very pretty M. le Chancelier educates her. Mlle Heker married last Monday a Mr Karter and is gone to Vienna with her husband and his mother I am afraid she will be very unhappy with her husband because they say he does not love her at all but married her out of interest because she is very rich and he is very ugly and stupid and disagreable.

Eugenia: 'I must now relate the naïveté of *Charles* de Bombelles which made us laugh very much. He said that the devil was called Satan and his brother said he was called Beelzebub. Ah, replied Charles, "that would be his Christian name". I learn from the papers that the French will become pagans. France is a hospital and if I went there I would think myself transported into a mad house. Are they indeed going to adore false gods? It is really too much this madness and it is inconceivable. We began again to have Salon every evening. We have agreed to meet all of us at half past seven.'

CHAPTER 8

MONDAY, 23RD APRIL. Papa haveing been very much tormented ever since he has come back from Ratisbonne of the piles, and having feared it to be a Fistula, has consulted a very bad physician but as he is not well, he is resolved to go to-morrow to Zurick for to speak to a good physician, Mamma goes with him.

APRIL 25TH, WEDNESDAY. St. Mark. As today was a great feast at Roschach and there was a ceremony we went to it with the Abbé and the boys. We descended at the Colonel's, who took us to a convent of monks where he gave us two windows that give on a courtyard where mass was said. There were 14 processions of 14 parishes from the environs of this town, which were reunited at Roschach. There were more than a thousand persons and this great number of people made a wonderful view to see. After the mass the excellent Prince of Diessentis gave us breakfast and showed us the appartments of the convent, and he then took us into the garden where we met the young ladies of Roschach. We saw the processions go back and walked home through the wood which was so long that we were arrived late and they were already at dinner. After dinner I embroidered a little, and then walked out into the wood where we thought to go yesterday, and sat in the shade on the moss on the edge of a little stream. In the evening we played cards, I lost a florin. Mr. de Regis is very sad because his goods have been taken away. After supper Mde. de Bombelles read *Le Philanthrope* which is as amusing as possible. The gardener gave me a little garden today which will amuse me very much in cultivating it. The weather is charming and nature of a ravishing beauty.

Eugenia writes: 'We returned rather late and I met on my way to Wardeck the small carriage which was going to Horn for the children and which had left after us. I met it and made more than half a mile, running always with all my strength, and I arrived at the house before the carriage although they made the horses gallop. I was all in a perspiration on arriving but was not very tired of my day's walk.'

April 28th, Saturday. I got up at 4.30 and at 5 o'clock went with Mde. de Bombelles, her three children, my sister, Mr. de Regis, La Bross at Roschach. We walked as there was charming weather, and we had breakfast with a good peasant which was excellent. We had fresh butter, cream and coffee, and I ate terribly. After having stayed some time on the mountain where we had one of the most ravishing views, we returned by Wienacht and went all round the wood in the Rheinthal. We stopped in a delicious place where we had once been with Clergé. I call this place the Hermitage because there is such solitude and tranquility there, that invite one to rest. At our return home which was 11 o'clock we saw Jaegle and Cimador who went off to Appelzel to the general assembly. A letter from Mde. Elizabeth to Mde. de Bombelles tells us that at last war is declared in France. After that country had been so long in the state of waiting this event will make things turn one way or another, and will settle them. The King declared it the 20th of this month. I think that Mde. de Louvois will not go as they say there has already been a battle where there were 300 nationals killed and only 30 of the others. I find this difficult to believe. We stayed in the courtyard until they called us for supper. Mr. de Regis told us his *Pierre and Adelayde* made by him which was more stupid than the first time.

Eugenia states: 'The new of war being declared made some people very happy, for me if I think it would do good I am pleased at it, but if not I am not, even if it should be made good. I dont know enough yet to judge for myself whether this new should cause joy or sorrow but what does give me pleasure is that the most part of the troops according to what they tell me, are for the King, whilst I think that those who thought to triumph will be defeated, and that at last Louis XVI will become once more master of the power which they wish to take away from him.'

April 29th, Sunday. I walked much before Mass, and directly after I made my toilette. During this time Papa and Mamma came back from Zurich. They brought back with them Mde. de St. Gracien and her youngest daughter Mlle. Cleofile. Papa is very well. The doctor whom he consulted does not think Mamma is in a good state of health. He wants to make an operation on her which will make her suffer much but from which he hopes for the greatest good. He has ordered her baths and we shall leave for Schinznach in the beginning of June and stay there two months. They say it is a charming place seven leagues from Zurich, where there is much society. Mamma brought me back a watch and a superb golden chain and the same to Eugenia. Mde. la Comtesse de St. Gracien will stay here till Wednesday. She is a very amiable woman, she is from Strasburg, and has married a Swiss gentleman in the service of France who resembles much, I think, my aunt the Countess of Rosenberg who is dead, but she is even fatter, and has not so much wit. Her little daughter of eight years old is very spoilt and she is outrageously fond of her. She is honest and obliging as much as it is possible to be. Mde. de Louvois dined here, she is decided not to go. The Grand Master of St. Gall came and made a little walk with us, after some music till supper. The weather was magnificent. The flowers already fall from the trees.

Eugenia writes: 'Mde. de St. Gracien is a little deformed by her fat, but the graces of her spirit replace admirably those of her face, although she is deeply pitted with the small pox there is something in her face that is infinitely pleasing.'

Eugenia relates: 'This afternoon I went with Mr de Salis in the carriage and Betsy and Papa went with Mde. de St. Gracien. I must relate all the misfortunes which happened to M. de Salis which had no bad consequences and made us laugh. Primo I must describe our horses, two mares which although only hirelings were half mad with excitement and a horse that kept on falling. We got on alright however till all of a sudden the horse fell full length and fell on the leg of the unfortunate postillion who was dragged some way as well as the horse. He was still a little lame after his fall. Another time during a descent I do not know what startled the horse but suddenly she began to make jumps and cries so much so that she nearly broke her legs. I saw on our way a most astonishing novelty the carriage of a monk of St. Gall the Stadthalter which we found was the town livery which was like this: the right side of the habit was black and the left white, the same side of his waistcoat black the other white, one half of his knickers [breeches] black the other white, one black stocking and one white, indeed it was all such a ridiculous sight that one cannot imagine it.'

SUNDAY, 6TH MAY. After breakfast Madame de Bombelle, Bitch, Eugenia and me went at Roschach at the great Mass. Miss Hoffman would absolutely make me sing, but as I had not studied, nor Eugenia neither any of the music that the Curé had given us she came with us during the sermon at the Col. Keebach, and there we studied a little an air a piece, and a trio, which we sung afterwards in the Church. Never was my voice so much admired, and my manner of singing as to-day. It must be the inhabitants of Roschach that heard it, and praised it, (as they knew nothing of good music, and of what is well sung) because in no other place where one has heard a good singer one could not come to praise my voice and my singing. . . .

We went after Mass at Horn. We found Madame de Louvois in bed very ill She has got a very great Cold in the breast, she spit blood last night, and has a violent fever. She is so much oppressed that she can hardly talk. One bidds her not to speak; but it is impossible for her to hold her tongue one moment. We came soon home, and found the groom from Paris come. (He is named Jack Hammon and seems very cunning, too witty for a groom) and Impertinent, but very clever in his profession. He will not absolutely have less than 4 guineas a month, not wanting to dine at home—Papa will not keep him for that price, to-morrow it'll be settled. I went in the afternoon at the village Stadt where there is a conjurer he did not play any pretty tricks, and I rather wearied myself there than amused. Passed the evening with Mrs. de B. a talking.

MONDAY, 7TH MAY. Eugenia staid in bed. Her fever increases and her cold is bad. Mrs. de Bombelles was so ill this afternoon that she could not come with us, nor at Horn, nor at the concert at Roschach. Papa and Mamma and me went to see Mrs. de Louvois, which is still very poorly indeed, they read while we were there the newspapers and the new that the Frenchmen had been beat near Lille by the Austrains, that they hang's the prisoners they took which were six directly, and they cut in pieces there General Mr. Dillon for to burn him. 300 of them has been killed, and but 30 of the German; this new rejoiced all the people which heard it, which did not think, I suppose, that *men* had been killed.

MAY 16TH, WEDNESDAY. It is today the vigil of a great feast at Venice but it is only a little feast here. The shoemaker from Stadt who was bitten came today to warn us that the inhabitants of the village wished to avenge themselves on the inhabitants of the castle which they believe are all French, and who they think are the cause that some of them are obliged to march on Basle. (As in Switzerland the Prince of St. Gall has to give 1000 men for a cordon is being made.) I do not fear them however. Papa shows himself very brave and in order to defend himself better he has put a sword and two pistols with the gun that he keeps at his bed-side. Some peasants who have already met persons from the Castle have made insults to them taking them all for French, even Messrs Jaegle and Loeben.

Eugenia: 'I took my music lessons with Betsi but she does not acquit herself as well as Cimador.'

MAY 17TH, THURSDAY. Ascension. We went to the great Mass at Roschach where we asked all the young ladies and young gentlemen of our acquaintance to come and spend the afternoon with us. We prepared a little refreshment in the meadow under some trees where we had a man to play the harp so that when the company arrived we all danced and then refreshed ourselves with milk, fruits, a tart and some wine. In the afternoon we played a lot of games, we ran about and amused ourselves. Mlle. Hoffmann and Bayer and the gentlemen were very pleasant and amused themselves I think as much as us. The peasants who came to see us were all given beer of which they drank 24 measures. I passed a most agreeable afternoon and was extremely diverted, we expected Mde. de Regis but she did not come. I went to bed almost directly after our company had left.

Eugenia: 'We received our guests in the meadow where there was a tea prepared, and the harpist, swineish and drunk, ready to show us his talent and make us dance. All the inhabitants of Stadt looked through the hedge which separates the little road from the meadow where we were. From some words that we heard the drunk peasant say we learned that they wished to burn our Castle but I think this is only Malicious Gossip.'

Eugenia: 'Mr de Calissane (a lawyer) arrived with Mde. de Regis and her child. She is tall, badly made and ugly and pitted with small-pox but she has an agreeable physiognomy, and seems to be an excellent lady but it is a pity that her health is bad. The child is not pretty it resembles its father.'

May 20th, Sunday. Papa and Mamma were coming back from Horn where papa had been when Papa was insulted by a man who spoke French, who said of him all sorts of insults and oaths. As it is a man from the Rheinthal Papa will go tomorrow to complain to the Chancellor. William who had been to Appenzel having been first taken for a Frenchman was insulted, but when he spoke German he was well received. He was told that the Appenzellers were furious against the inhabitants of this Castle and that we were the cause that they must go to make a *cordon* at Basle, and leave their families and their fields. They again said that they would burn the Castle. I confess I was very frightened.

MAY 23RD, WEDNESDAY. This morning I rode on horseback with Jack who has purged all our horses and put them in a good state and which prepared to go after tomorrow. It is nearly ten months since I rode and although I only went to Horn I was a little tired on my return. I amused myself and the weather was not too bad. I had a bad sore throat and the beginning of a cold. The man who insulted Papa on Sunday has been recognised and he will be sent to Mr. de Würz to be punished. I received a letter from Cimador written from Isola on the 17th of this month. Actually he will now be arrived at Venice. I wish he was already back for the lessons of Justina and Eugenia weary me much.

Eugenia: 'We learned from a private letter the atrocious cruelties made by the Ahlangs against the patriots. They set fire to a house where 75 of these miserables had taken refuge and made them die in a most cruel way by preventing them from coming out to escape. I think these unworthy actions. Whatever rights war gives, one should not abuse them.'

MONDAY, 28TH MAY. I took physic to-day it gave me the Belly ake all day and made hardly no effect I got up but in the afternoon the wearying and horrid Mrs Braun of Lindau came here, she will stay a few days. We played at many games not to weary ourselves but for me I was tired to death of all the stupid company. The weather was very fine, but my physick hindered me from walking out.

TUESDAY, 29TH MAY. The person that had insulted Papa lately came here this morning to beg pardon and to say that he was excited by the people of Stadt to do it. Papa pardons him and the matter is all over. Louis was very ill I never saw a worse health than his. Papa has got the Piles again and fears to have the Fistula.

June 1st, Friday. We left Winterthür in good time and arrived at Zurich not a little wet. We stopped at Mde. de St. Gracien who insisted we should dine with her. Her elder daughter Mlle. Athenais is very amiable. Mde. de Vasson was not at her house she arrived in the evening from Basle where she had seen her husband who has emigrated from France and will join the princes at Coblenz. After dinner I walked with Mde. de St. Gracien, we made some purchases in the town and then she conducted me to a publick walk which is on a hill in the town, never have I seen such a lovely view as in that place, on one side one sees the lake of Zurich which is long and narrow, and on the shores of it, hills, mountains and the glaciers of the Canton of Glaris. The town of Zurich is large but not pretty it is situated on a stream the Limat which comes out of the lake. Mde. de St. Gracien gave us supper and we came to sleep at the *Sword*, a good inn on the bridge.

June 2nd, Saturday. As our horses and our carriage return to-morrow to fetch the rest of our family we hired one which made us wait a long time. While waiting for it we made some walks across the bridge and I saw the senators of the town who were going to the council, their costume is so funny that I must make a description of it. They wear a sword, and a black bonnet on the head and round their necks they have an immense round ruff they wear a black cloak with sleeves and a long vest [waistcoat] in the antique manner with trousers. We went in a bad carriage with worse horses. We were obliged to stop in a village to refresh them, there we took milk, at last we arrived at Richterschwyl where we stopped at the *Angel*. The situation of this village is charming running always beside the lake which at its widest is a league and a half so that the other side which is all inhabited can be seen and gives most charming views. We had a good dinner at this place that is on the edge of the lake. As Papa slept, my sister Mamma and me went alone to Dr. Hoze who is a man between fifty and sixty years; he is separated from his wife and lives at Winterthür. He has his two daughters with him at present. One is married to a Frenchman and the other in the Vallais. They are both pretty and amiable. We went to bed before it was dark as Mamma and me had a bad cold. One sees a lot of pilgrims pass on their way to Einsiedlen, the pilgrimage is three leagues away in the Canton of Schweiz where I much want to go.

June 4th, Monday. On my return from the doctors I saw an old pilgrim sixty years who had broken his arms, he was full of troubles and was going to Einsiedlen. Mamma and me gave him some little pieces of money and he was so happy that he cried with joy, then Mamma seeing how poor he was gave him six francs this man could nearly not speak with pleasure and gratitude. He was so penetrated with joy. He admitted that since he lived although he had worked very hard he had never had so much money. I experienced real satisfaction at having succoured this unfortunate man and how wicked it is to spend so much money which would make so happy poor people like him! We left after dinner in the hired carriage for Zurich. We stopped at the *Sword* and went to Mde. de St. Gracien. As she had company we did not go up to her but waited in the garden until she was free, then she and Mde. de

Vassan, Athenais and another gentleman came to supper at the Inn with us. We had an excellent supper to which I did honour for I ate a great deal.

JUNE 6TH, WEDNESDAY. My two sisters and me went to breakfast with Mde. de St. Gracien with whom we spent the day. I heard Mlle. Athenais sing that she does not do well, her voice is false and not beautiful. She took me for a walk in the town on our return we found Eugenia, Louis, Mary and Clergé had arrived. The first two did not look well, Louis has been extremely ill but was better. After dinner we went back to Mde. de St. Gracien where was all our colony and Madame Escher came. She is a lady of this town very pretty and amiable, (and young). Mlle. Athenais, Eugenia, Amelie, Louis and I went to do some shoppings I then went back to the Inn as it was already late and the ladies and their daughters were very charming to us. Mde. de St. Gracien wanted to obtain permission from Papa to leave us some days with her during the fair which will be for ten days. This excellent lady has always the greatest attentions and politenesses for us. All the ladies of this town are charming. We left early with our horses and those that we hired for Schinznacht, the weather was not good but not bad. The roads are good and we went always in a valley and stopped at *Baden* an ugly town in a hole surrounded by mountains. As it was a great feast and as the place is Catholic we went to the great Mass. The costume of the peasants in the Bailiwic of Baden is very drole, they have a short bodice and petticoats and one sees their legs almost to the knees. We had some excellent coffee at this place and then we continued our route. We crossed the river at Reuss in a boat, it was very fast and much swollen and I confess I was a little frightened. Directly after having crossed it we were in the Canton of Berne and soon after we passed Brück a little town a league from Schinznacht where we arrived before midday. The innkeeper is very polite as is also his wife and daughter. There is only the house where we stayed and the baths that are a little distance from the house. The first is sad-looking and the baths seem dirty. The mineral water is tepid, it is heated for the baths, it stinks horribly, the smell is exactly like that of bad eggs. It tastes horridly. There are some very pretty ladies to take the baths, they seem amiable. All the people are more amiable than those at Roschach. The Inn is agreeably situated in a valley next the river Aar, there is a charming wood next the house and many gardens. There is not yet come much society, I made acquaintance with the doctor from Lausanne and his wife and also with a lady and her daughter called Muttach and a gentleman from Basle wished to hear me play the harpsichord. We did not have a good dinner but a good supper. Papa gave for the two meals 1 louis and what is left over is for the servants. He gave 12 francs for five rooms.

JUNE 8TH. I took my two lessons with Mr Jaegle, we began to read *Les Voyages du Jeune Anacharsis.* The little that I heard today pleased me enormously and the style is very fine. Our rooms are gloomy and on the ground floor, the outside of the house is large and fine. I played and made conversation with the ladies whose acquaintance I had made. There is yet very little persons here one hopes soon more will come. The peasant women have a very funny dress, their hair hung behind in two long plaits and there frocks are so short that when they stoop one has not the *finest* views.

June 9th, Saturday. Directly after dinner I went a walk with Mlle. Mattach and Vachet, Eugenia and Lewis, the weather being superb. After having taken my lessons I went with Mr. Jaegle to the Castle of Hapsburg it is up a very steep hill and it is very high although time has destroyed two floors. It is eight hundred years old and more and it is from here that the house of Austria takes its origin. The view was superb. We climbed the tower which is very high and from there we had a fine birds-eye view. In the castle we saw only a big room very ruined still its age makes one come to see it by curiosity.

June 18th, Monday. *Betsy*: 'We got to Zurich at 12 oclock where we soon after went to see Mr. Lavater whom I love with all my heart. He is a well-known physiognomist and he is venerable, modest, gentle and wise and impresses me with a respect that I can hardly describe how much I felt, and desired and wished to be equal to him; these feelings were inspired by the presence of this virtuous man.'

Saturday. *Eugenia*: 'Little Justina is entirely recovered of her fever and the eruption has since a few days already comenced. For me I have begun today to take cold spring water baths in a big tub into which Francis plunges me: the sensation I experience in the instant I am under the water is disagreable.'

Sunday, 24th June. We had the Mass this morning and the *agreable* company of the stupid Friar with the peasant his companion at dinner. There came many persons this afternoon we danced and I was very sorry to be obliged to do it with the disagreeable and unsupportable Mr. Vouchet. We drank some milk in the garden with Miss Renner I like very much this girl because she seems good and well bred. Mamma suffers exceedingly with her issue she does not know what to do with it. A young lady of Berne that is here for her health which she spoilt in taking care of her Mother when ill before she died, is very amiable. Justina's fever is passed the poor child takes Bark three times a day.

MONDAY 25TH. *Eugenia* writes: 'I continued to take my cold baths and I hope they will do me a great deal of good. I have not much to say for this day, therefore I wish to try and write a little about myself. How greatly am I inconstant in my thoughts! Now I love one thing, then a single chance word suffices to make me detest it. I thought Mr. Vauchet was amiable, I abhor him at present, and really he has done me no personal wrong. I loved his sister, but now I have known her brother, I find her a thousand faults where once I found graces. I am very stupid, but I cannot control my feelings. I am so changeable an hour suffices to make me or love or hate a person, what I think pretty now in an hour the scene changes and it becomes ugly to my eyes. I am impatient with myself. I have two persons in me, one scolds me and dissaproves of all I do, the other flatters my passions and counsels me to follow their dictates indeed I am an enigma to myself and wish to know myself in vain. I have the vanity of a devil. I have wit without wisdom (so I am told and I well believe it) I have in short a thousand faults which I long to correct but always the evil vanquishes the good in me.'

TUESDAY, 26TH JUNE. I was very much astonished to see Mrs. Renner this morning smoke. All men has that bad habit here and that disagreeable vice is so inveterate in this country that even women cannot help having it. It is a terrible thing.

WENESDAY, 27TH JUNE. I did not go out a walking at all, I only sitted in the Yard with the company.

Louis de Bombelles brought us bread and raspberry vinegar.

THURSDAY, 28TH JUNE. *Eugenia*: 'The new from Paris are detestable. In order to force the King to sign two decrees, many persons of the common people armed with bayonets and pistols climbed up into his room broke open the door with a cannon than forced him with the bayonet at his throat to drink to the health of the constitution, and to put the red bonnet on his head. The National guard behaved like the grenadiers of the King. One of them was wounded by a bayonet which his companion had turned aside. For one of these mad men was going to kill the King. Louis XVI showed on this occasion much more courage than usual although he ran a great risk. Of all this what afflicted Louis de Bombelles most so much as to make him cry was the decree to burn all the archives of nobility. I certainly do not approve this measure, but it is the least of the evils. Louis is a français tout craché one sees already in him not the noble pride which pleases but the cursed French vanity, false politeness and misplaced gentility. In short he is a silly boy who thinks more of a long genealogical tree than of a poor but noble and virtuous heart that is what I think of him and of nearly all french people in general. How the counts, Marquises, viscounts, barons, vibarons, and chevaliers will be desolated at losing their titles. I think if the Revolution can do a good it will be to root out from the heads of the french their foolish vanity by taking from them all that nourishes it. Silly Fools!'

TUESDAY, 3RD JULY. *Eugenia*: 'I saw today a peasant that has 100 year and who does not look to have more than 60. He has few wrinkles, a venerable physionomy, and a long white beard that goes down to his waist. How long peasants' lives are, and how strong and robust they remain! I should like to see a nobleman of 100!'

SATURDAY, 14TH JULY. Directly after my lessons I went on the Road to meet Mrs. de Bombelle we soon saw her coming with all her brawling children, why has she got any? I wish she had none. After everybody having talked a moment of her arrival that the conversation turned to Politic and continued on that subject the remaining of the day. It wearied me much. We had fine weather, what gives me great pleasure.

MONDAY, 16TH JULY. I have got nothing to say upon this day, so I must also try to make some account of the customs and fashions of this country. Everyone drinks tea after dinner in the English fashion. No ladye goes to pay a visit without bringing with her a working bag of which she makes hardly no usage. Seldom a gentleman goes without his pipe and it is always adorned with emerald and silver chains the Ladies has got as much pomp in their working bags as the men in their pipes they are all perfectly dressed when you go anywhere you are shure to find a tea and a good gouté prepared everybody is very sociable and amiable in short I would like better to live here than at Wartegg I do not know how I shall do to accustom myself to the rudeness of the stupid bears of Roschach.

WEDNESDAY, 18TH JULY. I passed the Aar for the first time and went at Schinznach for to see Mary Esmonds married to François Coudin the Parson of that place married them, it is the first marriage that I see made. I wish the Bride and Bridegroom all happiness which I fear they will not have. The village is big they reckon it a 1000 inhabitants the parson seems a good man his house is clean and pretty and his church too. Really Schinznach is much further than I thought from the baths, and it was so hot that I was very much fatigued of my walk. The other borders of the river are not half as agreeable as these. The earth is very bad. The Bishop of Coming and is two nieces came to see us this afternoon. The ladies are too old and ugly maids born in Spain and which seem to be excessively rich. We made music and the Bishop an old but amiable (for society) man Likes it exceedingly.

MONDAY, 23RD JULY. We had again the visit of the tiresome French ladies, they are like Catterpillars after us, I can not see them without being sorry them English people did not stay in their place.

CHAPTER 9

FRIDAY, 3RD AUGUST. I was quietly playing the harpsichord this afternoon when Mr de Calissane came and brought the new that the King of France had been kil'd the Queen and the Dauphin hanged. Mrs. de Bombelles was terrible afflicted and almost exasperated but when we knew it came from Mr. Merz we did not believe it—this man gives all the bad news. The Count de Thurn went directly at St. Gall and us all at Mrs. de Louvois where the Colonel Keebach was. Mrs. de Louvois and de Bombelles were both in a poor state they cryed, they cursed the Nationals etc, we hoped always it was not true and as it did not touch me much I was always in a mind to laugh, seeing all us women talk Politic with the Colonel which is a good man but a great stup. However we came home after I had wearied myself 2 hours at Mrs. de Louvois. I wanted to waite for the Count de Thurn but was too Sleepy so went to bed before he came back.

SATURDAY, 4TH AUGUST. The news is faulse, so much better for the poor Mrs. de Bombelles which has been so very affected the breakfast was gay and all the day passed in joy. Mrs. de Louvois came here to-day she is in better health and staide this last night.

THURSDAY, 9TH AUGUST. I was yet in Bed when Papa arrived this morning on horseback we went till halfway to Roschach for to meet Mamma we stopped for 2 hours upon a Bridge for to wait for her, but wearied to stop so long it beginning to rain we came back she arrived soon after and with a pretty good state of health. Mr Hoze sayes that she is almost well. Justina is much better, but the poor child always takes bark. The two eldest Boys are very well I am glad to see us all reunited.

Eugenia writes how 'all the gentlemen to mark their joy of mama's return made themselves drunk and were very noisy. We drank more Punch after.'

THURSDAY, 6TH SEPTEMBER. The Good Prince of Diessendies dined with us. This afternoon Papa my Sisters the two musicians and me went at Roschach at the Concert at the Lion this concert is composed of Few persons, and each has a Bottle of wine and some bread by him. There we all sung Papa's mass which he made at Padua and which we will sing next Sunday at the church. We came home when night and I played at cards with Papa before and after supper. It rained continually the wind was high, at last it was a winter day but not a summer one.

SUNDAY, 9TH SEPTEMBER. We sung to-day Papa's mass at the church but all the musicians are so bad that it did not make a pretty effect, Papa has given us leave to go at Einsidlen and we shall go away Tuesday. I am extreemly glad to go at that place which it is long I wish to see. Mrs de Louvois dined here as the master of Horn is coming back she is obliged to leave that castle and will come I believe to lodge at the good Colonel's which is very proud to have as he has not little friendship for her.

MONDAY, 10TH SEPTEMBER. To-day we sent away our cook Mary La Fleur, whose knaughtiness was come to such a height that nobody can bear her any more. She is a good cook but a great rogue. Papa will undertake to-morrow the voyage of Chambery he is going to visit Mr. Blair, and will travel with the Baron de Wrintz on horseback. I believe this last is a poor horseman his journey will fatigue him.

TUESDAY, 11TH SEPTEMBER. We set off all together

this morning, Mamma the three eldest boys of Bombelles and Chappuy we took a carriage of the Lion, with two horses. We pay for it 6 each horse and a florin for the man per day. The weather was very handsome this morning and our journey very agreeable. We passed St. Gal and Gossau then left the rode at Zurich and came at Oberdalt where we stopped a little to repose the horses. We dined with Papa and the Baron de Wrintz these two will come with us till Einsidlen and then will continue there way to Chambeisy through Lucerne. It rained very hard when we left this place, and the bad weather accompanied us. This country (the Tokenburg) is very handsome but full of mountains and very cold. Poor Baron de Vrintz has his behind broken for he is not accustomed to go on horseback.

Wenesday, 12th September. We left the Tokenburg this morning and came to a small town after which we passed the river Limat upon a curious Bridge and came through exceedingly bad rodes but dined at Lachen a charming village on the borders of the lac of Zurich in the Canton of Schwitz. We had a charming vew in perceiving this pretty lac. From Lachen we saw Rapperschwill at the other side of the Lac and the famous bridge which crosses it. But saw it much more distinctly in coming up the mountain of Einsidlen. We were obliged to walk a league and a half coming by the mountain which is very steep. The Canton of Schwitz is poor but seems to be handsome has it is full of mountains. We arrived at last at this place which I was so desirous to see I shall to-morrow give a little description of it.

Thursday, 13th September. Papa left us this morning. I wish he was already come back. I went to see the Church which is big and handsome, the chapel of the Vergin is in the middle of it I saw it, and it is beautiful very rich and pretty. This place is in an agreeable situation, it is I think a big village every house is an Inn and notwithstanding this very often there is not place enough for all the strangers that comes. The pilgrims are in great number and they all drink of each source of a fountain that is before the church, and washes their eyes in that Water. The fountain has 14 sources. There is a great superstition here, at the door of the Chapel is 15 holes, the peasants believe that it is Jesus Christ which printed them with his hands But I do not believe this. I went to see the treasure this afternoon it is very rich and especially the Virgin's Clothes, which are numerous are beautiful. There is here the Bishop of Chalon with different French Ladies.

FRIDAY, 14TH SEPTEMBER. It was the feast of this place to-day and there has been a great mass say'd last night at 12 o'clock; we went to another this morning and we comuned. We have found here a friend of Chappuis Mr. Collo a priest a very amiable good man he is much like Mr. Fries. This afternoon we went to see a convent of nuns that is very near this place of which Mr. Coxe gives a very good praise in his letters upon Switzerland but he exaggerates much because its situation is the only thing worthy going to see. Them nuns keep some poor french priests in their convent what is very odd is that they are of each sex 21 persons. We went to Vespers when come back and to-night the whole town has been illuminated what was a handsome spectacle every window was lighted and there was the martyr of St. Minard very prettily represented. We followed the procession which was fine then the primate of this place gave the benediction. I had great pleasure to see this ceremony which was celebrated with such ceremony that it inspired devotion to everybody.

There is more than 100 French priests here they are very poor and one must pity them. The convent is a beautiful building I did not see the prince nor any of the monks except one whose name Martin and who has been an officer, is only 34 years old and is now a monk since 8 years. He is a charming man by what I hear. We shall to-morrow leave Einsidlen which I am very glad of having seen.

MONDAY, 17TH SEPTEMBER. We were very well at Stein, last night and we left it as soon as it was daylight. We always come along the lac, which is named Untersee and is formed of one branch of that of Constance. All this country is charming. We arrived rather soon at Constance, a great town, in a Beautiful situation but almost desert. We found at the inn where we dined some poor French priests which coming through Belfort had almost been hang'd. 800 persons surrounded them and cried 'à la Lanterne'. Poor men, I do not know how any persons could not pity them, they looked so frightened and miserable. We went to see some Waxe figures but they were not very handsome, they are very ugly after having seen some in England. At diner there were some French gentlemen that seemed to me so rediculous that I cannot help saying in my journal what thing can be more unsupportable than that nation, during all the while they did nothing but moke themselves of everything that came on the table as it is *the French custom*. I did not see much of Constance but I think it a very dull place. We were obliged to stay at Horn the *Goldach* being so great that it was impossible to pass it. Mrs. de Louvois had the bounty to lodge us, what gave us great pleasure because we were very much tired and waite and we didn't know what to do.

FRIDAY, 28TH SEPTEMBER. We had some news from

Papa when returned at Lausanne he will be here Sunday. The French have made an Incursion in Savoy and it is said that they have taken Chamberry (this is n't sure) the King of Sardainia's subjects have all taken the French National kockade, the Swiz are all in arms for to defend themselves In the canton of Berne all the French that were in it have received order to quit the country I wish it would be the same here. At last the weather permit me to go out and I took a charming walk this afternoon. We came back down the wood and took some milk at Wartensee. My walk did me good and diverted me exceedingly. But what is a very tiresome thing is that you cannot go out without or being insulted or moked by the peasants. It is very hard to be always taken for French and so be obliged to suffer all the insults that they receive in all the countries.

MONDAY, 1ST OCTOBER. We went in the afternoon at Mikyhause to meet Papa but having stopped there till night, we came home. He came soon after and I was extreemly glad to see him returned in a perfect health and as gay as it is possible to be. He has left the Baron de Wrintz at Berne as this could not come as fast as him and as he had quarrelled with him many times. Papa cannot bear that man any more, I neither. I stayed up with him till near 12 o'clock as he told us all the particulars of his journey which amused us much. All his horses are very poorly. He has left his groom Samuel at Lausanne and has taken Charles Dibble a very clever one and which he likes exceedingly. All the English that were near Geneva goes away and Mr. Blair is unfortunately in bed with the gout what hinders him from going away and what afflicts much his family as they are in France and as that part is very dangerous now. Papa gave us so many news that I remember none. He has seen many of his friends which has treated him with much kindness especially Mr. Weston to which he passed two days near Lausanne. Lady Mary has given Papa a poney for us it gave me great pleasure as I will be able to ride it alone it will come with the Baron.

SATURDAY, 6TH OCTOBER. Mrs. de Louvois dined here before setting off we went to accompany her till down the hill. I could not help seeing her getting into her carriage without wishing to do the same when shall I have that great happiness? All the French here I cannot bare—I like and esteem Mrs. de B. but when her stupid children is with her I would rather live far from her than with her. I much fear that we will pass the winter in their company. Oh how I should be happy if Papa would decide to go away alone with his family if we stay here I shall pass a very tiresome winter.

SUNDAY, 7TH OCTOBER. I did not go out till after dinner then I went for the first time on our Gray Poney Charles (the English Groom) will learn me to ride he came out with me and he seems to be a very good man. Eugenia went to take Miss Muller and came back with her but this evening. I was glad to see that good girl, and she'll stay with us till Thursday. Mr. de Calissane will leave us to-morrow he is going at Mayence. I see that everybody goes away there is but Papa that notwithstanding the desire that he has to set off will I always fear more stay and pass an *agreeable winter* in company with these *French.* We have had many bad news but they are almost allways faulse now the best way is not to believe them so not to be afflicted nor rejoiced in vain. Miss Muller gave us an account of the manner that her Uncle had been kild, there can be nothing more barbarous than it.

1792

MONDAY, 8TH OCTOBER. As we had been Invited by the young persons of Roschach to go with them to take a walk upon the mountain. We were at Miss Hoffman's at 6 o'clock and her two brothers Miss Bayer her brother and herself we all set off on foot for to go at bird-catching two leagues from Roschach. We got there soon and had a charming walk. But what gave me most pleasure and what was a very curious thing was the Vew that formed the fog which covered all the lake and the plain. We were upon the mountain with the purest sky and enjoyed of the view of that for under us so It formed different aspects which I am not witty enough for to describe. We stay'd a little while for to catch Birds and we afterwards came to the village Ekersried which is one of the prettiest country in St. Gall. Arrived at this Village we began by eating and we afterwards played at many games till dinner time then we had plenty to eat but what we had the most was Birds. We played again a great deal in the afternoon till we set off. To come home we took another walk and after we had reached the top of a small hill we had a vew that I could not fatigue myself to admire. At one Side I saw very high mountains all covered with snow, and before me I had a charming plaine. All round us were some small hills all covered with cattle, fields, and cottages. I was enchanted of this charming country, and I much regretted not to be able to draw the country views because I cannot remember of having ever seen a more rural fine and agreeable prospect as this was. The way that led us down the mountain was pretty we had in many places some handsome vews over the lake. I have passed a very agreeable day and our Society has been as good as possible. The two Young Ladies seems very good Girls indeed. Though the young ladies at Roschach goes alone with the young gentlemen I do not think there is another place where they are more modest and where the manners are better. Miss Müller came to take us in the carriage at Roschach and we came back at Wardeck after having thanked our Company of all their kindness. We read to-day in the *Veilées du Chateau* I think that book very good for the young people.

MONDAY, 29TH OCTOBER. There arrived last night 3 French gentlemen Mrs. de Regis's brother and her cousin with his son they are named Bressac they come from the army and brought us many News. They all say much Bad of the Duc of Brunswick, and this a few months ago said to be such a Brave General is now but a rogue and an ignorant one! They give him all the fault that the armies was not victorious now the French have taken Back all what had been possessed by the Prussians and the Austrians and these are obliged to retire out of the kingdom for this winter. Mr. de Bombelles will soon be back with Mr. de Regis then Papa will decide where he will go. How happy I would be if he would leave this family? But that I fear he will not do. The French have taken Francfort and I daresay will have soon Coblentz. These gentlemen would not be astonished if they would come at Constance there visit would not please me at all. I amused myself very much this evening, as Mr. de Bressac told us many particulars of this war and of what they have done. He made us a description of the manner the two armies were placed, the character of Dumouriez, etc. At supper he sayed in what manner he treated the people of Verdun when taken. This was abominable and made me very angry. Because every day Mr. de Bressac himself or his footmen used to go at the Municipality to insult them all. He was glorious of this, and told it us with joy and pride. I can't conceive how men can be pleased in doing harm at one's neighbour even when it is an enemy. Mr. de Bressac has lived much in Italy and Naples and has much travelled. Mrs. de Regis' Brother seems to be a good stup.

TUESDAY, 6TH NOVEMBER. Mr. de Bombelles arrived this morning, what gave much pleasure to everybody. All what he told us of the conditions of the armies is really shocking. He is with Mr. the Chevalier de Verrac the son of the Ambassador of France at Soleurre. It is a very handsome young man. He was to be a priest and now has been in the armies and I daresay it won't chuse any more that first condition that he had taken. We made some music in the evening and I did not go to bed till midnight Mr. de Bombelles having given us an account at Russia which amused me much.

THURSDAY, 15TH NOVEMBER. I was very afflicted tonight as we thought the little Vixen (our groom's Dog) was going to die but the poor little thing was better when I went to bed. We all think she has been poisoned what can be very well.

FRIDAY, 16TH NOVEMBER. The Dog is entirely well what gives me the greatest pleasure because though it is but a Beast I am very much attached to it.

SUNDAY, 25TH NOVEMBER. I rode out on horseback to-day with Charles till Rhineck, and as it was night when I came home I found everybody in the Castle very much frightened that I hadn't been home sooner. Papa was rather angry for it and had made a great noise because Mamma had lett me ride with Charles alone. This is the first time that any harm has been found with me going out with the groom alone. But what made me laugh is that it was feared that Charles should run away with me. They must have a good opinion of me in this house if they can think of such a thing. At length Papa's passion passed a little and we amused ourselves very well this evening.

MONDAY, 3RD DECEMBER. Messrs. Vauchat and Walser breakfasted with us and went away soon after. The Chevalier de Verrac came and passed the evening here. I heard that all the French that were at Berne are going to live in this country as also the whole family Bressac. Indeed this new did not give me the least pleasure, we have got already enough French on our shoulders what will we do when we are surrounded by them emigrants I would rather live in a cottage in England than amongst these proud frenchmen Mary had to-day a letter from Charles Tanswell our last groom he has learned to drive and would like to come again at Papa's service.

TUESDAY, 25TH, CHRISTMAS DAY. I never past such a dull Christmas Day in all my life. I went to church at Roschach. It snowed all day. I recollected the amusing Christmas I had passed at Watcomb in England and was sorry not to be there now. But I much fear that I shall never see that country any More at least for a long while.

WENESDAY, 26TH DECEMBER. All the family de Verrac again dined here it is a good thing that they are soon a going at Lindau as we would certainly have had them here every day if they had stayd at Roschach. There is one more Inhabitant in the Castle it every day increases but never will diminish. This is a young man that is of one of the noblest but poorest families of France that Mr. and Mrs. de Bombelle regards as their Son. It is the Chevalier d'Opoule he arrived yesterday and will always stay here with the Bombelles. We really are too many to live together it is impossible to have the peace in your house when there is such a quantity of people if the masters live in good harmony the servants does not and there is many quarrels between these last. But it is to be hoped that it will not always last so and that Papa will at length see that it is not his interest to live with this family.

CHAPTER 10

WENESDAY THE 2ND JANUARY. Miss Hoffman and Mr. Martignon had the kindness to come and take me and my Sister in a *sledge* to go to Rheineck where great many persons of Roschach, were to go in a sledge—I like very much this manner of riding as it goes very quick and is not with a prudent driver at all dangerous—as soon as we all arrived at Rheineck we had some Coffee and as we were twenty persons we sent for some players and had the pleasure of having a good dance which was very gay after this small *Ball* we drank Tea and came back in our own Sledge at home. It was quite night and what was very agreeable is that the evening was pleasant and not cold. Miss Hoffman and Mr. Martignon staid half an hour with us and then continued there way to Roschach—I hope we shall enjoy more than one such parties in the course of this winter—the Sledges were eight in number, all very finely orned and there is always a man on horseback before the sledge to prevent any danger—I amused myself very much and had another occasion to day to admire the good conduct and modesty of the Young Ladies of this country especially Miss Hoffmann which really behaves as well as any aged lady.

MONDAY JANUARY 7TH. I begin to Believe that the King of France will not be Kild so much the Better for him! because although this world is like a City full of Crooked Streets I like it very well and would rather live in it than leave it so soon, and this is the manner of thinking of most persons in it.

SUNDAY JANUARY 13TH. The weather was very fine I walked much out. To night I had a little occasion to see how false the oldest son B. is My little sisters were found a keeping a very impudent conversation with the Boys they are no more to play with them for my part by what passed to night I have such a good proof Of the naughtiness of Mr. Louis that I shall have nothing more to say with any of all those Children. All the Vices that has Mr. L. is sayed Eugenia gives them him my Sister makes him a chaterer a Gamester and god knows what they say more. If he would imitate her in every thing they might be very happy! But He'll never be much good nor any of his Brothers. They can find some thing to say to others children But cannot see the faults of their own.

MONDAY JANUARY 14TH. It froze Very strong indeed to night and I could walk out to day as the weather was beautiful—The News very good to day—Papa can get no letter from England He has got no money I dont know whether the letters that he wrote have been lost or what's become of them however If we dont receive some Soon will find our Purse empty.

MONDAY JANUARY 28TH. At last arrived to day the fatal News that we feared to receive since such a long while—Unfortunately *Lewis Capet* was executed the 21 of this month—It is useless to say how much afflicted the Bombelles are I easily conceive their Sorrow, being persuaded that if I was to hear of the King of England's death it would certainly give me a great deal of grief, and I do not know King George and the B. were almost always with their King—The cruelty with which the vilains treated him is something shocking *Poor Lewis* I pity him sincerely. For the Queen and rest of his family the french will take care of—I walked out to day Every Body in the house is afflicted.

SUNDAY FEBRUARY 10TH. The vicomte de Fleurri left

us this morning—I was rather better and able to get up in the afternoon, then I went down and found these *poor afflicted* and *sorrowful* French all a dancing *Walses* and *Contredances* I was forced to dance a little too but was too weak to continue long —I came then up to hear a very famous concert Mr. de Regis de Hautpoul and Bressac all (poor players) made music, but what music! it hardly deserves that name indeed—I set us till supper time played at cards then was glad to do in bed.

MONDAY FEBRUARY 18TH. We received a letter from the good Mary my Sister that poor woman as been obliged to retire to a convent being so ill treated in her family. This new gave us all a great deal of Sorrow and we much long to know What obliged the young woman to take such a rash resolution.

TUESDAY FEBRUARY 19TH. We received all the particulars of Mary's separation with her husband— Her late husband wrote himself and has not got one thing against our good Sister Mrs. Michieli had been to Conegliano and treats mary like her daughter— I suppose that she'll have a pension and will live at Coneglian or Treviso. The reason of Mary's quitting that family is that Silvestro her brother in law was in love with her and she was used very ill in that cursed house—Cunning faulse Italians—The weather was horrid and I could not walk out at all—We were very uneasy on our Sisters account but the letters we had were a great consolation for us as we see that her conduct and behaviour is not at all to blame.

FRIDAY MARCH 1ST. The Spring is I hope begun: the weather is beautiful, the sun hot, the birds begin to sing and the Butterflies are seen—I was out almost the whole day as I had no lessons to take— Mr. de Rieux went to Lindau this afternoon and

Mr. de Bombelles went to St. Gall where we shall meet him to morrow morning—I know now the reason the B. have not to wish my sister to go with us—Eugenia and their elder son are often together they are both little chatterers and I dont know whether him or her take pleasure in being together but I think my sister (though not of such a great birth as him but being persuaded to be much more sensible reasonable and even witty than that vain boy) I think that she has it in her little head that she is much above him on these accounts however I hope and am almost certain that she is not fond at all of Louis the presomptuous Bo. are persuaded that these two young folks have a beginning of Love for each other, they talked to Mamma about it, Maman knowing which is Eugenia's manner of thinking dont mind it and laughs at the fears of the young boy's parents. As Louis is going too with us Mamma proposed Eugenia to accompany us but as they should be alone in a carriage Mrs. de B. answered that that was not her advice because one should not put *Straw near fire* a fig on their *fires* they may keep their fears for themselves but they would do better to hold their tongues and let one mind ones own children alone and not put into parent's heads non senses that never existed—When shall we be alone—The Emperor is I believe a going to war with the Swiss as it is probable that these will declare in favour of the French Republick—We would not then stay here.

CHAPTER 11

Monday, May 13th, 1793. Our farmer married this morning a young girl of 25 years old we all were invited to the wedding went to the Chapel and danced all the afternoon in the field with the peasants that were half drunk and smelt very disagreable I could not help pitying that poor young bride to be so foolish as to marry an old drunkard as the farmer is. Mr de Rieux left us this afternoon.

Thursday, May 23rd. I was left at home this afternoon as finding myself a little Ill I did not go with the rest of the Gentlemen and Ladies at *Thier Garten.* But I spent the afternoon very agreeably as I worked drew drank tea and wrote a couple of Letters I could not find time to weary myself—The gentlemen came all drunk at home and the Ladies all wet as it rained whilst they were out so I think I amused myself better alone than If I had been with our society.

Tuesday, July 2nd. I went this morning to Roschach to see there three girls take their oaths and make themselves nuns. We could go into the convent. No ceremony can be more dull than this it made my heart ache to see three young girls willing to shut themselves for all their life in A Convents As I was on the Organ I had a very merry sight to see a parcel of nuns each playing a different Instrument the one the trumpet another the Drum. I had a great deal of trouble to hinder myself from laughing but in the mean time I was in very low spirits the three young nuns which took their oaths being worthy all my compassion tho' no body forced them to take that profession. I walked in the gardens of the convent but could not see the cells. I heard that these nuns slept on Straw could never undress and that there was continually two of them that prayed: each had there time—Is it possible that there can be any body foolish enough to wish to undertake such a miserable State of Life. For my part I cant look at a Convent without horror and the only Idea of being shut up in such a small place would make me grow mad.

SUNDAY, SEPTEMBER 8TH. We at length set off this morning. Papa mamma and their four daughters all very much Satisfied—We stopped at St. Gall and went to church there then down to dine at Wyll where we had a monstrous bad dinner. We arrived at Winterthur before it was night lodged at the *Sun* where we have been very well treated.

MONDAY, SEPTEMBER 9TH. ZURIC. We had a pleasant Journey to this place were we arrived at ten in the morning Mrs. de St. Gratien and her family received us with her usual kindness and friendliness Mr. de Salis lodged us in his appartment and is very kind to us—I went this afternoon to walk in the great walk which is now a most delightfull place I had seen it in a bad time of the year now all the trees are full of leaves and the walk is in its greatest beauty I think I gave a little description when I saw it last; I shall only say something of the Tomb or monument which has been elevated in the honour of Gessner. It is a monument in black marble placed in the middle of the walk. There is a white Urn at the top of it. On one Side the image of one of his little Poems and on the other an Inscription. There was a great many persons in the walk and we stayed a long while in it—Mrs de Vassan is always disagreable I think her unsupportable. Athenais is a good girl but she is so cold and seems to love nobody. She'll make a very bad figure by the side of the two Miss d'Alberg's. I hope these will come to-morrow.

Thursday, September 12th. Lucerne. We left Zuric very soon and breakfasted at the top of the Albis a very high mountain which we had much trouble to go up whilst the horses were reposing we went half a league from the village on the hill to enjoy a most delightfull prospect. We saw all the Lac of Zuric and its neighbourhood of one side; of the other we could distinguish the Lac of Zug a very pretty and vast country—the whole was surrounded with monstrous high mountains—We had very bad roads till Lucerne what prevented our coming there soon—We directly went to see the Town which is Situated on the Lac and is amidst prodigious mountains Lucerne is not pretty we went on two Bridges which are across the Lac they are very Long; covered, and are all painted—One is full of battles the other of miracles. The Lac is very romantic and handsome it is 10 Leagues long and has a very drole form—The night prevented our seeing much of this place; the part of the town Situated on the Reuss which comes from the Lac is pretty as for the rest it is very dull—We were so tired that we Supped and went to Bed as Soon as possible.

Saturday, September 14th. We dined at Kilitsberg and came as soon as possible to Berne. The Country was equally charming, rich, and pretty. No high mountains but pretty hillocks; covered with fruit trees, houses, gardens, cottages, and Woods. Not such Sapin and Pine woods as in the Country of St. Gall but Oak's and all sort of beautiful Trees—The Situation of Berne is delightfull on a small hill which has the Aar at its foot. I was astonished of the cleanness and beauty of the Streets and houses of the town. The houses are all alike and the whole town is but like one building. They are very high and are elegant, simple and neat. The Streets are very large a small stream runs in the middle and on both sides there are large and clean Arcades which does not make the Streets the least Small but which are very convenient. As soon as we arrived at the Inn Miss Webber came to see us. She is going to marry a certain Mr. Prevot a parson of geneva which has left his mother country since fifteen years is gone to England where he had a small benefice and where he married an English Woman, which (he says) has made him very miserable he now has left his wife for Miss Webber and has promised to marry her as soon as he'll have undone his first marriage.

Tuesday, September 17th. Bois de Vaud. The road from Moudon to this place is very short and pleasant we arrived here very soon after having passed Lausanne a very ugly and disagreable town. We were received by Mr. Blair and family with much friendship. Bois de vaud is two miles from Lausanne at a distance from the Lac on a small hill in a pretty situation the house is excessively Small but good Mr. Blair gave us his appartment—Lady Mary is grown very old as she has been very ill. Mary is very tall and will be a handsome woman her brother Charles is a beautifull man—we took a walk in the morning and enjoyed a charming view over the Lac which is not quite as large as that of Constance but is much prettier. Having of one side the very high mountains of Savoy and of the other the charming pays de vaud. Miss Fellows and Dr. Ash came here this afternoon—We breakfast at nine; dine at three drink Tea at Seven and Sup at ten.

Wednesday, September 18th. I took a walk with Mary and her governess whose name is Miss Desruines. We went in a wood belonging to a Swiss which is the most delightfull garden we went too by the side of the Lac and then hurried home to dress for diner. Mr. Fouler a young man the son of the Bishop of Dublin dined with Mr. Weston here the last is settled here and is married to a Swiss Lady—Mrs Frazier her daughter Maria and Miss Dunford three English Ladies came this afternoon they are very amiable But have all the french manners and all the English men and women dress now like fools—Mr. Blair is very kind he certainly is the best man on earth—Mary and me are very good friends. Charles is grown very proud of his beauty he hardly is ever at home, being in love with Miss Frazier which is very ugly and only two months younger than me.

MONDAY, SEPTEMBER 23RD. Mrs Frazer her daughter and Miss Dunford dined and Supped here these are very amiable Ladies but are I am afraid and *certain* very bad company. Mary is very kind to us, but she is very naughty and her governess nor Lady Mary cant trust her to herself one moment; for all She is thirteen Years old. We Shall go Monday Mr. de Bombelles will be here Saturday. I am very sorry to see our departure decided. I kept by the fireside all day long with Mary as it was so excessively cold. I took my 2nd lesson with Mr. Pio a famous drawing master and I learn the perspective.

SATURDAY, OCTOBER 5TH. ST. URBAIN. We set off at eleven o'clock from Berne Papa suffers much with the Piles what makes him very Ill humoured, but I was much crosser than him. We stopped at Hindelbank to see the tomb of Mde. of Langahns a young woman of four and twenty which died in laying in at that age this tomb is cut out of one stone and represents the grave opening the last day and the mother lifts up her child and presents him to god.

It is very beautiful we dined at Kilchberg and arrived at night to this place which is a great Convent of Benedictine monks in the Canton of Lucerne. The chief abbot is called L'abbe de St. Urbain received us all with much kindness we could go in the convent where we Supped we then came to Sleep at a Small house belonging to the convent. The monks are very polite and live very well. Indeed they have none of the monk's manner and they live in the french way. This convent is very rich it is a great building and is said to be even handsomer than that of Einsiddlen. Its situation is very dull and ugly. There was here a Mr. Moro frenchman secretary to Mr. de St. Martin. There are too many french priests among which is the Abbé Glinglin a most tiresome chatterer.

SATURDAY, OCTOBER 12TH. We came to dine at Büren then proceeded our Journey to Wardeck and met at St. Gall all the Inhabitants of Wardeck which made a stunning noise in seeing us but showed much pleasure. Mr. de Bombelles staied at St. Gall and all the rest came to Wardeck where we arrived late. I was very glad to See the Good Jaegle which must have wearied himself sadly during our Absence. Mde. de Bombelles is grown very thick but enjoys a perfect health as does all the charming inhabitants of this Castle. I shall have much trouble to accustom myself to all of them but as it cannot be otherwise I must take patience.

TUESDAY, OCTOBER 15TH. Papa went shooting what he means to do every day he comes home late and dines at night.

FRIDAY, OCTOBER 18TH. If we shall spend the winter as *agreably* as we spend this season I dont know what I shall do as I cannot accustom myself to all these french faces which I hate most sincerely. I always keep up stairs and see the others but at diner and then have very little discourse with them.

SATURDAY, OCTOBER 19TH. I heard to-day that our Cook the ugliest dirtiest creature in the world was with Child of Mr. le Gout a monstrous blackguard. This is the fifth maid Servant that has been in this condition in two years time that we are here. I pity this unfortunate wretch as she has been most infamously deceived on all accounts.

MONDAY, OCTOBER 21ST. We had great many good news The lines at Wissemberg have been forced and the armies are only three leagues from Strasburgh We had been flattered with the noise of that town having given itself to the Emperor which thing will I hope soon happened. The towns Wissemberg Lautenbourg and it is said Landau and Marseilles have been all taken. Mr. de Bause a Saxon Baron which had served in France was sent from the princes to speak to the Marquis but as this was not at home he'll waite for his arrival.

FRIDAY, OCTOBER 25TH. The unfortunate Queen of France has been *aiguillotiné* the 16 of this month. She was condemned at three a clock and Executed next day in the morning. Lyon which had revolted and kept itself these three months has been now taken and thousand horrors are daily committed. The rogues of french will lay all waste except the manufactures And the Sans Culottes houses. Mama is very uneasy as her father and mother which had remained in Lyon cannot be found by her niece which is now returned in town and searches in vain all her friends and parents. Mde. de Bombelles is ill. Mr. de Bause and Badins from Constance came only to pay a visit.

FRIDAY, NOVEMBER 1ST. The cook began again her follies to-day there is no idea what a naughty monster she is she does all in the world to miscarry; she continues to speak most dreadfully of Mde. de Bombelles at last as one could not make her understand reason she was forced to go away and turned to Stadt where she'll be taken leave of. Mr. Legout is to be sent away too. It was excessively cold and bad weather.

MONDAY, NOVEMBER 4TH. It seems that the Covetous Lady of the house is tired of Mr. St. Gratiens Company but we will not let him go so Soon as he is the best man on earth and *as we pay* I hope that we can have what friends we chuse notwithstanding that Lady's dislike to it.

SATURDAY, NOVEMBER 9TH. Mr. de St. Gratien left us this morning we were sorry to see him go as he is very kind and best of men, but I dont think *every one* was of this same opinion.

WEDNESDAY, NOVEMBER 13TH. A real french Sans Culotte came here to-day He has been taken prisoner last year by a body of Hungarians but made his escape after having been Cured of his wounds which are in great number poor fellow! he had his head full of Scars. He was a Carpenter at Versailles and now wants to return in his country. We could easily perceive he was a bad fellow but he seems so bold and courageous that his discourse much amused me.

FRIDAY, NOVEMBER 15TH. We heard to-day that the Duke of Orleans notwithstanding the foul and vile manner in which he behaved to gain the Jacobites friendship has been *guillotiné* and died, as cowardly as he had lived. Hated by all mankind.

FRIDAY, NOVEMBER 29TH.

Nothing worth writing can I find
Except what passed in my mind
This place I hate with all my heart
It's inhabitants have their part.

Wednesday, December 4th. There is a very foolish custom in this country which is at the time of St. Nicholas to have the *Klauses* which are men dressed very oddly The naughty one, wips the children the good drest like a Bishop is said to bring them what presents their parents and others gives them at this feast. But this *Klaus* is the terror of all the children and their is even some instance, of children being dead with fear. This is a very stupid custom and I would like to see the charming Klaus well flogged instead of his having the pleasure of beating these poor little children.

CHAPTER 12

SUNDAY, JANUARY 5TH, 1794. The continual bad news makes us very mad. The armies have been obliged to pass the Rhine and the beastly french are at Spire, Landau which was on the point to be taken was delivered and what is now remained of this whole campaign but fort Lewis. How afflicting all this is a consolation amidst these bad things is the taking of St. Domingue by the English and Spaniards. Mr. Trepanié which has fortunately, there all his fortune is setting off for England from thence for that Island, and his good little wife is going at her mothers at Fribourg. I cannot help envying all those that go to England. Happy are they and unhappy me. But patience—*C'est écrit là haut*—as Mr. Jaegle Sayes.

MONDAY, JANUARY 6TH. We drewed the kings but this did not at all muse us, but I had a charming fun at Supper—Some players came we were all charmed at the pretty concert but how soon the smiling faces changed in the greatest anger when one of the players began to play *Ça ira* on his clarinette, every body started from the table cried *oh les gueaux les gredins* and went to Mr. de Bombelles to find some means of being revenged of the audaciousness of those musicians, but how catched were they seeing Mr. B. hear quietly this shocking adventure and ready to laugh at such a ridiculous passion. However one sent down to Start to know who were these persons and they said that some body having sent them away saying we did not want any music at this time of night, they played that tune to revenge and indeed were much in the right and all the french were in such a passion that they looked all as Turkies when they are angry.

TUESDAY, JANUARY 7TH. Unfortunately the news that armies have been obliged to pass the rhine are too well grounded to doubt the least on it and Mannheim is filled with Consternation and fear—Good god! how all this goes bad—What will become of the great quantity of poor Emigrants which are now in the greatest misery—For my part I Am very dull I cannot help reflecting very seriousness on all these misfortune—I always forgot to mention the death of the Duchess of Polignac. She is much happier now out of this Sad world.

FRIDAY, FEBRUARY 7TH. I went to Mde. Heckdes and found her in her Bed at three o'clock in the afternoon, the children told me that she is used to lay a Bed all the morning, and as two days ago she has been indisposed she thought it proper to be in Bed the afternoon too. I think her a lazy little Toad.

SATURDAY, FEBRUARY 8TH. There has been some little mischief between the young gentlemen and us; as they always would walk out with us, Mde. de Bomb. has told them that Mama has forbid it and that it was not well, what did't give them much pleasure—However they have taken their party very well.

WEDNESDAY, MARCH 12TH. A letter from Mde. Michieli gave us notice that as Mary Montalban during her abode at Venice had always been in good company, the Grazianis that was with her being jealous will have her no more at their house at Coneglian and now the poor woman dont know where to find a lodging.

FRIDAY, APRIL 11TH. Mama has been very much afflicted to-day with a letter from France which informs her of a terrible accident that had her parents. Her father and mother both of about the age of 70 were at their country house three leagues from Lyons at nine of clock in the evening fifteen men came with the excuse that they were sent from the *comunauté* to search all the house they asked for all the keys and whilst the rest were employed with stealing all they found four of them treated Mama's parents very ill made a great fire in the kitchen for to burn them alive, the poor old man had already taken off his coat not to Suffer So much in the fire, however through prayers and cries they were pacified and they took them in the Celar were they hung up Mama's mother, but the rope being new and coarse they could not do it very well so they threw the poor woman down kiked her about and made her suffer thousand horrors, they tried to hang her once more not with standing the terrible situation in which she was but as they could not they left her and her husband in the celar where they spent the night in the morning neighbours came to their assistance, but they are both Ill and have nothing left them. This is quite a Roman story and almost impossible to be believed but it is Mama's mother that wrote it herself—We walked out and went to see poor women which often have nothing to eat all day long as happened yesterday to one of them.

SATURDAY, APRIL 19TH. It was my birthday and I was sixteen years of age—This made me make many reflections; and all to no use but that of making me dull. We walked to Speck and went to Visit many poor old women.

MONDAY, APRIL 28TH. We only walked a little in the morning, and in the afternoon we went to a Gouter at Thiergarten; Mr de Reiux eat like a real Pig. I will not forget to mention that I had today my hair drest quite and that I am no more a Child.

WEDNESDAY, APRIL 30TH. After Supper Mde de la

Cote told us Some Charming Stories, especially one of a Lady in the Old Fashion which during her dinner at a Gentleman's was very uneasy; at last she cries to her footman; 'Jacques, cherchez ma puce', and Jacques put his hand in the lady's back and after having looked for it a long while he says 'La voilà, Madame', and She drowned it in her Wine-glass.

SATURDAY, MAY 24TH. Some news from Italy gave us some grief as it seems that my sister Mary do not behave herself Very well It is not astonishing that a young woman, that is left alone in a Country which is so corrupted, Should not follow the example of the all the women She sees.

FRIDAY, MAY 30TH. The news again bad the Duke of York has been beat and lost fifty Canons—How terrible it would be if these affairs would finish this Campaign. The prince of Dissenties dined here. the revolution in the Grisons Continues. the 10000 men which are said marches against that country never arrives. The Comte de Juinier returned to Constance. The good bishop left he goes first to Lindau, then to Naples. We had good news from the armies. The 22 May the french attacked the allies at six in the morning the battle lasted till past nine in the evening the french were obliged to retire but both parties lost Great many men. Never during this war has there been such terrible battle and never were both parties so furious and courageous.

TUESDAY, JUNE 3RD. A terrible conspiracy was happily discovered in England; where they wanted to make a national Assembly; and in the meantime the french should have landed 15000 men in the Island; which would have been Supported by 75000 men under Mr. *Rowan* which was at the head of this infamous plot; with the other conspirators—It is really dreadful. How is it possible after having Seen the horrors that the french have Committed to wish to follow their example. I hope that this conspiracy will have no bad consequences—All the power has been given to the king which being well advised by Mr. Pitt will take sufficient care that poor England should not become a prey to the infamous french maxims, that are now Spread over all Europe. Mr. Rowan has unfortunately broke out from his prison, and it seems that he is in France many others are taken and all precautions are taken that this beginning should not become fatal—The English have taken Guadaloupe and St. Lucia. Mad. Demontier is very amiable and has much wit. What a pity that She should have received such a bad education. Papa is gone to Zuric.

FRIDAY, JULY 4TH. We read a letter that comes from the neighbourhood of Marseilles and is wrote by a priest that is there; it is very interesting as it gives the detail of the manner that the persons which thinks well; profess their religion. They retire in Caves, woods and mountains, have fruits, bread and water for their food and are resolved to die for their religion. The priest that writes says the mass in Caves and says that there were 500 persons that came to it—I hope those poor people will not be discovered by the Jacobites as they would certainly be killed—I am not well yet my feet are very painful—The Abbé is always the same; If he had more patience and courage he would be better.

SATURDAY, JULY 5TH. The french on their taking Ypres accomplished the infamous decree which had been Made of killing all the English and Hanoverians and of making no prisoners. They fell 10000 in number upon a body of 1500 English and killed them all. The bad news puts us in very bad humour and I would wish to be far from all politic—I was not any better than Yesterday and I had again Some fever.

THURSDAY, JULY 17TH. Mr. de Farran and his Son a boy of 13, came from Constance. He is a man of Great merit, and has made a book upon the Revolution and the present circumstances which is said to be very good and well done. You can easily guess that this gentleman is an Emigrant As he looks very lean and poorly, and has a very ragged and old coat, he is an aged man very ugly, but has an honest and Good Look—He will Stay till to morrow—I continue to be very dull! indeed I have nothing that can give me pleasure! As I begin to fear that we Shall yet be a long time with this family, and indeed the Common Affairs go very ill. What will become of us.

SATURDAY, JULY 19TH. The Viscount d'Agout arrived to day He is now with a Polish princess of Nassau; which is going to Schinznach. He said she would be here to night and much wished to come to see us; Mr. Bombelles went to meet her for to invite to Supper but She only arrived at Roschach late at night. She is A very good woman and has much given to the french Emigrants She has now different french Gentlemen with her. The prince of Nassau her husband beats himself against *Cosciuskow* that heads the Polands. By what I heard the princess *likes* Coskinscow—I began to ride but this morning and I mean to take this exercice as often as possible. The french priests *La riche, Surville* that were here returned to Constance, there was another here that is now going into Russia but I forgot his Name.

TUESDAY, JULY 22ND. We had a very great quarrel here to day which might have had very bad consequences. Mr. de Bombelles disputed at tabel concerning the English with Mr. de Régis; as this gentleman detests that nation especially Mr. Pitt, instead of being Grateful for all the good the Emigrants received in England. Mr. de B. on the contrary finds that the English have conducted themselves as they aught to do. However the quarrel not being done when they left table Mr. de Régis prayed Mr. B. to speak no more about it on account of Papa the Marquis being in a Great passion; was quite shocked at the other's obliging him to hold his tongue took him in his Closet where they both told one another very hard things especially Mr. de B. that treated the other like a Dog; At length they went out for to *fight* but Mde. de Bombelles hindered this and they at last made it up. But Mr. de Régis wants to go Away. How easily a misfortune takes place; I could not have thought that such a reasonable man as the Marquis would have put himself at his age in the case to have a *duel*. I rode out this morning; it does me much good to goe on horseback of a morning. Martignoni dined with us he is sorry that we Should go away; and wants to come to see us at Ratisbon. We went this afternoon at the Bailifs.

MONDAY, JULY 28TH. The newspapers acquainted us with the fall of Namurs. I cannot conceive how the villanous french can always be victorious! A serious revolt is broke out in Geneva I have no doubt but all Switzerland will follow their example as the peasants are all as *Jacobites* as can be.

WEDNESDAY, JULY 30TH. I never go out but on horseback as every time we take a walk we *Carry home our pockets* full of impertinences which the peasants bestows upon us.

SATURDAY, AUGUST 2ND. Jaegle was very much afflicted as he received the news that his brother had been obliged to Serve the french had been killed at Landercy and lost his life in a shocking manner.

How terrible this war is! and the longer it will last the crueler it will be! Yet it is impossible to wish for a peace as that would cause still more blood to be spilt than the present war; and no kingdom in Europe could enjoy happiness and tranquillity; as the Spirit of Liberty has creaped in every country and if the French Jacobines are not entirely abolished every Sovereign may have in his dominions the same revolution that causes so much evil now—Letters from Italy has given us much displeasure as it seems that our Sister Mary behaves herself every day worse. She has left Conegliano and is gone at an *Arciprete* a man of bad reputation. What can have obliged her this Step! I hope and fear we should Soon know it.

SUNDAY, AUGUST 3RD. A french priest arrived to day and is the emigrant that has interested me the most. His lean and afflicted face, his miserable dress, Give easily an idea of a man that has much Suffered. He has only left France Since six months and Says that he has found the *Spirit* of the people worse out of that kingdom than in it; and that he has been more tormented ever since he is Out than before. His misfortunes has I think a little altered his senses; but notwithstanding he talks perfectly well with much reason and seems to have much wit. He will stay here one day or two to repose a little and will write a narration of all that has befell since his Emigration; which will be very interesting—I do not yet know his name. We had to day Martignioni's visit and that of the Prince of Dissenties.

MONDAY, AUGUST 4TH. The Monster Robespierre has been arrested with St. Just and all their party and it is supposed are by this time Guillotiné. It is impossible to describe how much pleasure it has given us all; No body has more deserved death than these infamous men. If it Could Give a better turn to Affairs as we hope how happy I should be. But I think that it will at least diminish the great number of persons that were *guillotiné* at Paris that was about 50 every day of all ages; and by Robespierres orders as he was the tyrant of France. We shall soon have more details on this event very Soon—The Prelate of St. Urbain came to see us with the Bailif of Rheineck and his Son. He is a very amiable man he has been to take the waters some where or other and is now returning at his Abby. We had to day a letter from Mr. Moreau he is with Mde. de la Cote at Rotterdam but will soon set off for England.

TUESDAY, AUGUST 5TH. News from Basle gives us notice that the persons that had been arrested had been Guillotiné the same day under pretext that Robespierre had conspired to murder the National convention; he and his party were protected by the *Commune* who brought *Cannons* against the Convention but the latter was victorious; and Robespierre, S. Just, Henriot, Couthon and others, all *guillotiné* the young Robespierre leaped out of window and was torn to pieces by the populace—The Same letter Says that Seals were put on all the papers of the Jacobites. This is a very interesting moment as if what we hope and have reason to Suppose; will realize in little time the fate of France can be decided.

MONDAY, AUGUST 18TH. The death of Robespierre has certainly been very advantageous to humanity; as the prisoners at Paris have been set at liberty and the *priests* are to be paid for. But I do·not much know what to think of this change in the french government but fear that it will affirm the republick and is not good for the emigrants how ever I am Joyous to See So many persons who suffered in prison delivered; and will only be happy of the present good without thinking of what may happen of course. Mr. Blair seemed decided to come to join us at Ratisbon; and this has given me much pleasure.

TUESDAY, AUGUST 19TH. Mde. Bombelles was very afflicted to day as we can not get a house with a garden and she fears that her *lovely children* will die for not having a place to run about and do like little blackguards. How foolish! as if all the other children that live in Town did not enjoy as good a health as hers! But they certainly are not so rude and blustering as these *nasty little Apes* that will make us blush very often when we will have some good company with us—I think there is some thing or other that will at last hinder our going to Ratisbon as the Count Thurn did all in his power to enduce the Marquis to stay here; for which reason I do not know! but I think that Mr. B. will not be welcome at that place. How ever I do not care where we will go as I am Sure we can not Stay any longer here and I shall be happy every where after leaving this tiresome old Castle.

SUNDAY, AUGUST 31ST. I forgot to write what happened Yesterday between our Gentlemen at Wardeck, which gives a good idea of the foolish french Character. Mr. de la Roche began to be impudent at table with Mr. de Régis who finding himself insulted answered, and gave a free Course to all his *morgue provençale* indeed the affair went so far that these fine Gentlemen (that always put their honour at the point of their sword) went in a wood in the Mountain and fought a most ridiculous *duel*; As Mr. de Régis *pricked* the *others* arm, he generously said *Sir you are wounded* and *I am contented.* the Chev. d'Hautpoule who was as witness finished the

Affair—But I cannot help finding it a true Comedy and it gives me a bad idea of Mr. de Regis as he is every moment ready to fight! I am not sorry that we will not have his company much longer the less french I shall see the better I shall like it as I cannot love that nation and how could I have any true liking for them! when I hear them all day long speak against the English. I cannot conceive how the Emigrants can be so foolish as to have a hatred for the best of nations and especially at the present time as certainly without the help of the English their affairs would be in a bad condition—Now, that there is no country where the french Emigrants has been better treated than in England, how can those nasty Creatures be so ungrateful. I declare when I hear them say something against *Pitt* and his nation I might scratch their faces and pull their eyes out but I think it better to despise their foolish talk; hold my tongue and at the bottom of my heart wish them to be happy but far from me that I may have nothing to do with them.

SUNDAY, SEPTEMBER 21ST. For all it was Sunday we began to embroider a waistcoat that we mean to give Papa and worked the whole day; thus I spent it agreeably. I always forgot to say that Our *Cher Colonel* is gone on a Journey which he says to Lucerne but every body knows he is gone on a journey to change his *Cross* and his honour for a Sum of Money.

THURSDAY, SEPTEMBER 25TH. As one of the three french nuns embroiders very well we went to take a lesson and spent the whole morning in the Convent after having been at the Christening of the child of our gardener which was born Yesterday and to which my Sister Eugenia was God Mother and had for God father the *Amiable* Bitch de B. I really did not weary myself in the Company of the nuns; I should like the tranquillity of Convents but all the rest makes me hate the thought of being nun indeed there is no fear that I should ever make myself one but *On ne peut Jurer de rein.*

TUESDAY, SEPTEMBER 30TH. Mamma Jaegle and my sisters we left Wardeck this morning very Soon and began the Journey with our own horses. Mr. de Bombelles and all the rest of our family will meet us at Memingen where we will stay one day for to see the Cury of Stolzheim Mr. Egg that will come to See us there We dined at Bregenz at the Crown where we had a good dinner, I got on horseback this Afternoon as the three Saddle horses are also with us and I had an unpleasant ride to Wangen where we arrived in the evening after having had detestable roads; and bad Weather. Mamma was very Ill and went to bed as Soon as she was arrived. We lodged at the —— which is a good Inn; new built on account of the two terrible fires that broke out in this town in one years time—Mr. de la Roche and the Cury that are going at Ratisbon arrived in the night in the Mail Coach of Augsbourg.

WEDNESDAY, OCTOBER 1ST. As the roads are excessively bad we took two post horses more to our Carriage that our own horses Should be too much tired. I walked great part of the way to *Lentkirch* a town one post and a half from Wangen, where we dined with the *Amiable* La Roche and the Cury. Our Carriage broke this morning; the roads are so very bad that I am afraid it will break More than once. I rode again this Afternoon till Memining and had an Accident which had no bad Consequences. The poney fell with me, near the Town, I was not at all hurt but I feared at first my horse was killed as he lay more than a minute with his head under his body and his four legs lay motionless in the Air. I was rather frightened and come on foot to the Inn *Le boeuf blanc*. Mamma arrived Soon After—The Master of the Inn is a great musicians he has an excellent Harpsichord and I mean to make some music with him to morrow. Mr. de la Roche and his companion continued their Journey.

THURSDAY, OCTOBER 2ND. I played the Harpsichord with the master of the Inn. Mr. Reinegg and I heard too Mr. d'Emmerick that plays very well indeed—We found here a Venitian named Count Corti that has been banished his Country for having Spoken against the Government; He has ever since travelled through all Europe and he finds himself well no where; he has been here eight months, and I do not know where he means to go now: he wants to pay us a visit at Ratisbon during the winter. I was very young when I Saw him in Italy So I did not remember him at All; he is an Amiable man— Our good Cury Mr. Egg Spent the whole day with us; I was very glad to See him; he looked as fresh and well as can be. He gave us new of many of our Acquaintances at Strasburgh. He is now at a convent of nuns *Heiligekreutzthal* where he lives as well as it is possible for a man that has been so unfortunate. Mr. d'Emmerick is a very ridiculous little figure as he is hunch-backed and Joins to his ugly body a more disagreeable face; but he is very Amiable and witty and really is an excellent Musician—. These Gentlemen Stayed the whole day with us and this Afternoon I took a walk to See the town which is neat and pretty. There are many very rich persons here, and we went to See a Country house belonging to one named Lamentz. He has expence a great Sum of Money and has a charming house and Garden near the town. Mde. de Bombelles her five Children the

Abbé and our Servants arrived After midnight— we Shall continue our Journey all together to morrow.

FRIDAY, OCTOBER 3RD. We left Memmingen at Six o'Clock and came the first post and a half with our own horses, which we left at Mindleheim where we took the post and Came to *Schwabminchen* which is a post and a half. As we had Sent an *Estafette* to order our horses (as we want fourteen) we found them ready and we arrived at Augsbourg where we were very sorry to be obliged to wait for Mde. de Bombelles that came again late— We lodge at the *Agneau blanc* which is an excellent Inn. Augsbourg is very handsome rich trading town. We shall to morrow leave Swabia and enter Bavaria. The Country we went through after leaving the borders of the Lac of Constance is ugly; and makes it very tiresome to travel through it as you only see meadows and woods of Sapin. The people look very Good and healthy. We met on the way a quantity of provisions that are taken in Switzerland for to send in France to the french. I was very Glad that Mde. de B. would not go as far as us and Stayed behind. We had a pleasant Journey to Geissenfeld, where we layed. We enterred Bavaria a league after Augsbourg, and the Country is not much prettier than the part of Swabia we Saw—Mde. *Schlich* came to see us as she thought Mde. B. was with us; She has been *femme de Chambre* to Mde. *Royale* is now in this Country She was very polite and amiable.

SUNDAY, OCTOBER 5TH. We found every where Good horses till Ratisbon where we arrived Soon in the Afternoon. Mde. de Louvois papa and Heckel came to meet us we then went at Mde Louvois where we dined. Mr. Bombelles has much Occupation and the houses are not quite finished but the Appartments that are furnished are charming and we will be very well lodged. I could not much see of the town which seems very old and ugly. Our habitation is in a charming position in the Island named *Unterwärts* on the border of the Danube we have three gardens, and are both in Town and in the Country which is very Agreeable I can not say how much pleasure I had when I heard that the *dear B. Buohl* was what I thought him to be, a cunning proud and bad man; he is him that received Mr. Bombelles the worst So I have nothing more to fear on that side. The Count of Thurn has behaved himself perfectly well he came to see us with the Baron B. Mr. de Beranger an ancient french minister; Mr. de Martin the Viscount de Meruy and other supped with us—We Shall be very well here, the good Mde. Louvois has received us with all possible kindness. She is not yet lodged at *Unterwärts* which will soon be. August is much grown. The Abbé Robert is no more with her and gives lessons in town.

MONDAY, OCTOBER 6TH. We went to the fair this morning we met there Mr. Taygue a Catholic Englishman that has married a German Lady Since Six weeks. The Princess which has married the Son of the Prince de la Tour Taxis; would get acquainted with us and we were presented to her at the fair. She is a charming princess. We had some visits this Afternoon Mrs. Taygue Mde. de Buchenberg her Aunt The tiresome french Lady Mde. de Bousselin and the Countess de Hohenthal which is the first house of Ratisbon after that of Princess's I played the Harpsichord to her and everybody persuaded me that I play better than the famous Mde. de *Tshadon* that is here but that does not go in the Good Society. Mde de Hohenthal is a fat aged woman but she is very amiable and it is her that makes up all the parties and that renders the Society gay and agreeable—Mrs. Taygue is a charming young woman She is not pretty but very kind and amiable—Papa is as gay as possible and amuses himself very much he has wearied himself enough at Wardeck for to find a little pleasure here. Every body treats him with all possible kindness and in Short we will be very well here.

CHAPTER 13

WEDNESDAY, OCT. 8TH, 1794. We did today what is called the *Tournee* and which is visits to all the ministers and *Grand* Families of this place. It was Mde de Homptenda that conducted us she is the wife of the Hanoverian Minister we were received nowhere except at Count *Gorts* the minister of Prussia which is an agreeable family Miss *Gorts* is a pretty and amiable girl—we finished the *Tournee* by Going at the Princess that received us and where we Spent the evening—The princess is very handsom and kind. She is of Mecklenbourg and a niece to the Queen of England there was many persons that I do not yet know. The B. Buohl, wants to make the amiable in Society and is a very ridiculous figure —We played at little games as princess likes it of all things.

THURSDAY, OCT. 9TH. Whilst we are very gay the news are bad the Austrian have been beat and have crossed the Rhine.

FRIDAY, OCTOBER 10TH. I heard the french were at Cologne! how bad every thing goes.

SATURDAY, OCTOBER 11TH. Every body almost speaks English here which thing gives me much pleasure.

SUNDAY, OCTOBER 12TH. After having been to Church and the Cathedral where there was a good music, I had a tooth drawn out and suffered excessively, as the tooth-drawer named Rathseler and which is excellent had a great deal of trouble to take it out. We only had Mde. de Homptenda Mde. Louvois and the Viscount Merci here this afternoon Mde. de Homptenda is a very good amiable and kind Lady.

We shall have great feasts Tuesday and Wednesday as it is the feast of the princess.

Tuesday, October 14th. We payed a visit to the Princess for to make her a Compliment as it is to morrow her *feast*. her husband is arrived, I have heard that he was very Stupid as all the family *Latour* is but I found him very kind and amiable for us—We directly afterwards went at Count Saylern the minister of Bohemia that gave a charming feast. he has beautiful apartments that were embellished by a great number of Ladies that all were very elegantly drest. As Soon as the princess arrived, the prettiest Ladies and Gentlemen drest in priestesses and priests came to the princess and gave her a *nosegay* as also to Mde. de Buckenburg whose name is likewise Therese, they were invited to go in the other Room; where there was a temple, that soon opened after the Priestesses had sung a Chorus and Venus was discovered holding love in her arms and the three graces, they all said some thing very pretty and it finished by a dance—Mrs. Teighe was Venus and the princesses son Prince George was love, the two Miss liliens and another Miss de la Phiné were the Graces they are all equally pretty. It really was charming and touching. We danced, had a Supper and after having danced a little more we returned home—We were acquainted with Mde. de Berbrick the Sister of the *nasty Baron Vrintz*; but she is much better than her brother for all She is very much like him—Every body is very polite for us, and we are treated with as much kindness as it is possible.

Wednesday, October 15th. We went after dinner to take Papa and Mamma that were at the *grand prévôt* de Lerkenfeld where they had dined with a parcel of *Jacobits* which are in great number here—All the family Lerkenfeld is not worth a fig, the young *Max de Lerkenfeld* is a handsome man but full of vanity and very impolite—After having paid few visits we came at the Count de Hohenthal, where there was a great feast—it begun by a play that was very well acted and that much amused me. It was the *Optimiste* and an entertainment very ridiculous but not very good. Mde. de Hohenthal Mlle. Ritter acted very well as also the little Comical figure Mde. de Biornsterna, which is very frightful on the stage. The Chev. de Brui and the Viscount Merci both act amazingly well—There was a great Supper after which we had a Charming ball but not long enough as we only began to dance at eleven and were obliged to go away at one as Papa and Mamma that dont dance weary themselves very well.—I saw again a great many new persons as almost all Ratisbon was here to night—Mde. de la Plinoy a french Lady that is here has 3 daughters full of talents the youngest which is twelve years old is a charming pretty little thing—The B. Buohl is always very rude for us, he is so extremely proud bu ti tgiv esm eaver ygrea tpleasur ea sineve rcoul dbearhi man dever ybody ylove dhi mmuch.

Betsy's Cipher: 'but it gives me very great pleasure as I never could bear him and every body loved him much.'

WEDNESDAY, OCTOBER 29TH. Mr. Fries will be here to morrow evening I am quite delighted with the thoughts of Seeing him—Mr. Blair having had the Gout has retarded his Journey and will only be here in the course of next month—We shall have quite an English colony, there is here the Bishop of Winchester with his wife six daughters and Son. They made the *Tournee* to day, the wife Mrs North is said to be a devil on Earth—and a nasty proud fool She plagues her husband and Children to death—We went in the morning at the princess where we had a repetition of a Concert that She will have to morrow at her house I wanted to walk out but the weather was So bad that I only went a little in the town and was glad to come back—I have got a bad cold so I Stayed at home in the evening, mamma went at Count Görtz, he has been very Ill, It gives him so much Sorrow that the King of Prussia Should behave so Ill and like a real rogue—He has made a peace a part, with the french—What will the Emperor do? Some fear he will do the same, then what can the English do?—How terrible it is—The Vendée continues very well that is the only hope the other Emigrants can have.

THURSDAY, OCTOBER 30TH. We went at the Concert of the princess—The English Bishop and is family were there—My lady North seems to be very naughty and is a tall stiff woman. Her two eldest daughters were with her they were kind to me but are both rather Ugly—The son seems to be a good young man; as for the old Bishop he does all that his wife will—The Concert was very good the band of music of the Court is excellent—I was obliged to play but hope I shall not always have to play at each Concert.

FRIDAY, OCTOBER 31ST. I enjoyed a very true and great Joy in seeing the Good Mr. Fries—He arrived in the evening and will I hope Spend a little time with us. What gave me still the greatest pleasure was to find him I think perfectly well; and not even to be *Constitutional*, what I had much feared as all his Seminary was and Jaegle is still so and as Obstinate as it is possible to be—But our good Fries is always the same honest, honest, excellent, amiable, lovely man as we had left him at Strasburgh—I hope he will *Convert* Jaegle as he always was his Oracle

—The princess came to Tea with us, and was very amiable and kind.

MONDAY, NOVEMBER 3RD. We gave a Charming feast to the prince and princess—We had a very numerous Assembly but Just as much as our Small Appartments could contain—Every body came at seven we danced till the Supper which was quite beautiful and Afterwards we continued our ball till two o'clock in the morning—Every one was much amused and I am Sure that the Princess will not so soon forget the evening She spent at Unterwarth.

TUESDAY, NOV. 11TH. I took a little ride at the Oberwarts, as the weather was more pleasant than it is usually. We are daily expecting Mr. Blair how I do rejoice to see them. But I fear they will not be here until after tomorrow. I am really now very happy, there is a good society of Englishmen; we have as many pleasures and amusements as I could wish to have, and I have nothing more to fear on account of the baron buohl as he is hated by all those that know him. There is only one thing that I would yet wish, and that is not to be in company of the Bombelles but as that can not be otherways I must take patience.

THURSDAY, 4TH DEC. This evening I played at the prince's Concert, and *Eugenia* sang—and indeed we had the universal Approbation and Praise which (I may say) were not undeserved—The Old Prince is vastly fond of music and understands it very well it is a pleasure to make him some His concert is very good as his very numerous band of music is excellent. I am very glad to have done my task, as I was really afraid to play before so many persons.

FRIDAY, DEC. 5TH: I took a pleasant walk in the morning and in the evening we went at Mr Teyghes where there was an agreeable society. Marchand was there and he is a most wicked and malicious devil his greatest pleasure would be to make me angry but that he will never do as I turn all his naughtiness in jokes but in the meantime my answers are as wicked as all he says to me. I do not know if he is jealous of me but I must take great care how I behave with him as he is monstrously naughty....

SATURDAY, 6TH DEC: Mrs. Teyghe walked out with us at Oberwörth she is a charming woman, but is not very happy with her husband who notwithstand he is a very honest and excellent man plagues her to death. It is but four months since she is married and it frightens her for the future. Papa has got a fit of the gout, he drinks too much ever since he is here and now he has got the gout after the Garlik had hindered him from having it a great while.

THURSDAY, 25TH DECEMBER. It is a great while I did not spend such an agreable christmas day, as I did this year. In the morning we had the three masses at Neidermünster the princess there is very kind to us. We had quite an English dinner at the White Lamb our family Mr Blairs, Mr and Mrs Teighe and young Mr North. It was very pleasant and it gave me much pleasure. This evening we went at the old princes where all Ratisbon was in the greatest gala. There was a concert and I amused myself much with the young ladies. As I now begin to get acquainted with them I amuse myself much more.

SUNDAY, DEC: 28TH. We went with Mrs Teyghe and the Boissiers that we had not seen for a great while. At the end of all it is a very foolish family the old man is a bore and a fool and the daughter is a wicked and naughty girl. This evening I much amused myself at the Blairs where Mr North and Mr Teighe were. father Maurus is always there he is a good young man but a bad monk.

WEDNESDAY, DEC: 31ST. This was the last day of this year that I began very bad and ended very pleasantly—I went to the Blair's and stayed there late. I always like Mr Blair more, but Lady Mary is not by half such a kind and good creature. She grumbles continually and gets very old which makes her quite childish—Father Maurus is always there and indeed I can not bear to see him as he is such a wild young fellow, that it is a real shame that he should have the monkish habit. Those bad Clergy men much wrongs our religion but there is abuses in everything nothing can be perfect in this world.

JAN: 1ST, 1795. THURSDAY. We had a great many visits to pay for New Year's day—This year began in a monstrous cold manner—I cannot remember since the year '89 that we were at Strasburgh of having had so much cold. We went at the *Grand Court* the princess and the old prince were there was a concert. It was a day of great galla and all the ladies had Sacks—the prince was covered with diamonds which he all showed us with great satisfaction, but I could not help laughing when he showed us his Diamond Garters as it was too ridiculous. The good old man is so stupid! The barometer is 15 degrees beyond Ice.

10TH JAN: SATURDAY. There is a great deal of noise among the English here. As we all want to give a feast the 19th of this month to celebrate the Queen of England's birthday. The Blairs Teighes Boissiers and us have come to an agreement but the wicked Mrs North does all in her power to puspone our feast and plague us. She loses the too goodly Bishops Character and behaves like a ridiculous fool. She wanted to give a ball the same day but all Ratisbon accepted our invitation so she was can no have anybody and is in a terrible rage. But I pity much the good Mr North he is so afflicted of all this and sees that his mother is wrong that I pity him with all my heart. He is such a charming and agreable young man and so misfortunate. He acknowledges to us that Mrs. North beat him once; poor creature, how can there be such a wicked beast as that woman.

11TH JANUARY, SUNDAY. Again the whole day there was nothing but messages from the Norths and the other English. I was at Mr Blairs morning and evening where we danced, played supped with young d'Omptada and Mr North But I wearied myself much as Lady Mary is very cross on account of all this noise. However we shall have a fine feast but it will cost 60 Guineas at least and indeed it is very foolish to expence so much money in that way when there is so many poor wretches.

12TH JANUARY, MONDAY. I went at Mde de la Pleisnoye in the morning and after much prayers I obtained leave that her young ladies should spend the evening at our house. She is rather whimsical and is very severe to her daughters. We amused ourselves much at our house as the princess, Mde de Hohenthal and all their society came. We danced as usually. The Bishop has at last consented to be in the list of subscribers. But Mrs North is very angry and will come to our ball only as a visitant.

13TH JAN., TUESDAY. We had a ball at Mrs Teighe's where the princess came. I amused myself vastly. Miss Norths and the Bishop came, poor girls they are worth the greatest compassion and these two unfortunate sisters are as miserable as it is possible as the nasty beast of a mother will not let them go out anywhere and the youngest is seventeen year of age. I wait with impatience our ball of Monday and I hope it will be very handsome and pleasant.

FRIDAY, JAN: 16TH. We went at Mr. Blairs in the evening Lady Mary has got a fever and it is feared will not be able to go to the feast. This feast has great many misfortunes we have every day more unluck.

MONDAY, JAN: 19TH. At last this feast that we waited with so much impatience arrived but I lost all pleasure of it as the Princess who was the principle object for which we gave it could not come her child the pretty little prince George being excessively ill. With her we were deprived of great many other persons and of all the Court which was a great pity but notwithstanding our feast was very handsome and pleasant. All Ratisbon of good society was there the ball was very merry and the whole charming. The Room was all decorated with garlands of flowers inscriptions *in transparens* for the queens praise and all the English had *God save the Queen* on the sashes and in the hair. It was very magnificent and I amused myself much but alas all the while the princess was in the greatest affliction for her child that is in great danger.

TUESDAY, 20TH JAN. The first thing that was told me when I awoke was that the little prince was dead and indeed it much afflicted me as it was a lovely Child, he had so much wit was so lively, pretty; and beloved by everybody. The poor Princess must be exceedingly grieved as she is such a good mother and lost already her first child. It is a great affliction for the whole family everybody is afflicted as it was such a charming little creature besides the family Taxis is much loved as they are all very good. I could but think on this all day, besides I was very tired of the dance and it had given me a bad Cold so that I staid at home.

FRIDAY, JAN: 23RD. We have to pay thirty guineas a piece for the feast which cost 150 Louis. How foolishly that money has been spent!

Friday, Feb. 6th. I could not go out anywhere as Mamma and my sister were very ill. What makes poor Mamma be worse is that she had a letter from Lyons where there is no bread and what her parents live upon is frozen potatoes done in Water. The people die of cold there as wood cost 400 frs. a measure. How shocking! Mr. and Mrs. Floyer were here a moment this morning, and poor Mrs Teighe whose husband played the fool yesterday getting drunk (has he does almost every day) and ducking a poor man in the street and quarrelling and being impudent with all the masks how unfortunate that good woman is.

Tuesday, February 10th. I went in the evening at a ball at Count Seilern where I was sorry to be present to a *scene* that does very little *honour* to Miss Blair. The Count Max de Lerchenfeld that is the greatest fop, the greatest blaguard of all Ratisbon and that gives a bad reputation and loses the character of all young ladies; had put it in his head to serve Mary Blair as he does all the others that pay attention to him; he courted her since three or four balls and Mary that is very foolish and found him a pretty and agreeable fellow showed him much preference—he would dance with her nearly the whole evening and as Mr de la Roche had engaged for a dance, that she preferred to dance with the Count Lerchenfeld, the two gentlemen had a great quarrel Mr de la Roche was insolent and by that got all the wrong on his side—it finished very ill as they would fight. Tomorrow we shall know the end of this sad stories that gives Mary Blair a very bad name all over the town, as she behaved like a real fool. This scene spoilt all the pleasure I had had the rest of the evening as the Ball was charming.

Wednesday, Feb. 11th. The first thing I heard this

morning was that the two fine heros were going to fight, but they made so much noise before that Mr. Bombelles and others ran after them and hindered them from it, and they made it up. Good God what bad consequences such a trifle might have had. It is a very good lesson for every young lady that will profit of it. Lady Mary dont know anything about the matter as Mary was under Mamma's care last night. The indifference that Mary showed to all this gives me a bad opinion of her. She is only affraid that her parents may come to hear of this as she loves the Count Max and is very proud to think that he wanted to fight for her but she mistakes those gentlemen only fought for the point d'honneur as they both make game on her. I went to the publick masked ball which was very pleasant everybody talks of this sad affair. Mr. de Buohl is very angry with La Roche, he is very impudent to him and Mr. Bombelles who though behaved as well as that young saucy frenchman behaved ill—What nonsense all this is! I am quite tired of it.

WEDNESDAY, FEB. 25TH. Mamma is very unwell. a letter that she saw of Mary Mantalban to the Count Abbé Montalban in which she shows the greatest ingratitude for all that Mamma ever did for her has quite made her ill and grieved her excessively—what a pity that that young woman should have turned so bad; she was once so godly so well behaving so good; an unfortunate passion she has for a certain Barbaro has changed her quite and made her forget herself in such a manner as that she is now blamed by all those that once loved her for her well behaviour and religion. It is too very humiliating to see that all the women of Papa's family should have lost their character in such a way and that must make us more than any one else be scrupulous for the least thing and *keep an irreproachable conduct.*

APRIL 7TH, TUESDAY. Mr. de Bombelles gave a breakfast to the princes and all the town, there was 76 persons we danced afterwards till 5 oclock in the evening and it was excessively pleasant, I hope it will give the idea to others of giving such feasts as they are very amusing and not so fatiguing as a night ball. Mlle de Diede the eldest is going to marry the Count Ranzou in a few months he makes a much better acquisition than she does as he is a cunning wicked devil. I am glad she should marry as she is a charming girl and begins to get old. It would have been a pity if she had persisted in her design of not marrying as it is said that she had refused many marriages already for to stay with her parents. I dont know whether it is true or not but I dont believe it she is twenty two.

MONDAY, APRIL 13TH. We went to the Blairs. Mary is not well and I saw very plain today that she is a bad creature she treats her mother like I certainly could not treat my maid.

SATURDAY, APRIL 18TH. I am quite sorry to think this is the last day I can say I am sixteen years old, I am very unpleased to see seventeen so near but patience it cannot be otherways. I went much to the fair today where I leave all my money, and I shall soon have no more. To finish my sixteenth year *most agreeably* I went at the Blairs.

CHAPTER 14

SUNDAY, APRIL 19TH. This was a day that made me reflect very seriously as I accomplished my seventeenth year and I must own I think it prodigiously old as it is not far from twenty. This made me spend a very dull birthday as at the bottom of my heart I was very sad to think I was beginning the eightenth year of my life and that till now I had wasted my time in a very foolish way but I took resolutions to begin to me more applied to things that will be of more use to me in future and to enjoy life as it is very short. I was quite Philosophical and mean to remain it.

MONDAY, APRIL 27TH. I went with my sisters to see the tumblers where I amused myself very well. Miss Floyer came there and I was much surprised to hear her praise so much at one of the Rope dancers the young one, that I really think she has a little liking for him. What a shocking thing it would be and how foolish but I am afraid it is true. I went to the Blairs in the evening. We saw a magic lantern there, that was as stupid as all those I have yet seen. Lady Mary begins to be a little better but Mr. Blair is very ill, and I dont know what is the matter with Mary, but she looks very unwell since a great while. She'll finish by having a great illness as she wont take care of herself at all.

TUESDAY, APRIL 28TH. What I had thought of Miss Floyer is very true Mamma told me today that she was passionately in love with the rope dancer, that she sent every morning to know how he did and that she was getting a blue sash embroidered in silver made for him. I declare I think the poor girl is mad, how is it possible to fall in love with such a creature, a rope dancer, besides that is not at all handsome. Now I begin to believe all that was told of her that she is an extravagant Romantic girl and that being abandoned to herself has made at many such follies.

WEDNESDAY, MAY 6TH. Mr. Blair sent for us to dine with him, *we did* and after dinner we went to take an airing but a violent storm obliged us to return very soon. We spent also the evening with them and I had much conversation with Mr. Blair that proved to me always more that he is a very good friend of ours. He said much of the B. and the foolish way we live, but to what use? I cannot change it. They have decided to go Sunday I wish we were going with them. How happy they are they will soon be in England.

FRIDAY, MAY 15TH. Old Father Dufresne came this afternoon and I went to draw with him from nature. Whilst we were drawing a great quantity of people that belong to the boat houses came around us and I was quite astonished that they were not rude to us. As they are in general like wild beasts they always live with their horses and sleep under a tent that they make with straw by their horses side out in the air. In Switzerland they would have certainly insulted us but these good people stayed around us, gazed at our drawings and were quite surprised and happy in seeing what we were doing. For all that, I did not much like all these admirers (especially as I feared they should make us some presents as for all they are very Good natured creatures they are not very clean and have a numerous family about them) so I went away and was surrounded in another place by a parcel of scholars with whom old Father Dufresne made a Latin Conversation, which was not very amusing. I thought the best was the return home.

TUESDAY, JUNE 2ND. We had a great many people at our house this evening and I was greatly embarrassed as I did not know how to be civil and how to satisfy all. Mlles. de la Villequiers (who are little devils and just as tiresome as Mlles. de la Plesnoye had told us they were) played the deuce for to dance, Mlles. de Diede who are quite the other extreme of these thoughtless foolish girls seemed to tire themselves much in our company, and would have much preferred to keep a serious (old womanish) conversation with the fine ladies than to stay in all the noise that the other society was making. I was greatly puzzled as I did not approve nor the one nor the other. I certainly love as much to dance laugh and sport as any young girl of my age but I find the way of Mlle. d'Aumont very ridiculous as they are so transported when they are a little at liberty that they are real devils, but in the mean time I have not by half as much reason as Mlles. de Diede and I should not like to resemble them as they are not at all what other young ladies are and dont take any pleasure in what amuses youth so that I think the consequences of all this is that young people should amuse themselves honestly and at the same time heartily but not romp about and show so much love for pleasure as to be justly ridiculed by everybody. We finished by dancing but quite against my wish as it really looked foolish but I was obliged to it. The Diedes made a foolish face and the others seemed devils that never any enjoyment before.

SATURDAY, JUNE 6TH. We had an assembly at our house. The Diedes Hohenthals etc. all for the Ambassador which is found here very amiable and is very much liked. We had some music Mde. de Hohenthal howld enough to frighten the cats and she has taken it into her head to make me sing, so that I was obliged to unfold that great talent of mine that I took care to conceal from everybody, for *very good* reasons.

SUNDAY, JUNE 21ST. The little Louis XVII is dead, this news was received with much indifference and it was easy to see that it gave the French more satisfaction than pain as they think now that all will soon end their king being out of France.

THURSDAY, JUNE 25TH. We were left quite alone at the end of the evening which was most tiresome. We shall be quite forgotten in society now as we cannot show our *pretty charming* faces for so long a time.

FRIDAY, JULY 3RD. We went to Kaffring directly after dinner, I rode there. The Lerchenfelds were very kind to us. It is a pretty country house, the garden is not ugly and there is a little wood, but altogether it is nothing remarkable. They must lead a tiresome life there as they are always quarrelling among them. Mary will soon return to Munich. Alexandrine is not very gay as she would wish I believe her marriage with the Baron Buohl to be quite settled and Walburghe is always as dull and as stupid. Count Max is the favourite and the happiest, but the worst of them all and I detest his foppishness and familiar way. We walked much about and I must own I tired myself to death. The stupid Count Max came on horseback with me almost till the town which did not flatter me at all as he thought it would, as I was alone and I did not like any body should see me with that *good for nothing Coxcomb*.

SUNDAY, JULY 26TH. How easily one gets tired of everything. I wearied myself horribly this evening as we had our usual society and were obliged to play the stupid *petits jeux* that I hate now as much as I liked them when I first came here. There came official news to-day of the taking of l'Orient and the remainder of the French fleet which had retired to Brest after the defeat the English gave them on 28th has been totally destroyed.

WEDNESDAY, JULY 29TH. I went in the morning to see a Jewish Matrimony it was in a yard and indeed much amused me. The woman was five and thirty and the man only seventeen which is quite ridiculous. The man first came drest in black with two of his relations and the two Rabies. He placed himself under a baldequin and covered his head with a veil. The bride came soon after very neat and elegantly drest with other women and was placed near the bridegroom under the same veil. After they had both drunk some wine and when the ring was given the two rabies sung a most ridiculous thing which made it very difficult for me to keep from laughing. Then the bridegroom threw a bottle against the wall where a star was placed. They have the superstition to believe that if they dont catch the star in the right place their marriage will be unhappy. As this did not happen everyone complimented the bridegroom and they all went away. There were many people to see this ceremony, the Jews gave a breakfast and all the company was invited to their ball and supper. They are very rich and both pretty. I was very glad to see the odd marriage as indeed it was a very comical thing, their dress and manners are all so different from what is commonly seen. We had a great number of company at our house this evening and had a very pretty concert.

MONDAY, AUGUST 3RD. Papa dont like us to be with him, his gout makes him horridly cross.

THURSDAY, AUGUST 6TH. The thunderbolt fell on the Cathedral and a boy of fourteen was struck dead in the spot, another work man that was working with him was also hurt. We were going to take an airing this afternoon after the storm was over and we met the man that was wounded that was carried to the hospital and we could not forbear going to see him, indeed it was shocking to see how the thunderbolt burnd part of his arm body and leg, he was horridly pale but for all that I dont believe it will be dangerous.

FRIDAY, AUGUST 7TH. We went to see the poor man that was wounded yesterday and the boy that was killed. It is a shocking sight the thunderbolt struck him on the temple and neck and he died immediately the other is much better, it will be of no consequence. The Hospital is kept very clean and they seem to be very kind to the sick persons. We afterwards went to the house when the fools are kept and it really grieved me to see the poor Karl Mde Seiglerns son in law, which talks as reasonable as any body else and his wicked wife to enjoy her liberty and his money says that his brains are turned and keeps him shut up in the hospital. It is horrid the poor man does nothing but cry and only wants to go into Saxony to his mother but his wife wont let him go. He is kept in a nasty dirty stinking room and it is the way to make him quite raving mad that nasty woman cannot conceive how one can be so cruel. Mamma will endeavour to do something for that poor man.

MONDAY, AUGUST 10TH. The Norths left for England.

WEDNESDAY, AUGUST 12TH. The English Minister Mr. Walpole arrived to-day. We did not see him. I am very glad he should be here as the Hanoverian minister wont give himself such airs as he did.

THURSDAY, AUGUST 13TH. Mr. Walpole came in the morning and spent an hour this afternoon with us. He is very much like young Mr. North. He has got his voice, his features, and all his ways. He seems to be very amiable and a little extravagant I think he looks old and I didn't know him again at all for all I had seen him at Munich seven years ago.

SUNDAY, SEPTEMBER 20TH. M. de Bombelles was much afflicted for Mde de Diedes departure. The poor man is indeed grown quite a fool as it is ridiculous that a man of his age qualities, etc etc. should fall in love. Everybody laughs at him.

MONDAY, SEPTEMBER 21ST. I went to Miss Cristina in the afternoon to take her to ride out with me but she was not at home and I only found there Count Alexander with whom I was obliged to stay for a great whiles alone which embarrassed us both excessively and made us both look very silly, I thought at last we were too stupid and proposed to ride till his cousin came home, I had time to take several turns with him till they all came home, I then went with Mlle Cristina in our favourite place, the Kuhwies and had a very pleasant ride with her.

THURSDAY, OCTOBER 22ND. The concert at the Princess' was terribly tiresome but after it we had a ball and supper. Mde. de Bombelles is again with child. She will never be tired to make such unsupportable brats? I am glad that I shant be here for her laying in.

MONDAY, OCTOBER 26TH. There is many complaints of us by the society, we seem to be proud, disdainful and are excessively rude to every body. I am very sorry they think we do but that's my manner of behaving and would not wish to change it and to take their hipocrisy grimaces and affectations. This has all been said at the Diedes, where harm is spoken of every body.

TUESDAY, NOVEMBER 3RD. Papa is grown a great favourite of the young prince la Tour. He always goes shooting and is continuously with him. This prince is a very good natured man. I don't think he is very witty but what is still better he has a good heart and a good understanding. He was telling Papa the other day that if he had any good chaces near Ratisbon he would give them all to him for his life time if he would promise to stay always here.

WEDNESDAY, NOVEMBER 11TH. Mr. Walpole gave a charming feast this evening for Lady Berwick. There was the most amiable persons of the town the princess looked beautiful and was drest with the greatest grace and elegance, we danced, had a fine supper and were very much satisfied. Mr. Walpole was very civil and Miss Louisa Diede behaved most ridiculously always running after him. Lady Berwick is going to Italy I am sorry that we will loose her for indeed she is very amiable in society I don't know what her character is in her family. Some says she is a devil it may be but certainly has affects quite the contrary and is very kind to everybody. As for her daughters I dont care for them a pin, they never talk and looks so stupid as can be.

TUESDAY, NOVEMBER 17TH. We went to an assembly at the princess' where a french Chantur sung many scenes of Oedipe à Colonne with the Count Hohenthal, his voice is fine but he dont sing well. Lord Bristol has been at Ratisbon since yesterday he had promised to come to the assembly this evening and has asked to hear me play but at last he did not come; which gave me infinite pleasure for all I would have wished to see him he is said to be such an original fellow. He is quite a fool, got himself in several scrapes in England he has been a great favourite of Mde. de Schaden, caused her to separate herself from her husband, he has been in love with the princess, told her to day in presence of her husband that he did not deserve such a wife. This curious fellow is to set off to morrow.

THURSDAY, DECEMBER 3RD. The concert at the Princess was very bad and tiresome this evening. Mlle. Fouchemoulin sung a french Cantata horrid bad, her voice is like that of a cat that one kills and she pronounces french like a pig, the french Chantre sung an Italian air which he pronounced with a french accent, and the whole was detestable.

FRIDAY, DECEMBER 4TH. We went to stay all the evening with Mrs. Douglas I wearied myself except when Mde. Bioloi came and that we talked of little Mary's wickedness. That always makes an agreeable conversation.

SATURDAY, DECEMBER 19TH. I was very sorry to hear today that Prince Charles Lichtenstein whom I had seen at Venice few years ago had fought an unhappy duel and had been mortally wounded. I was first acquainted with him at Mayence where he was the innocent cause of Papas making Mama a very disagreeable scene at a Ball. Such as many he made her the first years of her marriage. There are few years that this prince is married and it was in a very odd way that he got a wife he had fallen from his horse but was not hurt, a lady which was in a carriage had been so sadly frightened that she fainted away. This so much touched the prince that he married her soon after and he never had known her before. She was a charming woman and deserved him in all points. She is now very miserable and will remain a widow with two children. This duel was occasioned by a Russian young lady only 17 years old. She had induced a Chanoine Weichs to follow her from Italy to Vienna where she no sooner arrived than she mocked the Chanoine and played the fool with prince Lichtenstein. Mr. Weichts then despised her and for this reason the prince fought with him. He had first been wounded in the arm, and Mr. Weichs and him were satisfied, but the Prince's brother which is such a devil that he is named at Vienna the Abbé Monstre, forced them both to fight again, the prince already weak was wounded and now there is few hopes of his living. The young lady has left Vienna indeed she should not show her face any more.

THURSDAY, DECEMBER 31ST. We finished the year indeed very badly. The affair which happened today is quite surprising and a real comedy. As it gives the last stroke to the picture of the Marquis's character I shall relate it, although it is not necessary I should write to remember it, such a scene will never be wiped off my memory. The Valet de Ch. of Mr. B. a good for nothing man, who has dishonoured Nepomucks family, since we are here allways abused this poor man. They had a dispute in the morning and Nepomuck asked Mamma to speak to him, but as she did not like to meddle herself in their quarrel told him that when he would be impudent to him again he should give him a good beating. Nepomuck in the afternoon met the little Coxcomb Valet de Cha: in the street carrying his masters sword and a stick. On his being again insolent our Servant took hold of him, threw him down in the dirt and beat him as hard as he could. The coward did not dare to defend himself and cried for mercy. At last he was left on the ground and got up, took his sword and stick which he had lost in the fight and came home with a black eye. He is Mr. B's darling, confidant and friend and he never would consent to send him away for he could not do without him. The first reason is that the poor Man has a dozen false teeth in his mouth and nobody but his beloved

Barthelemi can arrange them for him. When he heard how terribly his Valet de Cha: had been treated he flew in a violent passion and came into Mama's room, with his hair half drest, his *powder mantle* a very comical figure. He was very saucy with her and on his hearing that she told Muck to beat his *valet* the *valet de Ch.* of a *Marquis* who has been *Ambassador* who has the Cross of *St. Louis* etc. etc. he was in such a rage that he went to take his wife to the present and to take his part, but on the contrary she was against him. He then said that as Mama could not give him satisfaction he would go to Papa to abuse him and thus oblige him to fight with him. This enraged Mde. Bomb. and Mama and there was a terrible quarrel, at last his wife took him away. I cannot say how angry I am about it. That nasty beast says he is our friend, and after the obligations he is under to Papa he will out of gratitude cut his throat, for a blackguard of a servant. This is of a *right* frenchman I never could have had the least idea of such a thing. Since a great while I disliked that man, but now I hate that hippocrite, that unthankful man, proud and vile, no I shall never forget his behaviour. Mde. de B. behaved on the contrary in this affair perfectly well. We have decided to leave their house as soon as possible, how can we live any longer with this brute. I long to know how this affair will finish. A very bad end of the year but very good if we consider that it discovers to us the vile character of this man who gave himself out for our friend and that it will be a very good excuse for leaving him.

CHAPTER 15

Saturday, January 23rd. I forgot to mention yesterday that Clergy the ancient Valet de Chambre of the poor french king arrived here and dined with us. It is about twenty days he has left France and he is now going to Vienna to join Mde Royale. He was kept in prison after his masters death and he found means to escape after the monster Robespiere ended his days. He gave us many details on that unfortunate Royal family. Louis XVI died with great courage and never showed a moments weakness. His neck being so fat his head did not fall at the first stroke and he was heard scream. The Queen had been kept in such piggishness during a great while that she was quite an eskalleton when she was killed. All her members trembled. Mde Elizabeth on the contrary was mild and calm and looked as fresh as a rose.

Sunday, January 24th. Mr. de Vernet one of the finest men that ever was seen, a favourite of the late french Queen, him that served her for postillion when she endeavoured to escape but was arrested at Varenne, breakfasted with the Bombelles. I was sorry not to see him as he is indeed a curious object to be acquainted with. He is of one of the great families in Sweden.

Saturday, February 13th. On accounts of colds and all the remains of the Carnival my sister and I stay at home. Papa and Mama go out every day and are very civil to every body to leave a good reputation behind them, when they'll be gone. The Marquis returned yesterday from Munic and endeavours to be civil and kind to us.

Thursday, March 3rd. This is the last day I shall

spend at Ratisbon and with the family Bombelles. I cannot say it afflicts me for the regret I feel to quit the amiable society of this place is so well compensated by the joy of being delivered of the French family, that I am quite happy. I went in the evening to the golden cross to hear a man who plays on an Instrument which ressembles very much the Harmonica. It has a most delightful sound. He after having played several slow tunes made a very extraordinary thing with glass. Throwing sand over a square of glass he then with a bow gave a sound and at the same time the sand instantly formed several figures stars, squares, rounds, etc. with the greatest exactness. We received kindnesses and bounties from every body. All the young ladies of our acquaintance came to take leave of us and all cryed. I was sorry to part with Marianne.

LANDSHUT, MARCH 4TH, FRIDAY. Many tears were shed and many wry faces made, but I resisted them all and did not cry. For all that I was sorry to quit Mde de Louvois, Louis B, La Brosse, and the old Chev. de B. as these persons have always showed real friendship to us, I have had too many proofs of the falsehood of the rest to be capable of regretting them. No, on the contrary I shall for ever think the day we got rid of them, the happiest of my life. With pleasure I got into the carriage and left the Unterwörth at six in the morning. The weather was horrid and dreadful snow but the roads good, excellent horses and came a very good pace to Landshut where we arrived at half past three and stayed the night.

FLORENCE, WEDNESDAY, APRIL 20TH. We made acquaintance with Mde Santini a very gay Italian lady good and kind to the strangers. Mde Fantastici comes often to see us. She is an excellent woman and in society you would not think that she possesses so great a talent for she is not at all affected. Mr Gordon came in the evening he is a Scotchman and a very good natured man, he is going to Venice. Poor Mde Lacaenca paid us a visit, I pity that creature much but I think she plagues also her husband, she does not seem to be very *good-natured* and *soft*. She is red-haired—that makes me think she is naughty.

SATURDAY, APRIL 23RD. As Papa will not absolutely stay at Vaninis we are looking for a house. We saw several this morning but did not decide any thing. When we returned home we found an invitation to go to a Ball given to-night by the Russian minister Ct. Mocenigo, Prince Corsini was to take us there, and did not come to fetch us till nine o'Clock. he came with his Lady Mde Sarastori a fine woman. I was quite surprised arriving to this assembly to find such a vast number of peoples, and all the women very elegantly and richly drest fashionably. Eight fine rooms full, all beautifully lighted. The dance was not amusing for the Italians dance so slow so ridiculously that I could not go on at all. I never saw any thing more comical than some of these Italian Ladies are, they have such foolish manners with the men. Mde. Sarastori is the most decent. This feast is really magnificent, but a small Ball would have amused me much more. All was over at twelve o'Clock.

TUESDAY, 26TH APRIL. I went this morning with Mde. Fantastini to see the Drawing school where there are some very fine pictures and statues. The latter are all copies from those of the Gallery. Mde. Fantastini dined with us and sung to us. She is one of the best women I ever saw, and at the same time quite gay and funny. She loves her husband excessively and he adores her. This seldom is the case in Italy.

FRIDAY, APRIL 29TH. Papa took at last a house which is rather small but very neat, Clean and pleasant. He will pay 18 zecchins a month without the Linon. It is in the via Annunziatina. I fear it will be exceedingly hot in summer. we will stay at Vaninis till the 8th of next month as the appartment is paid till that time. Mr Gordon, Beach and Penrose came to spend the evening with us.

I went with Mamma and Mr Biddulph to the Cachinis the Gentleman is a Catholic and is very much esteemed by every body, he is about forty. Mamma thinks him a saint and makes his praise to me all day long. I do not know to what purpose!

SUNDAY, MAY 1ST. Mr. Biddulph, Mr. Gordon, Mr. Penrose and little George Wyndham dined with us and stayed part of the evening. L'Abbe de Jou a cousin of Cts de Bressac comes very often to us he is a very good natured man. The poor french king has been obliged to quit Verona, the Republick sent him orders to go out of the Venitian estate. the reason is not known. He is going to join the army of Condé. He ought to have been there a great while ago. The French make a rapid progress in Italy. How it would vex me if they would come here and oblige us to go back to Germany. Affairs go on bad. Charette has been taken and suffered death with admirable courage.

SATURDAY, MAY 7TH. We paid a visit this morning to the Marchesa Santini, she is a very good sort of woman and saw a moment Miss Beckford. We dined for the last time at Vanninis as we came to sleep in our new house. We have taken Prince Chimai's cook and on this account the Prince is very angry with us and will not come any more to see us. It is not a great loss. This cook has been sent from Leghorn to this place for us the prince had taken him but the man would not stay with him so that it is very just that we should take him, he is a good and honest man. Mr. Gordon stayed the evening with us, he is gay and amiable.

MONDAY, MAY 9TH. We begun to be very uneasy as the duced French make such progress that we fear to have their visit here and though this is a neutral country and we have nothing to fear it would be a vastly disagreeable to find ourselves where those dirty creatures are. Mlles. de la Plesnoye spent the evening with us. Papa wants to go away, how sorry I should be.

SUNDAY, MAY 15TH. I went to the Cathedrale where there was a great ceremony, and the Grand Duke and Duchess present. Afterwards we went to see an illumination in the Church of St. Croce. It was very fine, coming home we heard all the news which were very bad and frightened Papa and Mama out of their wits. The french crossed the Po and has taken Milan. The Austrian army beaten and disheartened there is no knowing what is become of Beaulieu. The french are masters of all Italy now. They may go wherever they please Papa wants to leave this country and all is packing up. but where shall we go? To Venice we may meet the french on the road, He talks of going to Corsica to Spain etc. I dont care what he'll decide to do I should prefer though to stay here.

WEDNESDAY, MAY 18TH. Papa was less alarmed to-day. He saw Mr Wyndham who laughed at his fears and assured him that he had no occasion to be uneasy. We all went to the Cashinis with Mr Gordon our faithful Cavalier Servente. The weather being most delectable we walked in the woods and were delighted with the charming notes of the nightingales of which there are a vast number in that place.

Mde. de la Plesnoye came in the evening her daughters and we were very gay and laughed much at the stupidity of B. de Sel.

MONDAY, MAY 30TH. I was quite in distress this morning on hearing that Papa was quite decided to go away. Mrs. Newnham advises him not to stay here for she says Italy is lost. But different other persons Papa saw in the afternoon and especially Mr Wyndham said that it was quite foolish to fear the least thing. He was insisted upon waiting a little longer and in the meantime he will go to see Leghorn Mrs. Newnham goes there to-morrow. Papa and Mr. Gordon will follow her the next day. This lady came this evening to our house we had likewise Mlles de la Plesnoye Miss Santini and Mrs Caenea. We were very gay sung and danced all the evening There is here an american that came with Mrs. Newnham from Venice which is a very curious man. He is named Peerson he has been very long at Paris and means to return he seems to be a great partisan of the french. He has very free manners with young ladies and I do not like him at all. Ct. Montenari came to us to-day; he has at last obtained leave to travel and he is so happy to be out of Verona where he wearied himself to death, that he is quite changed. He is grown fat and is gay and foolish, but he is not any handsomer than he was before.

TUESDAY, MAY 31ST. Mr. Biddulph (*the dear Creature*) Mr Gordon, Ct. Montenari, Brunner, and the Doctor dined with us. We went in the afternoon to see Poggio Imperiale the *jolly* Mr. Biddulph took us there. It is a charming country house of the Grand Dukes. The outside seems very old and gives a very poor idea of the rest but inside it is very fine, a vast number of appartments very neat and nice. It is very agreeably situated and the view over the pretty hills round it is delightful. The garden is small and no great thing We met the grand Dutchess walking with the Dutchess d'Alve along the avenue. She seems to be an old woman of four score an ugly little lame and hunchbacked creature. I am not surprised the Grand Duke asked his brother the day of his wedding. 'Francis how do you like your wife? I think mine very ugly.'

SUNDAY, JUNE 5TH. The fears are again greater than ever and Papa wants to go. A letter that Mr. Ansley has received from Colonel Rook, in which it is said that Beaulieu is too weak to oppose the french that Mantua cannot stand for more than six weeks, has alarmed them all. It makes me quite mad. I went in the afternoon to the Cashinis and to the Pergola. The Morichelli sings divinely. If I was a man I should be passionately in love with that woman and would not mind her age.

FRIDAY, 10TH JUNE. We went this morning to see the Specula Cabinet d'historie Naturelle. It is a very curious and fine thing but terribly disgusting. There is every piece of anatomy done in wax, most beautifully but it looks like a butchery. It gave me much more pleasure to see the birds, fishes, marbles, minerals, and if we decide to stay here I certainly shall make a study of natural history and often come to this place but will not go any more to see the slayed corpses, the skeletons and all that dirty piece of work. It is very well for those who want to become surgeons, but for me it is no use.

MONDAY, JUNE 13TH. We heard to-day fine news I wish they were true. Beaulieu has beat the French by a stratagem they have recrossed the Mincio. The Peace with the Pope is certain. But all this does not put Papa in a good humour he hates Florence and Italy and is determined whether peace is made with

Rome and Italy never to go to those places and to return to his beloved Germany where he wants to take a Country house and where he'll lead a quiet country life, fine projects for him that cannot be a moment without any society. All this vexes me dreadfully, I like the town I wish to see Rome and Naples and should be sorry to return to Ratisbon at present.

TUESDAY, JUNE 14TH. Papa dined at Mr. Wyndhams where he got so thoroughly drunk that he was obliged to get into bed as soon as he returned home. We took a pleasant walk to the Cashinis, where we met Mr Wyndham he was vastly civil to us. He introduced us to Captain Herbert one of his relations a young man that is going to Gibraltar.

WEDNESDAY, JUNE 15TH. Papa was gay and in very good health to-day but he was ashamed to show himself and instead of going to the Cashinis he would go to the Gate of Bologna where he walked. We walked out again at ten o'clock it was quite pleasant and we were so much pleased with it that we mean to do so every night.

MONDAY, JUNE 20TH. Nothing can be compared to the alarm in which Papa and Mama were set, on their hearing that the French were at Bologna, that they wanted Leghorn and that they searched an occasion of breaking their neutrality with the Grand Duke. A visit of Mr Quintyn increased their fright exceedingly as he said their had been an insurrection at Leghorn which had obliged the French Consul to make his escape. This would be an excellent pretext says he for declaring against Tuscany. Manfredini, Myot and the Spanish Minister were altogether and the French Minister's secretary said that in a few days we should all hear a new that would surprise every body. What can this be? Mr Penrose seemed to be very uneasy at Mr Wyndham being in the country—he sent to him but he will only return to-morrow. he sent another express at Leghorn with orders to keep there all the English ships that are at present in that place, in case of danger. I was not by far as frightened as the rest. I do not believe all this as bad as it is said. It certainly is exaggerated—the thing that I dislike the most is that an old English young lady that was on her way here had been stript of every thing by the French at Verona. Mde de la Plesnoye came in the evening. Mr. Campos the secretary of M. de Las casas is going to Madrid. he came to see us, and is a vastly amiable man. He says the ambassador is exceedingly ill and they have little hope for his recovery.

Wednesday, June 22nd. Papa quite fixed upon going to Leghorn to-night—we were obliged to stay at home all day and to pack up and get ready as fast as we can—I cannot describe how sorry I am to quit Florence—besides I have not the least wish of going a sea voyage. God knows what will become of us at last. I could not see any of the feasts that were celebrated to-day for St. John the patron of this Town, in the afternoon there was a race of Charriots in the piazza of Sta. Maria Novella. The sights of it is said to have been fine. The Cuppola del Duomo was all lighted in the evening and there was an artificial fire—I enjoyed none of these amusements and spent a very dull day and evening expecting every moment to set off quit for ever Florence and my dear friends the La Plesnoye But how great was our surprise and joy when Papa returning in the evening said he had changed his mind and would stay I began again to be gay and happy hoping, from the news that were received to-day that it would not be at all necessary for us to leave this place.

CHAPTER 16

On board the Inconstant, June 24th. I did not long enjoy the pleasure I had felt Wednesday evening. Papa's fears began to be greater than ever Thursday and nothing could prevent him from resolving to set off for Leghorn in the evening, Everybody laughs at his being so great a coward and says it is very foolish to go away when there is not the least apprehension to be had at this place. I went in the afternoon at Mr Wyndham's to see a horserace, which took place. The race itself is stupid as the horses ran alone in a very foolish way, but the vast number of people and carriages offered a very pleasant and amusing sight. All this did not give me any pleasure as I was very much tormented with the idea of being obliged to go off in the evening. Mr. Wyndham and Mr Penrose were as civil and kind as it is possible to be. They assured us that we would return in a few days from Leghorn as they were fully convinced the French would only pass through Tuscany and not go to that place. This was some comfort to me as if we come back this trip to Leghorn will give me infinite pleasure, I did not take leave of anybody, being persuaded to see them all very soon. Poor Mary stayed behind with her child George and Hans Givry. In case we embark she will return to Germany and come over to us in England as soon as she can. Her husband, the cook and Muck came with us. We had a pleasant journey the night being light and beautiful I was sorry I could not well see the country as there is some very pleasant views which I could hardly perceive in the pale moon shine—We arrived to Leghorn at eleven in the morning we went to Mr Udney's and found there a most terrible bustle and noise—All packing up and getting on board the ships. We hardly had time to get a little breakfast, they hurried us so terribly to quit the place and Captain Fremantle took us on board his Frigate the Inconstant a most beautiful ship. The sight of the sea gave me great joy I had not seen it so long. I found the Inconstant so fine so clean so comfortable so many civil persons that I was quite delighted and regretted no more that the french had obliged us to run away. How kind and amiable Captain Fremantle is. He pleases me more than any man I have yet seen. Not handsome, but there is something pleasing in his countenance and his fiery black eyes are quite captivating. He is good natured, kind, and amiable, gay and lively in short he seems to possess all the good and amiable qualities that are required to win everybodies heart the first moment one sees him Two other English ladies came on board this ship Mrs Pollard and Miss Hood, they seem to be very good sort of women. We were very gay, the Captain though excessively busy and persecuted by everybody took the greatest pains to amuse us. He had promised to make us dance but something came in the way that prevented it. He had Mr Udney's Harpsichord come on board and we had a little music. It was intended we should go in the Gorgon but as we are not to sail to-morrow morning for Corsica Captain Fremantle was so obliging as to propose us staying on board his ship—he did the honor's so well, that we all got a good Bed or Cot and he had *none*, Jaegle had come with us but finding himself low spirit and sickly he had not the heart to remain with us, and returned on shore. I did not expect that after having lived so many years with us, the fright of the sea could be so strong as to get the better of his friendship for us and to make him take the resolution of quitting us.

SUNDAY, JUNE 25TH. I got up much earlier than I thought I should, but there was such a noise in the ship that there was no means of sleeping—I went to walk the deck, and the view I enjoyed there was most delightful. There is a vast number of English ships here, they are all going to sail for Corsica except the Inconstant which will stay to the Last and then will go to join the fleet off Toulon. We dined with Captain Fremantle who continued to treat us with the greatest kindness—just as if he had known us these great many years and we only saw him yesterday for the first time. Most alarming news arrived in the afternoon which put everybody in the greatest confusion. The Convoy received orders to sail at three in the morning. Captain Fremantle got us on board a merchant ship which is going to England. He assured us that we would be as safe as can be on it and that we could not get a better opportunity We left the Inconstant immediately after dinner to our great sorrow. One does not easily quit a place where one received so many marks of friendship and civility—not only the Captain but every one of the officers are equally kind and amiable. After having been on board that beautiful Frigate and having been quite spoilt by kind Captain Fremantle Captain Parishes ship the Achilles seemed rather small and unpleasant to us but I dare say we will soon get accustomed and be perfectly happy and comfortable—as the Captain is a very Gentleman like man. Captain Craven was so kind as to come with us. It is a strong and fine convoy going to Corsica. The French privateers assures that they will get some of the ships but as we have the

Gorgon, the Comet and other different armed vessels with us, I hope we will get safe to St. Firenzo. Jaegle returned. We were very happy to see him again. Poor man he says he could not live without us and would rather risk his life than leave us—so great a sacrifice proves us an attachment and friendship that deserves all our gratitude.

MONDAY, JUNE 26TH. We sailed from Leghorn at four in the morning but the wind being not fair we came a very little way. Notwithstanding we had the Comet, the Gorgon and Malagar to guard the convoy the detestable french privateers took two of our boats. We heard nothing but guns all day. The Republicans entered Leghorn and fired for some time at the Inconstant she immediately set sail and came to reinforce the Convoy which is now composed of 48 ships. Captain Fremantle came near enough to us for it being possible to speak to us, he is in a great rage against the French—and quite vexed to think that the English runs away from them. We are not very well accommodated on board the Accilies, and if Captain Craven had not been with us I really do not know what we should have done as Captain Parish not knowing to the last that we were to go with him had not provided nor prepared the ship for our reception. I hope at St. Firenze he will make it more comfortable. for my part I should much prefer to go to England on board a man of war. Why could not we remain in the Inconstant? Papa was very uneasy to-day as he was sadly afraid of the Privateers. All the Guns musquets and pistols were loaded and all prepared to make a vigorous defence, but we have nothing to fear and I went quietly to bed without having the least apprehension.

TUESDAY, JUNE 27TH. We were becalmed almost all

day and could not get along at all. Papa was again affrayed in the evening of the privateers, as we were near the island of Capriaia which is full of them, but the convoy is too strong for them to do us any harm. The two boats that were taken yesterday did not belong to the convoy and were coming from Corsica. We had Captain Hamilton's visit he commands the Comet and leads the convoy—he is a very civil young man—indeed all these gentlemen of the navy are kind and good natured. The Inconstant proved *inconstant* to-day as she kept at so great a distance that we never could see her without the glass.

WEDNESDAY, JUNE 28TH. The motion in the ship was terrible all night and morning It made Mamma sick and I was very near being it myself—I did nothing but eat and drink to prevent my being so and I found that a very good remedy. The Inconstant overtook us to-day—Captain Fremantle wished us a good morning and said he was going to the Fleet I thought we should never see him again or at least for a great while but how agreeably were we surprised by his coming on board our ship with Lord Garleys the Captain of the Lively a Frigate about same size as the Inconstant. He said he was very low spirited to be obliged to leave us and will endeavour to obtain leave from Admiral Jerveys to go to England for then he promises to take us on board his vessel. What happiness that would be for us! I cannot enough say how many marks of friendship we received from that excellent young man. He has an open, noble fine character I wish we would meet him again—but Alas—I do not much hope that it will happen—I was quite sorry to see him go—he left the Convoy and sailed towards Toulon. We came round Cape Corde and came into the Bay where St Firenze lays Towards evening we were surrounded by storms, we saw many lightenings and heard the thunder at a great distance. I feared the storm would reach us but after supper the skye cleared up and we were freed from all fears and anxiety.

SATURDAY, JULY 2ND. Lord Garleys came to take us with Mr. Foster to go on shore. We went to see the fine Town of St. Firenzo a most dirty, miserable, ugly infamous village, we took afterwards a long and pleasant walk in the mountains. which are very romantick. We dined on board the Lively, the Frigate is not as handsome as the Inconstant but kept in equal good order, I was rather low spirited to-day for I do not much like the idea of going to England in such a small and uncomfortable ship as the Accilies is—but the arrival of the Inconstant soon changed my sorrowful thoughts in the most agreeable ones. Captain Fremantle came immediately to us, we were at dinner and never was I more agreeably surprised. That kind best of men has acted towards us in a manner that can be repaid only by the most tender and sincere friendship. He has asked leave of the Admiral for to convey us on board the Brittannia a hundred gunned ship and he will take us in a few days to the Fleet, there we will remain till we have a safe opportunity of going to England. Our joy and Happiness is above all description—we have not now the least thing to fear and we will be as comfortable with the Britannia as we could be on shore. We were as gay as can be and had a most pleasant Ball in the evening on board the Lively. Mrs Pollard Mrs Darby and Miss Wood came. We had a famous supper and indeed the pleasures I had enjoyed to-day I had not enjoyed for a long time.

Sunday, July 3rd. Captain Fremantle is gone to Bastia but is to return tomorrow and has promised to give us a famous Ball. We again dined on board the Lively, Lord Garlies treats us with the greatest civility and kindness. He is rather more a man of fashion than Captain Fremantle but they are both equally good natured and friendly. Mr Foster is very unpleasant. He has very free ways and I dislike him exceedingly. We took a walk on the shore in the evening. We saw all the Corsican beauties in all their finery it being Sunday. We met kind Mr. Udney who gave me a hearty kiss in the midst of the street, which made me rather ashamed. He is going to Bastia. It was quite pleasant in the evening we took a long row in the boat but as we came too near shore, we stuck in some shoals and had trouble to get out of them. Lord Garleys supped with us on the Accilies and we had a little musick afterwards.

Monday, July 4th. We were greatly disappointed to-day for Captain Fremantle being detained by the Vice Roy wrote that he could not be back before to-morrow it did not prevent us though from having an excellent dinner on board the Inconstant and a pleasant dance in the evening. We should have amused ourselves much more had not good Captain Fremantle been absent. The wind blew very hard to-day and made it quite unpleasant for us to go from one ship to another however we got safe and were only washed several times by the waves that came into the boat.

Tuesday, July 5th. Captain Fremantle arrived early in the morning—he immediately sent to ask us to dine with him—he came himself to take us and we spent the day and evening with him on board the Inconstant. The Ball we were to have yesterday he gave us to-day, the deck was most elegantly drest up and looked really like a charming large Ball room all the guns being removed. We had a lively, gay dance. Mrs Polard, Miss Wood and Miss Berry and we were the only ladies the gentlemen were in vast number. Lord Garleys sailed after the Ball for the Fleet—he is an amiable man but not at all of an equal and steady temper. One moment he is serious the other quite foolish, and he proved to me at supper the greatest borer in the world for he quized me in a most tedious manner and I never could put an end to his unpleasant jokes. It is quite the revers with Captain Fremantle who wins every day more in my affection.

WEDNESDAY, JULY 6TH. Inconstant. The Ball having lasted last night till near two o'clock in the morning we rose exceedingly late Captain Craven breakfasted with us and Captain Fremantle came to ask us whether we would not take a walk on shore—but Mamma being very unwell, he took Harriot with him and we remained. He was again so kind as to want us to dine with him and he is going now to keep us on board his ship. Papa gave Captain Parish 70 pounds, it is rather dear but we cannot complain of that man for although he did not accomodate us as well as he ought to have done, he was vastly civil obliging and good natured. Whilst we were sitting very quietly at dinner Captain Fremantle received a letter from the Vice Roy which obliged him to sail immediately. Nobody but him knows where we are going, it seems to be something of great consequence for Captain Fremantle, looked very much disappointed, busy and occupied. For all this he was gay and kind towards us, indeed he behaves in a manner that deserves all our gratitude and friendship. I dare say had we not been on board his ship we could not have went with him, for he was in such a hurry that he could not wait for some of his officers that were on shore and remained behind. I cannot conceive where we are going, as long as we stay on board the Inconstant with this excellent man I do not care what part of the world we go to. It certainly is something very extraordinary however we were very gay, ate a hearty supper and slept sound, All together in the Cabin.

THURSDAY, JULY 7TH. It is a cruel thing to be Captain of a man of war. Indeed you never know from one minute to another what will become of you. The reason Captain Fremantle keeps his secret so well is I believe that the whole is a secret to him as well as to us. We could not discover the least thing to-day.

Captain Fremantle was not in a good humour and did not seemed pleased but we did not perceive that when he was with us, for he continues to treat us with uncommon kindness. The wind was not fair. We came round Cape Corse between the little island of that name and I begin to think we are going to Bastia and the Captain left us in the afternoon and went in a Barge to that place where I suppose he is going to receive the Vice Roy's orders. He will not have a pleasant trip there for he has 24 miles to go and he fears he will not get there before four o'clock in the morning. The poor man is far from being contented but his duty and service to the King must go above every thing—And indeed he applied to that alone, and is ready to sacrifice all for his King and country. He left us under the care of Mr Hutchinson his first Lieutenant, but this gentleman is such an enemy of women that we were likewise recommended to Mr French the Surgeon, Mr Boger and others, who are rather better disposed towards our sex.

Friday, July 8th. We were left all day alone Captain Fremantle did not return untill the evening. He was much fatigued and annoyed. He had been to Bastia left it early in the morning and spent all day on one of the transports. The secret is discovered now we found it out last night. The English are going to take possession of the Isle of Elba to prevent the French squatting there which is their project. We therefore sail now towards that island. Captain Fremantle is Commodore, and he is quite in a fever as the success of this interprize depends on him. Notwithstanding his uneasiness he was vastly gay with us. Mr Hutchinson has been uncommonly Gallant during the Captains absence. Indeed we have done wonders he is quite tamed.

Saturday, July 9th. We came in sight of Port Ferrajo only at noon. Commodore Nelson having joined us now has been a great relief to Capt. Fremantle and is likewise a great increase of forces. The Captain being a 74 gunned ship, another Frigate is likewise come up with us: the Flora she is just come from Smyrna and is in quarantine so that we only spoke to Captain Millerton at a respectful distance. The situation of Porto Ferrajo is delightful. It is uncommonly strong and lies on a charming hill in the most romantick country. Captain Fremantle went on shore with the Commodore and returned with the pleasant news that we should enter to-morrow Porto Ferraro and that the English would be received with joy. The 800 men who have been taken from Bastia landed without the least opposition.

July 10th, Sunday. We entered the harbour in the morning and the delightful situation of Porto Ferraro surprised us in the most agreeable manner. I saw few such pretty spots. The delightful hills that surround the town which is built like an Amphitheatre delights the eye with the most charming and various prospects. Coming from the barren Mountains of Corsica the sight of these rich and charming hills is still more pleasing. We went on shore with the Captain Mr French and Mr Boger. Satisfaction and happiness appeared in all the inhabitants countenances the English were welcome and received with the greatest demonstrations of joy. We walked through all the town. It is small and should only be called a Fortress but neat clean and pretty. The English and Tuscan troops are like friends together and indeed the pleasure that sparkled in all the faces, at being in the possession of the English gave me the most sensible joy. We dined on board the Inconstant we went in the afternoon to take a walk in the country. A good farmer took us in his house where we drank Tea. The Country is charming—and we had the most pleasant walk. The inhabitants of this place are the best creatures that ever lived. The good farmer and his wife gave us all they had. Their house is clean and they seem to lead a comfortable and happy life. We took a little walk in the town on our way back and as soon as we were returned on board the Inconstant unmoored and set sail. But there being very little water we got a shore and stuck so fast into the sand that we had trouble to get from it. At last we did but would not venture again and I was very much pleased at all this happening, as I do not wish to get to the Fleet. I cannot bear the idea of leaving this excellent man. He looked to be likewise sorry to have to part from us. Why dont he keep us with him? All this is a riddle that I should like to discover.

WEDNESDAY, JULY 13TH. Most luckily for us the wind

continued so unfair that we did not get to the Fleet to-day but alas there is no doubt but we will be there to-morrow. C. F. wrote a letter to M. In which he says the same things as yesterday. How very few men would have behaved like he did! We are all very dull even all the gentlemen of the Inconstant are sorry that we are going to leave the ships. They are very good honest creatures and were very kind to us. We paid them a visit to-day in the gunroom and went to see once more the ship indeed it is astonishing in what good order it is kept. I am sure it is not possible to attend better to Duty than C. F. does. He is active and always ready to do his business. Every body agrees to say that his ship is one of the best kept in the Mediterranean. Indeed he is very far advanced for his age and has reason to flatter himself, that he will reach to the highest for he is on a very good way but as he says an imprudent match at present would be his ruin and make him lose the fruits of eighteen years service and pain. What can be done! wait with patience.

THURSDAY, JULY 14TH. Off Toulon on board the Brittania. I felt the greatest pain as soon as I awoke this morning for the first thing that I heard was the fleet is in sight. Directly after being dressed I walked on deck found the poor C. F. who was still more afflicted if possible than I was. We both looked mighty stupid for we could not speak two words. Nothing so dismal as the breakfast we all sat down in painful silence and forced ourselves to eat. Mama and Tiny cryed much, I did not but was not less afflicted for that as soon as we had got near the Victory C. F. left us to go to Admiral Jerveys I really feared we should not see him again for he had said that he could not introduce us to Captain Foley as it would break his heart. I felt therefore no small degree of satisfaction in seeing him return but my joy was soon changed in sorrow when I perceived Captain Foley in the Barge with him. Alas I knew very well then that in a few moments we should leave the Inconstant. I made a very wry face when Captain Foley entered the Cabin however I endeavoured not to be quite so sulky, to that man who really was exceeding civil to us. C. F. said that the Commander in Chief was very well disposed on our favor, that as we wished to be conveyed to Gibraltar by the first opportunity we should have a passage in the Meleager who was expected and is going there. Till her arrival we shall stay in the Brittania. The Inconstant received orders to sail in the evening. She is sent to Algiers but is first going to Ajaccio. C. F. came with us board the Brittania and dined with us there I was not a little surprised when I first came into this ship as it is one of the largest that ever was made it has 100 guns 260 men a three decker of course. I find it like a Castle. Captain Foley gave us Sir Hyde Parker's apartment. We will have there as good accomodation as we would have in any house on shore. Nothing so fine as the sight of this Fleet always under sail and so near Toulon that you may easily see the town and the french shipping. I could not pay much attention to all these now for my head was full of quite different things. I was very dull and unhappy but the turn that all the matters took before C. F. left us made me much easier but not less afflicted. Papa has promised to wait at Gibraltar till the Inconstant goes to England and then to go in her. I am to correspond with C. F. and he gave me a ring to keep until we meet him again.

He did not say much to me but had much discourse with Mama. He recommended very much that I should not change in the least during his absence and he wishes to find on his return just the same as I am now. We parted with a broken heart. Before he sailed from us he wrote a note to me which made me feel exceedingly happy. As he made Admiral Jerveys promise him that when the Inconstant returns from her present expedition she will be ordered home. Now I have Nothing to do but pray night and day—that his cruise may be short and that he may be soon restored to our wishes. but that is not all yet for if we cannot get a fortune in the whole will be worse and worse. I trust in the allmighty who ever recompenses the virtues and indeed I may flatter myself that this man will be happy for certainly deserves to be it better than any other man in the world. The Inconstant was out of sight before it was night. The Lively arrived here only today she had sailed from St Firenzo the day before we did. We did not see Lord Garleys he was ordered back to that place immediately. Mr. Foster came on board the Brittania he did not bother me at all. Captain Foley behaves with the greatest kindness towards us. He is a man between thirty and fourty and seems very good natured and gay.

Friday, July 15th. We lead a very regular life here. Breakfast at 8 dine at half past two sup before 9 and go to bed at ten. Captain Foley keeps an excellent good table his ship is a little Town—you get all your desire in it. There are a vast number of officers who seem very good natured but I do not find them by far as amiable as I did the Gentlemen of the Inconstant. I am partial to all that belongs to that Frigate. The Commander in Chief was so kind as to send Captain Grey to us with a very civil message to Papa but a mighty gallant one to the

Ladies. We worked all day and walked on deck. The weather was beautiful and the sea as smooth as a mirror. But the evening it was horridly damp, There is always a Dew that falls in this country. which I think must be very unwholesome Papa feels a little gouty humour in his foot which puts him in very bad humour.

CHAPTER 17

OFF TOULON ON BOARD THE BRITANNIA. MONDAY, JULY 25TH. I had the pleasure of receiving to-day a letter from Ct^{n}. Fremantle dated the 18th from Ajacio which made me feel happy beyond expression but I was sorry to find that he had no hope of joining us before the month of October. When I think on so long an absence it makes me quite wretched for one person is so badly disposed that I cannot help fearing that before the happy moment of our meeting arrives something will happen that will change all our schemes and disappoint me especially in a most cruel manner. The news from Italy are so fine that Papa flatters himself that he will be able to return there and then his project is to get to his beloved Ratisbon as soon as he can. The idea of going to Germany grieves me to the utmost. I long for the arrival of the Meleager to get to Gibraltar for I think that when we will be there, we shall go to England to a certainty. However Pazienza as the Italians say. Without patience and hope one could not live in this world. Captain Grey and Sir Charles Knowles (an old bachelor who Commands the Golliath) came to dance with us this afternoon. Mr. Hamond who was Lieutenant in this ship left us he went into the Flora that sailed to Ajacio this afternoon where he is going in to l'Aigle. He was a good natured young man, but a little short thin wretched looking thing.

TUESDAY, JULY 26TH. I am quized most dreadfully by Captain Foley on account of Mr. Loring who is an excellent young man and has been so civil as to give me and lend me several things I was in need of.

But the old Gentleman[1] is very much in the wrong to laugh at his officers being gallant to me for indeed he pays some attention to me and I dare say should not be sorry if all the pains he takes to please were not useless. But for my part I think him the best creature that ever lived but look upon him as if he could be my grandfather. Captain Dakers of the Barfleur paid us a long visit in the morning, he is a great favourite of mine for he seems to be so fond of his wife and children, he always talks of his family. The French fired all the afternoon indeed poor Sir Charles got himself almost into a scrape he went so near shore that he was within gun shot and many of the shots even reached farther than the ship.

Friday, July 29th. Sir John Jervis wrote a note at four oclock in the morning to ask us to dine with him. We accepted with infinite pleasure of his kind invitation, and after having had several visits Ct. Ogle, Captain Hood, Captain Troubridge, the Commissioner from Ajacia (who brought us a letter from Captain Fremantle) we dressed to go to the Victory. The Admiral was on Deck to receive us with the greatest civility and kindness nothing stiff or formal about him and we were not at all embarassed as I feared we should be. He desired we should pay the tribute that was due to him at our entering his Cabin, this was to kiss him which the Ladies did very willingly. Lord Garlies came soon after us. The Admiral abused him for not having yet saluted us, the consequence was that we were kissed a second time. I was very glad to meet Lord Garlies here for he really is an amiable man, he has brought from Bandol fish and fruits that he got from

[1] He was not quite forty!

a French fisherman who came twice on board the Lively and was glad to get some money from the English. He gave all the news he knew which are of no great consequence. Nothing can express how kind, gallant and friendly the Admiral was to us, he is a fine old man, though past seventy, he is as fresh and brisk as if he was only thirty. He said that he would wish us to stay in the Fleet all the summer that when we were tired of Captain Foley we should go on board the Victory, however if we desired to go to Gibraltar he expected the Meleager any moment and he promised to give us letters for that place where he said we should be as comfortable as it could possibly be. He talked of Captain Fremantle but we could not make out where he has sent him to, he only said that we should wish him good luck for he was gone on a very enterprizing expedition. He made the greatest commendations of him and applause to Papa and Mama and said he would wish *him* to marry me Papa answered he had not what was necessary for the marriage state, any fortune, Sir John Jervis replied he was in a very good way to get one, and he was besides such an excellent honest man that he could wish nothing better for my happiness. The good Admiral has a very high opinion of me. He told me that I should make the best wife in England. And indeed he made me so many such fine compliments that I was quite at a loss how to answer them. All the gentlemen that had been to see us in the morning dined with us. It was a large party and we were very gay, laughed much and made a monstrous noise at table. The two Captains in the Victory, the first Mr. Calder, Captain of the Fleet, and Mr. Grey were very civil to us. We were obliged to sing a duet after dinner. We did not stay late for as

Admiral Jervis gets up at two oclock in the morning he goes to bed at half past eight. We got into the Barge to come to the Britannia at seven very much pleased with the kind reception we had met with from the Admiral and the kindly manner he treated us with. The Victory is a much finer ship than the Britannia, the same size but the apartments not by half as good and comfortable. On our return to our ship we stopped near the Courageous to hear some very pretty musick. Captain Hallow who commands that 74 (taken from the french the war before the last) has a very good band. They played the charming tunes and the flutes and Bugle horns made a most delightful effect. We had a dance in the evening on board the Britannia all the gentlemen that dined with us and Captain Hallow and Captain Sotheby who commands the Bombay Castle came. Lord Garlies was as usual remarkably merry, good humoured and amiable. He danced with me all the evening, and though he quized me and tormented me all the time I must own I found him very pleasant. At supper we had famous fun, but which finished bad and vexed me not a little. This all comes from his Lordship he told me that the Admiral had asked him whether Captain Foley was not much attached to me whether I was not engaged to him. On hearing this I screamed very loud and said it was the most ridiculous foolish nonsense that ever could be imagined, I should not have minded it if Captain Foley had not come to know what it was. I was then puzzeled to the highest degree, and indeed the old man was not a little embarassed Lord Garlies told me en confidance, many other things concerning Captain Fremantle and finished by saying to take care of him for he was a cunning, well speaking fellow etc.

This I must own I did not at all like from his Lordship if he was in Joke it was a very stupid one if serious it would give me a bad opinion of Lord Garlies. With all the nonsense we set late at supper, at last Lord Garlies went away he is going back to Bandol. I long for the arrival of the Meleager, since this—since this Joke with Captain Foley I am impatient to leave the Britannia—Mamma and myself had guessed this long ago, but now that it has been said out though laughing, it has quite made me angry. How can such ideas come into that old Gentleman's head especially since he must know all that has passed on board the Inconstant.

SATURDAY, AUGUST 6TH. I was delighted on hearing this morning that the Meleager has at last arrived, with the Excellent and a Convoy from Corsica. But I was not a little disappointed when I heard the Meleager had been ordered immediately to Barcelona and that there being almost a certainty of a Spanish War she would go no more to Gibraltar —what will become of us? I am greatly puzzled and vexed. We begin to find out where T. F.[1] has been sent to. He cruised to the Southern of Sardinia between that island and Cap Bon with the Dido and to endeavour to take all the ships that come for the french from the coast of Barbery. He may make some good prize money.

SUNDAY, AUGUST 7TH. I was miserable all day. I fear we shall have no other choice than going back to Italy, to Naples, from thence to Germany. Now all the game is lost, God knows whether, when or where we will ever meet T. F. again. This idea gives me so much pain that I am quite low spirited and unhappy.

[1] C. F. is 'Captain Fremantle', T. F. the more familiar Thomas Fremantle—one and the same person.

The whole Fleet has been exceedingly busy these two days to get all the stores out of the transports, we had fresh beef and a great many other provisions. The Barfleur is to take the convoy back. Captain Dakers who commands her came on board he asked us in joke whether we would not go with him, but indeed I fear the joke will prove true, for it seems Captain Foley thinks it best for us to go to Corsica and then to Naples as he says we have no chance of getting to Gibraltar and as for staying in to this ship till she goes home, indeed though he very kindly offers it we cannot think of being any longer so troublesome to him.

MONDAY, AUGUST 8TH. The Commander in Chief desired Captain Foley to tell us that as a Spanish war was certain we had no chance of going to Gibraltar therefore the best thing we could do was to go to Naples. We were very sorry to be obliged to take this last resolution and we prepared every thing to go on board the Barfleur, Captain Dakers came to see us and said he would get everything ready for us. I cannot express how miserable I was, going to Naples I had no doubt but we would soon go over to Germany. Our return to England in the Inconstant only a fine Dream. which will never be realized. What I suffered is not to be imagined. After dinner we went in the Ward Room to take leave of all the officers, they were uncommonly kind and civil and indeed felt unfeigned sorrow at our departure. I was not a little surprised on getting in Captain Greys cabin to find Captain Grey there with a very obliging note from Sir John in which he says 'The Amiables may remain on board the Britannia in case of Sir Hydes appearance they shall come on board the Victory till the convoy sails. All that has been said of their leaving the

Fleet is to be buried in Oblivion.' After many compliments with Captain Foley Papa at last accepted his kind offer to stay with him and now we are in the Fleet for a long time. I should like it very well if it was not the reason that makes us stay which displeases me to the highest degree. P. and M. both think that really C. Foley has some liking to me, he asked the Admiral that we should remain with him, I have friendship for that man and it would show a great degree of ungratefulness if I was not thankful for his obliging manner towards us but it does not flatter me in the least that he should pay more attention to me than any of the rest of the family. Quite the reverse I dislike it exceedingly and it makes our stay here unpleasant to me.

TUESDAY, AUGUST 9TH. Sir John desired to see me and Jenny this morning. C. Foley did not much wish to take us there, the reason I cannot guess but as were asked a second time we went with him and Papa. The Commander in Chief received us with his usual civilities and wanted us to be interpreters to some Germans soldiers he has on board who he wished to get in his Majesty's service and were to-day to take their Oath. We had a great deal of trouble to persuade these men, to swear, they do not like the sea, and say that *who swears on water remains on water.* Never were such stupid and idiots. They are all deserters and the Admiral told them that if they refused to enter the English service they would send them prisoners to Triest where they would suffer the due punishment as prisoners, some were frightened at this threat but many still were obstinate and chose to go to Triest, however when they saw the money which was given to those who engages, who had 5 guineas a piece, they all finished by staying. Sir John thanked us for the trouble we had had by a chaste embrace, the old Gentleman is very partial to kisses, he abuses all those who do not salute the ladies and always obliges all the Gentlemen that are present to kiss us. He spoke of C. Fremantle but what he said gave me great pain. He will not send the Inconstant home she is to be refitted at Ajacio. He added that C F should not be gone long. This in somewhat consoled me for it makes me hope that we may see him before we leave the Fleet. However I have not much trust in this pleasing hope and the unexpected new I heard disappointed and vexed me to the utmost.

Sir John Jervis got us all in a terrible scrape in the evening. He went exceedingly near shore it fell calm all at once and we were all within gun shot without a possibility of getting away. The french fired from all their Batteries, the Golliath being nearest they only aimed at her luckily for us, for we were equally near and some of the shots came so near to us that C. Foley was almost tempted to send us ladies in the Cockpit. We were though not in the least alarmed and looked all the time at this famous fire work that was quite a new sight for us and would have amused me if I had not feared it might have done some damage to the Golliath, as more than 120 shots were fired at her and they all went over her, we all fear she has been touched. We got at last out of the scrape with the help of boats. Lord Garlies came to see us in the evening. He was uncommonly pleasant this time, in the true humour. Not a bit too merry and he has quite left off quizying me, on the contrary he talked very serious and showing much interest for me, He promised to dine with us tomorrow which made us very happy.

WEDNESDAY, 10TH AUGUST. Lord Garlies had to look out all day we did not see him which thing disappointed us not a little. We danced in the evening, I did not share much of the amusement for I am not very well, I dare say I shall finish by being ill for two or three days, and besides my health is not in the best state, my mind is still worse.

FRIDAY, AUGUST 12TH. This being the Prince of Wales birthday it was celebrated in the evening by all the Fleet, Every ship fired 18 guns and a vast number of musquets We went on the Poop to see the firing and were not at all frightened at the noise but the smoak was mighty unpleasant and prevented us from seeing it well. Capt Frederick and Captain Suttons paid us a visit in the afternoon.

SATURDAY, AUGUST 13TH. We wrote to C. F. to-day but I fear there will be no opportunity of sending our letters how impatient I am to hear from him, I am always tormented by the fear of never meeting him again, and affairs tangle in such a manner that I apprehend all will not finish to my satisfaction.

SUNDAY, AUGUST 14TH. An unpleasant windy day, and I was tormented and vexed in a most cruel manner by C. Foley, as he cannot know from us how affairs stand with C. F. and me, he has written a letter to him in which he begs to be let into the secret, he showed me some parts of it but not the reason which makes him ask. This, I fear I may easily guess, it is too plain to be concealed. If C. F. had no intention to marry me I dare say the old Gentleman has some idea of it himself. It makes me quite miserable I hide this from Papa for he has a great partiality for C. Foley, he certainly would give him the preference. For my part as I do not think riches alone can make me happy my choice is in favour of the absent friend, I have friendship for C. Foley, acknowledge him to be the best man living, I dare say a wife would be perfectly happy with him, but I never could resolve to marry such a man, besides he is really too old for me, and I cannot help having a great liking for C. Frem. Alas, how will this matter end. If he does not make prize money, it will never do, I should not mind it but my parents would never consent to it without he gets a pretty good fortune. Captain Foley is continually quizying me upon this, I find his jokes unsupportable and I avoid speaking to him as much as I can.

MONDAY, AUGUST 15TH. Sir John Jervis came in the morning to pay us a visit which thing flattered us much, he told us a vast number of news he had just received by the Comet (which joined the Fleet in the morning and was ordered back to Leghorn immediately). This town must be now in possession of the English. The Austrians being by far superior in numbers and forces to the french in Italy gain great advantage and will probably soon be once more masters of Lombardy. In Germany all is in great confusion. The Austrians attacked in all parts the ennemy at once, but were every where completely beaten. The french are at Frankforth and advance at a great rate, The King of Naples' armistice is at an end and he walks at the head of a numerous army to defend his territory. As the Pope refuses to give any thing whatever to the English, and according to this shameful peace with the french will not allow any of our ships, to enter his ports, Commodore Nelson is going to Civita Vecchia to frighten him a little. I do not know what to think of all these news. I always fear we will finish by returning to Italy. How I should wish the Southern cruise to be at an end. We cannot hear from him nor have an opportunity of writing to him. It is the most cruel situation I ever was in.

TUESDAY, AUGUST 16TH. We spent the evening chattering in the Stern Gallery and admiring the moon and the beauty of the night. We had a long discourse and *all we fear* concerning C. Foley's schemes was so plainly explained that we can have no more doubts of it. Alas nothing can paint the state of my heart! I cannot express what I feel. Could I flatter myself to see soon C. F. I should be less miserable for his presence would put me in mind of all they said before he left us, which *things* unfortunately are forgotten in his absence. I wish I had never *never* come on board the Britannia. It would have spared me many painful and unpleasant things. What is to be done? What will happen? God knows, C. Fremantle's answer will decide the whole thing. If he says, as it in reality is, that his circumstances do not permit him to think of a match at present, then this *unwelcome* gentleman will doubtless offer *himself*. I am resolved not to have him. But Papa would certainly be delighted at the prospect and will I make it no doubt, do all he can in favour of this grey headed gallant. I cannot conceive what this man finds of so very pleasant in me. I never was so mighty stupid and sulky as since I am in this ship. Nothing amuses me I speak the less I can, and interest myself about nothing that happens. Any thoughts I have are always driving towards the South of Sardinia.

SATURDAY, AUGUST 20TH. We had Captain Obryan, Campbell, Rowley, Wells visit this afternoon, all very pleasant men. Ct Obryan is very musical and really understood it. Ct. Campbell is a very handsome man about 35. Ct. Rowley is likewise a very good looking figure, and Ct. Wells, Fremantle's brother in law! is said to be vastly amiable but the greatest quizz in the world. This I can say from experience for although I saw him for the first time he began quizzing me on account of Fremantle. Sir John told him all the story to my great dissatisfaction as Fremantle who had given us a letter for him on his supposing we should go to wait for him at Gibraltar had recommended to us not to tell his brother in law a word of all this affair, and desired me particularly not to let him quize me. I should have desired to satisfy his wish but patience. Mr. Wells looks to be very ill, I dare say he has been handsome enough but now he is as thin as a skeleton and looks miserable.

SUNDAY, MONDAY. We were disappointed of a Ball these last two days the newly arrived Captains had promised to come to dine and dance with us but the weather being rainy and windy it was not possible to visit one another. We kept within, M, as usual when it blows, seasick, and for my part as usual low spirited and ill humoured. I hate to be in such a state of uncertainty. The more I think of it all the more I wish I find it more difficult to succeed, poor Betsy! What will become of her at last?

TUESDAY, AUGUST 23RD. Captain Campbell and Captain Wells dined danced and supped with us. They are both indeed uncommon pleasant men, and C. Wells an amusing creature as I ever saw, He always comes out with a witty joke and says it seriously, this is just the way for when people laugh themselves at their wit it is then found stupid by other people. I was happy to hear our letters were come to Fr. When will they be answered?

WEDNESDAY, AUGUST 24TH. It gave us infinite satisfaction to see C. Dacres our very great favourite. He has brought the Ladies many excellent things from Corsica, plenty of fruit the only good thing that is to be found in that island. Indeed we are greatly obliged to him for the care he has taken of us. Captain Wells was here a moment in the afternoon. I was surprised not to find him in his usual good humour, he scarcely spoke two words. The poor man is very unwell everybody says he is astonishingly altered. Captain Rowley spent the evening and supped with us he was merry and pleasant.

FRIDAY, AUGUST 26TH. I think there is nothing so cruel as the situation I am in at present. Totally ignorant of what will happen fearing my wishes will never be satisfied having no hopes of seeing Fremantle again for these two months, and being obliged to stay until he returns with a *man* who by all he says and does wants to discover his attachment to me—Attachment I cannot return. I am miserable to the extreme, and I feel quite uncomfortable in the idea that we live here like beggars at this mans charge. Patience, it cannot be changed, I show as good a face as I can, at this so unpleasant game, and try to console myself in the hope of being one day or other agreeably surprised by the arrival of the Inconstant. I take pleasure in building castles in the air, but it is a very trifling consolation. The Meleager is at last gone to Gibraltar she left the fleet yesterday, Captain Ogle is now in her Captain Cokburn has changed in the Minerva which ship is gone to Barcellona a few days ago. What a pity we could not go to Gibraltar. The Spanish War is a great disappointment for us. But it will bring in prize money, a necessary thing for the accomplishment of my happiness.

TUESDAY, AUGUST 30TH. I heard some news to-day which made me quite mad with joy. Sir John told

Captain Foley that he believed for certain that we should at last go to England in the Inconstant and that he expected Fremantle back in the course of a month. Nothing can express the various sentiments that agitate my soul on hearing this, I wanted this beam of hope to set new life in me for I began to feel quite low spirited and grew daily more dull and sulky. Now I have recovered again my usual good humour, but this month will appear an age to me. When I think of the joy I shall feel when the happy moment arrives, it turns my head, I shall be fully compensated for all I suffered in his absence. The Captain joined in the evening with the Commodore's broad pennant.

THURSDAY, SEPTEMBER 1ST. Since I am on board I have never been so gay and good humoured as I feel now. From the moment I heard the admiral expects the Inconstant soon returned from her cruize my lonely thoughts changed in the most pleasing ones. All hopes of seeing Fr. before sailing for England had forsaken me, now I flatter myself soon to see the Inconstant join the ship. I am an odd girl! For all I only think of Fr. I can hardly live without him I scarcely believe I am in love. I should like to know whether he thinks so often of his Betsy as I do of him? and whether he wishes as much as I do to meet again? Surely if all he said before he went is true (as I cannot doubt of) it must be so.

TUESDAY, SEPTEMBER 6TH. I have been too sanguine. A few days were spent in joy and content but now my thoughts are lost again in sadness. I cannot bear from morning to night a man speak to me as if he hoped his love might meet return, he is always deriding the absent person he says he will not let us go on board the Inconstant unless it is a certain thing I marry Fremantle. Can I flatter myself this will ever happen, when both my parents speak against it! Mama says that I am not in the least engaged to him, and that the matter is far from being settled. Papa forgets his promise and even says he will not go home in the Inconstant for as he would never give his consent to the marriage, it would be imprudent to be again some time together. All this can but make me very miserable.

THURSDAY, SEPTEMBER 8TH. There was another Court Martial but as it blew fresh we had no visits. How anxious I am for the arrival of Capt. F. but I am sadly afraid there will be a terrible fuss. Papa is worse disposed than ever he swears he'll never consent to this match and even wont go home in the Inconstant, poor me, I am in great distress for I cannot help confessing I love that man with all my heart.

FRIDAY AND SATURDAY. We had these two days the most delectable weather. A fine Mediterranean skye the sea like a mill pond and only a little pleasant breeze enough for it not to be too hot. Captain Sutton and Sir Charles Knowles came both days to see us. The old Baronet is a real bore. Captain Sutton is a pleasant good sort of man. We danced Saturday evening with them but I was forced to do it, I heard something which quite broke my heart. Papa complained very much of me to Mamma. He says I am quite changed that I grow a downright Coquette, that he sees I shall be a second Montalban and with Fr. I was a great fool if ever I thought he would let me marry him. that I might do it if I chose but that he would never see me again if I did etc. and a thousand other such things. Good God, how mistaken he is if he thinks that I am flattered by the partiality shown to me and that I endeavour to please, far from it, Captain Foley's attachment is a torment to me, and it makes me wish still more for Fremantle's return. But then if Papa persists in his present resolution how miserable shall I be. All that I suffered till now is nothing to what is to come. Hope still keeps up my spirits a little. Papa changes so often perhaps he will yield to our prayers.

SUNDAY, SEPTEMBER 11TH. We paid a visit to Sir John in the morning he wanted us to see our Austrian recruits in all their finery, all the Marines were drest up most beautifully and looked superb. I went all over the Victory it was all very fine in the best order possible. Sir John told us Fremantle was gone up to Smyrna and would take the Convoy down that he expected him in eight or ten days. and that the convoy would sail for England at the latter end of this month. He did not mention the ships that are to go with it but I am sadly mistaken if the Inconstant is not one of them. He had proposed me to go to Triest in a Frigate he is going to send there. She had accepted the proposal but I succeeded in dissuading her from it and we have decided not to say anything to Papa about it for he certainly would take this opportunity of going to Germany. What could we do there? It is high time he should return to England and settle himself for ever there.

MONDAY. The Transports under convoy of the Southampton joined in the morning there is plenty of Beef and fresh provisions come. The goods were got from Gaetta though it is one of the articles of the Popes peace not to supply the english Fleet. *Money* procured us 400 bullocks from his dominions. Admiral Waldegrave came to muster the ships in the morning and dined with us, he is a gentleman-like pleasant man but I think rather too serious. The Britannia was in uncommon high order I went all over the ship She looked very fine. Capt. Dacres and Capt. Woodhouse likewise spent the day with us. The latter is lately come from Gibraltar. He is a remarkable talkative young man, very pleasant in conversation. A Brig and a Cutter joined likewise to-day, the one straight from England the other was sent from Gibraltar. Sir Hyde Parker is come from England with a convoy in the Queen it is likely he is gone to the West Indies with the Fame and the Valiant. The Brig sailed immediately to order the convoy to come here, Admiral Man's squadron is to return of which thing I am very glad.

TUESDAY. Two new lieutenants are come into this ship: one is Mr. Whyte out of the Cumberland a sprightly chattering young man, rather too forward, I think. The other is a Mr. Low, a brute as everybody agrees to say, always drunk. The Southampton and some Transports parted company, they are going for some wood to the southward of Corsica, where it is said all the insurgents are. The frigate is afterwards going to Trieste. Everything is very uncertain there is no knowing what will happen. I am anxious to know what will become of us. I dare say we will get to England some how or other, but I am exceedingly uneasy about what interests me the most. I am counting the days hours, and minutes and find that time passes very slowly. I am so impatient to see Fremantle after Papa's fine promises —to find him quite altered—however he may find my parents so he certainly will find me not in the least changed towards him. I even think I am more partial to him than I was before.

WEDNESDAY, 15TH. Honorable mention of Capt.

Foley to-day indeed I begin to think I like him better than ever I did since he begins to give up his schemes. He told Jenny that as he saw I was much attached to Frem. he had considered about it and really thinks himself too old therefore wishes me to marry his friend. I was very ill all day, a bad pain in my side and could hardly fetch my breath it is nothing but want of exercise. I danced much in the evening with hopes it will do me good. The Egmont went with the transports to Ajaccio.

THURSDAY, 16TH. I succeeded perfectly well last night and danced my pain in the side entirely off.

The last entry in the slim copy-book which is Volume 7 was on Tuesday the 27th. On the inside of the back cover, in an elderly hand, Betsey has written:

'The next book of my journal, from this time to Jan 1797 was lost on board the Inconstant. We went with the fleet to S. Firenzo, the Inconstant returned from Smyrna and took us to Porto Ferrajo, in Elba, where my father took a house and remained until the end of December, when we again embarked in the Inconstant for Naples.' Luckily *Eugenia's* journal covers Nov. 1796 to Jan. 1797, and her account of Betsey's wedding and departure are also given. She begins on Nov. 22nd, 1796.

CHAPTER 18

EUGENIA WYNNE'S DIARY. ELBA 1796

PLEASANT PROSPECT, PORTO FERRAJO, ELBA. MONDAY, NOVEMBER 22ND. The Hermit's life which I expected to live here is really such: as soon as a threatning cloud appears not a soul dares to come to see us. Thus did it happen to-day, tiresome enough, Sure the world is *depraved* and *bad* the race of men is a *race of vipers*, but however a little company now and then is not so *bad*. I wish that Fremantle would soon return, he was *our* evenings comfort and I had rather quiz him and my sister than play at Casino with Papa.

WEDNESDAY, NOVEMBER 24TH. The most provoking and tiresome weather all day. It is however worth notice to observe that at this time when Germany is covered with snow we have violent thunder storms here and are almost drowned with rain. Papa now forms new projects, If Leghorn is retaken as the politicians pretend it will be, a body of Austrians having marched against it, he immediately sets off for Florence, gets a carriage built there and sends Jaegle in the mail coach and finds his way to Vienna where he passes the summer. Castles in the air part of which I fear will be realised as Papa's aversion for England is excessive, *unbecoming* an English man and he sighs for Germany continually. This for no other reason but because he has left it! I shall not be astonished when I see him sigh for Elba. As to society this place is certainly not agreeable, nor for living neither, everything is excessively dear and even for money you cannot get a thousand things which would be of service: but with how much pleasure would I make shift if the prospective of going to England was within the bounds of the probabilities. But alas! I fear that I shall never behold again that beloved country, and if ever a bridal knot is bound for me it will be on the borders of the Danube and tied by *German* hands.

I read several elegies to-day, two of Shore the one on the death of his wife, the other on the loss of his child. His tale of woe is expressed in the most moving and natural fashion, and though you greatly admire the poet yet you must yield to the soft and sympathising composition of the widowed Husband and childless father. It is not so when you read Lord Littleton's complaint on his Lady's death, the poetry is beautiful, but less natural, less moving. He boasts with his grief, and indulges himself in some disgressions which show his extended knowledge, but are not natural, I think, to a mind wholly occupied with despair.

TUESDAY NOVEMBER 29TH. St Gratien came whilst we were at dinner and told the subject of a court Martial which was held yesterday upon a soldier of the 50th Reg. for killing his wife, the case happened as follows, He bid her get the dinner ready early and upon his return home at the appointed hour found nothing ready, the man young and passionate began abusing his wife and in his rage kicked her as she was stooping near the chimney. The unfortunate woman was far gone with the child, the violence of the blow caused her a great loss of blood of which she died an hour later. The soldier's despair of seeing himself at once the murderer of his wife and child, was boundless, he attempted to kill himself, whilst in prison but when he was brought to the trial he was absolved as the murder was not intentional. His own remorses will punish him more severly than the judge can and if ever that man marries again I would answer for him that he would not beat his wife. Though generally speaking people of his kind do not at all scruple to have a scramble sometimes between man and wife and are only the fonder of each other at last.

Wednesday November 30th. St Gratien came early in the morning and we took with him a very long walk to an encampment of 105 Swiss who are landed from the transports upon which they were obliged to remain till now and are encamped at the top of a neighbouring mountain where they are going to erect batteries. The walk is very fatiguing the road being steep. But the fatigue is nothing to the pleasure you feel in gazing over the beautiful prospects, to which each step you make adds new and more extended beauties from the top of the mountain you domineer over the whole country, the sea is opened to you from all sides and the varied and numberless beauties which you behold united in one point engross the soul with the most delicious feelings. During the way you meet with the most romantick spots and on all sides you see subjects for smiling landscapes, or magestic and beautiful in the highest degree.

The Swiss captain named Mohr a pretty young man received us with great civility and we returned greatly pleased with our walk but sorry to find that we had missed Lord Proby and Captain Giffard who had been here during our absence. Captain Mohr met with a lucky escape at Ajaccio he was sent with a few men to the pursuit of a deserter and saw him through the bushes at the moment when he was firing a pistol at him which failed he received a musket shot in his arm. The man that he took for the deserter proved to be a serjeant who had also been sent to pursue him and had taken the Captain for the deserter. He felt his mistake greatly but the Captain was very happy that at the expense of his wound he had missed the serjeant. The ball had never since been extracted and he suffers a good deal of his arm. Fremantle arrived in the evening. *Great was the joy at his arrival!* He brought us several presents and some letters from the Bressacs, Regis, and Mr. Gordon who unanimously try to persuade us to go to Naples. The king of Naples advised by the English has made his peace with France. What will become of us now I dont know? the fleet must or take Leghorn or leave the Mediterranean. I know what I wish, what other people wish, but what will happen I cannot guess.

The Bombelles have fled from Ratisbon to Brunn in Moravia. Their alarm must have been great. *Some* rejoice at their dissapointments and distress. I am far from it.

FRIDAY DECEMBER 1ST. Captain Fremantle dined here with Mr. French and Mr. Hornsey. The latter told us very innocently without thinking that he was betraying a secret that this Island would soon be evacuated. If so, what shall we do? Papa is confined to his bed with the gout, no news from François and no money but that which we owe to St. Gratien. However these thoughts will not trouble my sleep, God has till now protected us and the decrees of his divine providence may lead us further.

SATURDAY DECEMBER 2ND. We received this morning the unexpected good news that François has happily arrived at Longone in a Tartane which had been obliged to run in that harbour her main yard having gone to pieces in the boisterous weather of the night past. We sent him word by Jaegle to hire a Felluca and come in as fast as he could.

In the evening Jaegle returned and brought us a parcel of letters which gave me infinite pleasure, especially one from my friend Christine which is at Florence where she amuses herself very much. I wish we had never left Florence, our stay to the fleet, our stay here gives abundant subject to all the slanderous tongues to exert their skill and Betsy falls a victim to them, for my part it was so earnestly affirmed to Mlles de la Plesnoye that I was married to a sea Captain that they believed it. Comical enough that strangers should look out for a husband for me and spare me the trouble. My wish to see Christine and to quell by our presence all the stories which have been invented on our part is so great an inducement for me that I cannot help dwelling with pleasure on the thought that we may perhaps return to Florence if the English take Leghorn as it is very probable. There was a friendly letter from Mr. Bankes in which he acquaints us with Mary Blair's declining state of health, the poor girl is fallen in a consumption, abandoned by all the doctors, and irrecoverably ill. Her and her mother's situation really distresses me. Because not with standing her thoughtless temper, she has a very good and generous heart which amply compensates her faults. I am sadly afraid that I shall not see her again.

SUNDAY DECEMBER 3RD. We confessed and communed today. Fremantle Mr. Hardmann and Doctor Harness dined with us, with the help of Scot and Jack we were able to give them a tolerably well served dinner. The two latter returned to town in the afternoon, but Fremantle was constant to us, and our small party received an addition by the arrival of Mr. Huson, Mr Toliff and young Barry. Papa's gout is come in his thigh. I wish he would get well. François got here safe with the things. His poor wife has been very unhappy, Camille and Louis got the small pox at once, and her new born child a boy caught the infection at the moment when everybody had left Ratisbon, she found herself alone without a friend, three children with the small pox and herself with three holes in her breast for having attempted to suckle her child. The poor creature was greatly to be pitied. M. de Louvois is gone to Anspach with the Dutchess Villeroy. The Bombelles live at Brunn in Moravia in the same house with their mortal enemies the Boigelins and Kergorlay, what an infernal household this must make. Mde. Dumontel is at Vienna with Madame Bossiers and all the young ladies, Marianne writes word that she amuses herself very much there. Kehl and the Bridge of the Hunningue are fallen to the power of the Austrians. Old Count Brunner is dead The *Bonhomme* is gone to Spain. How many changements in so little time.

MONDAY DECEMBER 4TH. Fremantle came in the evening with Mr. French. I believe that he has some project or other in his head because he was very stupid.

TUESDAY DECEMBER 5TH. Bad weather, Mr. Hutchinson Mr. Boger Mr. Harford and Mr. French however came to dine with us, Papa was able to get up. Fremantle came to supper, he is certainly pregnant with some scheme, because he was still stupid. One thing which I am sorry to discover in him is that he seems to be perfectly cool on a *certain point* and I believe that *indifference* has taken the place of what he felt *at first*. The greatest part of the emigrés have been sent away today and the Curé of Toulons with them.

WEDNESDAY DECEMBER 6TH. I took a walk this morning the weather being beautiful. Fremantle was here this evening and brought us a new guest, Captain Hotham of the Dido (a nephew to admiral Hotham) He is a handsome and very young man. It seems that we are not to remain long here by all that is said and done. Our future fate is covered with a veil and which I have no curiosity, to draw. I wait patiently but not anxiously for the issue of all this and am ready to submit to any unexpected event that may take place. I read in the English Newspapers an attempt that has been made against the life of Louis XVIII as this unfortunate Prince was retiring from the armée of Condé (where the emperor would not suffer him to remain any longer) in order to take shelter in Saxony he passed through Dillingen where he arrived late in the evening, and he was taking the air at the window of the Inn when a carabine shot which came from the opposite side of the street struck him on the forehead. The Marquis d'Avaray, the Duke de Fleuri and the Duke de Guiche were with him, they showed the greatest alarm and distress in seeing their master in such a situation. He showed no fear at all and bore the accident with uncommon fortitude and patience. Luckily the wound was not mortal. Notwithstanding all the pursuits of the Magistrates against the assasin they could not find him out, but that villain is supposed to have been sent from the Republican army.

SUNDAY DECEMBER 10TH. Fremantle, Doctor French and Surgeons mate Alice, dined with us. The wind was so very violent that they could not return on board, Mr. French alone tried it, but Fremantle and the other remained as they did not like the idea of having to pull perhaps for four hours in the cold night before they could get on board. After having so many times been sheltered in the Inconstant we had the pleasure of sheltering them once.

MONDAY DECEMBER 11TH. After having eat a hearty breakfast Fremantle told us that he would not be here in the evening as he gave a dinner on board after which he would not perhaps be *visible*. All the gentlemen here especially those belonging to the army, drink excessively hard. The weather was beautiful we took a long walk on the road of Longone and met Mr. Hardmann and his favourite lady, at his arm, Mrs. Sanderson wife to a Captain in the Army, she has a lovely countenance and I must own it, though before having ever seen us she declared that we were all excepting the youngest, like little *crows* and *Jew girls*. She examined us with great attention, whether she found her ideas of us just, I don't know, but what I know is that as mine was the expectation of seeing a very pretty woman I found it by all means justified.

TUESDAY DECEMBER 12TH. The weather continues to be fair and we availed ourselves of it in taking a very good walk. Whilst we were at dinner we had three very welcome visitors, Mr. Hudchinson, Mr. French and Mr. Martin the surgeon of the Speedy, a young and excessively tall man, who has been particularly civil to Jaegle when he sailed in her. Fremantle was detained from coming here in the evening by a dinner which he gave on board but Mr. French and Hornsey came in his place, and cheered the gloom of our solitary evening, they will soon begin again now as the Inconstant sails tomorrow, and *there is no happiness without her.* I dont know where she is going to, Fremantle makes a secret of it, I wish his cruize may be successful and hope that he will fall in with a Spanish frigate and take her, of course attack and vanquish is the same thing for him. Laurels ever green grow under his steps and he has nothing to do but stoop and gather them round his temples. How Poetical!

WEDNESDAY DECEMBER 13TH. Fremantle paid us a farewell visit this morning; we accompanied him back to his barge and then took a walk with Mamma ruminating all the time on what may be the object of his cruize. I suppose he is going to look into Leghorn and Toulon, that he may afterwards send true intelligence to the Fleet. For the purpose he has taken with him the Fox cutter and the Speedy brig has also attended him. He sailed very late in the evening part of which we passed in Mr. Clarkes company. He is a very good man but rather tiresome. Mr. Harness called here in the morning.

THURSDAY DECEMBER 21ST. Captain Harness called here with Captain Woodhouse who is returned from his Petterell from St. Firenzo where he had been cruizing. There he ran ashore during the bad weather and in order to get her loose, he was obliged to throw his wine and water overboard, meanwhile the Corsicans fired at him with musquetry and one man was wounded. The Petterell however though slightly endamaged got herself safe out of the scrape. We took a very long walk to a very high mountain to the summit of which we were led by a very fatiguing and dirty but amusing walk. There we found the ruins of an old Convent of which a Chapell alone remained and escaped the destruction of time. There is also a resounding in a well in which all your words are answered by the most perfect echo. The sight you have over all the country is above all praise and as the mountain is higher than that one upon which the Swiss are encamped, the prospect you enjoy from St. Luna is of course more extended and more beautiful. On our way back we met with an object which greatly hurt my feelings both as a girl and as an English girl. A poor dog which had been shot in the leg that very instant by some English soldiers who were hunting. It is so barbarous to trie ones dexterity on a harmless creature, so shameful for an English officer. No punishment would be sufficient for such a villain. We stopped at a farmers house where a sweet young girl with a most healthy, delicate complexion, pleasing countenance and good natured manners, sold us some eggs. When we returned home Captain Woodhouse returned on board and Doctor Harness remained with us for dinner. He told us that General de Burgh is to give a Ball for the new year day. These words make my heart beat as if it would jump out of my breast. Beat for anxiety, wish, fear. I wish to go, I fear not to be asked, and if I am asked to stay at home, then I hope, then I fear again, and can think of nothing else. God forgive me if it be a sin.

FRIDAY DECEMBER 22ND. No visitors. The Ball, the Ball always trots in my head. I cannot help it but I am always thinking of it.

As we were going down to the Chapell in order to prepare ourselves for the confession of tomorrow we met all the Swiss officers of the camp and those from the town among which were the Colonel Durler and Mr. Capol whom we have known in Switzerland. I would never have known him again had I not guessed that it was him alone who could come and tell me *Je n'ose me flatter que vous me reconnaitre*. He is so much changed to his disadvantage in his personal accomplishments, and to advantage in his manner. He has brought upon himself illnesses which have made him grow ugly, old, dejected, gave him a difficulty in speaking, but as for his manners he has left off that too lively familiarity and foppish way which was not to his advantage and he is very civil polite and gentleman like. Captain Mohr was there, we asked him to breakfast Sunday. Betsy and me we held a council of war about the gown cap sash shoes we want to wear, if we are asked to the Ball. Womanish, childish will a rigid censor say, but very natural I think. The IF alone torments me. Because I know that our solitary way of living here makes us appear like savages in the eyes of every body, and I am sadly afraid that that idea, may prevent General de Burgh from asking us, which I own would be a severe disappointment for the two Damsels.

SATURDAY DECEMBER 23RD. I am confessed and communed. The vicar of Toulon is chosen for our Guide in the path to Heaven. I own I dont like him so well as the Curé.

SUNDAY DECEMBER 24TH. Captain Mohr and Lieutenant d'Ebener heard Mass with us here and then eat a hearty breakfast at the end of which Fremantle and Mr. French arrived. They were seen with pleasure. Soon after a herald on horseback (Captain Wyndham) came to summon us to my infinite satisfaction to a Ball which General de Burgh gives tomorrow. How great was my pleasure I cannot express. The preparatives for the Ball were all done in an instant and nothing but anxiety for the weather was left to me and it was amply justified by the abundant rain that fell this evening. French, Joliff and Barry dined with us.

MONDAY DECEMBER 25TH. When I woke, my eyes instead of being pleasantly struck by the welcome rays of a brilliant sun, were obliged to employ all their power in order to see through the gloom of the clouds that surrounded and threatened with a deluge of rain. I went to church with a sad heart for I was sadly afraid to miss the Ball. On our return from Church the Vicar made me as mad as possible in pretending that we should give up the ball, and make a sacrifice of it, take it as a mortification etc. and God knows what stuff. I made no answer, but thought, my friend, if instead of that black robe you had a petticoat on, if instead of the weight of fifty years you had only seventeen, you would not speak so. Fremantle came to see us in the morning, comforted us and promised us the barge. Whilst we were at dinner he sent Mr. Joliff up to tell us that the Minerva was come in with Commodore Nelson who was going to take the command of this place. We had a very civil and amiable letter from Sir John Jervis, none of Foley, it was dated 10th from Gibraltar. It is supposed that the Fleet is going to England, again what will become of us? A letter from Mr. Bankes is most distressing on account of poor Mary Blair, there is no hopes for her, unfortunate girl, unfortunate mother, unfortunate father! Their fate breaks my heart. I never saw parents more unhappy in their Children. Pepoli, the extravagant young Pepoli is dead of the rougeole. The Empress of Russia has finished her brilliant but guilty career I am glad for Christine's father.

On his passage from Gibraltar to this place Com. Nelson fell in with a Spanish frigate which he took, another attempted to retake her, she was terribly beaten both by the Commodore's valour and the violence of the weather when finding himself involved by the whole of a Spanish squadron,

Nelson was obliged to give up the prize he had taken and the one which he was going to take and had nothing left to him but the Captain of the frigate, a poor prise at last the barge arrived in the afternoon, and we went over to the town. (It rained) We dressed at the Cantinis, when our toilette was over, Fremantle Commodore Nelson and Captain Cockburn took us to the Ball room. It was at the theatre and we had to trot about in the dirt before we would arrive there. It was very prettily decorated General de Burgh received us with great civility, we danced a great deal and amused ourselves very much. Many pretty French girls were there and thinking that we did not understand the language in talking to one another they gave us several praises which I am conscious we do not deserve, and yet to have been flattered by. The Ball consisted of 300 persons it lasted till three oclock in the morning, after which we trotted back to the Cantinis and at last returned home very tired.

TUESDAY DECEMBER 26TH. Unexpected changement in our fate. Commodore Nelson and Fremantle called here in the morning. The latter is to sail for Naples after tomorrow, my idea of it is that he is to fetch the Viceroy and take him home. The former without telling us why advised us as a friend to avail ourselves of the good opportunity and go to Naples. It is then decided we will go though Papa is still very poorly. I own that if the Bressacs were not at Naples the prospect of going to Naples would be pleasant to me. But I fear that they will get us again among the french and that Papa will put himself in the hands of the Ct. de Bressac and then adieu to all that is English, as to all those that we have known in the Navy who had laid upon us so many obligations and to whom we owe sentiments of everlasting regard and friendship, I fear that no sooner we'll have touched the Neapolitan shore, we may bid them an eternal farewell, and a farewell which will certainly lay very heavy on my heart as with it are buried all the hopes which I nourished with regard to Fremantle. I thought that I should see in him the Creator of my sisters happiness. But I hear that the contrary may soon be said of him though he is the innocent cause of it, he has always shown in his behaviour to us the most disinterested kindness, friendship good will and the most scrupulous delicacy. I believe that this Island will soon be evacuated, that the good ships will be sent to the West Indies and the old ones home, of course the Inconstant must go for she has been condemned these two years passed then I conjecture farther that Fremantle will take a good ship, go to the West Indies and probably we shall hear no more of him.

WEDNESDAY DECEMBER 27TH. Great preparations for our sea voyage which will be but too short. In the midst of them we were surprised beyond measure by the arrival of Mrs. Sanderson, with Mr. Hardmann and a Mr. Hunter. The visit was short and rather formal on both sides. Mr. Hornsey who came up with the sailors who had the trouble to carry our things on board, dined with us it was the least that we could do for him, to give him a bad dinner for all the pains he took to keep his men sober, a thing in which he did not totally succeed, you may as soon keep a fish from drinking as a sailor. Commodore Nelson, Fremantle and Capt. Cockburn were here in the evening, always kind and good humoured.

INCONSTANT THURSDAY DECEMBER 28TH. We had a deluge of rain all the morning however we all got safe on board by dinner time. Not without getting excessively wet and having our foremast carried away by a puff of wind. Papa was saved from these accidents by the cares of good Lindsey who was better than a nurse to him. The wind being much against us we were not able to stir from the harbour. I felt a mixture of joy and pain in finding myself once more again on board the Inconstant. I not only enjoy the present moment but remembrances sweet like those of Nicolas and Blanche come to greet my mind and then my pleasure is troubled by the idea that I shall never see this ship again. Oh God I declare I will not look farther than my nose or else I should make myself very dull.

SATURDAY DECEMBER 30TH. The most beautiful day but a perfect calm, it was so warm, so mild in the evening without having any fire in the cabin, we were obliged to fan ourselves all the while and this the 30th December. We did not get on a great deal but perceived plainly the fair Italic shore a sight which is not at all tantalizing for me. Fremantle was uncommonly amiable and good humoured in the evening. I cannot bear the idea that we shall perhaps never see him again, that thought seems to strike and hurt him too. Captain Foley again dined with us, he is a handsome young man.

SUNDAY JANUARY 1ST. NEW YEARS DAY 1797. Good God how swiftly time passes and if now that I am only seventeen I complain of its rapidity, what shall I do when I am thirty? To how many moral reflections must this thought naturally lead one. It is a pity that a thought is not a deed, and that in such a giddy head as mine, the impression of one thought is soon effaced by the more lively impression of another. The weather was fine but perfectly calm, I believe that B's ascendant over Fremantle continues to be the same, but he is always undecided, he would and would not, she would, and would heartily, how will it end?

MONDAY JANUARY 2ND. No wind, I went all round the ship to take my last farewell of this frigate when the people were at quarters, I saw the light room a place very deep under water where the candles which are to light the magazine are kept. It is very narrow lined with tin and the candles are kept within a sort of tin grate, with so many precautions you should think it impossible that ever a ship could be blown up, and yet it frequently happens, the descent to the magazine being too difficult for us Damsels we could not see it. The new purser of this ship a Mr. Buckingham dined with us, he is a very ugly humped back little deformed man and yet, he is married.

TUESDAY JANUARY 3RD. No wind, or if there is a little it is foul. Fremantle is a riddle to me. I cannot doubt but he is in love, all shows it, the most trifling incident a new proof of it, and yet he does not talk of marriage and if he does he contradicts himself again the next moment. Mr. Baring the Russian officer and Captain Foley dined with us. We talked at dinner of the custom which the *Cavaglieri serventi* have at Florence to pay five sequins a month to their ladies, at Venice the contrary is practised and though less munificent it is not less ridiculous the ladies give half a ducat to their *Cavaglieris*..

WEDNESDAY 4TH JANUARY. I had again a great deal of talk with Fremantle, he gives his word that his intentions, his sentiments are the same as they were when he went to Smyrna, and then he adds what would do if you was in my position? as far as delicacy will permit it, I try to hint to him what I would do, if I were in his place. He understands me perfectly and says that he does not want inclination but power to do it. I own that I am quite out, yet the idea of seeing him a member of our family, is too dear to me, is grown too favourite, that I should give it up at once. So many unexpected things happen! and since some time I have been taught to look only towards improbabilities, therefore why should I give up the hope? I am afraid that if time does not justify this hope B. will have forfeited her happiness, because she is far gone, her affections are very deeply engaged.

FRIDAY JANUARY 6TH (THE KINGS). This morning early we were very near the charming Island of Ischia and thought that we should soon enter the Bay of Naples. But the wind blew quite out and there was no means of getting in. We had a very jolly party in the evening and drew the King in the Captains cabin with all the officers of the ship. They were all amiable or at least good natured. We played at cards and then supped, everybody was obliged to sing a song at supper, they did it well and all good humouredly and that is enough. The gaity was rendered more sprightly by our having cast the anchor and entered the port in the middle of the supper.

NAPLES. SATURDAY JANUARY 7TH. I got up very early in order to enjoy the charming scene which the brilliant rays of the rising sun promised me. Nor was I disappointed in my expectation. Nothing can be compared to the beauty of the situation of Naples, of the adjacent country, and of the Vesuvius, whose crater we could so plainly see. This majestic Landscape rendered more awful still by the gilded colour that the beams of the sun reflected upon it caused me the greatest pleasure imaginable.

JANUARY 8TH. Nobody could get on shore until a man

of the Customs house came with what they call (La Practica) after breakfast we left the ship and landed near a very fine Inn the Brittannia where we were shown in an elegant appartment adjoining to that in which Prince Augustus lives. I saw him on the Balcon, and found him grown very fat since the time I saw his R.H. at Venice. He has married Lady Augusta Murray but his marriage has been annulled and if he goes to England or if she comes to Italy the King stops his pension. He passes his time with his music masters. No sooner arrived but we went to see the Bressacs and Regis. I shall not say I was glad but I was sorry to see them. The company of frenchmen is grown intolerable to me. I passed the rest of the day on the balcony from which we have the sight of the Corso and a Public walk near the Sea shore. Fremantle and French dined with us, the Bressacs and Regis came in the evening to us I cannot, cannot accustom myself to them. I forgot to mention Mr. Gordon whom I saw this morning; we dont treat him any more so well as we did at Florence, and I believe that he perceives it. The Court and Lady Hamilton are both at Caserta.

SUNDAY JANUARY 9TH. This morning after having been to church we had the visit of the Colonel Drinkwater and Mr. Hillary who were both introduced by Fremantle, after them came the Baron de Senft who told us that his friend Ct. Geissler suffered a great deal of his eyes, and next to him, Huson, Boger and Captain Foley called upon us. We took a ride in the carriage with Fremantle and passed through the famous grotto of Pausilipo it is a very long passage cut through the rocks in the middle of which you are involved in the most profound darkness. This immense work of art and industry deserved great admiration and mine was readily granted, Fremantle was rather stupid as he acknowledged it himself during the walk, and gave several hints as if he would speak to Papa, if he were certain not to meet with refusal. I wish he would say and very soon too. Captain Foley, Huson, Boger, French, Hornsey, Barry and Fremantle dined with us. We had a very fine dinner served with great cleanliness and neatness at the end of which Mr. Regis and L'Abbé de Tour came, I must make honourable mention of them, they both behaved with great honesty and real friendship towards us. They warned us from B. telling us that he was everybodys enemy here, and that to keep acquaintance and familiarity with him was the mean of breaking off with the whole town. They added to this, that they would themselves come to see us very seldom, for fear of wronging us in the eyes of Lady Hamilton and the other English here. By the by of Lady Hamilton she sent us a very civil message this morning by her secretary Smith and said she would be in town Tuesday. For my part I am outrageous against B. he is the cause that we shall leave this fine Inn where we have been so well served and could have continued to be and he makes Papa appear like a shabby and mean man, in taking up his lodgings in a dirty horrid Inn. The french must meddle in every thing. I cannot say how much I was shocked today in going through the streets to perceive everywhere objects of disgust, you meet with a quantity of beggars, miserable wretches the greatest part of them are deformed rebukes of Nature, and there are so many of them that you cannot give to all, yet the frequent refusals they meet with from me hurt me as much as they must hurt them. The streets are bordered with old and young Lazaronis and Lazarone who are employed in the pursuit of those insects who delight to nest in their head. This view is the most disgusting of all.

Monday 10th. I was very low spirited all day. I cannot help thinking that in all probabilities my sister will be soon torn away from me, and notwithstanding the thought bathes my cheeks with tears of grief I cannot help wishing that the affair may soon be brought to a conclusion because I shall always be ready to sacrifice my own private interest to her happiness. Fremantle was here in the morning, he charged Mr. French with a letter for Papa in which he made him his proposals but had as yet received no answer. We waited for his return in the evening with the greatest anxiety. Papa was serious and silent. He came in the evening and told us that Papa's answer to Mr. French was that he had no objections but that he would consider upon the subject with Mama. That answer is decisive enough, I have no doubts that my sister will be very soon Mrs. Fremantle. I smile at her happiness whilst my own distress exacts my tears.

11th Tuesday. The top of the Vesuvius was covered with snow, a sight which much surprised me. Hutchinson and Alin dined with us—Fremantle was here both in the morning and evening, he spoke to Papa who behaved very handsomely in granting him my sister and 8000 pounds—But he is to take her away after tomorrow and that idea breaks my heart—The marriage is to be at Lady Hamilton's who will take care of all. For my part I have never been so unhappy as I am now, I had never till now known what sorrow was, I know it too well at present. I can do nothing but weep till my aching eyes have no more tears to bestow. My poor Mother, my poor Father, are both deeply affected and I can give them no comfort, I am only fit to mingle my tears with theirs. The dear companion of all the moments of my life, the dear partaker of all my joys, of all my pains, her who made the principal charm of my existence, her to whom I have always unbosomed myself, is going to leave me, and God knows for how long! I shall never be happy without her. My only comfort is the persuasion I am in that she will be perfectly happy—a man like Fremantle must make her so; his amiable qualities, his affection to her cannot fail to assure her happiness.

12TH WEDNESDAY. Lady Hamilton was here in the morning—a beautiful and amiable woman. She was excessively kind to us and insisted upon the ceremony being performed at her own house tomorrow. I made a very stupid figure during the visit, I could not restrain my tears my heart was so full. She showed the greatest interest to us all, she is a charming woman. Gen. Scheel came in that evening.

13TH THURSDAY. After having equipped ourselves, the Bride and me, in a Nuptial garment, (white crepe), we went to Lady Hamilton's where the ceremony was soon performed by an English Parson. It was awful and was gone through in great style, Prince Augustus being the one that gave my sister away, and Sir William Hamilton, Sir Gilbert Eliot, Mr. Lambton (one of the richest private gentlemen of England) with their wives and Colonel Drinkwater having witnessed. The dinner was merry and many toast were drunk to the happiness of the Bride and Bridegroom. The greatest attention and regard was paid to them by everybody but especially by Lady Hamilton and the Prince. In the evening we went to the Opera. It being the King's Birthday the theatre was illuminated and all the Royal family was there. I cannot say much for the Opera. Before the second act we returned home where Lady Hamilton, with Sir Gilbert and Colonel Drinkwater were so good as to accompany us and where the newmarried couple received the blessing of a Catholic Priest. We have had a great deal of trouble to obtain this—the greatest difficulties have been made by the Cardinal, and this blessing has been granted, but with the condition that a dispensation shall be got from Rome and that they then will be married again.

14TH FRIDAY. We passed all day in retirement and received only Lady Hamilton in the evening. Fremantle and my sister both appear excessively happy—I rejoice at their happiness with all my heart—but the thought that they must soon leave me is killing me.

15TH SATURDAY. I went a shopping all the morning with Fremantle and my sister. He made me a very handsome present of a gold Venetian chain. Upon our return we had Lady Hamilton Mr., Mrs. Pollard and Mrs Darby's visit, the former told us she would present us to the Queen, this amiable Princess having heard of the difficulties that were made against my sister's marriage, took it upon herself to make the Cardinal consent. At four oclock we went to Lady Hamilton, she took us to the Queen, who received us as if we had been equals, with that ease and noble familiarity that wins the hearts of all those who know her, during an hour and a half that we were there she kept up the conversation and did not miss an opportunity of showing her regard and esteem for the English. She is not young but full of vivacity, has many children, one of her daughters sits on the Imperial throne. After having taken leave of her Majesty we returned home where Fremantle and my sister were married for the third time by the hands of a catholic priest to the great annoyance of the first. When the ceremony was over we went at Lady Hamilton's where we had a very pleasant ball. I danced to shake off my sorrow, but when I came home I felt it the more for it, and the idea of to-morrow quite overpowered me.

16TH SUNDAY. I saluted this cruel day with my tears. My sister and Fremantle breakfasted with us—we went to church and then returned—Lady Hamilton came, the moment of bidding farewell was arrived, it was heartbreaking, too moving to dwell upon. They took me on board with them, everything was perfectly arranged for her reception. I helped her to put her things to rights. At last arrived the Viceroy and Drinkwater—they dined on board—in the middle of the dinner we were surprised by the arrival of the Prince—he was as ever very civil. When he was gone I retired with Fremantle and my sister, he spoke to me with the affection of a brother. I shall never forget all he told me, and the idea that I have a warm friend in him is of great comfort to me. It was dark before I left the ship—I had not the heart to tear myself away.

Colonel Drinkwater accompanied me home, he is a very civil, good and agreable man. I found my Mother bathed in tears complaining of my sister's indifference, of her want of love for her. I tried to excuse her but I own I was myself surprised at her coldness, for she did not shed a tear—yet I know her too well to doubt her affection. But the sentiment which now occupies her heart leaves no room for any other feeling.

CHAPTER 19

'Man's love is in man's life a thing apart, 'tis woman's whole existence' wrote Lord Byron. Fremantle's diaries for the years 1793–96 have been preserved, and the following extracts will serve to prove how right Lord Byron was.

MAY 1793. Wed. 22. Agreably surprized at S. Hyde Parkers coming into my Room and informing me I was app. to the Tartar, calld on Lord Hood, graciously received my commission—my coxswain ran away from The Friendship, took all finest things for L 20.

Mond. 27. With the mermaid took the General Washington, French privateer of 22 Guns, a great beast could not sail in the least. She fired her guns and struck, none of the shot struck the ship. The mermaids boat got on bd. first.

JUNE 1793. Sun. 16. Find the surgeon to be a mauvais subjet, talk much to him. He crys, and promises to amend.

SEPTEMBER 1793. Sat. 14. Make Mother Ceyan sleep below. She does not like it. My famous goat given me by Wm. B. drank wine and died in the greatest agonies. I am much annoyed at it—and can't drink tea.

JANUARY 1794. Mon. 13. Went to the little island of Portreross to wood and water. Made the Ship fast to the Rocks. Got plenty of good beef and vegetables. No bad thing at sea.

Fri. 17. Capt. Van Kensjsen and his wife, Mr and Mrs and Miss Groyme dined with me. The eldest girl beautiful. Fell in love with her. They stayed supper and played at domino; burned olive leaves & wood in the fire. Famous fire and smell.

Sat. 18. Sent an officer and 50 men ashore to pull the embrazures of the forts down. The forts the oddest construction possible, perfectly round and a hole at the Top to descend by a ladder only. Have the appearance of state prisons than castles with ditches and drawbridges.

FEBRUARY 1794. Mon. 24. Went on board to Nelson. Sutton very savage about his Bowsprit wounded, and a shot in his quarter gallery. Persuades Nelson to let him return to Lord Hood. After som argument, Nelson agrees.

Tues. 25. With great good humour, Nelson tells me he had rather be without a ship, unless they are desirous of staying. Rather indignant with Sutton and with cause. Lord Hood joins us.

MARCH 1794. Wed. 30. Went on shore to see the ladies, bought two goats. One fell down the main hatchway and killed himself. Took the command of the gun boats, and went off the Town after dark. Stayed there till daylight, dining at the Sans Culottes. They fired from the batteries but did not hit us. A good deal tired with being up all night. Saw some holes in the Houses and went to see Nelson, who is cruizing in the offing.

APRIL 1794. Tu 19. Dine with Nelson, take a view of the new Battery at Toga. Walking with Nelson from thence a shot knocked him down and covered me all over with dirt. Determine never to go the short way again.

Wed. 20. Got my stove down. Have not had a fire for many days. Cabin dirty with the smoke.

Th. 21. The Neopolitan mortars not worth a farthing. They crack. The shells don't fit them, very pretty in the nights to see the shells flying.

Fri. 22. Went to the upper post. Many of the houses unroofed with our shells.

Sun. 24. Some of the cutters crew got on shore. Robbed a church. Sacreligious dogs. Gave them a good flogging for it—called in the Parson, an old man of seventy. He gave me a flask of wine of his own making. Old man begd hard to have the men forgiven.

Fri. 29. The ships anchored in a semicircle round the town of Bastia. We came too in 60 fathoms. Ord'd by Wm. Inglefield to send a boat to the Victory complain'd of the hardship, his hectoring manner, more like the bully of a bawdy house than a Gentleman.

Sat. 30. Write to Nelson in consequence. He condoles with me, and offers to take day and day about with the Agamemnon. Very civil but decline. Before we make the enemy line, one shot over us.

May 1794. Sat. 28. Was introduced to the King, at his country house. Saw the horse race. Dine with Sir Wm. Hamilton. My lady an uncommon treat, tells stories about the King. Paget and I go together, W & M with the H's.

Sun. 29. Dine with Sir Wm. Hamilton. Look at his collection of antiques, very extraordinary. Go to the opera. Lady H's maid the prettiest woman in Naples. The Queen the ugliest. Lady H. protects Wm. Bollinger.

Mon. 30. Dine with Sir James Douglas. 2 very pretty daughters. Both married. He is a civil creature enough. Copley dined with us, who appears more mad than ever, and is the greatest democrat at Naples.

November 1794. Fri. 7. The Abbé taught me to sing two Spanish songs. He is quite happy at the idea of getting on shore so soon at Corsica, had some conversation in the evening with Mr Kent about Neti.

Tu. 18. Dined at Currigo with Nelson Hood Lister

and Hotham. Went afterwards to the opera as before, found Nina, who is the prettiest little woman in Leghorn. After the opera was over I went on board and got the ship under way, it was near one in the morning.

DECEMBER 1794. Wed. 3. Dined at Nelsons and his dolly—called on old Udney, went to the opera with him. He introduced me to a very handsome Greek woman.

FEBRUARY 1795. Wed. 25. Arrived at Leghorn. Adml. Hotham to my great joy orders me to anchor which I did directly go on shore. Dine with all the Lads at Curry's, went to the Comedie. Very bad.

Thurs. 28. Very pleasant on shore. Take up my abode at the Lion Rouge, no room at Coulsons. Lord Proby dined with me on board. Gave him a lecture.

MARCH 1795. Sun. 8. Dine in the gun room. Read the Articles of War to the Ship's company. Mr. Duncomb leaves the Inconstant. Mr Hutchinson joins. The admiral makes the sign to unmoor at night.

Wed. 11. The French fleet seen by the Moselle. We repeat the signals. 14 sail of the line and 6 frigates.

Fri. 13. Engaged with the Ça. Ira. 3 killed, 14 wounded. The enemy consist of 15 sail of the line. 6 frigates and 2 brigs.

Sat. 14. The squadrons engaged, about noon the Ça Ira struck. Am angry with Reeves. Let the French officers come upon bd. They are annoyed at the conduct of their countrymen, who certainly behave very ill—send prisoners to the Palace.

Fri. 27. Dine at Currys. The Consul & Henryman dine with us. Nelson made me many *compliments.* I know why!

JULY 1795. Thurs. 3. French prisoner attempted to desert. Caught him.

Called on an uncommon pretty Dolly whom I christen Mrs Hill, via Speranza, 967.

Fri. 4. Dined with Drake. Genoa very quick. Promised to send my prisoners on shore, which they are very thankful for. The French Consul sends me his compliments.

Sat. 19. The Adml. informs me I am to go to Leghorn, with a cargo of Admirals. Rather dislike the trip but can't help myself.

Thursday 24. Find that Mrs Hill is at Leghorn, pay her a visit and make future arrangements.

Saturday 26. Dine with Pollard, stupid enough. Take a ride with Mrs Hill in the evening, quarrel with a — man who gives me a good dubbing.

Sunday 27. Dine tête à tête with Plampin at Currys, I call on Mr Johnston who is at the hospital sleep with Mrs Hill.

AUGUST 21. A convoy arrived from Genoa. Dined with Nelson. Dolly aboard who has a sort of abcess in her side, he makes himself ridiculous with that woman.

AUGUST & SEPTEMBER 1795. Fri. 27. Carrying sail all day to get the prizes two of which I had in tow into Vado. Anchored about 9 at night.

Sat. 28. Dined with Nelson and his Dolly. Shields seriously ill and is in my opinion determined to go home.

Th. 4. Bothered great part of the night with a Spanish Sloop of war. Fired several shot at him and made an officer come on board.

Sun. 27. Dined with Nelson & Dolly. Very bad dinner indeed.

Mon. 28. Dined at Nelsons. Went to see at the theatre a man who was blind play upon a flute, well enough. Nelson sailed in the Agamemnon.

Wed. 30. Have serious conversation with some of

the officers who stay on shore more than they ought to do.

October 1795. Fri. 9. Very unpleasant rainy weather. Anchored at Vado. Nelson Brisbane & Elphinstone dined with me. Sent the cutter on shore for Magdelena. She was very seasick.

January and February 1796. Wed. 27. Dined with Trowbridge, & went to a ball at Mr. Abbotts. uncommon pretty women.——at Mr. Moody's. The Governor opened his gates for us.

Fri. 29. We dine with Middleton and drink more than we ought to do.

Mon. 8. Anchored at Smyrna. Find there has been an accident, a great bore.

Sat. 13. A grand fete at Wilkinson's, which by the bye was much about as stupid a business as I have been at some time—called to see a Venetian dolly—ravenous *bitch*.

Sun. 14. Dined with Trowbridge—went in the evening to the Consul's—called on the Shute's, gave both the girls rings—am much smitten with little Mimi.

June 1796. Wed. 15. Can't find Madalina. Called on the Governor.

Thursday 16. Went to Pisa baths, called on Adelaide who was quite recovered and looked well.

Sat. 25. Went on shore in the morning, receive the Wynns from Wyndham's recommendation. They dine and sleep on board, as does Mrs Pollard. Adelaide came off in the evening**.

July 1796. Sat. 2. Arrive at Bastia after 18 hours. Find the Wynns at dinner on board the Lively. Go to them and call on Nelson, receive a very famous letter of thanks from the factory.

Mon. 4. Stay at Bastia all day. The Wynns dine on board the Inconstant with Lord Garlies. I dine at Bastia. very rude of me to send an apology to the Wynns.

Fri. 8. Met Nelson off Elba. The Soldiers very undetermined and very jealous of us.

Thursday 15. Give a dinner and ball, rather pleasant. The Wynnes will come on board, that's positive.

Sat. 9. A long consultation about landing the Troops. Nelson & I offer to take the Town with the Ships. Damsels uncommonly pleasant. Am very dismal all day on account of the damsels leaving me so soon. Had much conversation with Mrs Wynne.

Wed. 13. Serious thoughts about Betsey. If I was not such a poor wretch. The Old Man and Old Woman cry much, but approve much of my reasons, &c.

OCTOBER 1796. Mon. 10. Bore away for Porto Ferrago, arrive at 4 o'clock. Nelson Sutton & Cockburn here. Find the Wynnes are still on board the Brittania.

Tues. 11. Went on shore & look pratique dined with Montresor and got mortal went to a ball & fell asleep—it is somewhat surprizing but I always drink too much the first day I go on shore.

Thurs. 13. Those that remain in Port dine with me. Little Cayen likewise. A very pleasant ball at Montresor. Was in great spirits and made Love to a Miss Watson.

Fri. 14. Got under way at daylight. 14 sail under convoy. The wind very moderate. Heard somewhere that Broughton died at Gibraltar, a good thing for him and his family.

Sat. 15. Make little progress. Wind fresh from the Westward. Am not a little annoyed to find the Wynne's are still on board the Britannia.

Tues. 18. Anch. at S. Firenzo, went to the

Blenheim where I found all the Damsels at dinner. Went at night to the Britannia where I had much talk with Foley. Find he is violently smitten. Letters from Lord Spencer.

Thurs. 20. Took a walk on shore with the damsels, more talk with Betsey. They went out to the Inconstant. dined with Foley. A pleasant day enough. Get under way at one in the morning. Mrs W offers 5000 & 10 at his death.

Fri. 21. In the middle of the night fell in with the Spanish fleet, dogged them till daylight when they chased me. Ran into S. Firenzo and told the Adml. 37 sail. Went to sea again immediately to cruise for Adml. Mann. Did not see the damsels.

NOVEMBER 1796. Sun. 20. Anchor at night at Naples. Blew rather fresh during the day. Ran in twelve knotts. Found the Adriatic and Sardinian Squadrons at anchor.

Mon. 21. Took up my lodgings and dined at the Grand Brettagna. Went to the Opera & dined at Lady H. Called upon Hacketts where there was a Musical party.

Tues. 22. Dined with Sir William Hamilton. All the great people there, and a very pleasant dinner. Get on tolerably with my lady, whom I dislike.

Wed. 30. Anchored at Porto ——, went on shore to see the Wynnes who are uncommon.

DECEMBER 1796. Thurs. 1. Dined with the General. Went with some of the young folks to sup at the Wynne's.

Fri. 2. Dined with the General. Supped as usual at the Wynne's, who are more pleasant than I can describe.

Sat. 3. Forget where I dined. Supped with Mrs. Sanderson. Pleasant enough.

Sun. 4. Handman and I dined at the Wynne's. Was very happy until Evening with them. Miss B uncommonly well dressed and beautiful.

Mon. 12. Hannah dined with me on board tête à tête, uncommon——.

Tues. 13. Gen. Horneck dined with me, a very large party. Tolerable decent dinner. Supersede the Master of the Navy Transport.

Fri. Hannah dined with me, got mortal. Got an order for the Master of the Alliance to go on shore. Much quizzing.

Wed. 26. Nelson came in the Minerva, a grand ball given by the General. Mr. Cockburn and the Spanish captain dine with me. Did not get to bed until 3. Very bad weather.

Thur. 27. Nelson Harneck Anna dined with me. Carried Dolly on shore at one o'clock. Found Elphinstone with his brat on the chair. Persuade the Wynne's to go to Naples.

Fri. 28. Court Martial on Old Harrison. Dismissed his Ship. We all dine with Captain James on b. the Dolphin.

Sat. 29. Got the Wynne's on board. Terrible weather. Dine with them tho I was engaged to Pringle.

Sun. 30. Sail early but make little progress. Damsels uncommonly pleasant. Don't like the idea of parting with Madlle. Get serious fits.

Mon. 31. Uncommon all day. So warm in the cabin the damsels were obliged to make use of their fans tho there was no fire. Old Wynne very ill indeed. Am amazingly attached to Betsey, but cannot make up my mind to marry. I can't say I have on the whole behaved very well.

January 1797. Thurs. 10. Sent a proposal to Mr Wynne about marrying his daughter. Everything concluded as I could wish. Everything to be finished the 12th.

Sat. 12. Was married to Elizabeth Wynne at Sir Wm. Hamilton's, where we dined. Prince Augustus, Mrs. & Lady Anne Lambton, Sir Gilbert Elliot was presented in the morning to the King of Naples whose birthday it was. Dressed Ship and fired 21 guns.

Tuesday 15. Went on board at 12 o'clock with Jenny and Betsey.

Wed. 16. Make very little progress. Came to blow hard during the night. Ship rocked a great deale.

Mon. 23. Nelson Cockburn & Hope dined with me. Had a Court Martial on Lieut. Pigot who was dismissed his ship. Determine to send Antony to the right about he is so great a blackguard.

Tues. 24. The Granets dined with Betsey on board. I dined with Cockburn, where we drank large quantities of champagne. Took too much. My Betsey uncommonly good humoured about it.

March 1797. Sun. 19. Dined with Betsey in the Gun room. The wind got moderate in the even. Weather fine. Busy at letters great part of the day.

April 1797. Wed. 19. Betsey's birthday. Great difference of opinion respecting her *real age*. She acknowledges 19. I allow her three years more. I allow I am eleven years older. Got the harpsichord out of the hold.

Thurs. 20. The Wind to the Westward. My passengers I think improve a little but the Genl. is certainly very costive. He requires laxative emolients, one man belonging to the Royals died on board.

Fri. 21. Fell in with Adml. Nelson in the Captain.

May 1797. Mon. 15. Make little progress but the weather is very fine. Captain Lydy ** came from Adml. Nelson who has 18 sail with him. He sleeps on board his ship not in. Sight it in the morning. Send him by the Speedy.

JUNE 17. Dined at home tête à tête with Betsey, walked in the evening to the dockyard.

[That is Fremantle's last entry, although the diary is ruled and dated until September 8th.]

CHAPTER 20

[*Betsey's Journal.*]

MONDAY, JANUARY 9TH, 1797. What a day this was for me. Till the evening I was in the most anxious expectation. Fremantle made Mr French speak to Papa in the morning and as Papa did not mention one word about it to anybody at home, I concluded that he had refused. The evening my surprise and happiness were beyond expression at hearing that on the contrary Papa had given a very favourable answer. It is now decided that I shall marry Fremantle, I could say much on this subject but what I must feel on this occasion is not easily expressed.

TUESDAY, JANUARY 10TH. Fremantle spoke to Papa and all was settled. We are to be married on Thursday and sail immediately after Though I must acknowledge that this event makes me perfectly happy, yet I dread it and the idea of leaving so suddenly my Father Mother and sisters, distresses me I can hardly make up my mind to it. I was quite miserable after the whole was determined upon. Mamma and my sister burst into tears, I did not know what to say, what to do. I was very low spirited myself, poor *Eugenia* does nothing but cry, How shall I accustom myself to live without them? Oh God, I wont think of it, it must to happen, it is for my good and happiness. I wished it myself and now that what I desired might happen, it frightens me and I think the undertaking almost too great.

WEDNESDAY, JANUARY 11TH. Sir William Hamilton and his Lady came in the morning. It is impossible to say how civil they were, especially Lady Hamilton, she is a charming woman, beautiful and exceedingly good humoured and amiable. She took all the management of this affair, and the wedding is to be tomorrow at her own house. I never felt more miserable than I did this morning, I was almost sorry that my marriage was to take place, I feared I should not have courage to undertake so much. However I made up my mind to it Happy I am sure to be with Fremantle, it certainly is dreadful to be obliged to leave my family but it will be but for a very short time, I dare say this will make Papa come to England, he promises to do so as soon as possible, we will stay till Saturday. this has made us all again contented. After I had got the better of the fit of stupidity I had in the morning I was the rest of the day and evening in very high spirits. Mama is exceedingly kind to me herself and Papa behaves indeed very handsomely towards me and more than I deserve, what I can never repay. It is with heart-felt sorrow that I think of leaveing my family, and still more when I think what a loss I shall be to them, how much it afflicts them. In this sorrow however, there is something that gives me infinite satisfaction, how flattering it is for me to find how much I am beloved, not only by my father mother and sisters, but even by Jaegle and all the servants. They all feel very much concerned at my leaving the house. Fremantle was here almost all day, my felicity is encreased at finding that he is happy.

For the last time I shall write as Miss Wynne, what a day tomorrow is—I dread it.

THURSDAY, JANUARY 12TH. NAPLES. At one oclock we all went to Lady Hamiltons where the ceremony was performed by Mr Lambton's Chaplain. What I felt at the wedding is not to be described. Prince Augustus gave me away, Sir Gilbert Elliot, Sir William Hamilton, Mr Lambton, Colonel

Drinkwater were all witnesses. We all dined at Sir Williams, went to the opera in the evening and returned to the Albergo Reale where we intended to be married by a Catholic priest. But we could not persuade the scrupulous Bishop to give us a dispensation. At last we found a priest that gave us his blessing and appeased Mamma's conscience.

FRIDAY, JANUARY 13TH. I never felt better and happier in my life than I did today. I did not chose to see anybody and the weather being horrid we could not go to see any thing of Naples, so I did not go out of my apartment. The family is not so dismal and Papa in quite high spirits. Lady Hamilton came with Sir Gilbert in the evening, it is not possible to express the many civilities she has shown us as well as every other person here.

THURSDAY, JANUARY 14TH. Went with Fremantle and *Eugenia* shopping in the morning, had to come back early to dress, dine and be ready to go with Lady Hamilton to the Queen at 4 oclock. We met with the kindest reception there never was a woman more affable, civil and amiable. She had something to say to every one of us and we spent an hour with her in the most agreeable manner. We returned to the Albergo Reale there to be married a third time. The Queen was kind enough to take the management of this affair herself and has persuaded the ArchBishop to permit the ceremony to take place. It made Mamma quite happy. She has fretted herself to death these three last days on account of Religion. A Ball at Lady Hamiltons in the evening where I saw Many handsome Neopolitan women, but what manners? Indeed I felt no great fancy to dance, I feel very unhappy in the idea of parting to morrow from my family.

SUNDAY, JANUARY 14TH. The emotions I felt today are

not to be expressed. I took leave of my father mother and sisters with a broken heart. *Eugenia* came on board with me dined with us and only left me in the evening, poor sweet girl how miserable it makes me to leave her. Sir Gilbert Elliot, Drinkwater and Pozzo di Borgo are of our party. Prince Augustus came on board he has been uncommonly civil to us as well as every body else.

INCONSTANT. MONDAY, JANUARY 15TH. We sailed last night, had fair weather and pretty good wind all day. I find it quite odd to be alone here. I dare not think on those I left at Naples for it makes my heart swell with anguish, however I can make no complaints for I am as happy in my situation as it is possible to be. Fremantle is all attention and kindness. I have got a comfortable little cabin where I can do what I like. The Vice Roy and Colonel Drinkwater are a pleasant society for us.

PORTO FERRAJO, ELBA. SUNDAY, JANUARY 22ND. TUESDAY AND WEDNESDAY. We had a long and tedious passage. Very blowing weather, poor Pozzo de Borgo very seasick, Sir Gilbert not very well. It did not affect me, it increased my appetite and I laughed at everybody else. We only came to an anchor this morning at three oclock. I begin to get accustomed to the life I lead and find myself comfortable and happy.

The general report here is that this place is going to be evacuated but General de Burgh and the Vice roy are against it, a council of war is to be held in the evening to determine. I walked a shore with Fremantle met Captain Hope, Cockburn, Giffard, all very civil and the *sposa* received so many fine compliments of congratulation that she was quite at a loss. The weather delightful quite pleasant, Commissioner Coffin and Captain Elphinston dined with us. I spent the evening alone and I amused myself very well with my Harpsichord and books. It has been determined that Fremantle will remain here with the command l'Utile, Blanche and other small vessels all the rest go down to Gibraltar with Commodore Nelson. For a thousand reasons I prefer staying here to going immediately to England Fremantle likes it as well, we are both contented. I daily think more and more that I have ensured my future felicity by marrying one who so well deserves my love and regard nothing on my part will be wanting for us both to be happy.

TUESDAY JANUARY 24TH. Took my usual walk, had Mde Granets and her daughters to dinner. Fremantle dined on board the Minerva where they had a drinking party, he assured me when he returned on board at nine that he was tipsy but I found him perfectly sober and even had he been tipsy he behaved so kind and good humoured to me, begged I should forgive him with so much good grace, that it could not have given me the least uneasiness.

WEDNESDAY, JANUARY 25TH. St. Gratien came over from Rio and stayed the whole morning with us. The weather was bad and in general this, a dismal day and unlucky, last night the ships company all got drunk and behaved horridly ill. Much flogging this morning which made Fremantle ill and broke my heart. I could distinctly hear the poor wretches cry out for mercy, from the cabin. A man broke his leg. After all this misery I was glad to get out of the ship and went over to the town.

THURSDAY, JANUARY 26TH. A Court Martial to try three Mariners of this ship. The weather so bad that I could not go on shore, stayed quietly on board with Fremantle, who spent the evening with me, he gives me daily new proofs of his attachment and gains more and more in my affections.

FRIDAY, JANUARY 27TH. The weather horrible impossible to get out of the ship, I occupied myself all day and spent my time as agreeably as I could wish with Fremantle.

SATURDAY, JANUARY 28TH. I was quite miserable all the morning as the three Mariners were punished and flogged along side of every ship, some men flogged likewise on board.

SUNDAY, JANUARY 29TH. It was with inexpressible satisfaction I received letters from Naples, but nothing can equal the mortification and pain I felt in reading the one Mamma wrote to me. It make an impression on me which I shall never forget. She expresses how unhappy it has made her to see her daughter leave her without shedding a tear which proves so much indifference and ingratitude on my part and will ever be a sorrow and chagrin to her. But how ill she knows me. How bad she has interpreted my feelings! If she can suppose me possessed with such an unfeeling heart. Though at my taking leave I did not cry, I certainly did not feel less for that, I know how much I am indebted to so indulgent so good a parent. I shall ever have regard and love for the best of Mothers and ever be thoughtful for all she has done for me. I took a walk in the morning. Captain Donelop and his lady and Major Probin dined with us. Matrimony has not agreed I should think with this lady for she looks older and uglier than ever she did. She is vulgar and stupid.

WEDNESDAY, FEBRUARY 1ST. Fremantle attacked me for some nonsense or other I am too *inanimate*, but we were very good friends at last, I see that very little is required to make him uneasy and must be still more on my guard.

WEDNESDAY, FEBRUARY 8TH. I behaved very foolishly towards Fremantle caused him much uneasiness and made myself very unhappy, certainly not intentionally I was very angry with myself afterwards but it was too late, all for a trifle and nonsense.

THURSDAY, FEBRUARY 9TH. Was unhappy all the morning as I saw I had given F. real cause to be angry with me however it was better explained and we were friends again. The Blanche is going to Porto Ferrajo with the prize.

FRIDAY AND SATURDAY. Continually in chase but did not take anything. I find time passes very quick, and I like being at sea almost better than Porto Ferrajo. The honeymoon is over but it finished almost better than it began, I flatter myself that the months that are *to come* will all be *honeymoons* for me.

SUNDAY, MONDAY AND TUESDAY. A pleasant passage back to Porto Ferrajo, the weather continues fine.

WEDNESDAY, 15TH. I was very ill indeed all the morning and obliged to keep my bed. We took a French boat going from Bastia to Leghorn with 90 people in her, some deserters of Dillon's corps and some Swiss. We came to anchor at noon the Blanche and Fortune soon after us got practique immediately but they all say we have put the island in quarrantine. I was a little better in the evening and exceedingly happy as I received many letters from Naples answers to my last, Mamma writes to me in the kindest manner imaginable assuring me that she had never acused me of having a bad heart but could not help being hurt at parting seeing me show so little chagrin. The news very bad, Mantua taken and the french on their march to Rome. The Bombay castle was lost in entering the Tagus and the Zealous so much disabled that she is ordered home. The Courageous was also lost a little time ago at Gibraltar. Nothing but misery from all parts. It makes me quite low spirited.

FEBRUARY 16TH. *Eugenia* left Naples for Caserta. The Queen was given a white satin gown, locally made and embroidered, which the king has bidden her wear at the next ball, not only in order to encourage the manufacture, but to give a good example to the other ladies who instead of wearing silk always wear lawn. I waltzed and received from his Majesty many undeserved but loud *Bravos*.'

FEBRUARY 17TH, FRIDAY. INCONSTANTS COTTAGE. We dined on board and came to our new house in the afternoon, tho excessively small it is very nice and comfortable. The weather very cold and blowing very hard which did not make Inconstants Cottage very pleasant in the night as it was miserably cold. French and Huson stayed the evening with us. The Rose Cutter sailed for Naples and carried my letters.

FRIDAY, 17TH. *Eugenia* receives 'a packet of news from Betsy. She is returned from her cruize during which they only took one merchantman, and have taken a little casino near Porto Ferrajo. She is always contented and happy, her husband is full of attentions for her, and has even left off snuff for her sake.'

TUESDAY, FEBRUARY 28TH. Returned this morning to our cottage and never enjoyed it more, coming from the stupid dull town. St. Gratien and Captain de Wyl, and General Horneck called, I spent the whole day and evening tête à tête with Fremantle, it was cold and we wrote letters till supper time. I never thought of the Ball, last year I should have been distressed and miserable to finish the carnaval in my room but now I am never so happy as when alone with Fremantle and have not the least desire to enjoy any other pleasure.

THURSDAY, MARCH 2ND. Mamma sent me a most charming gauze gown, some musick and many other things, I was delighted with it. I went over to the town and spent half an hour with Mrs Stephen and walked back. Mr French dined with us and we again took a pleasant walk in the evening. Nothing more pleasant than the life I lead now, quietly in a little cottage, I feel daily happier.

FRIDAY, MARCH 3RD. Rode over to Longone with Captain Cousins and Woodhouse and went to see General Day, the only curiosity in the place, he is a fine old man, monstrous fat and I really think a fool, he affects great singularity, has pretentions to wit but says the most trivial stupid things, he pinches everybody very near breaks ones fingers and stuffs every body with sweetmeats and wine. He made me laugh as he is the greatest original I ever saw, his wife is a poor miserable thing, the daughter a good looking fatty, our visit was short as he dines at twelve we were not sorry to take our leave and we rode over to Rio. The country is beautifully romantick and Rio delightfully situated on a hill a few miles from the sea. St. Gratien (who is here Signor Commandante and has four hundred Swiss with him) received us with his usual good humour, we walked to the mines a pretty walk but the mines did not answer my expectations, I found nothing very curious nor very interesting a Cave all of iron but people that dont understand it like myself would never take it to be iron. I was more pleased with the look of the country the charming prospects than with the mine. I found the walk back dreadfully long, was much fatigued and starving with hunger.[1]

[1] The same day *Eugenia* visited the Lago d'Aqure, and returned home with an appetite to dinner.

MONDAY, MARCH 13TH. Came to breakfast on board and was delighted with the Cabin. I wrote to Naples where the Petterelle is going.

WEDNESDAY, MARCH 15TH. We got under weigh this morning and after having worked out of the harbour the main top sail split which obliged us to return the weather being bad. [On March 16th *Eugenia* and her parents were sent for in a hurry: Lady Hamilton was going to exhibit her attitudes. 'She is beautiful in them, I much admired her.']

THURSDAY, MARCH 16TH. It rained almost incessantly and blew very hard it was lucky we were in harbour.

Fremantle has fitted out two little cabins below where we sleep it is much better for me at sea on many accounts.

FRIDAY AND SATURDAY. Sailed Friday morning only spoke an American ship from Falmouth.

TUESDAY, MARCH 21ST. We took a prize in the night a Spanish small ship with 9000 dollars who was going to Cicely (*Sicily*) for corn. It blew very hard indeed and the motion so violent that we sat in the cot all day, dined and supped in our cabin below. I walked the deck a little, tho I was not at all sick, as I had not slept all night I was very stupid.

TUESDAY, MARCH 22ND. I had a restless miserable night could not sleep till morning. The noise of the Bulkhead and the motion annoyed me more than anything else. The weather fine and the prize money shared.

THURSDAY, MARCH 23RD. Quite a summer day. Spoke to Ragusen who says two Spanish Frigates are going to convoy a valuable prize down. The officers are building castles in the air and think already they have taken (with the Inconstant alone) the two frigates and their prize. Indeed nothing amuses me so much as to hear them, they are in expectation of getting immense riches.

FRIDAY AND SATURDAY. A charming westerly breeze and delightful weather boarded two Danes these last two nights.

SUNDAY, MARCH 26TH. Dined in the gunroom where I am always ready to fall asleep.

MONDAY, MARCH 27TH. The wind shifted off Cape Corse and is now right against us.

TUESDAY, MARCH 28TH. It blew rather fresh and we were driven in the night almost off leghorn.

THURSDAY, MARCH 30TH. Again bad weather in the night. We came to an anchor early and I was delighted to receive all my letters but I little expected what I heard. It gave me at first very great pain. But on reflecting a little I thought it was a lucky event. Ct. Senft is much in love with *Eugenia*, she is passionately fond of him, he asked to marry her but Papa who began by encouraging this amour declares himself against it. Mamma of course is very unhappy. Eugenia has lost all her gaity and cheerfulness, and will be miserable if Papa persists in his present resolution, but I think he will finish by giving his consent. Ct. Senft is only 21, too young for Eugenia, Tho from the knowledge I have of both their characters, the amazing love they have for one another, all make me hope it will ensure her future happiness, but still I cannot help having some doubts about it, and as I could never have resolved on marrying a German and living with Germans I fear *Eugenia* will get tired of it. However Ct. Senft seems to be a good quiet, peaceable man, she will entirely domineer over him.

THURSDAY, APRIL 6TH. I was on shore from nine o'clock in the morning until ten in the evening and was heartily tired of it, I called on the Cantinis, Mrs Stephens, Granets and dined at Mrs Dunlops. Talked of nothing but her pregnancy, of children, etc. and when her husband and some officers were there the conversation was only upon Mrs Beneditti, her sister and all that noble set, which discourse I did not find at all proper in the presence of Ladies, and I was shocked that Mrs Dunlop gave her opinion on that indelicate subject, but she is to be excused. Every body is very busy about the embarkation. It is wished it should remain a secret and is of great consequence it should be kept so, but the new will soon be spread all round the country.

Tuesday, April 11th. The Speedy returned from Naples and brought me many letters. Poor Eugenia is in great distress. Papa will not give his consent. I cannot blame him for it, it was a very disadvantageous match for her, but everybody says he behaved very ill, he certainly did in allowing it to go so far. Ct. Senft is gone to Rome but is coming back in a fortnight. I hope Eugenia will not see him and more and will forget this unhappy event, at present she is exceedingly miserable, and seems to be passionately fond of that young man. It makes me very uneasy.

Thursday, April 13th. Captain Hotham dined with us, he is returned from a cruize of three weeks and again took nothing but a chest of oranges, he is either very unlucky or very awkward.

Saturday, April 22nd. As the convoy is so strong now Fremantle had my pianoforte put up in the cabin. Mr. Brinley plays upon the Flute, not well but he understands musick.

Tuesday, April 25th. A charming fair wind I have a bad cold do nothing but sneeze all day. Captain Montresor shows me how to paint in water colours.

Major Brinley accompanies me on the Flute every evening.

WEDNESDAY, APRIL 26TH. I think our passengers altogether not pleasant.

SATURDAY, APRIL 29TH. I was quite well again I am delighted to find I am getting exceedingly thin.

SUNDAY, APRIL 30TH. A foul wind all day it had all the appearance of blowing hard in the night. Fremantle went on board with Admiral Nelson and I slept alone in the cabin all night, the first night I have slept alone since I have been married, did not like it. Fremantle composed a very pretty song which he set to musick.

SUNDAY, MAY 21ST. We came over to the coast of Barbery, and a delightful country it looks like, highly cultivated and some charming prospects. The current is in our favor, and we have gained considerably though the wind is foul.

MONDAY, MAY 22ND. A fair wind and we saw the Rock of Gibraltar very plain at sunset.

TUESDAY, MAY 23RD. Were close to the Rock by daylight, and I was struck with the appearance of this place. Came to an anchor before breakfast and ran on board the Meleager, Fremantle much annoyed by it, Captain Murray, Noakes etc. came to see us. The admiral was here and got under weigh soon after we arrived. The convoy is all safe except Philips brig and our Spanish prize that were seen in the evening and were taken by the Spaniard.

Colonel Hill dined with us, he was kind enough to offer us his house on shore where we are going tomorrow, he is an old acquaintance of Fremantles, and a very well behaved pleasant young man. Fremantle was quite low spirited and unhappy all day, he heard of a Mutiny that happened in the Fleet at Portsmouth, the consequences of which he dreads very much he has no more thoughts of changing into the Sea Horse who by the by got on shore on Europa point and was near lost, Captain Oakes very poorly wishes much to get to England, and has wrote to the Admiral about changing with Fremantle. Our Passengers all left us, thank heavens, the cabin was quite comfortable and quiet without them.

WEDNESDAY, MAY 31ST. GIBRALTAR. Breakfasted at General Frigge with Mrs. Stephens and was hurried away by Mr. Day who told us we were to sail to-morrow morning early. I had not been home long when I heard Fremantle had changed into the Sea Horse and Captain Oakes was going to take the Convoy home. I am glad it so happens. I dined at the Convent where I went with Colonel Hill. Fremantle was so busy that I saw nothing of him till the evening. Mrs. Pigot was there and exceedingly civil. Old General O'hara is all attention and kindness to me. I met Fremantle as I came home. He is not pleased with the change Captain Oakes forced him to it.

MONDAY, JUNE 5TH. Colonel and Mrs. Hall and Captain Boyne dined with us. I like Mrs. Hall amasingly. Went to a Ball in the evening which I did not find pleasant. I was exceedingly unhappy to have done something that vexed Fremantle.

WEDNESDAY, JUNE 7TH. Mr. Adams, Mr. and Mrs. Wood in to dinner, the stupidest of all women and insupportable and tiresome, the husband drank too much and talked nonsense all the evening.

SATURDAY, JULY 1ST. We drove last night at single anchor and as the wind was Easterly got under weigh and ran on the Portuguese Frigate, we joined the fleet in the morning. Captain Grey Troubridge and Sutton came on board immediately I dined on board the Ville de Paris. Sir John Jervis very gallant as usual, to accommodate me he is going to send this ship home and we are to carry General Stuart from Lisbon, but I am sorry for it. . . .

MONDAY, JULY 3RD. Anchored with the advanced Squadron, Admiral Nelson and Captain Martin came on board. Captain Foley dined with us. Fremantle was out all night he went with Admiral Nelson to bombard the town, much firing all night. I was anxious for Fremantle and did not go to bed until he returned. Spanish gun boats and a barge were taken, many people killed and wounded. Fremantle received a blow.

WEDNESDAY, JULY 5TH. Dined on board alone with Fremantle and some of the officers. One of the many Fishermen came on board it is said not a woman now remains in Cadiz, but the night before last a bomb went into a house and killed a child in the mothers arms and the woman lost her arm. They again went to bombard the Town tonight. The gun boats did not venture out, but they fired most amazingly from all sides. The bomb almost knocked to pieces and great many men killed and wounded. Fremantle did not return till four oclock in the morning I was quite unhappy all the time he was away, and sat up till three, Hornsey was near killed the half of his hat knocked away by splinters himself bruized he had a miraculous escape.

THURSDAY, JULY 6TH. Very much tired and sleepy all day. Admiral Nelson Captains Miller, Martin and Foley dined with us. The Admiral wrote that this bombardment must be given over, Thank God, it was sacrificing men for nothing, he did it out of avarice as he heard 4 millions of piastres should be sent out to him.

FRIDAY, JULY 7TH. Captains Foley and Martin come every evening to us. We hear the Spanish Fleet talks of coming out, but they are too great cowards to do it.

SATURDAY, JULY 8TH. Thank God it seems we are going to have peace. The news from England much better and Fremantle in much better spirits. Captain Hall is returned from Gibraltar and belongs to this squadron.

FRIDAY, JULY 21ST. Captain Miller came on board with 350 of the Theseus' men they are all to land in the night but in order to keep out of sight it was late when the three frigates got in shore and day light by the time the troops were landing, they therefore returned without doing any thing, I was unwell as usual, slept below, had a woman with me the sail-maker's wife.

SATURDAY, JULY 22ND. We anchored in a small bay at a short distance from the town but out of gunshot. The troops landed again this morning and had a most tiresome and fatiguing day, for no good what so ever they went at the top of a high hill the enemy on another of them they stayed till the evening, almost dead with fatigue hunger and thirst, they were obliged to return on board. The Thesus men the most tiresome noisy mutinous people in the world, they annoyed me amazingly, and Fremantle still more, I was quite glad he did not go to day Captain Miller returned very much dissatisfyed of this day's expedition as every body else was. Captain Troubridge that commands the whole was almost dead with fatigue.

SUNDAY, JULY 23RD. The Signal was made to weigh and we went to join the Admiral and line of battle ships that have been cruizing all this while, had they been with us the place would have long been taken, A German that was brought off yesterday says the Spaniards have no force are in the greatest alarm all crying and trembling and that nothing could be easier than to take the place, only 300 men of regular troops, the rest are peasants who are frightened to death, Fremantle went on board the Admiral, to morrow night he is to go himself and land in the Town. It blew very hard all day I was better than I have felt for some time and hope to get soon quite well.

MONDAY, JULY 24TH. I was pretty well today. The Leander joined and the whole Squadron came to an anchor in the evening. The Admiral supped with us, he then went with Fremantle on their expedition. They are all to land in the Town, As the taking of this place seemed an easy and almost sure thing, I went to bed after they were gone apprehending no danger for Fremantle.

TUESDAY, JULY 25TH. The troops landed at two oclock this morning, There was much firing in the Town, but from the ships it seemed as if the English had made themselves masters of it, Great was our mistake, this proved to be a shocking, unfortunate night Fremantle returned at 4 this morning wounded in the arm, he was shot through the right arm the moment he had landed, came off in the first boat, and stayed on board the Zealous till day light, where his wound was dressed. Thank God as the ball only went through the flesh he will not lose his arm he managed it so well that I was not frightened, but I was not a little distressed and miserable when I heard what it was, and indeed he was in great pain and suffered cruelly all day but it was fortunate that he did get wounded at first, God knows if ever I should have seen him again had he stayed on shore, It was dreadful, poor Captain Bowen killed on the spot, The Admiral was wounded as he was getting out of the Boat and most unfortunately lost his arm. The fox Cutter was lost and poor old Gibson drowned Captain Thompson is likewise wounded. All the rest remained on shore very few people returned to the ships in the morning. As they threatened to burn the Town they had their own terms and were sent off in the evening Captains Troubridge, Hood and Miller came on board, they are all safe. They could not stay long as Fremantle was in very great pain at that moment. All our Officers are safe and came on board. Mr Douglas only was shot through the hand, few men of this ship have been killed. All the prisoners are to be sent off. The Spaniards behaved exceedingly well.

This is the most melancholy event, I cant help thinking of poor Captain Bowens losing his life just at the end of a war in which he had been so fortunate. At the moment he was continually talking of the happy life he should lead when he returned home. His first lieutenant was likewise killed.

Fremantle was in great pain all day but I hope he will soon get well.

All the ships were obliged to get under weigh this morning as the Spaniards fired at us and the shot went over us. A shot went through one of our sails, I would not go into the Cockpit tho Fleming asked me twice to go.

WEDNESDAY, JULY 26TH. Fremantle had a very good night's rest he has no fever at all, his wound was dressed at twelve oclock and Fleming says it looks very well, It is a wonder how nothing but the flesh was hurt as two musquet balls went through the arm, about 15 of our men are wounded and two dead we are lucky as the other Frigates lost about 20 men a piece and some of the line of battle ships a hundred. The Admiral is coming on very well, he wrote me a line with his left hand.

THURSDAY, JULY 27TH. Fremantle is doing as well as can be expected, but he is still in great pain and cannot get up. All the people are come on board and the loss not so great as was feared. Hornsey is gone acting Lieutenant in the Terpsichore.

FRIDAY, JULY 28TH. Captain Troubridge and Hood came on board in the morning Fremantle is doing very well, I am still sick of a morning.

Fremantle's wound looks as well as possible, but he is almost always in pain and is very low indeed.

SUNDAY, JULY 30TH. Captain Troubridge came on board. Fremantle was pretty well and in better spirits.

THURSDAY, AUGUST 3RD. Fremantle was in good spirits and very well in the morning but in great pain all day. I am pretty well sick a little generally before breakfast. I am quite anxious to be able to hear from my family and to be able to write to them. Fremantle's only wish now is to get to England. I wish it as eagerly as he does.

FRIDAY, AUGUST 4TH. Captain Troubridge came on board in the morning he was quite angry to find Fremantle so low and weak, The Surgeon of the Zealous came on board they all agree to say that he does not live high enough and abuse Fleming for not giving him Bark and Port wine, he took some in the course of the day and found himself much better. Admiral Nelson will ask to go home in this ship. We are glad of it, but fear to be a long time getting to the fleet. There is no wind at all.

SUNDAY, AUGUST 6TH. Still becalmed. This hot weather very bad for Fremantle. He was not at all well yesterday. I wrote to the Admiral he answered me a long note he is astonishingly well.

MONDAY, AUGUST 7TH. Chased a ship this morning which proved to be the Emerald. A charming fair breeze in the evening. Fremantle not in as good spirits as I should wish, but his arm comes on well.

TUESDAY, AUGUST 8TH. Bark does not agree with Fremantle and his arm is always very painful.

FRIDAY, AUGUST 11TH. Were sent in chase of a Portuguese Brig no news.

SATURDAY, AUGUST 12TH. The ship has so much motion that Fremantle cannot get up, he is very low spirited, his arm very painful but it is coming on as well as possible.

SUNDAY, AUGUST 13TH. Chased again a ship. which was a Genoese. It blew rather fresh and Fremantle could not move out of his Cot. The motion hurts his arm much, and the noise of the guns annoyed us both beyond conception.

TUESDAY, AUGUST 15TH. A fine day, the ship steady and Fremantle was up all the afternoon, he was stouter and better today than I have seen him yet.

WEDNESDAY, AUGUST 16TH. Joined the fleet at three oclock in the afternoon, I was much surprised to see Captain Wells he came with four sails of the line lately. We had all the Captains on board. They were uncommonly attentive and kind, We are going to take Admiral Nelson home, which makes Fremantle and myself exceedingly happy. I received a letter of Mamma and Eugenia of the 13th May. Papa had consented to the marriage but found the gentleman's fortune so trifling that he has persuaded him to put it off for some time and sent him to Dresden. He is in hopes that in his absence he can persuade Eugenia not to think any more about him. Mary Blair is dead and poor Lady Mary more wretched than anything ever was, I shall be glad to see that unfortunate family.

THURSDAY, AUGUST 17TH. Fremantle was much the worse for all his visitors yesterday, he had a bad night and saw but very few people to day. The Earl St Vincent wanted to come on board but on account of Fremantles being so poorly we sent to him to ask him not to come. Fremantle's wound is doing very well, but is so uncommonly painful.

Saturday, August 19th. Lindsay is made Boatswain of this ship. A man was hanged in the fleet this morning, the Boatswain of the Emerald. Fleming has been appointed to that ship as Admiral Nelson takes his surgeon with him. I am glad of it as Fremantle had no great confidence in Fleming. He was better today but poorly in the evening. Foley dined with us.

Sunday, August 20th. Fremantle was very unwell, this morning, he heard that Lord St. Vincent was determined to come on board which made him quite nervous and miserable. However he did not come at last, but Captain Wells, Foley and Martin were with me all the morning and all the others came to take leave of us as the ship got under weigh. Admiral Nelson came on board at twelve oclock, he is quite stout but I find it looks shocking to be without one arm. He is in great spirits. Fremantle was pretty well in the afternoon. Mr Eshelby the surgeon seems a sensible young man, he gave me some pills to take, for I am not well at all, but I dont mind it as it is easy to guess what is the matter with me.

Wednesday, August 23rd. Fremantle's wound is larger than ever, exceedingly painful and does not heal at all. This ship is worse than an hospital, a number of sick and wounded from the Thesus, from morning to night and from night to morning you hear nothing but those unfortunate people groan. If Fremantle could but get rid of the great pain he has in his hand that prevents it from healing.

Thursday, August 24th. A foul wind which makes

the Admiral fret, he is a very bad patient, poor Fremantle is still the same, no sign of the wounds healing up yet.

FRIDAY, AUGUST 25TH. A good deal of rain and almost calm. Therefore we are in great hopes of getting a fair wind. I am anxious to get ashore as I am sure Fremantle will get better much sooner. I am quite distressed to see him so poorly.

SATURDAY, AUGUST 26TH. A fair wind which is the only comfort we have, as Fremantle suffers cruelly and the Admiral is far from being well.

SUNDAY, AUGUST 27TH. Fremantle is no better, his patience is almost exhausted and he is wretched. It makes me miserable to see him so.

FRIDAY, SEPTEMBER 1ST. Had a fair breeze and I was delighted with the pretty Isle of Wight tho the weather was so hazy that we could not have a good view of the country about us. We came to an anchor before dinner. Fremantle better and walked about by himself he was quite stout. The Admiral went on shore immediately after dinner, the weather was so bad that we had not a thought of leaving the ship today.

PORTSMOUTH, SATURDAY, SEPTEMBER 2ND. The weather bad and cold all the morning. Captain Drury came on board he went to look for some lodgings for us and as soon as he had let us know he had found one Fremantle immediately left the ship and we came on shore. He was able to walk to the house and we both were quite delighted with our lodgings. Mr. Leeds an old Messmate of his who was surgeon of the Brunswick brought the surgeon of Hasler hospital (Mr. Fitzmaurice) to see him. They dressed the wound and found nothing alarming in the appearance of it. They are two very clever people and exceedingly obliging and good natured.

CHAPTER 21

SUNDAY, SEPTEMBER 3RD. Fremantle was much better tho his hand continues to be very painful. His brother William's arrival in the afternoon affected his nerves considerably and quite upset him again. He sat up with him till very late in the night as his brother goes to morrow. He is going to be married in a fortnight to a widow, Mrs. Felton Hervey, a woman about three and forty with five children but very rich. He is only thirty and a very good looking young man.

MONDAY, SEPTEMBER 4TH. Fremantle was worse than ever, had a restless miserable night and kept his bed all the day. The surgeons say he must not see anybody, not hear any news and be kept very quiet and continually alone. Mr. Fitzmaurice Leeds and Eshelby dined with me. They are good sort of people and so exceedingly attentive to Fremantle, that nothing can be more so, but I found them highly stupid society at dinner as they talk of nothing but medicine wounds and fevers.

TUESDAY, SEPTEMBER 5TH. Spent the day quite alone with Fremantle who was something better. I received the kindest letter from Lady Mary wishing us very much to go to them.

WEDNESDAY, SEPTEMBER 6TH. Fremantle's eldest brother arrived this morning. We had a letter from his Mother saying she will be here Friday. Fremantle complained much of his hand the wound comes on very well, I like his brother Jack better than William he is not half so formal, and I got much sooner acquainted with him.

THURSDAY, SEPTEMBER 7TH. I walked out this morning with Jack F. and called on Lady Parker who is

I think the most civil kind woman I ever saw. Sir Peter very kind likewise, but the oddest figure in the world and would make a most excellent caricature. They are both very fond of Fremantle, have known him so long and Lady P. was a mother to him in the West Indies.

Friday, September 8th. I walked to the Camp with Jack F. and had the pleasure to see Mrs. Fremantle arrive a little before dinner. It affected Fremantle much at first but he was in great spirits all day. He had some leaches applied to his hand this morning. I like his mother amazingly, she must have been very pretty and does not look at all old.

Sunday, September 10th. It is a determined point now that Fremantle has the gout in his hand. He is much easier since they have persuaded him it is so. I walked out with Mrs. Fremantle and Jack. William F. and Mr. Bishop arrived in the evening, the last is married to Fremantle's youngest sister. He is the ugliest little fat curious man much too old for her. They stayed the evening with us.

Friday and Saturday. Continue in the same way. Fremantle is one moment better and one moment worse. If his hand could but get well, he is coming on so well in every other respect.

Sunday. Mr. Cathcart arrived to day and set F. in a fidget. He is married to F's second sister, uncommonly good humoured and pleasant.

Monday, September 18th. Mr. Cathcart stayed the day with us, he set out in the mail with Jack F. who I am sorry has left us as he is the best natured creature in the world. Fremantle was very ill all day and would not even see his brothers before they went. He was distressed about it afterwards, cryed much, what relieved him and he was better in the evening.

Wednesday. Poor Fremantle had again a bad day.

The wedding has been put off till tomorrow, I should like to be present such a young man to so old a woman.

Friday, September 22nd. Mrs. Fremantle had a letter from Mr. Cathcart describing the wedding. The *happy* pair are gone to Worthing.

Sunday, September 23rd. Received a letter from Eugenia and never felt happier in my life. That dear girl has behaved like an Angel and has given up all thoughts of Ct. Senft seeing her parents were so much averse to the match. I love her still better now than before. Wrote to her. Mr. Hudson called in the morning, he is appointed to another ship.

Monday, September 25th. Fremantle wrote to be superceded, his wound is almost quite healed but the pain in his hand continues as violent as ever and his patience is quite exhausted.

Wednesday, September 27th. Fremantle has determined to go into the country where he will be out of the way of everybody and will not be so much annoyed. His mother is to leave us on Friday and we shall go Saturday.

Thursday, September 28th. Walked out with Mrs. Fremantle and called on Lady Parker who was not at home. Poor Fremantle attempted to take a walk but was in such pain that he was obliged to go into an old man's house and lay down till he was well enough to come home. Mr. Eastman has found us lodgings at Purbrook a village six miles from here on the London Road.

Friday, September 29th. Mrs. Fremantle left this morning after breakfast. I am sorry she is gone as she is a worthy good creature and very kind to me. By the bye she gave me an exceedingly pretty diamond ring. Fitzmaurice dined with us. Captain Foote called in the evening.

SATURDAY, SEPTEMBER 30TH. The weather was bad, we left Portsmouth at two o'clock. Fremantle was in great pain in the carriage but much better when we arrived at our little cottage. He was delighted with the place, the house farm and all pleased him and he walked out all the afternoon, and was better than ever I saw him yet in the evening. Old Mrs. Sharpley seems the most good natured soul in the world. She is to manage everything for us.

MONDAY. Fitzmaurice dined with us and dressed Fremantle's arm for the last time. The wound is quite dry now and wont require another dressing. Fremantle complained rather more of his hand today but he walked as much as usual. He walked in the morning in Mr. Busigny's gardens. He is an ugly Batchelor and has just bought a very pretty house opposite Mr. Sharpley's with very pleasant walks and gardens about it.

TUESDAY, OCTOBER 3RD. I was most agreeably surprised by Mr. Blairs coming this morning. He only stayed ten minutes but promised to come another time. He looks very well, I was delighted to see him and to hear from him that Papa was quite determined to come to England as soon as the road was free. Fremantle's nerves were worse today, Mr. Blairs coming by surprise in this manner hurt him much tho he was much pleased to get acquainted with him.

FRIDAY, OCTOBER 6TH. Fremantle was worse today which was occasioned by his taking no opium in the night, a little laudanum in the afternoon eased his pain immediately. Miss Fortnum a young lady who is here for her health dined with us. Her father keeps a grocers shop in London, she is a well behaved pretty little girl.

SUNDAY. Miss Fortnum dined with us. Sent to Portsmouth yesterday for a Piano Forte and played all the afternoon. F. something better today and Music did not at all hurt his nerves.

WEDNESDAY, OCTOBER 10TH. Poor Fremantle again in great pain, and bad spirits, thinks himself worse instead of better, but I think he is undoubtedly better since he left Portsmouth.

SUNDAY, OCTOBER 14TH. Some more news about the defeat of the Dutch.

MONDAY, OCTOBER 15TH. Had all the particulars about Admiral Duncan's victory. Eleven of the Dutch ships and Admiral de Winter and two other Admirals are taken, but it was a most severe action and the number killed and wounded considerable.

WEDNESDAY, OCTOBER 17TH. Walked to the Commissioners house and found him there. More like a Boatswain than a Gentleman. Mr. Busigny dined with us and Mrs. Turner came in the evening.

THURSDAY, OCTOBER 18TH. We had an illumination in honour of the famous victory.

FRIDAY, OCTOBER 19TH. Hear of nothing but the defeat of the Dutch and of illuminations, etc.

SUNDAY, OCTOBER 21ST. Took a ride in the carriage as far as Porchester Castle where we saw the French prisoners, there are 3000 of them they are industrious and make all kinds of little works. We bought a Guillotine neatly done in bone. Fremantle bore the carriage very well and is determined to leave this next Saturday.

MONDAY, OCTOBER 22ND. Fremantle is getting much better. We spent the day as usual, walking, working and reading, I am never tired or at a loss when we are both together.

THURSDAY, OCTOBER 25TH. I received a letter from *Eugenia* of the 1st of August which made me happier than I can express as she thinks no more of Mr. S.

who it seems was only in love with her money, and behaved extremely ill. Dined at Southwick with Lady Calder, she is a clever pleasant woman but a bore for such a stupe as myself, she talks of nothing but ships and sea service and of the red ribbon that was given to Admiral Nelson, instead of very properly bestowing it on the great Sir Robert, who, however, is to look up to something better now. The dear lady drank half a dozen glasses of wine after dinner, which made her still more talkative than usual. She is an uncommon civil attentive creature. Fremantle tho in more pain to day managed very well.

Friday, October 26th. Very busy packing up and paying everything as we are going to morrow. I received another letter from Naples of the 6th of June. Mamma writes me a long and good letter giving me the most excellent advice. *Eugenia* talks hardly of nothing else but the stupid B. S. François has been sent away, and I am sorry to hear Papa would not give him a character. Justine does everything. Eugenia and Mamma help as well as they can and Pigge for last ressource. Jaegle is rather annoyed.

Saturday, October 27th. Left Purbrook after ten o'clock and Fremantle bore the journey very well. Came as far as Ripley, 42 miles. We left Scott behind F. discharged him for being drunk yesterday. I was monstrously fatigued.

Sunday, October 28th. A horrid bad day, got to town early dressed and went to dine at Mr. Bishops where Jack F. and his wife met us. Mrs. Bishop a pretty little woman I like her better than Mrs. J. F. They are all good humoured and kind. Mrs. B's children are sweet little creatures. The old Grand-mother came in the evening.

Monday, October 29th. Went out in the morning

with Mrs. Bishop and Mrs. J. Fremantle. Saw the plate given by the Leghorn merchants, it is beautiful. Dined at home with old Mrs. Fremantle and Mr. Jack Butter Mrs. Fountain and her daughter, Mrs. B. and F. came in the evening. Miss Fountain sings well enough. Cimador has been her master.

THURSDAY, NOVEMBER 2ND. Went out shopping in the morning and saw the Shakespear Gallery, dined at Mrs. Bishops he must be a mighty tiresome plague of a husband. I admire his wifes patience and good humour very much.

FRIDAY, NOVEMBER 3RD. Went to see the King go to the House. Very grand and amusing enough. Called on Lady Nelson, not at home but saw the good Admiral.

MONDAY, OCTOBER 6TH. Jack Fremantle breakfasted with us and went back to Chelmsford. I went out with his wife and Mrs. Bishop and dined at Mr. Bishops. Mrs. J. F. is going out of town again tomorrow. She is an odd woman. Fremantle saw Ld Spencer who was very civil. He certainly is to have a pension.

FRIDAY, NOVEMBER 10TH. Lord Minto called in the morning. Went to Englefield Green with Mr. Fremantle and his wife. They were very civil. The two Miss Herveys both exceedingly tall, which makes the bride look rather oldish. She is a tall elegant figure talks much and well.

SATURDAY, NOVEMBER 11TH. A fine day, walked on Englefield Green, the country delightful, Mr. Fremantle very loving to his wife who is uncommonly attentive to him.

MONDAY, NOVEMBER 13TH. The Duke of Rutland and Mr. King came to dinner, a good looking young man, Mr. King a horror but very clever.

THURSDAY, NOVEMBER 16TH. Mrs. Bishop dined with

us we went afterwards to the play at Drury Lane. Fremantle went to Surgeon's Hall where he was much annoyed and pulled about by the surgeons, who said however his wound was equal to the loss of a limb. He could not stay with us at the play and went home in great pain. I liked the play well enough, it was '—— a wife and have a wife, The Devil to Pay, and the trip to the Nore.' The two Miss Cottons were of our party.

SATURDAY. Went out shopping the whole morning and dined at the Bishops. Fremantle is to receive a years full pay as a gratuity he has sent a memorial to the King for a pension.

SUNDAY, NOVEMBER 19TH. Could not get away till near twelve o'clock. It snowed very hard we found the roads so exceedingly bad that we could not get on at all and as it was quite dark when we arrived at Dunstable, we determined not to go any farther.

MONDAY. We got to Linfold by three o'clock, Fremantle's mother was glad to see us at last.

THURSDAY, NOVEMBER 30TH. Fremantle received a letter from Mr. Gascoigne saying his petition was complied with and that he should have £200 a year in addition to his half pay.

FRIDAY, DECEMBER 1ST. It rained and thawed fast this weather agrees better with F. than the frost, we shall leave Lady Cave tomorrow to go to Stowe. She is a worthy, respectable woman, and is uncommonly kind to us. Mrs. Fremantle likewise said many kind and affectionate things to me, about her attending me in March when I shall be brought to bed. I wrote to Mamma, I am distressed I don't hear from them.

DECEMBER 2ND, STOWE. We got to Stowe by three o'clock. A most magnificent place. Lord and Lady Buckingham, exceedingly civil, Lord George and

Lady Mary nice and clever children. Mr. Finche arrived whilst we were at dinner.

DECEMBER 3RD. Nothing can be more attentive and civil than Lady B. is to me. She had the most pleasing and engaging manners. She was good enough to take me all over the house and walked with me in the gardens. There are some most beautiful paintings, several of her own doing, likewise that are very fine. We called on a Mrs. Dardies that lives in a small cottage in the garden. A Catholic, she is uncommonly big with child.

FRIDAY, DECEMBER 8TH. Mr. Bernard draws remarkably well. We had a drawing party in the morning, the weather being too bad to walk. Miss Macnamara and Abbé Martin arrived today. She is a Catholic and a great favourite.

SUNDAY, DECEMBER 10TH. Had Mass in Miss Macnamara's room where there is a nice little chapel fitted up. Lady B. does not show herself but is present. Lady Louisa continues to be uncommonly kind and attentive to me. She is the most unaffected and pleasing woman I ever saw.

SATURDAY, DECEMBER 16TH. I go to Mass almost every morning in Miss Macnamaras room. Mr. Martin is a charming old man, quite a saint.

SUNDAY, DECEMBER 17TH. Fremantle is much better and Lady B. says we must stay until he is quite recovered.

MONDAY, DECEMBER 18TH. I have a very bad cold and am quite stupid. Mrs. W. F. is to be here the 16th. L. B. is delighted with the idea of My *Younger* sisters coming, it is the standing joke. (Betsey was still only 19.)

SUNDAY, DECEMBER 24TH. Sir Watkin W. Wynne is here, an awkward, rather stupid gentleman. Had Mass at Midnight in Miss Macnamara's room.

MONDAY, DECEMBER 25TH. Christmas Day. Near 300 poor people dined in the house. I confessed to Abbé Martin. Was very tired and unwell in the evening.

SATURDAY, DECEMBER 30TH. Lord George's birthday. He gave a supper to 60 poor children that can read, as no others are admitted to the feast. It was a pretty sight, he sat at the bottom of the table, his sister at the head, and gave them a shilling a piece before they went away.

TUESDAY, JANUARY 9TH. BOLTON ROW. Left Aylesbury and got to town in very good time. I was delighted with our house it is nearly finished and furnished with much taste and neatness. I walked to Russell Place, unfortunately Mr. and Mrs. Bishop did not dine at home, we got some dinner however and went afterwards to call on the Fountains. Fremantle went to Mrs. Prestons and walked with his sister Marianne to our house. She looks very big and is quite distressed at being again with child.

THURSDAY, FEBRUARY 8TH. Was out all the morning with Mrs. Wells, dined with Mr. Bishop and went to the play at Drury Lane to see Hamlet and Blue Beard. We had an exceedingly bad Box up one pair of stairs, nothing but fine *Damsels* about us, which I found not a little annoying. Blue Beard is vastly pretty but it was interrupted in the most interesting part by a great noise and cry of fire. All the ladies fainted away and were greatly alarmed. I was not much frightened. It proved to be nothing but a boxing match. Our Beaux chose to leave us alone in one of the Lobby boxes whilst they went to look for the carriages. Two drunken young men came in and were exceedingly impudent taking us for other sort of women. I was very much alarmed but we got however rid of them.

THURSDAY, MARCH 1ST. I went to the Chapel in Soho

Square to confess. Fremantle went to the drawing room with Lady Minto. Dined at home alone. Cimador, Dragonetti and Mr. Heck came in the evening. Had much music. Mr. Preston Mrs. Wells and Mrs. Bishop came likewise.

FRIDAY, MARCH 9TH. Dined at Mrs. W. Fremantle's to meet Lady Cave. These ladies say I shall very soon be brought to bed, I am exceedingly well, had the monthly nurse in the house.

SUNDAY, MARCH 11TH. I woke in great pain this morning, continued poorly all day, but minded it as little as possible. To my no small happiness and everybody's surprise I was brought to bed by seven oclock in the evening of a boy, before Dr. Savage had time to come, the nurse delivered me. A small child but a sweet boy.

Betsey's infant was, from the first, a model child, and Betsey herself recovered with quite amazing rapidity. Two days after its birth she writes:

TUESDAY, 13TH MARCH. 'I am doing extremely well, so is the child, who was *half* baptized this morning by Mr. Cathcart, and is called Thomas Francis. I got up to have my bed made this afternoon.' And on the following day she records:

WEDNESDAY, 14TH. 'My little boy begins to suck very nicely and I am not at all troubled with my milk, he is a charming child and never cries. Got up for half an hour in the afternoon. Our house was broken open last night. John heard the noise and called the watchman: I fortunately heard nothing of it.'

On the 15th there is 'comfortable news from Naples': Papa has at last 'determined to come over to us very soon, and we are to take a house for him'. By the 18th she is up all day, but finds it 'very tiresome to be so much alone, and the nurse's gossip a great bore'. On the 22nd she received a crib which 'little Lord George' (Temple-Grenville) had made for 'my child' fitted up by Lady Buckingham. On the 23rd she was well enough to amuse herself a little with her pianoforte, and on Sunday 24th, there is the triumphant entry: 'I dined with F, in his little parlour. I am getting stout quite fast and my little boy improving every day.'

She went out for the first time and was churched on the 31st of March, and from April 1st there is the regular note: 'went our airing with the Baby.' There is a charming comment on the 6th: 'called on Mrs. Bankes who, tho' civil to me, treats me I think rather too much like a child. I gave Eliza warning—she is a giddy impudent thing.' (Betsey was not yet twenty.)

Gradually news of her family's journeyings reach her: Papa writes from Leghorn, and later she gets a letter from Eugenia from Padua, and later still from Munich. Meanwhile the new Mrs. W. Fremantle gives great offence by not asking any of the family except Betsey (who has the prudence to refuse) to her 'rout', and at Lady Ongley's rout, which she found a great bore, the prudish Betsey comments: 'The fashion now is to be almost naked, even old women show all their necks and back.' The Turkish Ambassador provides 'Otto of Roses' on the 11th of March and says English-women are pretty, but *don't dress half enough.* And so the London season goes on, and Betsey frequently attends the Opera, which she much enjoys, though nothing 'can be more tiresome than getting away from it. There is always an amazing crowd, the *fashion* being to go and be squeezed, almost to death, in a very small room. I could not get the carriage until one o'clock tho' the opera was over very early.'

At last, after many disappointed expectations, on May 24th Betsey writes: 'At four o'clock I was agreeably surprised by my family's arrival. I was delighted to see Mama look so well. The children are much grown. Papa I thought is very much altered and is uncommonly thin. Jaegle remained at Hamburgh they would not have known what to do with him in England. My sisters are really very nice girls: Eugenia sings better than anybody I ever heard that does not sing on the stage, Justina and Harriet likewise very prettily.'

[*Eugenia's Diary*]

THE 30TH MAY. Mama set off this morning with Papa and Fremantle to go and make the choice of a country house, and I left ours of Curzon Street and went to my sisters where I slept.

31ST MAY. *Chaperoned* by my sister and Fremantle I went to a ball at Mrs St. George's (one of their acquaintance's, who very civilly asked me no sooner had she heard that I was returned from abroad) I found the fête or Rout, very brilliant and pleasant. I danced all the time I was there (thanks to those that got me partners) but own I did it very awkwardly, for I found the style of dancing quite different from what it is abroad. In truth, I find myself here as if in a new world obliged to alter everything, my behaviour, my dress, my manners, all is out of fashion—and my figure into the bargain. I think I must appear perfectly ridiculous.

CHAPTER 22

[*Betsey's Journal*]

ASTON ABBOTS, 10TH JUNE, 1798. SUNDAY. I left Bolton Row at nine o'clock and travelled in the *coach* with our own horses, the children, the baby, the nurse and all the lumber. I dined at Berkhampstead. I sent for Charly and Robert Bishop and Johnny Fremantle—these three boys made such a noise I could not keep them in order and they got tipsey.

The road from Aylesbury to Ashton is very bad—I arrived in good time—and I think it a nice comfortable house—I was rather tired.

30TH JULY. MONDAY. We all went to see the house Fremantle wishes to buy, it is two miles from Winslow, about two miles from the turnpike road in the village of Swanburn, very agreeably situated on a hill, it is a very nice place which would suit us on all accounts. It is to be sold for 1,000 guineas but we are endeavouring to get it for less—it is very cheap even at that price. Mamma was very ill indeed.

2ND AUGUST. THURSDAY. Mr. Cathcart called in the morning—Fremantle returned to dinner—Master Fincher came in the evening with *the answer* about Swanburn—which we are to buy for 900 guineas—it is worth £1,200.

6TH AUGUST. MONDAY. Went with Mamma to our *Estate*. The more I see the place the more I like it and find it a good bargain—as there is three little fields with the house and a good kitchen garden.

5TH SEPTEMBER, WEDNESDAY. Eugenia, Fremantle, Capt. Hutchinson and myself called on Mrs. de Salis at about twelve o'clock to go with us to Great Brickwell. It was a great disappointment to everybody that the day was showery as it would have been a most charming sight, but the rain prevented our seeing the yeomanry making the sword exercises etc.—. We dined under tents and had a charming ball and most elegant suppers—. Nearly all the County was there. We danced 24 couples till past four o'clock in the morning—I was well entertained but much fatigued.

13TH SEPTEMBER THURSDAY. We all went to see the great meeting of the yeomanry in Berryfields, it was a most charming sight, unfortunately it rained all the time. We were all quite delighted to hear that General Lake had defeated the French who had all surrendered—not an officer killed or wounded. Mr. Praed was obliged to give his dinner to the yeomanry at the Swan at Newport as the tents were blown down the day before yesterday.

LINSLADE, 18TH OCTOBER. THURSDAY. Fremantle drove Mrs. John F. over to Swanburn, but coming from Aston by himself the horse fell down at Wing, cut one of his knees and broke the gig all to pieces—he did not hurt himself in the least, but was much mortified, especially as it unfortunately happened to be one of Papa's horses.

19TH OCTOBER. FRIDAY. Fremantle is quite out of humour about his accident yesterday, he has taken to turning again and is all day in his shop—but it hurts his hand much.

BATH. [They all go to Bath, for poor Papa to take the waters. But their efforts are in vain.]

26TH OCTOBER. FRIDAY. Papa gets weaker and weaker every day—he keeps nothing on his stomach and as the Doctor says that neither the waters nor any medicinal assistance can be of any service to him, he wishes that we may endeavour to persuade him to go home—but we fear to frighten him by that, and must therefore do it with great management. Blair is obliged to go back to the Downhouse to-morrow, but he has promised to return here on Tuesday that he may help us to get poor Papa away from here on Wednesday and will go to Linslade with us—. Papa continues to be in good spirits, it seems as if he did not wish that we should know he is ill—indeed I do not believe he knows it at all himself. He was out in the carriage with us in the morning and sat up till the evening, but he was about teatime taken exceedingly sick and that he regularly is every day.

31st October Wednesday. Nothing that I can say can paint my horrid feelings on this wretched day—poor Papa seemed to be out of his mind in the morning and did not know us. We sent an express to Mama. Blair and Miss Fane arrived, just in time to be witness of a scene of misery, of which I cannot speak—and shall only say that our unfortunate father seemed in a sound sleep all day—but never waked again—and at twelve at night Fremantle who was as much afflicted and distressed as ourselves, told us we had nothing to do but pack up our things and go away.

Thame 1st November Thursday. At daylight Eugenia and myself left Bath, overwhelmed with affliction which was doubly felt on our meeting poor Mama and the children (only four and twenty miles from Bath)— This meeting was heartbreaking and dreadful, poor Mama is truly in despair, as she wished to get home as soon as possible we made the best of our way, but finding no horses at Thame, stayed there the night.

Linslade 3rd November Saturday. My dearest little boy is the greatest comfort to us, poor little innocent creature he is perfectly ignorant of all the misery of this world, and can only laugh and smile at everybody—he is much improved and is my delight.

4TH NOVEMBER SUNDAY. Mama continues much in the same state, very poorly and low. We had a letter from Fremantle, this *morning* the ceremony of interment was to take place—it was a new cause of grief—. F. will be here on Tuesday morning. [Mr. Wynne was buried in Bath Abbey where there is a plaque to him in the porch. Poor Fremantle was very disappointed, on his wife's account, at the sad state of his late father-in-law's finances. In lovely copper plate hand, the lawyers' letters were most melancholy: all the four daughters got was £23,000 equally divided amongst them.]

BOLTON ROW, 2ND APRIL, 1799. TUESDAY. Poor F. had a very severe fit of the ague today and obliged to send for Bagot and go to bed. As he had got a box at the opera for us, I went with Mrs. Bishop and J. Fremantle. Banti could not sing as she was *brought to bed* in the middle of the day—the comic opera ill sung and tiresome—the new Ballet Tagliore excessively pretty.

12TH APRIL. FRIDAY. Was very busy packing up.[1] Dined at Mrs. Bishop, a large party, Lady Mansfield, Col. Greville, Mr. Greville, Mr. and Mrs. W. Fremantle, Miss Hervey, etc., etc. Went in the evening to hear the musical child at Admiral Young's—it is a little boy not four years old that plays very tolerably upon the pianoforte—I played and heard some singing. The three Nivettes were there and sing exceedingly well together.

SWANBURN, 5TH MAY. SUNDAY. The road so heavy I was obliged to have four horses. F. met me at Aston

[1] To go to Swanbourne.

where I stayed an hour. Got to Swanburn by four o'clock, the house much improved since I saw it and the paint smells very little.

16TH MAY. THURSDAY. I walk about a great deal—it is astonishing the number of old people there is in this village.

21ST MAY. TUESDAY. Fremantle was sent for on account of a riot having taken place at Dreyton occasioned by the people of the canal. Twenty-six of them were taken and are to be sent to Aylesbury jail tomorrow. Our magistrate was delighted in having this opportunity of showing his *great skill*—Burne's Justice is never out of his hands.

My new nurse came.

13TH JUNE. THURSDAY. I was surprised and frightened at being taken ill in the middle of the night as I did not expect to be brought to bed till the end of the month and my nurse was not to come till the twentieth—I called up the women at four o'clock in the morning and sent immediately for Dr. Tooky—it was all over at a little after six—the *Cook* was *head nurse* and dressed the child—it is a nice little girl but owing to her being born three weeks before her time is very delicate and small.

11TH SEPTEMBER WEDNESDAY. Fremantle for the first time in his life shot a bird, but could not show his prize as he lost it in the corn.

19TH OCTOBER SATURDAY. Received very distressing accounts from Eugenia, poor Mama is almost quite out of her mind. She is obliged to take 120 drops of Laudanum a day, and this convulses her in a shocking manner and at times deprives her of her senses. Eugenia is so terrified that she never dares to sit alone with her. Fremantle dined at Aylesbury.

UPPER BAKER ST. 12TH NOVEMBER TUESDAY. Our unfortunate mother's sufferings were put an end to this morning, she expired at seven o'clock. Eugenia was called to her but she could not speak one word and died in her arms. We left the house almost immediately and removed to a lodging only three doors from it. It is a great comfort to us all that we came to town. Though it is shocking to be present at this scene of distress. Still I feel much less the shock of having been near her than if I had been away, as I should always have feared that she might have wished to see me in her last moments.

22ND NOVEMBER. FRIDAY. Eugenia will continue in her house in Baker Street, Bankes approves of it, but does not seem inclined to her taking a governess for the girls which I think very necessary. They will return to town the 16th.

24TH NOVEMBER. SUNDAY. Paid Justina a cruel trick, in writing a letter to her acquainting her her ticket in the lottery is come out as a prize of £10,000—she is taken in like a goose.

11TH DECEMBER. WEDNESDAY. Discharged the cook who has been cross and sulky of late and seemed to do all in her power to provoke us.

[For Christmas they go over to Stowe, to the Buckinghams.]

STOWE, 17TH DECEMBER. I got safe to Stowe tho' I did not think I would, as it has snowed incessantly since yesterday morning. It was Lady Buckingham's birthday. Lord and Lady B. were exceedingly kind to me and insisted on having Tommy down to coffee. We were more than thirty to dinner and after we went to see the dance and supper that is given to all the neighbouring farmers—the Ladies danced with them till 10 o'clock.

18TH DECEMBER. Three hundred poor people dined here today on the remains of last night's supper. Everything goes on at Stowe exactly as it did two years ago Lord George and Lady Mary are grown monstrously large and shockingly fat. Tommy is taken a great deal of notice of and much admired.

21ST DECEMBER. There is mass every day as three priests are now in the house. Mr. Glover, Lord George's tutor, is an unpleasant man. Lord Buckingham, who is all kindness and attention to me makes me play every evening on the harpsichord tho' he does not understand music he is very fond of it—at least pretends to be.

24TH DECEMBER. I drew all the morning. Had mass at midnight in Miss Macnamara's room where we have a most complete chapel.

30TH DECEMBER. Today was Lord George's birthday. He gave a supper to the poor children and a shilling apiece; there was 80 of them, the servants danced.

12TH MAY, 1800. SUNDAY. Payed as many visits as I could. Found Ly. Shaftesbury at home who was very civil. Dined with Fremantle at Eugenia's—poor Justine & Harriot cryed when we went. I did not like to take leave of them poor little things, I hate the thoughts of their being sent to Chelmsford.

SWANBOURNE 13TH MAY. MONDAY. It was past eleven before we could get away, what with Nurses Children & lumber. I thought we should never be ready. Tommy behaved very well in our post chaise all the way. Emma was with the women in a hack Chaise. Dined at Berkhamstead & got home by seven o'clock. The house is very clean & nice but feels cold.

31ST. SATURDAY. Fremantle was to have dined at Aston but as I did not feel very well he stayed with me. I walked a little after dinner but as I felt worse & worse I was not sorry to see Nurse Emy arrive at about nine o'clock, she just came in time for I was soon obliged to send for Mr Tookey, and I was delivered of a nice boy.

JUNE 1800. 5TH, 6TH, 7TH. THURSDAY, FRIDAY, SATURDAY. Fremantle has been dining out every day, & I spend my time extremely stupid in my bed, the Nurse is a dreadful bore, I only got up to tea on Saturday. I am however as well as possible & the baby thrives nicely.

14TH. MONDAY. Mrs John Fremantle, Mrs Philimore & Ann Ongley dined with us & several Gentlemen. The Miss Lowndes & Miss Bennet came to Tea & to see our sports. Fremantle chose a delightful spot for the running. Few girls ran for the Smock as they pretended to be shy—the Ass & Poney race & men trying to catch a hen with their teeth was the most amusing part of the whole. The sight was really pretty as there were a very great number of people & the situation of the ground was delightful.

29TH JULY. TUESDAY. Fremantle has a number of workmen at present employed & was amused in seeing an old Barn move about 30 yards on rolers—at the other end of the yard opposite—nothing in it broke.

1ST AUG^st.^ FRIDAY. My dear little baby grows exceedingly, he is almost as big as Emma & I think him a pretty child but Fremantle calls him an ugly dog.

21ST. THURSDAY. I was much distressed at Fremantle receiving a letter from the Admiralty to day appointing him to the Command of the *Ganges* a seventy four at Portsmouth—he is to go early Sunday morning. I feel quite miserable at his going from me but still cannot help being flattered that he has so good a ship. It threw us in great confusion & misery. I wrote to Eugenia & asked for the girls to come to me for I should be sorry that she should leave Dorsetshire so soon, I fear however Mr Bankes will not like them to come away from Newhall yet, as they have been there but so short a time.

23RD AUGUST. SATURDAY. Such miserable cold weather that we had fires yesterday and to-day. Mr. Howard and Mr. James Lord dined with us. I need not say I never felt so unhappy during all my life as I did this evening.

24TH AUGUST. SUNDAY. Fremantle went early with Hutchinson this morning, I feel quite at a loss and wretched alone—poor little Tom distressed me many a time in the course of the day enquiring when his Papa would come home again. I kept Mr. Maudonit to dinner. It rained incessantly and the weather quite dismal.

25TH AUGUST. MONDAY. The weather was so wet and bad that I could not stir out of doors which made it still more dismal for me. I employed myself in different ways and spent the day better than I expected.

26TH AUGUST. TUESDAY. Heard from Fremantle who seems much pleased with his appointment as the *Ganges* is reckoned as good a ship as any that sails. Mrs. and two Miss Heslops called and asked me to spend a few days at Adstock.

[Fremantle wrote personally to his patron:]

Capt. T. F. Fremantle to the Marquis of Buckingham.

Ganges, Portsmouth.
30th August, 1800.

My ship is to be quite perfect I am told. I have every reason to be perfectly satisfied with her and my appointment, as both Lord Northester and Lumsden were making applications for her, I hear. My officers are all appointed and I have not a single person of any description that I ever sailed with before. We are getting on very fast and preference is given to ships of the line. I keep very steady to business and if it was necessary, could be ready in a very short time. Nothing can be more gratifying to me than the accounts I hear of the state and discipline of the fleet. I feel as much confidence, and there seems as much respect and obedience in every ship here as at any period of my service. It is said there are three or perhaps four ships in the Channel fleet that are not so well regulated as they ought to be but I think a short time will see an end of them. I have had the good fortune to get four tolerable midshipmen and a coxwain from Wallace, out of the *Brunswick*. My lower masts are rigged and we stow our ground tier on Monday. *Ville de Paris* goes to Spithead on Monday. She is in high repute as to discipline, fitting, etc. I don't think they have lost three men since she has been in the harbour. The *Triumph* is in dock but will be out next week. I dined with Captain and Lady Louisa Hervey yesterday. The ship is so well manned and so established that a few days after will equip him for Spithead. Our Commander-in-Chief here is a perfect imbecile; he never gives an order and seldom admits anybody into his house. Before I left Swanbourne I endeavoured to get some boys from thence, Winslow and Mursley, to go with me to Portsmouth, and though I talked to the overseers of the parishes, and the boys themselves, particularly two from Winslow, who came to me for relief, the sons of a man of the name (I believe) of Higgins, whom you discharged, at my request from the militia; still I could not persuade any one of them to go, nor did any one of the overseers dare to urge them on the subject. I can only say that I should most willingly receive any lads from Buckinghamshire who are, in my opinion, preferable to the wicked vagabonds that are to be picked up at Portsmouth. By way of inducement to the boys to go, I consented to take the son of a farmer at Swanbourne, whose name is Hutchings.

29TH SEPTEMBER. MONDAY. Set out with Miss Maria Heslop after seven o'clock for Buckingham and called in my way on the Miss Lowndes who much against their inclination stay at home, as their brothers Richard and Thomas refused going. Mr. Rogert was of a different opinion, and *blamed* by every one for going. Miss Hannar who was to have gone with Miss Lowndes, accompanied me. She looked very handsome but *has bad manners*. The ball turned out better than I expected but I found it rather stupid as I could not dance being a nurse —the supper was tolerable, but the Gentlemen would pay for it, which was unpleasant for those that went without a *beau*. Mrs. Pigot was there, I dislike her manners, she tyed her garter in *public* and told her partner what she was about. It was five o'clock when I got home and just daylight. Charles had been good.

CHAPTER 23

[The anger of the 'neutrals' in the war now raging (1801) between England and France was roused by the English Navy's insisting on the right of search, and also partly by the Emperor Paul's mad yearning for Napoleon's friendship. The second Northern Confederacy meant three navies for England to contend with, and Sir Hyde Parker was sent to the Baltic to break up the new combination of Russians, Swedes and Danes. But he was old and jittery, and could not make up his mind how to attack. There were two ways: through the Sound, or round by the Great Belt. The Sound was the more direct way, but it was fortified. At the council of war, Nelson, who was Parker's fiery second-in-command, said 'Let it be by the Belt, by the Sound or anyhow, only lose not an hour.' Later, he wrote to the admiral 'The more I have reflected, the more I am confirmed in my opinion that not a moment should be lost in attacking the enemy. They will every day and hour be stronger, we never shall be so good a match for them as at this moment.' For the Swedes were busy fortifying the Sound, and it was vital to attack before their preparations were completed. The Admiral changed his mind several times, until Nelson became almost frantic and very rude, but at last on March 26th the order was given to prepare for battle. The forts at Cronenburg were supposed to give the Danes the uncontrolled command of the passage of the Sound, but actually, as the British fleet passed, the Swedish forts remained silent: to the general surprise not a shot came from them, they were incomplete and had only a few guns mounted. The Danish batteries opposite blared away, but the British fleet, by keeping well over to the Swedish side of the channel were able to make their way past, quite unharmed. The last ships were off Copenhagen by noon on the 30th. During the night Nelson, Riou, Hardy, and a few others marked the way out by buoys. The story of the battle has been told many times, and Fremantle's account adds little to that of Colonel Stewart or Midshipman Millard. But it insists, as all the others did, on Nelson's personal part in the victory. And the battle, together with the murder of the mad Emperor Paul, which so immediately preceded it, successfully broke up the Northern Confederacy.]

SWANBOURNE, 23RD JANUARY. FRIDAY. It snowed and the weather has got quite sharp and cold. Mr. Selby walked here with Mr. Harman—the old gentleman has given me 50 Beech trees. He had a fit of gallantry this morning.

26TH JANUARY. MONDAY. I had a letter from Sr. Thos. Troubridge who knowing it was Fremantle's intention to send for me to the neighbourhood of Torbay, writes to inform me some regulations had been put in force since he sailed which induced him to request I would not go until I heard from him again. I fear it will prevent my journey to Torbay, and since this coalition of the Northern powers, I am afraid I have no chance of seeing Fremantle for a length of time.

SWANBOURNE. 6TH FEBRUARY. FRIDAY. I was dreadfully alarmed in receiving a packet of letters sent express from Aylesbury, and indeed the contents distressed me more than I can express. Lord Temple wrote to say they had just received a letter from Mr. Grosvenor, who says he had no more hopes for poor John Fremantle, and he had every reason to suppose the mortification had extended to the bowels. Capt. Brown likewise wrote the melancholy news and enclosed a letter from Oxford that gave him the same hopeless account. Expresses had been sent to William Fremantle and Lord Ongley who passed with his brother through Aylesbury yesterday.

SWANBOURNE, 18TH FEBRUARY. WEDNESDAY. Walked in the village—much distress and misery. Lent begins today—fasted for the first time.

22ND FEBRUARY. SUNDAY. Mr. Maudonit came before breakfast as I confessed. The weather was charming. I was much distressed to hear from Ld. Buckingham that the *Ganges* was ordered to join the Baltic Squadron and is coming into Portsmouth immediately with some other ships from the Channel Fleet. But their stay will be so short that I do not think it is worth while for me to go to meet Fremantle.

OXFORD, 2ND MARCH. MONDAY. I had a letter from Portsmouth—poor Fremantle is worried to death, as he is to sail again in two or three days. He has been obliged to take 80 men of the 49th Regiment on board and they are going on some grand expedition.

OXFORD, 3RD MARCH. TUESDAY. The weather is delightfully mild and we walked all the morning with Mrs. Fremantle and Mr. Phillimore. Saw most of the colleges—some of the buildings are very fine. Called on Mrs. Cleaver and met her walking with her three little girls; they are as hideous as herself. Col. Fremantle looked much better to-day, he was rather overcome at seeing us yesterday. I had a letter from my husband today. Portsmouth is all bustle and confusion, they are to sail today for the Downs. Lady Nelson is sueing for a separate maintenance. I have no patience with her husband, at his age and such a cripple to play the fool with Lady Hammilton.

SWANBOURNE, 27TH AND 28TH. FRIDAY, SATURDAY. I am

in daily expectation of a letter from Fremantle and feel quite anxious and miserable to know how they have succeeded in their expedition. Eugenia wrote me an account of poor Mde. de Bombelles' death, who died the 27th September, about a fortnight after she had lain in of her eighth child. Her husband was absent at the army of Condé and her resignation was equal to a Saint's—poor soul, she is a great loss to her family, and I feel for her poor little Caroline, who is to be put in a convent at Vienna and the Queen of Naples will pay her pension there.

SWANBOURNE, APRIL 1801. 3RD AND 4TH. FRIDAY, SATURDAY. Since the weather has been so much milder I have dined earlier and walked out before Tea; visited all the poor in the village, some are truly starving and look the picture of death. Tom walks with me and grows a dear little sensible boy.

APRIL 16TH. THURSDAY. Tom and Emma are exceedingly riotous with their Aunts. This morning's post brought me most delightful news from off Copenhagen, where the English have gained a complete victory. It seems to have been a most dreadful engagement on the 2nd inst., but thank God Fremantle is safe. Two Captains were killed and 1,000 men (including the wounded)—17 of the Danish ships have been taken or destroyed out of 18. The *Ganges* was stationed next to Lord Nelson's ship, the *Elephant*.

SWANBOURNE, 17TH APRIL. FRIDAY. I received today the plan of action which Fremantle sent me. He writes a most satisfactory account—and Lord Nelson had been on shore with the Crown Prince. It is hoped an armistice will be concluded—and as Emperor Paul is in reality dead I hope there will be no more fighting in the Baltic. I am quite delighted since the news of this grand victory and hope it will not be long before I see Fremantle again:

Ganges, off Copenhagen.
4th April.

My Dearest Betsey,

I send you for the information of your County acquaintance a plan of our mode of attack with the orders given by Nelson; he has conducted himself towards me with the same kindness he ever did, and made the *Ganges* his second in the action. We anchored where we were directed and Lord Nelson himself hailed me when to let go my anchor. We have been more fortunate than any ship that was so long in action and I can account for it in no other way than by saying that the vessels we were opposed to did not hold us much more than ¾ of an hour. The 2 ships immediately ahead of us, the *Monarch* and *Defiance* were exposed to the Crown batteries, which made dreadful slaughter on board those ships, but the most remarkable part of the whole business is that one man only, the Pilot, should be wounded, before we anchored. The Master was killed and the Pilot lost his arm, so that I was obliged to con the Ship myself. Our Masts and Rigging are very much cutt indeed, but I am in hopes to keep them together with the assistance of some good fishes which the Carpenters are putting up. Every merit is due to Lord Nelson for his policy as well as bravery on this occasion; as soon as the ships abreast of the *Elephant* and *Ganges* had struck he hailed and desired I would come on board. I found him talking with some Danes in his Cabin, and telling them how he longed to see the Russians down; at the same time he was sending an officer with a flag of truce on shore to tell the Prince that if he did not cease firing from the batteries he should be under the necessity of burning all the ships with the people in them. This produced a cessation to the very severe battle, which was certainly as convenient for *us* and the Enemy, as we had several ships on shore and most of the Ships engaged so completely crippled that it was with difficulty they could sail out.

Lord Nelson has been on shore with the Prince; he was received by the Multitude with Cheers and *Viva* Nelson; on his going to the Palace they were more loud in their applause, so much so that the *Government* did not seem well pleased with it; he embarked in the same way and is the life and soul of the Squadron. The Signal is made for letters. I am well and am busy as a man can well be. I have daily every reason to be more satisfied with my Ship and Ship's company, and I do not think there is a probability of the *Ganges* returning to England until we have settled with this Northern confederacy. God bless you and the children. I write another letter for *yourself* by this conveyance.

Ever yours most affly.,
THOS. FRAS. FREMANTLE.

Addressed:
Mrs. Thomas Fremantle.

[In the same packet was another letter for Lord Buckingham.]

CAPTAIN THOMAS FREMANTLE TO THE MARQUIS OF BUCKINGHAM

Ganges, off Copenhagen, April 4.

My Lord,

For our action, I shall refer you to Lord Nelson's letter, which, in confidence, he *dictated to me* on board the *St. George* while I wrote it; but to make the business more clear, I inclose a draft of the situation of the Danish ships and ours as opposed to them. The fatigue of firing so long was great, but our unexampled good fortune in the *Ganges* is surprising. I felt much flattered at being appointed second to Lord Nelson, as well as to the Commander-in-chief. We followed the *Elephant*, and I dropt my anchor in the spot Lord Nelson desired me from the gangway of the *Elephant*. In passing the line, my master was killed, and my pilot had his arm shot off, so that I was obliged to carry the ship in myself, and I had full employment on my hands. The *Monarch* and *Defiance* are dreadfully cut up, as they were exposed to the Crown batteries; the *Bellona* got on shore on both sides the channel, and, notwithstanding all that may be said, never could fire a shot with effect. They, however, did fire, and her loss of men was principally occasioned by the bursting of two guns on the lower deck, which hurt the ship much. I visited Sir Thomas Thompson with Lord Nelson this morning, and he is doing as well as can be expected. The *Russel* got on shore and could do nothing; *Agamemnon* totally *hors de combat*; so that we were but nine sail of two-decked ships. I consider all this business as Nelson's, to whose ability and address we are certainly indebted for a conquest instead of a defeat.

The first mode of attack, I was attached to the command of the flat boats, but when I found a larger force was to go against the batteries, I begged Sir Hyde to allow the *Ganges* to go. After getting by the middle ground I dined with him; and at night with Riou, he planned the attack, a copy of which I received at eight next morning. At nine we weighed, and at ten we began. When the ships abreast of the *Elephant* and *Ganges* were completely silenced, Lord Nelson desired me to go to him. He was in his cabin talking to some Danish officers out of one of the ships captured, and saying how anxious he was to meet the Russians, and wished it had been them, instead of Danes we had engaged, &c., &c. At this time, he put into my hand a letter, which he meant to send immediately to the Prince in a flag of truce, threatening to burn every ship captured if the batteries did not cease firing. At this time he was aware that our ships were cut to pieces, and it would be difficult to get them out. We cut our cables and ran out. The ships were so crippled, they would not steer. The *Elephant* and *Defiance* both ran on shore. We ran on shore, and the *Monarch*; and at this period when the batteries had not ceased firing, we counted no less than six sail of the line, and the *Désirée* fast on shore. Luckily we had to contend with an enemy much beaten, and who did not take advantage of our situation; otherwise all those ships must have been lost. They are not all off, with great exertion, but as you may imagine, what a state a ship must be in, with so many wounded people on board, and so much crippled. We are all fitting as if we were at Spithead, though within five miles of Copenhagen. The carnage on board the Danish vessels taken exceeds anything I ever heard of; the *Ça Ira* or Nile ships are not to be compared to the massacre on board them. The people generally were carpenters, labourers and some Norwegian seamen. Luckily we have been enabled to keep our flag of truce up until now that I am writing, which is of great advantage to us. The Danes are between two fires, and the difficulty is great for them to decide on. There are not 5000 troops in Copenhagen, but I have no idea they can submit to the terms proposed to them. I have recommended stopping up the Sound with these hulks, and having no passage but through the Belt, in which case, a small force will defend that pass; and the Russians have not seamanship enough to get through such an intricate passage.

Our masts and rigging are cut to pieces, but I think in a few days I shall be as effective as the day I left Yarmouth. The *Monarch* is so bad, she must be sent home; one gun burst on board her, and another in the *Isis*. The frigates behaved most gallantly; poor Riou had just cut his cable, and was going off when he was killed. I was much pleased at Lord Nelson's manner on board the *Elephant*, after we ceased firing; he thanked me before everybody on the quarter-deck, for the support I had given him, &c. I have to attribute our good fortune in losing so few men to the bad gunnery of our opponents, and beating them most completely in less than an hour.

Lord Nelson, with whom I breakfasted this morning, has just been giving me an account of his reception on shore, when he went to treat with the Prince. He was hailed with cheers by the multitude, who came to receive him at the water-side, and 'Viva Nelson' resounded until he got to the palace, much to the annoyance, I believe, of his royal highness and his ministers. During dinner, the people were allowed to come in to look at him, and on going down to the boat, again he was saluted the same way. The populace are much in our favour and the merchants already feel the total want of commerce. I just received a letter from Otway, who is going on shore for a categorical answer, after which he will return to England; and as he is a particular friend of mine, he will, I am sure, give you any information you wish. He will call on my brother William.

Your most obedient servant,

T. F. Fremantle.

Ganges, off Copenhagen 5 April (1801.)

My Dearest little Woman,

I send you all the public news and am most delighted at having my ship so little hurt as to loss of men. I went through the action without reflecting *much* on those who were so much interested in my welfare but when everything was over I could not suppress tears which at this time again flow from my eyes. You know my regard and attachment to you, which your very proper conduct so justly entitles you to; I remain so perfectly satisfied with everything you have done and am so assured of your judgment in whatever relates to yourself and the children that I shall not enter into any detail. Whatever I possess in this world is at your devotion; make yourself happy and easy, and do not become too parsimonious; if you see Hutchings tell him his son behaved exceedingly well, and will in time I hope make a good Seaman. I hope the children continue well, and you may now rest satisfied that whenever we do return into port, I shall have an opportunity of seeing you as we want a new fore Mast, a new Main Mast and Bowsprit. The anxiety I have undergone and the continual movement we are in will not allow me to be steady. If you were to copy the plan I send you with Nelson's orders, and send them soon to Sr. Jonathan Lovett and say I desired you to do so he would be much flattered. God Almighty bless you, and my poor little children; be assured of my tenderest regard and sincerest affection, and that I am ever yours

THOS. FRAS. FREMANTLE.

[No address or endorsement.]

Paper endorsed:

LORD NELSON'S ORDERS TO CAPTAIN FREMANTLE.

The arrangement of the attack is as follows, but as the Vice Admiral Lord Nelson cannot with precision mark the situation of the different descriptions of the Enemy's floating batteries and smaller vessels lying between their two decked ships and hulks, the ships which are to be opposed to the floating batteries &c. &c. will find their stations by observing the stations of the ships to be opposed to the two decked ships and hulks.

LINE OF BATTLE

These ships are to fire in passing to their stations.	*Edgar* *Ardent* *Glatton* *Isis* *Agamemnon*	
	Bellona *Elephant* *Ganges* *Monarch* *Defiance* *Russel* *Polyphemus*	Are to Lead in succession & take their stations & anchor as is prescribed by the following arrangement.

The *Edgar* to anchor abreast of No. 5 a 64 gun ship hulk. The *Ardent* to pass the *Edgar* and anchor abreast of No. 6 & 7. The *Glatton* to pass the *Ardent* and anchor abreast of No. 9 a 64 gun ship hulk. The *Isis* to anchor abreast of No. 2 a 64 gun ship hulk. The *Agamemnon* to anchor abreast of No. 1. The Memo. No. 1 begins with the Enemy's first ship at Southward.

No.		Rate	Supposed no. of guns mounted on one side	Station of the line as they are to anchor and engage
1		74	28	*Agamemnon**
2		64	26	*Isis*
3 } 4	Low floating batteries ship rigged lay within the line		10 } 10	**
5		64	27	*Edgar*
6 } 7	Pontoon / Frigate hulk		10 / 12	*Ardent*
8	Small. No guns visible		—	*Glatton*
9		46	30	
10	Ship, Gunboat of 22 guns		14	*Bellona****
11 } 12	Pontoons or floating batteries		12 / 9	
13		74	36	*Elephant*
14 } 15	Pontoons or floating batteries		12 } 12	*Ganges*
16		64	30	*Monarch*
17		64	30	*Defiance*
18		64	30	*Russel*
19		64	30	*Polyphemus*
20	Small ship supposed a boat		11	

Notes in a further column:

* The *Désirée* to follow the *Agamemnon* and rake No. 1.

** It is hoped the *Désirée* will not only rake No. 1, but also rake these two floating batteries. C. Rose is to place six gunbrigs, to rake them also. [i.e. Nos. 3 and 4.]

*** [*Bellona*] To give her attention to support of the *Glatton*.

The six gun boats Capt. Rose is to place with the *Jamaica* to make a raking fire upon No. 1. The Gun boats it is presumed may get far enough in shore of

No. 1 to rake No. 3 and 4, and C. Rose is to advance with the ships and vessels under his Orders to the northward as he may perceive the British fire to cease, where he is first stationed.

No. 1, 2, 3, 4 being subdued which is expected to happen at an early period the *Isis* and *Agamemnon* are to cut their cables and immediately to make sail and take their stations ahead of the *Polyphemus* in order to support that part of the line.

One flat boat manned and armed is to remain upon the offside of each Line of battle ship.

The remaining flat boats with the boats for boarding which will be sent by Admiral Sir Hyde Parker under the command of the first Lieutenant of the *London* are to keep as near to the *Elephant* as possible, but out of the line of fire and to be ready to receive the directions of Lord Nelson.

The four launches with anchors and cables which will be sent by Admiral Sir Hyde Parker under the command of a Lieutenant of the London, to be as near to the *Elephant* as possible ready to receive orders from Vl. Admiral Ld. Nelson.

The *Alcmene Blanche Arrow Dart*, the *Zephyr* and other fire ships are to proceed under the orders of Capt. Riou of the *Amazon* to perform such services as he is directed by Lord Nelson.

NELSON AND BRONTE.

To Captain Fremantle.

CAPTAIN THOMAS FREMANTLE TO THE MARQUIS OF BUCKINGHAM

Ganges, off Copenhagen,
6th April.

My Lord,

The note Lord Nelson sent on shore before the action was over, is such a leading feature in this affair, that I have begged it of his Lordship, and shall copy it for your information.

To the Brothers of Englishmen, the Danes

1. Lord Nelson has directions to spare Denmark, when no longer resisting; but if the firing is continued on the part of Denmark, Lord Nelson will be obliged to set on fire all the floating batteries he has taken, without having the power of saving the brave Danes who have defended them.

2. His Royal Highness, the Prince of Denmark, has sent Adjutant-General Landholin on board His Majesty's ship *Elephant* to Vice-Admiral Lord Nelson, to ask the particular object of sending the flag of truce.

3. Lord Nelson's object in sending the flag of truce was humanity; he therefore consents that hostilities shall cease, and that the wounded Danes may be taken on shore. Lord Nelson will take his prisoners out of the vessels, and burn or carry off his prizes, as he shall think fit. Lord Nelson, with humble duty to his Royal Highness the Prince of Denmark, will ever consider this the greatest victory he ever gained, if it may be the cause of a happy reconciliation and union between his most gracious Sovereign, and his Majesty, the King of Denmark.

(*Signed*) NELSON AND BRONTE.
On board the *London*, 6th April.

After much communication between Sir Hyde and the Danish government, I conclude the *ultimatum* is now on board this ship. I have just brought Lord Nelson from the *St. George* and we shall know in an hour or two, whether we are to commence hostilities or not; at all events, Otway will go in an hour. I do not presume to judge the propriety of our terms to the Danes; but I know and feel as a seaman, that great sacrifices in our present situation should be made, sooner than to declare openly against them again. Should we begin with their bombs, little will be effected, and our fleet must positively return to Leith or Yarmouth for water and stores. We are now with above 100 prisoners each, eating and drinking us out; and the ships could not have been fitted out, if we had not found a great quantity of stores on board the ships captured, all of which ships are to be burnt, except one, which Sir Hyde has commissioned as a hospital-ship. They are very fine ships, particularly one of the seventy-fours, which is much larger than the *Ganges*. You may, perhaps, be shown several plans of our engagement. I took some pains in *placing* the ships; and all the others that I have seen are taken from *mine*. Lord St. Vincent's, is from mine, and is very fairly done without a scale. If we arrange *well* with the Danes, Lord Nelson will wish to proceed with twelve sail of the line to Revel. If so, I shall not I think be left out; and I am in hopes, on my return from this campaign, I shall obtain leave to go to Buckinghamshire for a few days.

Thursday, 23rd April 1801.
Off Moon Island.

I was obliged to leave off writing as the look out frigates made the signal for seeing a strange fleet. The signal was made immediately for a general Chace, so that as you may imagine I became very anxious; on our near approach we perceived The Swedish fleet at Anchor in Carlscrona consisting of seven sail of the Line and some frigates, but so environed with batteries and guns, there was no probability of our being able to attack them. We therefore hauled off from the Land and have ever since been keeping to the Northward of the Island of Bornholm. Sr. Hyde who is all kindness towards me allowed the *Ganges* alone to anchor off a little bit of an Island called Ertholmar, and I was all day yesterday on shore with the Governor, who is a plain honest, stupid Dane. This little Island, or more properly these 7 little Rocks together do not cover more than a mile of Ground, and is inhabited principally by fishermen; there are nearly 1000 inhabitants, who seem very comfortably situated and the children are innumerable; one of these Rocks the largest is quite near another, so as to allow a floating bridge from one to the other, and the water is so deep between them that a 74 Gun Ship might be hauled in. The place is so barren that there are only a few Gardens on it exactly like those you may recollect at Gibraltar; on the whole I was much amused with my Governor and a walk on shore did me much good, as I had been very unwell with cold and bile for some days before. On my return on board I find a letter from the Captain of the Fleet saying Sr. Hyde had received information from the Russian minister that matters seem likely to be adjusted between the British and Russian Courts, and informing me at the same time he was proceeding to Kioga bay, near Copenhagen. I am at this instant leading the Lee line, and near to the *London*; thus I think this Campaign, at least as far as relates to these Seas completely at an end, and you may expect I think to hear of our return to England in 5 or 6 weeks; our masts are so crippled that we must even if the war continues remain some time in port and you may rest assured I will not go to sea again without seeing you and my little ones. I suppose Swanbourne is quite gay now and that all your roses are nearly in blossom; I should like to peep in upon you whilst you are perambulating in your parterre and giving your uncontrouled directions. I am quite annoyed to hear you have got some Methodist preachers in the Village; I wish they were here for an hour or two. I shall make a point of bowling them out of the line when I return. I hope Eugenia received safe all the Music &c. I sent in by the Cruizer (too) and that you were pleased at the account I sent you of our action off Copenhagen; it has given the Northern Nations a great opinion of our determination, and the Swedes are outrageous with the Danes for making an armistice with us; if we had had the good fortune to have fell in with the Swedish fleet at Sea it would have been glorious for us, but I cannot help thinking it is highly impolitic in us to oppress either the Swedes or Danes, but the Russians if you please, and as much as you please. Were you not rejoiced to hear that Paul was dead? He and Robertspiere will meet in the next world if they have their reward; so much for politics.

I shall only say in addition that I believe we are generally all well satisfied that this Campaign is drawing to a period; I think with satisfaction of meeting you soon with the dear little ones and remain as always my very Dearest Woman.

Your most affectionate husband,

T.F.F.

Ganges.

[The last of this series of letters was from Captain Thomas Fremantle to the Marquis of Buckingham on April 22nd from the *Ganges*, off Möen Island.]

My Lord,

I wrote by Colonel Stewart, who left Copenhagen the 6th instant. We remained in the Road until the morning of the 13th, when twelve sail of two-decked ships weighed and ran through the Grounds. I had brought the *Ganges* to draw only twenty-two feet two inches, and led the fleet the whole way. We just touched ground once, but never stopped. The *Raisonable*, endeavouring to pass us, struck the ground, but got off again before night. It made me, I confess, very nervous to be running four miles in four fathoms and a half water, frequently in less. The *London* got all her guns out, but struck hard several times, though reduced to draw only twenty-two feet seven inches. She had knocked off part of her gripe. Most of the ships touched; but I do not hear of any very material damage being done. The whole squadron were at anchor in Kioge Bay at night, except the *St. George* and *Agamemnon.*

The 16th, the wind continuing southerly, Lord Nelson left the *St. George* and hoisted his flag on the *Elephant.* The 17th we weighed from Kioge Bay, and on the 19th arrived off the harbour of Carlscrona, where the Swedish fleet of seven sail of the line and some frigates were anchored. Since which time the squadrons have been cruising between Carlscrona and the Island of Bornholm. Yesterday, Sir Hyde received letters from Copenhagen, and among them, a notification from the Russian Minister, that the differences between the Courts of Petersburgh and St. James's, were likely to be adjusted &c. This has, I believe, determined Sir Hyde to return to Kioge Bay, where I conclude he will remain until he hears from England. He has made the signal for letters, so that I am apprehensive I shall not know more until the vessel has sailed from the Fleet.

The ships begin to grow short of water; and it strikes me, that had we been under the necessity of proceeding to the Gulf of Finland, we should have been much straitened for it. I anchored yesterday, with leave, off the Small Island, on the rocks of Christiansoe, or Entholmar, which lie to the northward of Bornholm. The seven rocks together do not cover more than a mile; but should it ever be found necessary to send a Fleet of men-of-war in these seas, we ought to possess ourselves of this island, as the top of them are full of water preserved in tanks, which by conductors may be brought down to the boats. Besides which, two of these rocks are so near each other as to make a harbour for small vessels, and on occasion would serve to heave down a seventy-four gun ship—there being twenty-six feet of water. It is very strongly fortified, and contains more than 1,000 inhabitants, who are all under military jurisdiction, and live in barracks, They all fish; and vessels from hence are sent weekly to Copenhagen, laden in the same way as the Dutch boats, with wells in them. There is a light-house on the top of the rock; and it is a place much frequented by English merchant ships trading to the Gulf of Finland. 24th, I just return from the *London.* The *St. George* and *Agamemnon* touched in coming through the Grounds. We shall, I expect, anchor tonight in Kioge Bay; and if anything material occurs before the vessel goes I will write again.

[Twenty-two days after the battle Fremantle received this letter from Nelson, which is still at Swanbourne, and sent it home to Betsey:]

My dear Fremantle,

If you don't come here on Sunday to celebrate the Birthday of Santa Emma, Damn me if I ever forgive you, so much from your affectionate Friend as you behave on this occasion.

NELSON AND BRONTE.

St. George, Apl. 24th, 1801.

Ganges, off Copenhagen.
(1st May 1801)

My Dearest Love,

Your letters of the 19th and 23rd reached me on this day. If you feel happy at hearing from me, judge how gratified I must be at knowing of the welfare of you and my Dear little ones, indeed, it is a great sacrifice being absent from those we so dearly love, but when *we* consider it is for the advantage of those who are so beloved by us, and is our duty to protect and provide for it will not bear reasoning with you, much as I wish to be with you, I am convinced it is for my interest honor and reputation to be where I am, and I reflect with heartfelt satisfaction on the happiness I shall enjoy when we meet again—*and I cannot repeat this too often.*

I have just been performing as disagreeable a piece of duty as I think ever occurred in my service, namely being desired by Sir Hyde Parker to take on myself the care and charge of removing poor Sir Thomas Thompson from his ship the *Bellona* to the *Isis*, in which ship he is to go home; figure to yourself the removing a poor man, whose leg is just amputated from the side of one ship and having him hauled up the side of another, his agonies were great, and it brought to my recollection what I once suffered, and the never ceasing attention you showed me, let me at this distance once more thank you for that kindness and goodness of disposition with which you attended to me, and be assured that neither time nor circumstances can efface from my mind that benevolence which so strongly marks your character and conduct. Thompson is very ill, if anything can support him it is his spirits which are very good.

I went yesterday on shore in company with Foley

as attendants on Lord Nelson, who by direction of Sir Hyde has made an armistice for four months with the Danes, so that we shall as soon as we have got some fresh beef and water proceed up the Baltic in quest of the Russians, who will not I dare say feel very bold after the example we have made of the Danes. The Squadron are all refitted, and except the *Monarch* and *Isis* who will be obliged to return home, we shall all proceed through the Gerunds in a few days. I am much pleased at the attention shown your sister, and I wish you to go to London for three weeks or a month, either to Marianne or Eugenia's, I will not allow you to stay at Swanbourne alone, you will torment yourself to death, therefore my Dear Woman, do as I wish you on this head, I will give you credit for it. I request you will be generous to the poor at Swanbourne, as they do not annoy you, they ought to be requitted, and God knows it is not charity ill bestowed, I hope to make £200 prize money by taking these floating batteries off Copenhagen. It is really quite flattering to me to be living on such very friendly terms with all the leading features in the Squadron; if it only leads to seeing you and my Dear little ones well and happy when I return, I shall think myself well repaid, God in his goodness preserve you and them, and reflect sometimes how miserable I feel inwardly at being deprived of the society of her I love so much and so ardently as I do you, kiss the children and be assured of the affection

of your faithful husband, T.F.F.

We dined with the Prince of Denmark, and if the weather had not been so cold and rainy we should have passed a very pleasant day. The Court of Denmark is not even so splendid as Naples. The Ladies of the Court came to the door during dinner to see

Nelson, and he was received on shore by multitudes. He went in my barge.

St. Petersburgh.
May the 9th, 1801.

My Dear Betsey,

I arrived here yesterday, and as you may well imagine have hitherto scarce had time enough to turn myself round this metropolis which is beautiful beyond description. I am happy to think that matters are likely to be soon settled between these two Countries, and I have every reason to be pleased with the attention I have received both here and at Cronstadt. Our passage hitherto was rather longer than I had expected, but had we been much sooner we could not have proceeded up the Gulf of Finland as there was much ice off Hogland as we passed it, if this should reach you before you hear again write to my brothers and say I am here, I conclude Foley wrote to you soon after I left the Fleet, Kiss all the children for me and believe me always your most affectionate

T.F.F.

Addressed:
Mrs. Thomas Fremantle,
No. 6, Russel Place,
Fitzroy Square,
London.

And re-addressed:
Swanbourne,
near Winslow,
Bucks.

Endorsed: Peterstovr and Foreign office, July 1.

Ganges, off the Island of Bornholm.
May the 21st, 1801.

My Dear Betsey,

You will have received I dare say the letter I wrote you about ten days ago from Petersburgh, I could only there mention that I was well, as had I wrote anything of importance the letter would have been stopped, I left the Squadron under Sir Hyde the 26th of last month and in the *Lynx* sloop, arrived at Petersburgh the 7th May. I was exceedingly well received by Count Panin the Court Minister and Prince Korakin, the Vice-Chancellor. With the former I dined twice, with the latter once, during the four days I remained at Petersburgh; I saw the whole of the Winter Palace, the Hermitage where the Museum and all the fine paintings are; I likewise went to see the Palace of the late Prince Potemkin, that of Oranienbaum where Peter was prisoned, and the Palace of St. Michel where the late Paul was strangled, to relate you all the modes he had found out to torment and tyranise over his subjects will fill a folio volume, and I am only surprised to think he was suffered to live so long. The affair of his decease is much spoken of at Petersburgh where it is generally spoken of and the conspirators pointed out, several of whom I had conversation with. I am sorry to say that the Courts being in mourning, did not allow me to be presented to the new Emperor, who has the character of being a mild tractable young man, but with not sufficient firmness of character to govern Russia as his grandmother did; he has, however, a very able counsellor in Count Panin who is the particular friend of Lord Whitworth and Mr. Grenville. The Russian Fleet are mostly laid up at Cronstadt, and have no idea of meeting us at sea, they are however putting the Port in as defensible a state as can well be imagined. The fleet from Revel left that place and arrived at Cronstadt only a few hours before me. I hope you continued to write tho' Foley must have informed you I was gone to Petersburgh. Yours of the 19th April reached me yesterday.

In my opinion we must make our peace with Russia, tho' they seem to stickle a great deal about this armed neutrality, I met Lord St. Helens in the *Latona* going to Petersburgh and as it is so much the interest of both countries to be at amity, he will I make no doubt make a treaty with them, none of the English ships or seamen were released when I left Petersburg. I can only add that I am well and satisfied with my trip to Petersburgh, and the attention I receive from Lord Nelson is flattering beyond what I can name. The insult of the Admiralty to my friend Sir Hyde is scarcely to be named without feeling detestation to the person who occasioned his recall in such a way as *Treason only* could have rendered necessary. God bless you.

Ganges at Dantzig 10th June
1801.

My Dear Betsey,

Here I am again traversing the Baltic from one end to the other, and I am quite gratified at having had an opportunity of seeing so much of this country in so short a time; I have certainly availed myself of what has offered, as I think it is not very probable a Squadron will be sent here again for many years. The manners of these Germans I think more congenial with the English than any I have seen in Europe. I am much pleased at what I have seen but I don't think there is anything that can induce me to come again. Our conquest I may call it of Egypt will

I hope tend to make an advantageous peace if such a *thing* is to be presumed, which I have very much doubt about. Whilst the war continues I think there is little probability of our living much together; however, happen what will, I am resolved to steal away for a few days when we return to England which I calculate will be very soon. Captain Otway in the *London* is here with me and we have a very good society at the tavern on shore when we can get there. I am quite well and the weather is so hot I have left off my flannel waistcoat. I shall leave this place in four or five days.

Dantzig, 18th June, 1801.

You will find by the date of this letter I am still at the place where we have made very little progress on account of the very bad weather we have had. I have lived generally on shore and if I could have spoke German should have been well amused. Lord Nelson I just hear is just going home and is superceded by Admiral Poole. I cannot imagine our Squadron will remain in this sea much longer. You must be aware that in corresponding by post one cannot say half what we are desirous of doing. I hear there are several letters on board the Admiral ship for us. I expect many from you as I have not heard from Swanbourne for some time past.

I know nothing of the operations of the Fleet, as I have been absent from them some time. I shall only (say) that I am well, and that I leave this place in a day or two. God bless you and the children and be assured of tender regards and sincere affection of yours most truly

T.F.F.

SWANBOURNE, 2ND AUGUST. SUNDAY. Had a letter this

morning from Sr. Thos. Troubridge, to say Fremantle was hourly expected in England.

Reading, 7th August. Friday. Heard from Fremantle to say he could not get leave of absence and wishing me to meet him at Portsmouth. I left home at about twelve o'clock, with Eugenia and little Tom. I went through Missenden, High Wycombe and Great Marlow, to Reading where I stayed the night. It was an excessive hot day and very uncomfortable travelling, being four in the chaise.

Portsmouth, 8th August. Saturday. Left Reading very early and was excessively well drove all the way through Winchester to Portsmouth, the country in Berkshire beautiful, and the harvest plentiful. Met Fremantle in the street who showed us to our lodgings which are very comfortable. He is looking very well and is not quite so fat as when he left us. He was delighted with little Tom who knew him again. I was much fatigued from the journey but quite delighted to meet again after a twelve months' absence.

[Fremantle gave Betsey his diary of his visit to Petersburg after his return.]

1801

Sunday, 26th April. Dined with Lord Nelson in honor of Lady H$^{s.}$ Birthday—all the Admirals and Med$^{n.}$ Captains there, left them at 6 o'clock and embarked on board the *Lynx* to proceed with dispatches to Petersburg, the Wind Easterly and quite mod$^{e.}$

Friday, 8th May. Was awoke in the Night by Mr Boker, who informed me I had permission to proceed to Petersburg, got up very early to call on Adm$^{l.}$ Hennekoff to get a pass which he gave me as likewise an officer to attend me to the Capital. We left Cronstadt at 40 ms. past 7 and arrived at Orianbaum 20 ms. past 8—Neither horse nor Carriages ready for us, which was an inducement to see the Palace, famous for the confinement of Katherine and for the Death of the Emperor Peter. The Palace not large but very pretty, in a Summer house there were some very pretty pictures of the Italian School, after sauntering round the gardens, we got a coach with four horses a-breast, this with two sorts of Carts to carry Servants and baggage conveyed us safe to Petersburg, where we arrived about one o'clock at the house of Count Panin Minister for foreign affairs, we were stopped at least half a dozen times in our journey at the different ports to have our passes examd. and on our arrival at the Barrier gate, the Town Mayor and an officer of the police were sent to receive us, and in this stile we were conducted, Count Panin received me with great politeness, and having perused the letters of Sr. H and Ld. H. seemed well satisfied of the good Disposition manifested by the Cr. in Chief in returning to Keoga bay, he begged me to dine and immediately went to wait on the Emperor while we escorted as before took a Walk, and went into the Shop of Mrs Hoy a great English house that sells *everything*—Called in the Evening on an English Mercht. Mr Wagriene who walked with us around the palace and showed us the outside of the Palace of St. Michel—We returned home completely tired, I took with me McDonald a Mid$^{n.}$ of the *Lynx*, got a Valet de place named Frederick took lodgings at an Inn called the London and hired a carriage with 4 horses. The English were in great hopes my arrival from the fleet would cause the English ships to be released.

Sunday, 10th May. Went in the morning to see the palace of Prince Potemkim, which is now converted into a barrack and the flooring &c. totally destroyed, the Garden which is quite in the English stile is very pretty and laid out with much taste, but now much neglected. Dined with Prince Rerakin. About 30 people at dinner everything in good stile, and well served. After breakfast we went to the Parade, the Emperor and Grand Duke Constantine both there, The Troops very fine indeed, Many of the *Consprs.* were pointed out to me on the parade—After dinner an officer was sent to acquaint us the Emperor allowed us to see the Winter Appartments in the palace. Went with him but saw nothing very remarkable. Went home by myself and to bed as I was quite fatigued. Called on Count Panin who was not at home.

Monday, 11th May. Called in the morning on Count Panin, who informed me he should be ready to receive me at h. past 8—at that time I received his directions for Sir. Hyde and took my leave of him—None of the British Seamen released, and the English Merchant Ships decaying daily—Their Sails quite decayed and rotten for want of being aired.

28TH AUGUST. FRIDAY. All the Holloways, Otways, Lamberts, ourselves and a large party of Captains dined on board the *Elephant*, and Captain J. Murray who arrived this morning from Town and is going to join *L'Oiseau* to which ship he is just appointed. Danced on the quarter deck after dinner, I return early on shore with Fremantle, who was in better spirits about his ship.

PORTSMOUTH, 4TH SEPTR. FRIDAY. The letters unfortunately only came at one o'clock, and to my surprise Fremantle writes his ship is detained at Portsmouth and wishes me to return with little Tom. I made all the hurry I could but could not set out till after three o'clock, the distance being 65 miles I despaired to arrive at night and I had no Servant—I thought it however a pity to stop on the road, and got safe to Portsmouth at a quarter after twelve just before the gates were shut. All the world was asleep at the Fountains Inn, but Fremantle who was in bed at our old lodgings opposite, heard the carriage and we drove to the door. He was much pleased at my having come on as he fully expected me. Dear little Tom was very good humoured tho' kept up so late and not at all troublesome in the carriage.

Portsmouth, 6th Septr. Sunday. Dined at Adl. Halloways, met Capt. and Mrs. Lambert and Capt. and Mrs. Murray. Mrs. Otway has been a widow ten days, Capt. Otway sailed with Capt. Foley to join the Channel Fleet. She does not seem au desespoir. The fever has broke out again on board the *Ganges*, but the marines are alone affected who first brought it in the ship.

"Ganges" St. Hellens, 9th Septr. Thursday. Stayed the night on the *Ganges* with little Tom. Came on shore at one o'clock, dressed, crossed the water to Gosport, then went on in a post chaise with Fremantle to Mr. Stowes' country house, where we dined and stayed all night. Fremantle enjoyed the country extremely, the Miss Stowes rather vulgar.

"Ganges" St. Hellens, 10th Septr. Friday. Returned to Portsmouth after breakfast, and went with Mrs. Whitelocke to a dejeune on Portsea Bastion given by Lord Belgrave. Several marquees were pitched and an elegant collation provided. Dancing was attempted on the Green, but the wind was cold and I felt quite sick and miserable in the midst of this gay scene, I made therefore soon my escape with Fremantle and came on board the *Ganges*.

Kingston Hall, 14th Septr. Monday. Fremantle went to get his ship under way before I could set out. Arrived early at Kingston Hall, but fatigued and dismal enough.

Down House, 20th Septr. Sunday. Left Kingston Hall and got to the Down House at four o'clock. Lady Mary was much affected at seeing me. Mr. Blair is confined to his room upstairs with the Gout, but is as happy and full of spirits as ever. Miss Fam and Miss Mitchell are at the Down House, Mr. Charles Mitchell came to dinner. Little Tom was much admired and is on his good behaviour.

Down House, 24th Septr. Thursday. Went in Lady Mary's gig to call on Mrs. Baker who was not at home, walked all over her house which is most comfortable. Called afterwards on Miss Beckford; she is as pretty and unaffected as when I saw her at Florence. She show'd us her miniature paintings, they are most beautifully done. Met her father out a shooting, he has very much the look of an Italian. They have not been returned many weeks to England.

Down House, 27th Septr. Sunday. Went to prayers at Blandford and afterwards drove out with Ly. Westmoreland in her Baroutsch; she does not get up before one o'clock, as she complains of being very ill, she is again breeding which greatly vexes her for she hates children and is every instant pretending to be in hystericks.

Down House, 3rd October. Saturday. No words can describe the universal joy which was spread on learning that Preliminaries of Peace with France were actually signed. I was most truly delighted and the more so as it was an unexpected happiness.

Claydon, 5th November. Thursday. I had a short letter from Fremantle of the 23rd Octr. and I was truly miserable to find he had been detached with four more ships from the Channel Fleet with sealed orders, he was much out of spirits and did not expect to be at home for ten weeks or three months. Mrs. Fremantle left us.

Swanbourne, 24th Novr. Saturday. I was most delighted in receiving a very kind letter from Ld. Buckingham to say the instant he had heard the *Ganges* had been detached from the Channel Fleet he had requested Lord St. Vincent to recall Fremantle. He assured him he did not even know he had been sent on this duty till he heard it from Admiral Cornwallis, and would recall him immediately. Ld. Buckingham says I may expect to see him very soon which is a great comfort to me. Col. and Mrs. Fremantle came to dinner; he is looking very well. They think Emma and Charles much improved. Played Loo with Mr. Blick in the evening.

Stowe, 12th Decr. Saturday. Went to Stowe immediately after breakfast with Tom, who was particularly asked in two notes from Lady Buckingham. Met with a most kind reception. No one else but Miss Macnamara, Mr. Talbot and Lord Ebrington. The French princes arrived at about seven o'clock —*Monsieur* (late Count d'Artois—the Prince of Condé and his son the Duc de Bourbon. Everything in great style for them, the saloon lighted up and band playing. Prince of Condé is a charming old man, Monsieur talks a great deal, but is pleasant enough, the Duc of Bourbon seems more affected by their misfortunes than the others who seem to possess all the usual French levity. I played on the pianoforte to them in the evening. Ld. Buckingham has bought a very good new instrument for his new library which is a delightful room. I made my escape before supper—a formal dinner of three hours was quite enough for me.

Stowe, 13th Decr. Sunday. I am quite delighted with

the prince of Condé; he is a most interesting and pleasant creature. All the State apartment was lighted up this evening and the House looked to great advantage.

STOWE, 17TH DECR. THURSDAY. Walked with Ly. Buckingham, called on Mrs. Perry to see a Mulatto family just come from Barbadoes who are great quizzes.

STOWE, 26TH DECR. SATURDAY. Lord Buckingham who is all attention and kindness to me has proposed to send Monday his carriage to Swanbourne to fetch Emma and Charles, as he imagined I wished to see them, and should then have no excuse to shorten my visit. Went in the garden chair to Buckingham.

CHAPTER 24

STOWE, 1ST JANY., 1802. FRIDAY. Mrs. John Fremantle heard that poor old Mrs. Fremantle continues in a very low way and seems to get weaker daily. I fear she cannot live through the winter. Little Tom is a wonderful favourite, and most excessively admired, he is a good little boy and much more sensible and clever than Lord Cobham.

[Betsey goes home to receive her in-laws on the 10th January.]

SWANBOURNE, 13TH JANY. WEDNESDAY. Mrs. John Fremantle went to Warden, and does not return till Saturday, she has left her husband under my care till then. We heard this morning that his poor Grandmother died last Monday night. I am quite sorry as she was a dear little old woman. Played Chess all the evening with him. He seems to enjoy himself much more here than at Stowe. The children are all indifferent with colds attended with fever.

21ST. THURSDAY. I was most agreeably surprised and much delighted in receiving a letter from Fremantle from Spithead where he arrived in the *Ambuscade* Frigate with Capt. Foley on Tuesday. I expect him home to-morrow.

SWANBOURNE, 22ND JANY. FRIDAY. Went with Eugenia to Aylesbury to meet Fremantle who did not get there till five o'clock owing to his being taken to Woodford instead of Watford. He is looking very well, but was quite ill in the West Indies, the wound in his arm having broke out again which made him apply for leave to return to England immediately and leave his ship. Capt. Foley has done the same and is in very indifferent state of health. Fremantle is delighted with little Emma and admires her excessively.

SWANBOURNE, 23RD JANY. SATURDAY. Mr. Lulby and Miss Lowndes called for a few minutes. Fremantle was obliged to go to Stowe to dinner and stay the night. Eugenia and myself were much interested in reading the trial of Governor Wale who I recollect seeing at Florence—he is condemned to be hanged for flogging a man to death when Governor of the Island of Goree about 20 years ago. He seems to deserve his fate but it is a horrible thing for his wife and family.

SWANBOURNE, 4TH MARCH. THURSDAY. Eugenia has agreed for a House in half Moon Street and goes to Town the 18th. I believe we shall go with her for a week only.

SWANBOURNE, 5TH & 6TH MARCH. FRIDAY–SATURDAY. Mrs. Heslop called and sung all the morning with Eugenia Marcello's Psalm. Fremantle returned quite dismal from his morning's ride having heard there is every appearance of the war breaking out again.

9TH. TUESDAY. A general impress throughout the Kingdom and every appearance of war. Buona-Parte a treacherous monster.

14TH. SUNDAY. I am in the agonies of looking out for a cook again, mine which suits in every respect will not stay without a kitchen maid and exhorbitant wages. Servants are great torments.

16TH. TUESDAY. Mr. and Mrs. Langston called; she looks very weak and ill. Fremantle rode out with the Fox Hounds, and dined at Mr. Selby's.

25TH. THURSDAY. Fremantle rode out to meet the Fox Hounds. We have bought a Jack Ass for little Tom who is highly delighted with it.

WEDNESDAY. The Cook went, they none like the country. Mr. Selby called to drink Madeira in the morning. Mrs. Howard was brought to bed yesterday, the third girl.

SWANBOURNE, 15TH APRIL. THURSDAY. Eugenia writes that as Justine continues in an indifferent state of health, change of air has been recommended she is to have good advice in Town and then to come to me. Harriot must wait till June for her holy days.

17TH. SATURDAY. The new building was compleatly roofed today—the alteration in the parlour is to be begun on Monday.

7TH MAY. FRIDAY. I began to feel so uncomfortable as soon as I went to bed that I was obliged to get up before one o'clock in the morning and soon sent for Mr. Tookey. I was rather worried at not having Nurse Emy with me and sent towards morning for Mrs. Feasey—however, all was as well as I could wish and another boy was born at half past eight in the morning. I rather suffered more and longer than with the others and the child did not seem quite well at first.

8TH JUNE. TUESDAY. I was much distressed in hearing from Eugenia that her house was broke open on Sunday evening at ten o'clock at night when she was at Mr Bankes's. The Plate chest entirely stripped £15 in money & several of her laces &c were made off with. It seems to have made her very nervous & is a most unpleasant circumstance.

SWANBOURNE CORPUSCHRISTI, 17TH THURSDAY. Mr Delanos came over before breakfast, he will not be able to come for some time as Lady Buckingham returns to Stowe to morrow. I was quite sorry to hear of the death of poor Mr Blair.

23D JUNE. WEDNESDAY. Fremantle went with my three sisters to the Buckingham Ball, I stayed quietly at home, with my four brats.

28TH WEDNESDAY. Heard from Fremantle Capt. Foley

is to be married in a few days to Lady Lucy Fitzgerald.

30TH FRIDAY. Fremantle returned this evenᵍ from Town. He has ordered a new carriage & new gig prices £160 & £80.

SWANBOURNE, 2ᵈ AUGUST. MONDAY. The poor Chimney Sweeper's wife was brought to bed last night of two children a boy & a girl. Worked for them, tho' they are not likely to live. Inhabited the new nursery it is quite dry and very comfortable.

4TH. WEDNESDAY. Called again to see the poor twins, the misery of the house quite heartbreaking.

19TH. THURSDAY. Eugenia had a most satisfactory letter from Mrs. de Salis who very kindly undertakes to procure her lodgings at Hastings and strongly recommends the place. They leave us on Monday.

20TH AUGUST. FRIDAY. Eugenia is to have our old carriage for her journey and has purchased it for ten guineas. It is undergoing a few necessary repairs at Swanbourne.

4TH JULY, 1803. MONDAY. Fremantle threatened to take Tom to sea with him but I have endeavoured to dissuade him from it—the poor child certainly is too young. We had a note from Mrs. John Fremantle to persuade us all to join her party to a play at Aylesbury on Wednesday, there is a tolerable good sett of actors.

HARRIET

WEDNESDAY, 6TH JULY. We dined in great haste and Capt. Fremantle drove us to Aylesbury in *grand ton* having two Servants *riding behind*, I sat on the Dicky with him. We arrived in the town not knowing where the playhouse was, as C.F. had heard they were to perform in the town hall but it was not true, after travelling about for a good half hour, we at last got a guide, and reached a *barn* which was the Theatre . . . with a number of Gentlemen filled up the box which was very dangerously situated as the Gallery over it was *cracking* at a famous rate, being crowded with people. The pitt was *pretty* full —a beautifull out of tune Symphony, consisting of hair-dressers, butchers, &c. opened the play which was the Mountaineers, the Subject very stupid but pretty well acted, the principal Actor was a Mr. Lacy who is Amazingly tall, being at least seven feet high and very thin which augments his height. The Farce was very pretty and a scene between Doctor Lennity and a Baronet was very like the one in the Poor Gentleman when *Ollopod* went to pay his morning visit to his friend Sir Charles Cropland. After our ears had been affected with a few screams, we got up to depart, we had promised the M. Chaplains to sup with them which we did after affronting poor Mr. Browne who departed in *anger* at our not accepting his *mal a propos* invitation—We eat a good Supper, and C.F. drove us back half way but finding the wind too cold he readily gave up his office to *Olleps* who kept on his steady slow pace so that we did not reach Swanbourne till near three. Poor Tom has been unwell with a cold and fever; Betsey was up with him almost all night. We slept very well.

Betsey

10th July. Sunday. Capt. Fremantle went to Stowe to take leave of Lord Buckingham, as he received to-day a letter from the Admiralty to announce his appointment to the *Ganges* and he is to take up his Commission at Portsmouth. He really goes to sea quite *à contre coeur* as he was now so comfortably settled here, and I feel not a little anxiety at being left alone with five such young children and so much to manage.

12TH JULY. TUESDAY. Fremantle made application for three Lieutenants who were in the *Ganges* with him before, and they have immediately been appointed, which will be very pleasant for him. He takes David with him, who is delighted to go to sea, our Groom James, who has once been on that element and never wishes to encounter it again, remains as my Servant, we shall sell the saddle Horses, and tho' the poor man is very awkward now I hope in time he will make a tolerable *footman.*

HARRIET

SWANBOURNE.

WEDNESDAY, 13TH JULY. Capt. Fremantle was much affected during dinner and cried so that he was obliged to leave the room. We were all very dull at the thought of his going away.

THURSDAY, 14TH JULY. After breakfast Capt. Fremantle left us. I need not nor cannot describe what I felt in taking leave of him. Betsey behaved much better than I should have expected, poor thing, I pity her sincerely. We worked the whole day for the poor people and made a frock between us.

FRIDAY, 15TH JULY. Justinia frightened me in the Night and woke me out of my sleep in telling me that she saw a man go to Tom's bed. I was greatly terrified. At last, taking courage, I got up to encounter the ennemy which proved nothing else but Betsey's gown.

BETSEY

15TH JULY. FRIDAY. Mrs. Hutchings called with her boy George, who is much grown but has not lost his stupid look. He brought me two Cocoa nuts, and assured me Capt. Mackenzie and the Carpenter say the *Ganges* must be six months in Dock.

17TH JULY. SUNDAY. This was Swanbourne feast and many fine white gowns, feathered and flowered bonnets and parasols were exhibited.

18TH JULY. MONDAY. No less than eight or ten Gipsey fiddlers, a tabor and fife paraded the village.

HIGH STREET, PORTSMOUTH, 24TH JULY. SUNDAY. I left Sunbury at seven o'clock and came into the Portsmouth Road at Ripley. I found it dreadfully dusty, particularly from Godalming to Liphook, it was like a deep sand the colour of brick dust. I suffered much from the heat and dust, as well as the poor children and arrived at Portsmouth quite fatigued at seven o'clock. Fremantle did not expect us so soon and dined at General Whitelocke's, he came to drink tea with us. The house he has taken is extremely small but tolerably clean and when we were a little settled we shall find it comfortable enough. We were not so on our arrival, the children being cross and tired, Nurse ill and obliged to go to bed where she was soon terrified at being attacked by a regiment of Bugs, and I could scarcely persuade her to lay down again. Fremantle has written for our Cook to come directly.

HARRIET

THURSDAY, 28TH JULY. Was very idle all day though I pretended to be busy with packing up, went to bed at past twelve, took a kind of farewell of my Dearest Sisters. I regret much leaving them, but it is of no use to complain and I must conform myself to the will of heaven. I shall find plenty friends at New Hall, who will make up in a kind of way for my disappointment of seeing so little of the persons I love the best in the world, ungrateful; I did not doat on theirs, they are all kindness to me. May I one day be worthy of deserving all their goodness; it will be my chief Study, and *goodwill* will not fail I am sure. I never felt so lonesome in parting with anyone. The Cocoanut did not agree with me and its effects did not contribute to make me forget my approaching journey on which I looked with pleasure for some reasons and the contrary for others.

FRIDAY, 29TH JULY. Set off very soon after taking a heartbreaking leave of my Dear Sisters, may God grant them every happiness and blessing is my sincere prayer. I betrayed great *weakness* and was quite vexed with myself for tears are my abhortion even shed for good motives. But I generally have got over partings much better than this time. Nelleh and we were very witty. Allen drove very well and got to town in good time. After doing all the commissions I went to bed early enough.

BETSEY

PORTSMOUTH, 30TH JULY. SATURDAY. We were greatly alarmed in the night, as Nurse came into my room saying the Watchman was crying out fire and on opening my eyes I saw an amazing blaze at the back of our house. It appeared very near us indeed and we hurried out of the house with the children, Nurse without shoes nor stockings, we went to a house the opposite side of the street, where we heard the fire was in a timber yard in St. Thomas's Street, and tho' near us we were in no danger at present. We could see it very plain, but fortunately it was in the course of an hour entirely put out and we returned to our house which we found in great confusion as everything had been removed to carry away had it proved necessary. The house we went to was a wine merchants, Mr. White, whose wife and daughters were extremely civil to me and the children. I felt rather nervous all day after this fright and walked to see the place where the fire broke out, it is in the midst of wooden buildings and it is wonderful no greater damage was done. One house and two stables were burnt, and two horses and one dog burnt to death.

PORTSMOUTH, 7TH AUGUST. SUNDAY. I dined tete a tete with Justine, and went to walk on the walls, where we were not a little surprised at seeing a great concourse of people on the beach, the yeomanry out, guns frequently fired, signals made, the tellegraphes at work and many sails in sight. On enquiring I was told it was supposed the French were effecting a landing as numbers of the flat bottom boats were seen making towards the shore. This created a very great alarm. Fremantle and his dinner Companions returned immediately from Badhampston, and every precaution taken, as if really the French were approaching. I felt much alarmed myself, but as everything appeared quiet towards twelve o'clock we went to bed in hopes some mistake created this great bustle.

PORTSMOUTH, 8TH AUGUST. MONDAY. I was very happy to hear this morning that a fleet of coasters who had been becalmed at the back of the Isle of Wight had occasioned our alarm, and that no appearance of an enemy remained to-day. We spent this morning on board the *Windsor Castle*, Capt. Bertie's ship, where we found a large party from Southampton, and sailed to Spithead. We had a cold dinner at Spithead and then returned on shore.

26TH AUGUST. FRIDAY. I went in the morning to Haslar Hospital where Fremantle was with Capt. Vashon on a Survey. Dr. Linde showed us all over the Hospital which is a very fine building, with 2100 beds, all very clean and comfortable and the bedsteads of Iron—there are at present only 100 sick in it. I went through one of the wards, and tho' there was but one man in bed it struck me as a melancholy sight.

2ND SEPTEMBER. FRIDAY. After walking down to Mrs. Holloway's, who is going to-morrow to Southampton to attend Mrs. Otway's accouchement which is daily expected, Fremantle drove us to the Camp at South Sea Castle and to Cumberland Fort, which is built by the Convicts; it is a melancholy sight to see so many wretches at work with heavy chains to their feet, and I was much shocked to discover among them numbers of quite young Lads fourteen or fifteen years of age.

EUGENIA

KINGSTON HALL

MONDAY, 5TH SEPTEMBER. A sad accident happened here this morning which shocked us all very much and particularly poor Mrs. Bankes who was witness to it—she heard screams and a violent noise in the stables, as she was walking in the garden, and immediately flew to see from whence it proceeded, having at the same time the precaution to call for assistance. She found the Coachman under one of the Coach Horses covered with blood, the animal most furiously kicking at him, while one of the footmen was standing by and thro' extreme terror was unable to assist. The horse was so wild and maddened, that it was some time before they could extricate the unhappy man from under him—the Carpenter walking over the side of the stall cut the horse loose—by that time the Coachman's skull was fractured in a most shocking manner, one eye nearly knocked out, and the use of one side quite gone—immediate assistance was sent for, he was trepanned, and there is a chance of his living altho' the surgeons do not venture to give hopes—this accident has shewn me several of the individuals of this family in a truly amiable light—as for Mrs. Bankes, had the man been her own son, she could not have shewn more interest or bestowed more care.

FRIDAY, 9TH SEPTEMBER. Mr. Meeke went away this morning, and Ld. Westmoreland left us for Dulish—We none of us felt in spirits for a Ball, the idea of a fellow creature stretched on the bed of pain and perhaps of death as the unhappy man is (who met with the accident), is well calculated to unfit one for gaiety. However we all set out this evening between eight and nine (for Milton Abbey) which is about 15 miles from hence. We found the Ball already *en train* by the time we arrived; it was hot and crowded, and the whole county was there. I soon got in spirits and driving all melancholy ideas out of my head, danced the whole night. Ld. Dorchester went carried about, from one room to the other to do the honours of his fete but retired early. The supper was laid out in the Gothic Hall, which had a charming effect. Mrs. Pickard was not well enough to come—there were many quizzes amongst the company, as must always be the case at a general county ball like this—Mrs. Morton Pitt was not there (she is at Cheltenham) and poor Ld. Digby look'd very much out of his element. Neither Horace Beckford nor Ld. Rivers were there—the men were not *des plus elegans*. Ld. Westmoreland came from Dulish, as well as his brother, Mrs. Fane and Miss Strohne, the bride elect of Mr. Robert Snow—Captn. Digby who was to have delivered a message to me at the Races, from Portsmouth, at length plucked up courage, and spoke—Mr. Butler and the boys returned home—we slept at Milton.

SATURDAY, 10TH SEPTEMBER. Before we left Milton Abbey this morning, I admired the beautiful Gothic building, the many fine pictures it contains, the grounds about it, and the Abbey itself—only finding fault with Ld. Dorchester for planting fruit trees against the walls of the Abbey—I renewed acquaintance with Ly. Georgiana Buckley, who has been very beautiful—on our return home, we found the Coachman rather worse, but alive—Mr. Smith came —I felt horribly tired.

Lord Dorchester to my great surprise this morning at breakfast, was rallying Ld. Digby in the coarsest manner about Mrs. M. Pitt.

BETSEY

ST. HELENS, 15TH SEPT. THURSDAY. Fremantle dined on board and came to us in the evening. We met him on the sands, which is our usual walk. He said the Prince of Wales drank six glasses of Cherry Brandy at Luncheon with a bottle of muld port wine, he sat at dinner till eleven then went to sup and sleep at the Commissioners.

21ST SEPT. WEDNESDAY. It rained the greatest part of the morning and blew hard at sea but it was pleasant on shore towards the middle of the day and I walked out a great deal with Fremantle, who missed for the first time visiting his ship as the weather was to bad for a boat to come for him. An Officer came in the evening with some orders which greatly worried him, as of the 80 men of the Goliaths he had given him a few days ago all the Seamen among them are to be sent to the *Excellent*. His ship is not half manned and he will lay here probably a month or two longer.

25TH SEPT. SUNDAY. We all went on board the *Ganges* by eleven o'clock to prayers and to stay dinner.

Fremantle could not unfortunately stay with us, as his signal had been made to go to the Admiral early in the morning and I fear to receive orders to go to Sea. His cabin is very comfortable and nice and his ship getting in some order. Mr. Lond, Mr. Kidd and Mr. Burns (the Parson) dined with us Fremantle returned at five o'clock—he is ordered to get ready to sail as soon as possible, and Cork for the present is to be his station. He is going to-morrow to Spithead and the *Britannia* is to take the *Ganges* place at St. Helens. These sudden orders have upset all our schemes and I shall take my departure for home early on Tuesday. We returned on shore early having all been made stupid by this disappointment.

18TH OCTOBER. TUESDAY. I begin to be half alarmed at the attempt to invade this country which is now daily expected to take place, and these horrid French are such desperate wretches that I quite dread their attack, tho' I trust it will prove unsuccessful. Received two letters from Fremantle:

Off Cork Harbour, Sunday Night.
9th of Octr., 1803.

My Dearest Love,

Your letter of the 2nd came to me this day and I think you managed uncommonly well in making your Journey so soon and you need be under no kind of anxiety about Charles who will not long remain stupid or heavy with such lively Companions as Tom and Emma, keep them as much in the air as you can and don't bring them up to be delicate and tender. Depend on it nothing will make them so healthy as exercise in the open air, and with such a *beautiful* parterre before you, there can be no danger. There is one word in your letter which I am sure you will excuse me for taking notice of, as you would prefer my doing it, to anyone else; it is *unsatisfied* instead of dissatisfied. I am sorry about my two Cape Sheep, but I beg you will set Henley's heart at rest as I know it was not his fault. As to the pointer dog, tell Mr. Robt. Lowndes that as he was so good as to procure it for me and I have no immediate occasion for it that I beg he will dispose of it among his sporting friends, of the Newfoundland dogs, I think you had better consult Henley, if the puppy given me by Mr. Tookey seems to be promising you had better give away the one at the farm, if not return the puppy with many thanks to Mr. Tookey, and if he don't want him give him to anybody. I have been drinking tea without milk, and have had no new bread since we sailed, besides that I find Martin a very bad maitre d'hotel tho' I believe a very good Servant. Would you believe that he gave me for dinner *four dishes of meat* (all I have every day) of Beef, Roast at bottom, Stewd. at top, Beef Stakes one side and Beef steak pye on the other, this you agree as a housekeeper was not good management, and obliges me to look more to my menage. Blacky is grown quite humble and is as stupid as a brute—My cook understands nothing but Roast and boild. but as he is young and I am no great Epicure I must continue endeavours to improve him.

Yours always and ever truly,
T.F.F.

Cove of Cork, 15th Octr. 1803.

My Dearest Love,

Tomorrow I expect we shall sail from hence. Our station I imagine will be off Bantry Bay, where we shall resort in the very heavy gales on this coast during the Winter. We have three dozen of Turkeys on board which cost us only two shillings a piece, fowls half a Guinea a dozen. I have got a nice Cow for ten pounds and we begin to bake very tolerable bread, in short taking it all together I am much more at my ease than I expected to be, and as I must in every case have been separated from you whilst the war lasts I am perhaps as well here as anywhere.

HARRIET

SWANBOURNE

TUESDAY, 25TH OCTOBER. Was very busy the whole morning putting up our things and did not leave Swanbourne much before five. The roads were intolerable, Betsey and Justina did nothing but cry out *misericorde*. We at last reached Linford after tea we trimmed our gowns and talked and laughed till past twelve, when Mrs. Fremantle and Mrs. Cathcart arrived storming against a drunken Postillion who almost broke their necks driving them from Mr. Pratts. We stuffed down a chicken and were not in our nests before one.

BETSEY

16TH NOVR. WEDNESDAY. I received to-day a very long letter from Fremantle dated 5th Novr. in Bantry Bay; he is much pleased with his men and particularly with his officers who are so extremely attentive to him he says he never was so comfortable:

5th Novr. 1803. Bantry Bay.

Tho' I know I can trust you with everything, still at this moment I am not at liberty to state to you my conjectures as to our probable movements, suffice it to say that I feel myself perfectly satisfied in every respect, both with my situation, and the progress I make in the Ship, I have not lost a single man by desertion, and I hope that time and attention will establish that confidence with those around me I wish,—I have got one of my old boats Crew to be Coxswain, and a little time will bring me comfortable in that respect,—I am very glad to find you visit the farm daily, and that Music forms a part of your occupation and amusement. You will I am sure consider that your conduct will form a very leading feature to your Sisters who are now living with you, and that you will not indulge them in Idleness,—but if there is any subject on which I feel diffident, it is that your kindness and affection for the Children will lead you to take *too much care* of them, believe me that nothing tends more to health than exercise and Air, and that the more they are out of the house the better. I have this day been in several of the Cottages, where the poor wretches of Children of a year and a half old take care of themselves, and are infinitely more healthy than any Gentleman's Children I ever saw, if you Nurse them too much be assured they will ever have cause to lament it, and that they will not be able to undergo the vicissitudes of this life,—If I thought any man could have a more real or sincere Love for his family than I have I should not have ventured to have expressed what I now do. Consider what your boys must undergo before they arrive even at Manhood, and I am sure you will agree with me that it is not wise to bring them up too tenderly. I shall conclude with the assurance of my sincere regard and attatchment to you and yours, and that I remain your most Affectionate husband and sincerest friend,

THOS. FRA. FREMANTLE.

SWANBOURNE, 4TH DECR. SUNDAY. We went to bed as usual at eleven o'clock and I had just got asleep when Eugenia came into my room and said there was an extraordinary smoke rising through the boards in her room near the fireplace for which she could not account as she had been in the library and all seemed apparently safe. I went with her and found her room in a dreadfull smoke; we immediately called up the servants who on looking in the library chimney saw a blaze of fire at the back of the glass. The carpenter, Henley and three other men were soon alarmed and came in a few minutes, the glass was taken down and the fire having by this time worked nearly through the stucco, the wall was broke in and with pails of water safely extinguished. It bore at one time a formidable appearance and I truly feared the house would have been burnt down. The fire had reached the beam which supports the floor of the bed room above and Taylor said if it had remained half an hour unnoticed the room must have fallen in. Eugenia and indeed us all had a most providential escape. We went to bed again at three. Eugenia behaved with most courage. I was anxious for the children and Justine was frightened Harriet should catch cold.

SWANBOURNE, XMAS DAY. SUNDAY. We had midnight Prayers and a Reveillon. It rained most wretchedly and blew violently. I had a letter from Fremantle, who had been on a short cruize in which they had dreadful weather and the ship was in great danger; they split every sail and ship's head was completely washed away:

Ganges Bearhaven near Bantry.
24th November 1803.

My Dearest Love,—We have since I wrote you last been on a short cruize, when it blew hard the whole time and I was as sea sick and miserable as my enemies could have wished me. We are now however safe at an Anchor here and are already joined by the Northumberland. The Squadron is to be reinforced, and to consist of 10 Sail of the Line and Sr. Robt. Calder to be the Admiral. The *Brittannia Goliath* and *Prince of Wales* are already named but what the other two Ships will be I cannot guess—every day we get here I consider as autant gagné from the Winter—I think you may now rest satisfied that Buonaparte will not venture to make a landing in England. I am of opinion all his efforts will be exerted against this Country, which will in course keep us in continual hot water,—We have been very Sociable and pleasant whilst at Anchor here, I am living in great habits of intimacy and friendship with Captain Jervis and Lord Amelius Beauclerk, who are both very good fellows, —the former you know lives quite en prince and we benefit much by his hospitality and good Cookery—indeed I think we all live too well, but the occupation of the Mind keeps us in good health. We have had a most unpleasant disorder raging in the Ship, namely a severe inflamation in the Eyes which has gone almost through the ship, it attacked me at first but slightly but as I did not pay attention to it and kept on Deck, I became worse and was so ill for four days running that I was obliged to have recourse to Leeches, and to sitt all day with a bandage and Night Cap drawn completely over my eyes, the pain was not so great as you would expect, but the misery of not being able to go on Deck, or to read or write was more than I can describe to you, I am now nearly recovered but my eyes look very red and feel sore,—I was so ennuyed at my blindness, that one evening I made the Chaplain read me four Sermons, which alleviated my suffering for a time.

Yours only most affectionately

T.F.F.

My Dear little boy—I am very much pleased that you have wrote me such a very pretty letter, it is so well wrote that I can find out you have been very attentive to the Lessons your Mama has given you, —I dare say I shall admire Emma's Rug—be a good boy and obey all your Mama's instructions, and then I shall love you very much when I come home,—give Emma three peepers *for me*, and tell Emma to give you three *for me*, I am my Dearest boy Your affec. father

THOS. FRA. FREMANTLE.

Ganges 1st December 1803.

My Dearest Betsey,

Disertion from the Ships here is so prevalent that not a man can be trusted on Shore. I have hitherto kept so good a look out and am realy so well attended to by the Officers that not a Single Man has left us, this I do not flatter myself arises from any regard the people have for the Ship but from the attention that is paid, and which occupies much of my time, and which is in Lent with many regulations I am making my principal source of amusement.—Yesterday I gave a Seaman permission to go on Shore to be married to a poor woman who was attending the woman who sells slops and different articles to the people; they could not get a licence to marry according to our worship as they were not residents, nor any Surrogate near, the consequence was they went to father O'Flarty the Lady being a Jolly Catholic, who refused to unite them until after advent, but my Comrade the Sailor by name Jones in his way to the Village took a fancy to a younger and prettier girl, and begged to marry her instead of his intended, this as you imagine has caused us much amusement and has proved a lucky circumstance for the original bride, who is a poor harmless creature that serves for two Guineas a year. There are two famous priests here, father O'Flarty and father Mullahoon. The former an old Drunken wretch who is completely the Governor of the lower Order of people. We called on him at 11 o'clock in the morning and found him drunk and in bed, having as he said been at a Wedding the preceding night. Father Mullahoon is of the social sort but much more the manners of the world, and more the conduct of a gentleman. The natives are almost savages, and have a species of low cunning that is incredible. We are, however, well supplied by them with turkeys, poultry and potatoes which are abundant and cheap.

5th December, 1803.

I am rejoiced John Poulet has the liberty of hunting and shooting, his visits to Buckingham will not lead him *into good Company*; I have had a very civil letter from Macdonald desiring to sail with me in the *Neptune*, and I have wrote him for answer that nothing could give me greater satisfaction. He seems to me to have selected a wife quite young enough for him. I forget what James's wages are, but I would not for two Guineas risque his leaving you, paga the good Servants, the expense and trouble of changing is intolerable. My menage is now rather better but the difficulty is to find sober people. I have now for Maitre d'Hotel a Canadian who is sober and speaks French like a Native. I am getting on rather better, the servant who succeeded David was very badly wounded and continues still very unwell. I would have you by all means give David a character for honesty and sobriety; it is the Women that turned that fellow's head. My Mother must have been in high fidgets at Fanny's accouchement chez elle; I desire you will compliment Mrs. Cathcart for me on this occasion. You are like me, I always think I do not half answer your letters, which is true in part, but I have an excuse in being frequently so hurried and having so little notice. I should like to peep in upon you all sitting over the fire and quarrelling for places; I suppose Eugenia does nothing but loll in my large chairs.

CHAPTER 25

Betsey

Swanbourne, 13th February. Monday. Lady Buckingham arrived soon after nine o'clock with Lord George, Lady Mary and Mr. Martin. We breakfasted in the Library and she admired much the House. She saw all my brats and was very civil to old Mrs. Fremantle who had not seen her for some years. She left us at eleven and the moment she was gone I was busy in clearing my room for this evening's dance, preparing the supper table &c. We dined in Capt. Fremantle's dressing room. Miss Chaplin came in the morning and little Harriet Howard who I asked to please her Mamma and is the ugliest little ape I ever saw. We all dressed after dinner and our company began to assemble at eight o'clock—Miss Heslop, Miss Bennett and her brother, five Miss Pouletts and their brother, General Poulett was ill but paid me a great *compliment* by sending all his children—Mr. and Mrs. Howard, Dr. Millner, Wodley, the Blicks, Capt. Brown, Mr. and Mrs. Harman, five Lowndes, a Mr. Oddy and another friend they brought, in all we were thirty-four. Dancing was kept up with much spirit and thirteen couples had just room enough in the Library. We supped at twelve, our table in the dining room held twenty-two, the rest were in the Dressing room. Supper was very good and all went off better than I expected. Dancing soon recommenced and was kept up till half-past four; I was so lame I could not dance and played Casino with Mrs. Fremantle. Everybody seemed much pleased with the party.

STOWE

TUESDAY, 14TH FEBRUARY. Lord George went out of hunting and Lady Mary, Doctor O'Connor and I rode. We had not got far when a heavy shower began, and in returning my horse ran away; I lost my hat, the wind blew me about and I was nearly killed. A gate however stopped him and we returned wet through. On its clearing up later, we took a walk, and rowed the Doctor in the boat—almost drowned him. Hardly had time to dress. Oh! fie for shame in the evening.

SWANBOURNE

TUESDAY, 6TH MARCH. We went and remained to see three trials, the Poor Man who killed the other is sentenced to three months' imprisonment and a fine of one shilling. The little girl received no punishment in Public, but I believe a good whipping will prevent her ever stealing again. The young Carpenter who stole the watch was pronounced not *guilty* to the blame of the Jury, in everybody's opinion, it was very wrong. We returned home in good time found an entertaining letter from Eugenia and all the children well.

[Betsey, who accomplished the annual move to London with the usual bustle, was hardly settled there before she received a letter from Fremantle:]

Off Gibraltar, 3rd April 1804.

My Dearest Tussy,

On the 15th I anchored at Gibraltar, to you who know what sort of place it is I shall not enlarge, suffice it to say that to a man who has been 16 weeks at Sea, I found it very pleasant, immediately on my landing I called on Genl. Drummond and dined with him, and from that time until this day it has been a continued Scene of festivity and good living, to bring the Detail of my proceedings at Gibraltar into as small a Compass as possible, I shall divide my days into separate Columns and I think you will say I have been amused.

Day. Mon.	*Dined.*	*Evening.*	*Observations.*
15	Genl. Drummond.	Mrs. Drummond.	Very pleasant Card party with Cold Supper.
16	Col. Airey	Mrs. Airey	Very pleasant; I live much with Captn. Ogle of the *Unite*, an excellent good man married to Miss Gaze.
17	The Commissioner. Middleton.		
18	Genl. Smith	Mrs. Smith.	Genl. and Mrs. Fox were of the party; 22 at table in a small room etc. However the same was amusing enough.
19	Genl. Grosse.	Mrs. Sweetland's card party.	He was Comg. Officer at Botany Bay and is a great friend of Bishop's I am again on good terms with him now.
20	Genl. Fox.	Mrs. Fox's ball.	Very grand indeed; upwards of 40 couples and a magnificent supper.

Day. Mon.	Dined.	Evening.	Observations.
22	Col. Fyars.	Genl. and Mrs. Fox dined alone.	Stupid enough in the Evening.
23	On bd. 16 at dinner.	Mrs. Drummond	Mrs. Fox and a large party to prayers, and a Cold breakfast afterwards.
24	On bd.	On bd.	Gave my ball which was gay enough; the weather not at all congenial.
25			
26	Genl. Fox	A public ball	Very good indeed, afterwards supped at Col. Airey's.
27	Col. Ross.	Mrs. Fox's.	Mrs. Ross very pleasant and very handsome, rather bad figure, they are Scotch.
28	Col. Fyars	Good party.	
29	Genl. Fox.	Ball at G. Fox to	Sr. Sydney Smith and Compliments, who danced with all eagerness.
30	Comr. Middleton	Mrs. Drummond.	Very pleasant party at dinner; a coze in the evening.
31	Major Wright.		Sr. Sydney Smith of the party, some very good singing in the Evening without accompanyment.
1	Col. Stirling.	Mrs. Drummond's.	
2	Col. Mc-Cloud.	Mrs. Airey's.	Both pleasant and quiet.

HARRIET

WEDNESDAY, 25TH APRIL. William Fremantle called to ask Betsey to chapron Miss Hervey to the play, she therefore accepted and at about 7 we went to Covent Garden. It was the Merry Wives of Windsor and Valentine and Orson. The first was very laughable and the latter surpassed everything in scenery; really in their last scene the stage appears a sole mass of gold; I was excessively entertained as well as Emma but Tom was sleepy and stupid. The box being small I was stuffed to death. Kemble was admirable in his part of Ford. Mrs. Siddons was in the box opposite and looked quite ugly. It was a very shewy evening and the music pretty.

THURSDAY, 3RD MAY. Mrs. Blair and her party came to dinner and we afterwards departed for the Opera. Billington sang delightfully, as for Grassini I never heard so bad a singer. She certainly is very pretty and an uncommon good Actress. Deshays danced admirably; he is excessively light; the Ballet was stupid. I got out very well handed by Sir John Burney. The round room was very full. We safely arrived to the carriage and got away very well. I amused myself the whole way by treading on people's feet. Poor Col. Fremantle was so tired that he left us soon. I spent a charming day and felt very warm the whole evening.

BETSEY

4TH MAY. FRIDAY. I received a second letter to-day from Ferrol tho' of an ancient date it was very satisfactory:

Ganges off Ferrol:
11th April, 1804.

I received a most friendly letter from Lord Nelson a few days ago dated the 6th of January. Of course, it contains nothing new, but is a proof of his attachment. As I have not lately dealt much in the *Sermonizing* line, and I know no man in Europe who has less occasion to do so to his wife than myself, still I am convinced you will feel better satisfied at hearing my opinions on many subjects, which will perhaps enable you to form further conclusions, and this I do not do from Vanity or any superior understanding, but from the experience of years, and of course longer intercourse with the world. In the first place I shall promise, by observing that situated as you are, you must consider yourself as responsible for every act, and for the entire conduct of your sisters, and I charge you whenever that is not consistent with your Ideas of what is strictly correct (in appearance I mean) for I never can insinuate anything else, that you will find some plausible excuse for going into the Country, it will not satisfy me or the world at large to say you were persuaded to let them do Idle things, use your own discretion and be firm when you are right, all responsibility will be attatched to you, and will ultimately, if you are unwise in this particular, be felt by those who are devoted to you by every tye of gratitude Love and affection.

T.F.F.

Lord Buckingham is come to Town. We are to have a change of Administration. Addington is out and Pitt is expected to come in again.

Ganges off Ferrol
27th May, 1804.

My Dearest Betsey,

You will be surprized at my writing three letters, three days following but as another opportunity may not occur, I don't like to let any Ship go from hence without communicating with you. If there is one thing that I feel distressed about, it is the want of Tooth powder and brushes for my teeth. I beg you will promise me a pretty large assortment well packed up, and send them directed for me at Mr. Glencross's Plymouth Dock.

June 22nd at Sea off Ferrol. (1804)

My Dearest Betsey,

I wish you would by some means endeavour to procure and send me a Sonata I believe of Mozart with an accompanyment of the Violin, if you recolect it was one played by Miss Tate at our house in Clifford Street, and I have frequently requested you to play it since, it is so pretty that I wish to give it to the Consul's Daughters. I hope you recolect it, I am now singing it.

2ND JULY. MONDAY. It was hotter to-day than I ever remember having felt it in England before. The wind rose very high in the evening and threatened a change of weather which greatly alarms me for my hay.

HARRIET

NEW HALL

MONDAY, 2ND JULY. A gentleman, lady and two sweet little children came. We all admired the Monsieur for his fatherly behaviour, but unfortunately he was not supposed to be the husband, and our praises were of no avail. Mr. Van Ham did not come; he is gone to London to gain the indulgence for St. Petrus Paul. God grant he may return comme il faut.

BETSEY

SWANBOURNE, 4TH JULY. WEDNESDAY. The hay-making is going on prosperously. I walked to the hayfield this morning. There will be a most abundant crop this year.

STOWE, 6TH JULY. FRIDAY. Lady Buckingham proposed at breakfast our going to see the corpse of their Under Butler, a young man of 21 who died of a consumption. Lady Mary was at last prevailed upon to pay this not very agreeable visit—the sight was unpleasant and *offensive* to the *nose*. In the afternoon we all attended the burial with Lady Buckingham—the scene was extremely affecting, the poor old father and the sisters of the deceased following the coffin in deep distress; almost everybody cried. *Eugenia sobbed* in the Church, and the end was still more tragical as the old school mistress was so overcome that she went into strong convulsions and was carried senseless out of the churchyard.

EUGENIA

STOWE

MONDAY, 9TH JULY. Ld. Buckingham went to Aylesbury after breakfast to see how the Election is going on. Ld. Temple is there canvassing for Mr. J. Grenville against Ld. George Cavendish's Son. Ly. Mary, Justina and I, in spite of the burning heat at midday, set out on a frolic, dress'd like gipsies, and ran all over the gardens, frightening children, and enraging gardeners, from whom we received plentiful abuse. I returned much fatigued and as if I had been bathed in a pond.

BETSEY

WOTTON, 22ND JULY. SUNDAY. I took the entire round of the gardens, three miles and was much delighted with the walks, which are much more natural than those at Stowe. Lady Buckingham seems to be very partial to this place, where she spent the first years of her marriage. We were invited by Lord Bm. into the Boat who was rowed about the lake by his two sons, and were some time upon the water.

EUGENIA

WOTTON

WEDNESDAY, 25TH JULY. We went in a boat, on a very fine pieces of water which they have here, several charming Islands rise in it. We enjoyed many beautiful *point de vues* there is a number of temples, bridges, pavilions, about this place, the whole is laid out with infinite taste.

I am silly enough not to be able to sleep in my room, it looks like a receptacle fit for ghosts to keep their midnight revels in—dark and gloomy to a degree—a bed—red crimson velvet furniture of the same, long window curtains, black doors, black cabinets, etc. and what is worse, a woman hung herself at the foot of the bed and Mrs. Grenville died in it. If that is not enough to conjure up black imaginations I do not know what will.

BETSEY

SWANBOURNE, 18TH SEPTR. TUESDAY. The letters made me quite cross and miserable. Fremantle hopes to be in England towards the 20th but he says if he comes to Plymouth we have no prospect of meeting, if he gets to Portsmouth he will try to obtain a few days. Justina is triste—tant mieux—son père est maitre d'ecole dit-on!

Off Ferrol, 19th August, 1804.

My Dearest Betsey,

The loss of the Election at Aylesbury has given me real concern, and I am sure must have affected

Lord B. very much. I shall not say one word to him on the subject. I advise you by no means to take more than one child with you to Stowe, you know how often we have had occasion to censure our neighbours, for such an excess of kindness on the part of Ld. B.—I received Henley's accounts, as also yours for June and July, but I have not as yet found time sufficient to examine them minutely, however, I think I may venture to say you have succeeded very well, and I make no doubt you will improve in farming, particularly as it seems to answer your purpose. I am rejoiced that Heslop is going to leave our neighbourhood; I think we can't get a worse neighbour. I have received the box with the tooth powder and brushes, and thank you for the Sonata, which will now not be of as much consequence as it would some time ago, for the Damsel to whom I meant to present it, sixteen years of age, has thought fit to fall in Love with an ugly, ill-looking officer, a Lieut. without a shilling and with a very bad character, and contrary to the advice of her parents is determined to marry him, this the father in course objects to, but the Young Lady is so headstrong that she is determined to go to a Convent until she is of age.

I can't say that I think the parents have been very prudent in allowing the fellow to have access to the house for near two years, and will with one other instance be a sufficient inducement to us to guard against an evil, which is the complete destruction of all Social intercourse in the family for evermore. I confess I am not a little surprized at Genl. Paulet's being on the Staff, and what a General can have to do in Buckinghamshire is truly astonishing,—Lord Buckingham is a Traitor to show you my letters, notwithstanding, I forgive him most cordialy as I am sure he did it from the most friendly motives, what I expressed to him I hope to see verified, tho' I am not too sanguine on that score.

To tell you how we pass our time here would be to repeat what I have already so frequently detailed. We go on Shore almost every day either to walk or to dine under a tent, tho' lately we have taken possession of a Friars garden where there is a Stone table with Seats, and covered entirely with vines, which makes the Scene rural and pleasant, besides which there is a deep well of very good water in which we cool our wine, etc. My menage goes on well, but I have lately purchased so much wine that I have impoverished myself, my Stock is very large, and my dinners by no means contemptible. —You don't say a word about the Madeira or the Old Nurse, for the former if it is not yet bottled let it remain until I come home.

LIPHOOK, 1ST NOVR. THURSDAY. I received a letter from Fremantle and as he cannot procure a leave of absence immediately, I sett out for Portsmouth at three o'clock with Tom and Emma leaving at Sunbury Mr. and Mrs. Wm. Fremantle and the Miss Herveys and several morning visitors who came tres mal a propos. I travelled the two last stages in complete darkness, and the wind was so high, at the formidable part of the road called the Devil's Punch Bowl that I began to be alarmed, but we arrived very safely to Liphook at nine o'clock, and as I had had no dinner, I got a good supper and went tired and fatigued to bed.

PORTSMOUTH, 2ND NOVR. FRIDAY. I left Liphook at day light and arrived at Portsmouth before twelve, I travelled in great anxiety in the fear of not finding mon mari, but he was at Starkeys and is looking extremely well and I was delighted to hear he would be some months in England. I was tired and stupified with my hurried journey—the children not much fatigued and Fremantle much delighted with them.

Portsmouth, 7th Novr. Wednesday. Fremantle was rather annoyed as an anonymus Letter has been written from the crew of the *Ganges* to complain of the Officers, &c. in consequence of which there was an Enquiry on board the ship to-day, which turned out much to his satisfaction.

Portsmouth, 9th Novr. Friday. I went on board the *Ganges* in the morning to see the Cabin which is very nice and comfortable—the ship is found so bad that she will probably be paid off.

Portsmouth, 10th Novr. Saturday. Fremantle has applied for a fortnight's leave of absence which will enable us to take our departure to-morrow. My sisters are to be at Swanbourne on Wednesday.

Harriet

Swanbourne

Wednesday, 14th November. We set out at nine, had a stupid journey, it rained a great deal in the morning. Poor Justine was much frightened all the stage from Brackley to Buckingham, having kicking horses and had to walk the whole eight miles. We reached Swanbourne at six, found Charles, Harry and Augusta looking rather pale but pretty.

Thursday, 15th November. We buzzled the whole morning preparing the house to make it look smart for the reception of the nice little couple. We waited with impatience till near seven o'clock when at last they arrived. Capt. Fremantle is not altered in the least and looks quite fresh and blooming. We sung, played and chatted very late with him. Justine and I are to go to Portsmouth for certain.

Betsey

24th Novr. Saturday. Fremantle heard to-day that

the *Ganges* was ordered to be paid off which will oblige him to sett out for Portsmouth to-morrow. I hope he will not be employed so soon again and that he will spend the winter at home. It snowed incessantly all day, and the weather looked so cold and comfortless that I rejoiced we should not have to remove to Portsmouth at this inclement season of the year.

EUGENIA

THURSDAY, 12TH DECEMBER. Fremantle arriv'd to a late dinner—and remained quietly at home with Betsey, who has a cold, while Justine, Harriet and I set out rather in an ill humor for the Buckingham Ball—we however liked it very well when we got there and carried 15 dances without ceasing—Gnl. Poulett was there with his son and Lucy and made a very good natured Chaperon.

HARRIET

STOWE

WEDNESDAY, 19TH DECEMBER. This is Lady Buckingham's birth day. In the evening we all danced with the tenants. Mr. Winfield was my partner, I laughed a great deal to see the different mixture of people. We could hardly breathe it was so hot and the smell was beyond anything. We danced Sir Roger de Coverly, attended their supper &c. Delighted were we to go to bed.

BETSEY

STOWE, 22ND DECR. SATURDAY. We were all very much shocked to hear to-day the death of poor Lord Proby, of the yellow fever—all the officers of his ship have shared the same fate. General Poulett's family arrived to-day. The Band of the Royal Bucks played this evening, and the young party danced.

28TH DECR. FRIDAY. I began by sending Tom and Emma home. Great confusion and preparations all the morning for the arrival of Monsieur, who came at six with the Duke of Berri, Duke d'Harcourt Le Chevalier de Puisegure and Baron de Rolle—43 at dinner in the music room, the Band playing all the time. Monsieur is very much out of spirits having lost the last year several of his friends, his misfortunes have turned his mind very much to religion and he is quite an altered man, tho' equally pleasant in society—his son seems a good humoured little body and very fond of music, I played in the evening and Eugenie sung.

STOWE, 29TH DECR. SATURDAY. Monsieur and his party went out shooting. The state appartment was lighted up this evening and we all danced in the long Gallery. The Duke de Berry only danced one dance and a Walz with Eugenie.

HARRIET

MONDAY, 31ST DECEMBER. Le Chevalier de Pisuguse walked out with us we went on the ice; every body tumbled but I, a Mr. Becket was there. He is a parson from Wooton. We all beat him for attempting to kiss us whilst our Chevaliers were skaiting after a rat. It was delightful. Skylois pushed Lady Mary, Winfield Justine, Lord George Lucy and Mr. Poulett pushed me. We afterwards went all over the house with the Chevalier who is very entertaining. We danced in the evening again in the State Gallery. Le Duc de Berri waltzed with Eugenia and Le Baron de Rolet with Justine. Monsieur goes to-morrow to the regret of all, but he will not remain longer. Capt. Browne dined here and there is to be soon another Buckingham Ball.

CHAPTER 26

Eugenia

Cottesmore, Thursday, 3rd January 1805. I found Ly. L's horses at Uppingham and arriv'd here soon after four—poor Miss Lowther is very lame with the rheumatism and looking not at all well—Ld. and Ly. Lowther seem extremely well—Miss Seymour Coleman, the maid of Honor is here, Mrs. Tom Smith, and a north Country Clergyman, Mr. Satterthwaite.

Friday, 4th. I feel once more quite *at home* here and have entered into the new spirit of the House so different from that of Stowe—Miss Coleman is very agreable, and Mr. Smith a good humored young man but not handsome—

Harriet

Saturday, 5th January. We went down to see the Children's supper which Lord George gave in honor of his birth day. I had a most singular conversation with J. who certainly was rather tipsey and I made a kind of promise which I shal fulfill six months hence if he continues in the same mind. I never spent a more pleasant evening it was heavenly. Four boys acted a play, Lord George gave a shilling to all the Girls and Lady Mary did the same to the boys. We afterwards went three *pairs* of us to see the servants dance, but upon being summoned up we reluctantly mounted. We danced and I may say with truth that this was by far the pleasantest day I ever spent here. Capt. F. went to Buckingham with John. My supper was likewise delightful in fine je ne puis que regretter qu'il n'a pas quatre Ans plus que moi.

MONDAY, 7TH JANUARY. All the Gentlemen went out of hunting, returned very late danced in the evening. I was dull at the thoughts of going to morrow and J. was miserable. We talked a great deal together and Lady B. at last found out that I liked him. She spoke both to Capt. F. & Betsey about it. I danced the first dances with him and he had no other partner the other four but Albinia. Mr. Mrs. and Miss Barnett came. Lady Buckingham played us a trick about the *changeling*. Hetty was put under the bed with her head on a cushion and her forehead was painted as a face. We were all left in the *dark in the passage*. After laughing for some time in her room, we drew King and Queen. Mrs. Cleaver was Queen and her son King. I was Lady Marrowfat. We did not laugh much about it. Our supper was dullish.

SWANBOURNE, TUESDAY, 8TH JANUARY. The breakfast was very pleasant. I talked a great deal and appeared merry although very dull. Many a promise was made me, but I fear they will soon be broken. All the Cleavers went away before breakfast. Lady B. spoke to me about my love for John, it was horridly stupid untill we went which was at twelve. John, Winfield and Major Talbot handed me in the   . I was some time alone with them. Capt. Fremantle stopped at Buckingham to pay Mr. Mcdonald a visit. The evening was shockingly dull the Children have bad colds and we were all sleepy and cross. Went to bed at ten. Heigh ho!

EUGENIA

THURSDAY, 8TH. Immediately after breakfast I went with Ly. and Miss Lowther to Apthorpe for a morg. visit we found Ly. Westmoreland, Ly. Viliers, Ly. Borringdon, Ly. Maria and Ld. Borringdon at home —*The two Brides* are looking very handsome, in spite of bad colds and Ld. Borringdon is grown *beautiful* since his marriage—Ly. Westmoreland was all civility, wanted me to stay, begg'd me to go on Thursday, etc. we return'd home to a late dinner after a drive of 42 miles.

MONDAY, 14TH. Ld. Lowther, Mr. T. Smith and Mr. Satterthwaite left us, very early, for London where the meeting of Parliament summons almost every Man—yet this was a fine day for hunting—I rode out with Miss Lowther who is only able to ride a double Horse—Mr. Finch came—

TUESDAY, 15TH. I rode out again to day and the loss of our Beaux does not affect my spirits—I live in an *imaginary world* best part of the day—

THURSDAY, 17TH. Poor Betsey has a *houseful*, a sick Child, and no hopes about herself, which I think dull enough—*Marriez vous mes filles*, as poor Mama us'd to say—

BETSEY

SUNDAY, 20TH JANUARY. My sisters flirt with Macdonald & John—faute de mieux—les filles sont d'etranges choses. I have not been at all well for this week past, being most wretchedly sick & sleepy—c'est un mauvais signe!

EUGENIA

THURSDAY, 31ST. A very bad snowy day—Ld. Henniker was to be elected Member for the County at Betham in the room of Ld. Carberry who died lately at the age of 36, of a total break up and decay of constitution—it is shocking to reflect how the Men of our days grow old before their time and shorten their lives.

BETSEY

MONDAY, 4TH FEBRUARY. Capt. Gaff and Mr. Macdonald went back to Buckingham, as Fremantle was engaged to dine at Hardwick Mr. Aubrey's. We are much surprised & annoyed at that miserable wretch Macdonald having the stupidity to leave with Justine what he said was a copy of verses he had made, & which she found to be the most ridiculous declaration of Love. We thought the best way would be to take no notice of it when he comes again on Thursday.

HARRIET

MONDAY, 4TH FEBRUARY. I never laughed more than I did for Justine received a love letter from Macdonald, the most sentimental which ever could be written, in which he acknowledges a passion makes her an offer of his heart &c. After they were gone we told this to Fremantle who was as much amused as we were, we intend taking no notice of it, and he returns on Wednesday. The Man must be a complete idiot.

THURSDAY, 7TH FEBRUARY. Macdonald came and looks more foolish than ever, he really seems mad and does not know what to do, both Justine and I cut him completely.

SATURDAY, 9TH FEBRUARY. That monster departed after breakfast and looks quite disgusting.

[Fremantle received from Lord Ongley an enchanting example of the use and abuse of patronage.]

'I have received,' Lord Ongley wrote, 'a letter from a J.P. of the County of Bucks, desiring me to let a thief, who is now in Bedford jail, return to his place where he is much wanted. He was only sent there last Monday at the finish of Quarter Sessions, and his punishment was by a mistake more lenient than was intended. The J.P. admits the man highly culpable, and I confess I feel surprised at his wishing a man to return to his place whom I was not only obliged to discharge for ruining my garden but also to prosecute as a thief. It is said that the man is particularly missed at this season at Hartwell: that is impossible, for a worse gardener and greater scoundrel does not exist: during his stay I scarce had vegetables enough for the family and had I been at home this winter I must have purchased them. As to fruit, cucumbers and the like, it was out of the question he sold the cucumbers and made all the currants goose-berries etc. into wine which was sent to London. I think my dear Sir that you will be of opinion with me that the Justice is wrong in asking for the release of this villain.'

[Alas! Fremantle's reply has not survived!]

WEDNESDAY, 13TH FEBRUARY. I was very busy the whole morning, we dressed early and at four left this. We found the Papa and Miss Poulett in the room and soon after Lucy and Johnny made their appearance. We had a very good dinner I sat between the General and Miss Poulett. John sat at the bottom of the table looked ugly having cut his hair so short on his forehead. We did not remain long at table and retired to the drawing room. We told the Miss Pouletts everything about Macdonald at which they were greatly amused. Lucy gave me a number of patterns and drawings, and we both went up to *tiff* and had a long conversation in her bedroom. She told me of a plan which John had settled, and which was so ridiculous that I laughed a long while about it. Jane and Charlotte looked very nice and the latter particularly pretty, Vera likewise étoit très joli; at about nine we set out Betsey Miss Poulett and Justine in Betsey's carriage, Lucy Vera and me in General Poulett's, and the General with John went in a Hack. I was merry the whole way talking over old affairs. Miss Beecher did not dine with us under pretence of being too unwell to come down. The room at Buckingham was very full, and we had no sooner entered the room, but Macdonald in full Uniform came flying up to me to remind me of my engagement, he looked just like a Corporal, and I could have thumped him. My two first dances were stupid to a degree which was not supportable. My two next with John were much better, I then danced with Robert Lowndes, who kept teazing and plaging me the same as usual. We went to supper at one J. begged me to let him sit by me but I could not as I had promised Lucy to be by her and I danced with Robert it was therefore impossible for me to *allow* that honor, he sat by the two Miss Chaplins, to whom he hardly spoke. I was stupid enough at the top of the table. General Poulett was elected Stewart for the next ball which is to be on the 13th of March, I am quite mad about it and could cry with vexation. I danced with J. after supper, and rested two dances talking to him, and then we closed the ball with Sir Roger de Coverly when I danced it again and it was five before we left off. Macdonald behaved like a Jack Ass and provoked me a great deal, he would hand us in the carriage. J. promised to call soon. He was particularly drole to me and told me of all his mechancetés. It was near seven before we got to Swanbourne I was tired to death and sleepy beyond measure therefore delighted to get to bed.

FRIDAY, 22ND FEBRUARY. John Poulett called at one we were out when we heard the bell but soon returned he brought me a nice note from Lucy which I answered and then walked round the garden with him and Justine. He was come all by himself and notwithstanding his father having strictly forbid any horse going out of the Stables. The General was gone to Aylesbury but was to be back by three. John told us all his Misfortunes, and I pity him most sincerely—really to be kept in the way he is at the age of sixteen is a most cruel thing, he quite made us dull with all the things he told us. I was left a minute alone with him in the Garden, Justine went to fetch Macdonald's letters, but he like a wise boy never said the last word to me. He is in hopes of going to town, but Alas! I know not what to say about it except that I wish it most sincerely. He made a number of awkward excuses for not shewing himself on Tuesday, but I can see threw it, and can easily guess the motif which induced him to act so. He left us at half past two, and I hope he may not be found out.

Friday, 8th March. Sir Thomas Troubridge and other *Bucks* called. We went out in the Carrige and to my joy and great surprise Justine declared she saw John Poulett walking Arm in Arm with Major Talbot in Bond Street, I thought she was playing me a trick but on our return home we found he had really called. I am so delighted that I hardly know what to do. Betsey wrote them a note to invite them for Sunday but they answered saying they could not go out before Monday. I am very sorry, but I must not grumble as their coming to town is really a thing I did not expect in the least.

Friday, 22nd March. John at last called at twelve and made himself tolerably *amiable*, his Sisters came whilst he was in the room. The General has a dreadfull inflammation on his eyes and cannot go out of town, this gives me real delight. We heard of poor Colonel Fremantle's death. Mrs. Wiseham payed a tremendous visit, and Betty Morgan likewise. John and I laughed much about the Old Maid. We called for the Pouletts at nine and made our entrée at Lady B's together I remained with them the whole evening. Deace was there and so many people I knew that it was quite ridiculous. Lord Southwell spoke to me the whole evening, a thing qui rendit mon Jean un peu jaloux ainsi il fit la meme chose avec Fanny Talbot.

WEDNESDAY, 1ST MAY. The chimney sweepers begun their gambles and proved rather troublesome. I did not go out in the evening to rest for to morrow. Viganoni and Cori came.

THURSDAY, 2ND MAY. Sir Jonathan Lovett, Sir William Young, Admiral Berkeley, General Hastings and a Mr. Hanford dined with us. Betsey and Eugenie went to Grassini's benefit. We looked very smart in our sarsenet Gowns and at nine Mrs. Lloyd called for us. Mr. Lawrence the famous painter and the handsomest man in London was of our party. I never remember seeing a greater number of quizzers than we witnessed. All the hair dressers shoe makers and taylors of London were invited. The women were terrible. I danced very little feeling tired and n'ayant aucune émulation pas comme je sentois a Stowe ou a un bal de Buckingham. My partners were the ugliest men in the room especially one who was very like me and sported a smart pair of spectacles on his nose. The supper was quite magnificent, and altogether very well managed. We departed at four, I was not much tired, as I really did not enjoy it sufficiently to induce me to figure away with a horrid quiz.

BETSEY

TUESDAY, 7TH. We dined at Mrs. Douglas, Fremantle came home to dress to go with us but just received a Letter from Lord Garlies (who is now one of the Lords of the Admiralty) to inform him Ld. Barham had this day appointed him to the *Neptune* 98 guns, which is coming into Plymouth in a few days. I fear he will be obliged to join her very soon.

CHAPTER 27

[Fremantle had indeed to leave soon, and at the summer's end was Trafalgar. Betsey had not realised how terribly near Fremantle's departure was; but next day enters the following:]

WEDNESDAY, 8TH MAY. We were very busily employed in preparing for our little Concert—& poor Fremantle in getting information about his ship & making arrangements for his departure. He dined at his Brother William's & came to our music late. Dragonetti dined with us another very good second violin & Bartolozzi came to play Quatuors & accompany. Our company did not come till near ten & the party was very select & brilliant—about 130 in all. The Amateur performers were Mrs. W. Jerningham on the Harp, myself on the Piano, the Chevalier La Caema who really sung delightfully, Mrs. Peploe, Miss Fanny Cornewall, Eugenia & Mr. Mercer. We had asked all our best acquaintance & *very charitably* left out the Quizzes. Our party ended very dismally as after every body was gone poor Fremantle who had looked very unhappy all the evening announced to us he should be obliged to sett out to morrow for Plymouth to join his Ship. I wish he had not been employed so soon but at any time it happen'd I should have disliked it, therefore it is perhaps better while we are in Town than had he left after my return to Swanbourne.

SATURDAY, 11TH MAY. I heard to day from Fremantle from Portsmouth where he made every arrangement about his Wine & Cabin Furniture, & expected to get to Plymouth to morrow, His ship is quite ready for sea, so that he will sail immediately. We all stayed at home, I feel *low & not quite well.*

MONDAY, 13TH MAY. Princess Sophia again asked for Tom & Emma to go to her to morrow morning to the Queens House with Miss Heryey. I went this evening with my sisters & two Miss Cornewalls to Cramer's benefit. It was very well attended & a good selection of music. Mrs. Billington played a Lesson on the Piano with Cramer remarkably well.

TUESDAY, 14TH. Tom & Emma were very much pleased with their visit to the Princesses & were taken to the Queen, who admired Emma, but said her shoes did not do justice to her foot & that she should send her shoemaker to make her two pair. Princess Sophia gave Emma a necklace and fan & Tom had some trifling present likewise.

FREMANTLE

FRIDAY, 17TH MAY, NEPTUNE, OFF USHANT. I begin my journal with saying that I have passed as miserable a day and night as I could well expect, tho' I have no particular reason why that should be the case as everything goes on very smoothly—I have just met the *Lotus* returning into port but as I wrote yesterday I shall not communicate by her,—Oh, Night, I am just going to bed having walked myself quite tired, I have been worrying a parcel of fellows cleaning my cabin not before it was wanted, —Saturday, 18th, I dined with Young Hastings only on a fowl and some salt pork, as triste as a gentleman need to be I get rather more seasoned to my misery, but feel the want of furniture and linen,—A propos, you should call upon Mrs. Cunningham who is a relation of Lord Carysford's, make *le gentil* to her as her husband has been very attentive to me,—I think she lives at No. 17 in Harley

Street, 20th. All misery, it is now blowing very hard and I am sea sick,—You know that Capt. Cunningham is a Commissioner of the Victualing,—I dined with Sir Ch. T. Cotton on board the *San Josef*, the day before yesterday there I met George Martin and some old acquaintances, Lord Gardner was very gracious, but I saw him only for a short time, Mrs. Martin was waiting for her husband at Plymouth, I don't see much prospect of this meeting,—he very honorably gave me up my 7 midshipmen which makes me feel somewhat more at home, they have all behaved very well,—This morning a Squadron of nine sail of the Line under Adml. Collingwood left the Fleet, for some place, where we have to learn,—The Loire frigate joined us yesterday and made the signal for having been chased by 5 sail of the enemy's ships, I hope Adml. Collingwood is gone after them, the wind is now favorable for our Squadron and will hinder the french getting into their own ports, we want something to raise the spirits of the country,—I wrote a few days ago to Mr. McArthur the Agent for the Toulon prize money desiring he would pay it into the hands of Mess. Morland & Co. whenever it becomes due, I should imagine that will be the case in a week or two,—I am certainly to return to Plymouth soon that the ship may be paid, and I have great satisfaction in saying that I continue perfectly satisfied with any appointment my mind hangs constantly towards you and your children, and I am at times so low I cannot hold up my head, this sort of ennui and indolence makes me as bilious as possible and the want of the ordinary comforts deprives me of the society of my Officers entirely,—I envy you your occupations at Swanbourne how I should have enjoyed a month there and making all my little arrangements, my only hope is in a peace, which I trust in God may be brought about through the mediation of Russia, These french Rascals will never come out and fight but will continue to annoy and wear out both our spirits and constitutions.—If I judge right here is a cutter coming that will bring me something from Cork Street, pray let me hear from you regularly I beg.—Remember me most affectionately to all your sisters kiss all the children for me and believe me ever most faithfully and truly yours,

T.F.F.

Another letter from Fremantle:

May 23rd, 1805.
Off Ushant.

My Dear Tussy,—

I wrote to you only this day a sort of pitiful letter which I had not time to finish, I began again in order to be in readiness to avail myself of the fresh opportunity that occurs. The weather has been so cold all day that I am coddling myself over a fire, which is better company than none, I get on quietly and comfortably, and have already found out a great deal more care in a three decked ship than one of two,—my low spirits are excessive and I do nothing but take snuff and read Shakespeare, when I am off the deck,—thank you my dearest woman for your attention in sending me the newspapers, I had wrote to Richard Butler on the subject,—I could wish to have the *Morning Post Morning Chronicle* and *Cobbet*, settle it with Richard Butler on a sure foundation, to be *permanent*, and have them directed for me at Mr. Kent's, you can't think how much I enjoy these periodical papers, and daily ones,—6th June—I this instant receive your very interesting letter of the 1st of May, everything contained therein is so very much as I could wish it to be that I have no comment to make on it. The Toulon prize money rejoices my heart, there is £2114 to be paid on account for what I borrowed, the rest is to be placed to my account and you will do the needfull with it, Stephens the Upholsterer must be paid as soon as convenient—Turner at Portsmouth has been annoying me to pay him £200, I wish my mother could spare me as much just now, as I can't bear owing so much to him, I think I shall muster courage and write to him some of these days.

I am quite flattered at the King and Queen's attention to my children, it will quite turn Mrs. Emma's head, how I long to see you all, but—

I am getting the curtains up in my cabin and am at last making myself as comfortable as circumstances will allow me to be, indeed I am quite reconciled to my ship inasmuch as that I prefer her to any in the Navy—I acknowledge I am glad your nurse is not going to leave you, I hate new faces,—

David's head is worse than ever, he has left my mustard pot in London, and missed three coats on the road, the latter I have got, and will get some sort of a mustard pot at Plymouth, a propos I wish you would send me nine yards of livery lace with some small buttons, I want to make 4 jacketts for my boys, the cloth I can get at Plymouth,—I must conclude immediately, give my best love to your sisters and peepers to the brats,

ever your most afft. husband
T. F. FREMANTLE.

HARRIET

FRIDAY, 14TH JUNE. It rained all day nothing but bills to pay, I remained at home without stirring *once*.

SATURDAY, 15TH JUNE. We afterwards went to the

Opera and to our sorrow had again La Clemenza. Paul and Virginia pleased me as much as last time. We only had the Second Act of Ossian and when the Green curtain fell down, being only 20 minutes past eleven a scene of riot took place which perfectly astonished me. The *Beaux* in the pit clapped for some time that the entertainment might continue, but upon nobody making their appearance they jumped upon the stage tore down the curtain and scenes, broke every instrument, threw chairs at the chandeliers, in fine the whole house in a few minutes was left in total darkness. We remained quietly in the box attended by Mr. Salisbury and Tom Smith, and got away very well a long time before this scene of vulgarity ended. Kemble was collared and obliged to make an appology and the name of Goold resounded from every quarter, but he was in the country and could not make his appearance. We left the *Monsieurs* busily employed in tearing up benches and only four Lustres escaped their fury. The damages cannot amount to less of 5000 Pounds.

[Eugenia says:]

SATURDAY, 15TH JUNE. I never witness'd such a Shameful Scene of riot, and never could have thought that a *Mob* of gentlemen could be so tremendous a thing —We staid till past one and they had not finish'd their work of destruction then—they must have done damage for at least £500—one gentleman had his arm broke—I only wonder the house was not set on fire—Dragonetti ran away with his Contrabasso on his back the moment he perceived symptoms of a riot—Mr. Charles Manners seem'd to me very active in doing mischief—

[And Betsey explains the cause of the trouble:]

The Bishop of London having some time ago

insisted the Performance should be over by twelve o'clock the Ballets have in general been curtailed on a Saturday night, but this evening the Green Curtain having dropped at twenty minutes after Eleven, after only the second act of the Ballet of Ossian, the first having been left out, a great noise & riot commenced.

Betsey received a letter from Fremantle, dated

June 14th, 1805.
As usual off Ushant.

My Dearest Love,

I just receive your letter of the 4th, which you have the modesty to say contains nothing, I on the contrary think it contains everything as I am assured of the health and happiness of all I hold dear in the world, indeed I think it most interesting, and you can have no idea how an arrival revives and comforts my spirits which are not so good as they used to be, in fact I am by no means so comfortable in point of *acquaintance* on board as I was in the *Ganges*, altho' I have no very serious cause to be dissatisfied, the duty does not go with the same good humour, where there is not a mutual understanding, and I don't see how it can be amended, my only consolation is in the recollection that au dernier resort, I shall have the happiness of returning to the arms of the most affectionate wife, and children any man can be blessed with, I am horribly worried at times with ennui and bile, and still I flatter myself I am getting more reconciled to this dog's life. The times appear to me getting worse daily, and I am really quite a croaker about them,—in looking over my books I find the cypher you and I used to correspond with, tell me if you have got yours, as circumstances may occur that may make it necessary for me to communicate in that way—11 o'clock the wind increases and I am getting sleepy, Good night, I shall not seal this up perhaps for some days,—

16th. the signal is made for weekly accounts and I will venture this altho' it contains nothing very material, I have not yet got either my linen or my mahogany writing table, Mr. Kent writes me, he shall keep them until the *Neptune* arrives in port so that I am absolutely at this instant without a table cloth a towel or a clean shirt.

[And another shortly after, dated:]

Neptune off Ushant
18th June 1805

My Dear Tussy—

Today we have been pitching about a great deal and I have a most complete fit of the bile which I have been endeavouring to get rid of by drinking large portions of lemonade, but I am still stupid and heavy, I am very considerably annoyed to find you do not get my letters so soon as other people I cannot account for it as you are perfectly aware I never let any opportunity of writing to you escape, nor have I at any time ever wrote to Lord Buckingham without writing to you, I am sure I need not say more to convince you of the truth of what I have stated, and I should be miserable if I thought you could for a minute suppose I was wanting in that respect indeed my Dearest Woman you and my children employ many hours of my thoughts every day, and I build castles in the air, and fancy a hundred things that I hope may be realised, be assured my whole happiness is centered in you and yours, which I trust you are fully pursuaded of,—

I received yesterday a very kind letter from Lord Buckingham, dated the 13th consequently only 4 days from town, with it a newspaper containing the debates on Lord McCodle's business, which was very interesting to us. We have had some change in the order of sailing which pleases me, and is not worth explaining to you,—

If I judge right you will be tomorrow or next day on the road to Swanbourne bag and baggage, what an undertaking almost equal to the constructing of a 2d. rate.

[Yet another follows hard upon the last:]

Saturday night, 22nd June 1805.

My Dear Betsey—

My letter of this days date you will have received eer this, but as I am not very sleepy, I will converse with you five minutes before I retire to the gentle arms of Morpheus, you see I am poetical, you can have no idea how anxious I am to have your next letter which will in course be from Swanbourne,— You have not said one word about the carriage, whether it is well fitted or to your liking,—if I knew Eugenia's address I would certainly have wrote her a long letter, I am occupied a great deal just now in reading a new novel called *Family Secrets*, it is a compound of unnatural occurrences but being embarked on it, I am doomed to wade through five volumes, it belongs to the Purser's steward. My will which I was so anxious to have finally arranged, has been received by Mr. Baxton, who has by my direction deposited it with Lord Buckingham's at Mr. Box's the banker at Buckingham, should anything happen to me I trust my Dearest Woman you will feel satisfied with the arrangements I have made for you and yours, it will prove were it necessary to add that proof of the sincere regard, as well as of the high opinion I have of your good qualities and understanding, it is the most consoling as well as the most gratifying feeling possible under the separation we are doomed to suffer, to reflect on the sweetness of your disposition and your unvaried attention and kindness to me and your children, but I will drop a subject on which I assure you I could enlarge, but it is too melancholy to indulge in,—These cabins are so large, that two wax candles are not perceived in them, it gets late I shall therefore wish you a good night altho' I think you are by this time in bed with the little Emma, as fast as a dormouse.—

Monday night 24th. all yesterday I was worrying to make my people more cleanly, I dined in the Wardroom and went to bed rather earlier than usual with a fit of the bile,— This morning I got up early and have been the whole day with all hands setting up the rigging and putting matters to rights,— The *Rolus* is arrived from Plymouth and newspapers, of the 21st. No letter from Mrs. Tussy, but I had one so lately that I did not expect one, a letter to Nagle from his agent mentions a change of Government and that Lord Grenville is to be first Lord of the Admiralty, and Lord Spencer to go to Ireland, I can't flatter myself this can be true,—

Tuesday night 25th. today the *Glory* with Rear Admiral Sterling joined us from Portsmouth and the *Ville de Paris* is gone to Plymouth for some purpose, I hope it is not to bring Cornwallis here, he is so unaccomodating there is no getting papers or letters when he is in command, I have got everything except my Gigg which is still at Portsmouth, the two frigates that were at Weymouth last year and will I conclude go there this summer are now with us, my message is rather better than it was, mais mes gens sont si extravagants qu'ils ont mangé ou volé plus d'un livre du Thè chacque semain, c'est trop cela n'est pas ma Betzi, et coute un demi guinea le livre, diable, I have had a letter from the d—d copper people for £2.10. I wish you would pay the rascals and have done with them.—Jinny Jinny Jinny Jinny Jinny, I think very much of that dear girl, who is certainly a very different character from you, I could find in my heart to write her a saucy letter if I was not afraid, but I am cold and tired, and to bed I shall go, so good-night again, I shall not send this away until I can find enough to fill two sides more.—

I am sorry the poor Mace is dead but I can't cry, her value was not great, and our accidents of that sort are not in general very numerous, I should be sorry if anything happened to the coach horse, you must spare the hack horses when you get home as much as you can, you don't tell me whether the waggon brought Mrs. Jns. Fremantle's things to London,—I am afraid my dear Betsey you had drank a little too much when you wrote, for you talk of Mr. Butler's bill that was enclosed, of Lord G: Grenville's letter that was enclosed, neither of which have I ever sett eyes on, but patienza, I should have liked to have seen the latter, because you say it was amusing. I forgot to tell you I have got my tooth brushes and powder.

23rd. There is a signal flying for letters and tho' it is only two days since I wrote you as you are a good little girl and that I know my letters make you happy I shall send this off,—Malheur, the only poor goat that was in the ship fell down the hatchway yesterday and I am obliged to drink my breakfast without a drop of milk. I don't know it is I have been all this day thinking of Emma, tell her I am dying for a great number of peeps, but I must seal up,

Harriet

Swanbourne, Monday, 24th June. The horse was at

last well enough to permit us to smell Winslow air. When we got near the dwelling of the *Miss Nymphs* We met General Poulett who told us his daughters were coming to us—We first asked if the Miss Lowndes were at home, and as they had just set out for Oxford we continued our route and as we got up the lane we met John looking quite hidious, with his hair in powder, a pink neckcloth blue Waistcoat nankin inexpressibles and blue coat, he really was a sight, and soon went on, and when we got to the turning the Miss Pouletts were just coming—We stopped and I got in their carriage and they took my place and I had a very pleasant journey home talking the whole while, they remained some time with us and after making us promise to dine with them on Thursday—They departed—I gave Lucy a little cat and she is to give me a Canary—John was to inspect the volunteers and was not of the party here—he declares he never will call here if his Sisters discover his intentions—Lucy played him a trick about the famous promise—We walked out almost the whole evening.

Neptune, Plymouth, 24th July 1805.

My Dearest Betsey,

I am in hopes of getting a very famous band, who have offered themselves to me, they are the 2nd Devonshire Militia band, the Regiment being reduced, I hope I shall get them, tho I shall not cry if I do not as it will certainly lead me into some expense, as I go on rarely with my Ship and if I succeed in my band, I shall indeed be en grand Seignieur.

I have been on board all this morning and am so pleased not a Complaint of any sort, and a sober good boats crew who begin to creep into my ways and good graces. Mr. David is more idle every day I must get rid of him soon. I cant write any more, for I am tired and worried a little, God bless you all, peeper the dogs for me ever affectionately yrs.

T. F. FREMANTLE.

Plymouth 27th [July 1805].

My Dear Betsey,

I am just come in from the *Dock yard*, and the weather is so sultry that my hand shakes so much I can hardly hold my pen,—I shall not be sorry to go to sea again, which I think will be about the 2nd or 3rd of next month, and we shall go I understand first to the Fleet and from thence off Ferrol,—I think any place better than being with Cornwallis, I shall be with Sir Rob. Calder who has now a very large fleet with him.

I dined yesterday with Adml. Sutton and went afterwards to a ball given by the Lieut. Governor at the Citadel, it was gay and elegant enough with all the principal people, but still I did not enjoy it in the least, I was the only person that did not dance,—I think I shall get my ship fitted out well which is no small consolation,—I am going to dine with Commissioner Fanshaw today he has a very large family of amiable daughters, I believe four married and four single, who do you think I met at Genl. England's ball, but the Miss Stephens's whom you must recollect quite children with their mother in Corsica Elba and Gibraltar, the youngest who was then an infant is now literally as tall as me, I talked a great deal with them the eldest is married to a Major of Artillery.

I am afraid I shall be disappointed about getting my band of music, as I have not heard from the man since I wrote you—this new fitting out will cost me a great deal of money but I can't help it, I wish to heaven's the war was over and I was safely landed at Swanbourne,—pray continue to write twice a week, I shall want every sort of news more than ever.—

I am really so tired with the heat and setting up so late last night that I am quite stupid, I promised to spend the evening with the Miss Stephens's on Sunday, and I dine with Mr. Kent and his five daughters the same day.

Adml. Young is very civil to me, as is also Sutton, but the terror of perhaps four months at sea does I confess not afford much prospect of real happiness, however I am so much better off than many of my neighbours that I must not repine, Whilst you are confined, I know Harriet will have the kindness of corresponding with me, Eugenia's letter is gone to sea, I shall find it when I join the Fleet, kiss all the dear children for me my Dearest Woman, and believe me ever most affectionately yours

TH. FRAS. FREMANTLE.

My Dear Betsey—

I write to say two Spanish Ships prizes to the Squadron under Sir Robt. Calder are just arrived, it has made all bustle and joy here, the action was not very severe, only 40 killed and 147 wounded in all, I am to be paid on Thursday and to sail on Friday.

God bless you,

ever affy. Yours,

THOS. FRAS. FREMANTLE.

HARRIET

STOWE, FRIDAY, 9TH. Mr. Tom Grenville came—and to my surprise and joy, Lord Temple and Lord

George came during dinner, *My* boy is quite tanned —*He* walked out with us in the evening but we did not stay very late on account of Lady Mary having a little sore throat—Lord G. has not spoken to Mr. Arundell since his return and I fear he has been set against him by his brother during his stay at Aylesbury—

BETSEY

THURSDAY, 15TH AUGUST. I walked through the rooms which are all finished & have a very splendid appearance, the appartment fitted up for the Duke of Clarence is very handsome in the Egyptian style, & quite a State Bed put up for him, which is extremely elegant. The Portico is quite an orange grove, being filled with orange trees in the finest blossom and green House plants. We had a sort of dinner at three o'clock as the Prince was not expected till eight, but he arrived much sooner than was expected & made his appearance soon after four o'clock when Ld Buckingham was alone ready to receive him. He brought with him the Duke of Clarence, Mr. Fox, Col^{l}. Calcraft and Major Bloomfield. The Duke & Dutchess of Bedford arrived a little before him. We all met at half past five in the State Gallery where we stood in a formal circle for an hour before dinner was announced—the going into dinner was no less formidable, the Band was playing in the Saloon above, & there was two rows of Servants in their full Liveries & valets de Chambre in dark blue Coats covered with Gold Lace. I contrived to get to the side Table where I sat more at my ease. The Princes table was layed for forty & we were about 18 more at a Side Table. Nothing could exceed the splendour & magnificence of the Dining room especially when the candles were lighted. We had music in the evening in the State Drawing room & my performance met with great success.

FRIDAY, 16TH AUGUST. We breakfasted at eleven in the State drawing room where two tables were layed. The Prince walked afterwards with Ly Buckingham to the Flower Garden, & was drove by her in the Garden Chair, The Duke of Clarence with Lord Buckingham followed in another, they returned at two when all the equipages & Horses came round to the North Front, two Barousches & six, several with four Horses, besides Curricles. They all drove in the Park, I did not like to venture for fear of fatiguing myself. Dined at six & soon after nine, the Grotto being illuminated & the greatest concourse of people possible being assembled in the gardens, we all followed the Prince in Procession to the Grotto, among the shouts of the multitude, who crowded so much upon us we had some difficulty in reaching to the destined spot, which had the appearance of enchantment, the Grotto & surrounding scene being illuminated most brilliantly, the Bridge & Obelisk on the water had a charming effect. Several Maskers were pitched on the banks, & groupes of Morice Dancers, the Bands of the Pandeons, Savoyards, & of the Regiments who were on the water played in succession, & enlivened the scene, the crowd was so great, there being at least 10,000 people present that I remained in the Grotto, with Mrs. Berkeley, while the rest of the party walked quite round the water. On the Princes return to the Grotto the Fire works commenced & succeeded wonderfully well, the water rockets had a particular good effect & the whole went off with great éclat. I sat snug in the grotto by *Charles Fox* & had a good view of the whole. The Prince & Grandees, such as the Dutchess of Grafton, Ly

Euston &c. supped in the Grotto, the Knyvetts sung Catches & Glees during the supper. I went to one of the marquees, & did not get home till one o'clock.

HARRIET'S

account of the splendours is as follows:

FRIDAY, 16TH. We breakfasted in the Music room Lord Althorpe is excessively pleasant as well as Major Bloomfield who made us pass a most delightful breakfast—We then sung and at one Lady B. drove the Prince in the garden chair round the park, Mr. and Mrs. Jerningham Ly. Mary, Mr. Arundell and I followed in Lady Temple's barouche and six, We had excellent fun the whole way, and laughed much—We went in to dress, and afterwards prepared for our evening entertainment—At nine Mr. Arundell with Ly. Mary of one side and I of the other followed the Prince to the Grotto—The evening was beautiful, and luckily, it only threatened rain, which thank God never made its appearance—It was with great difficulty we got to the distant spot, but our trouble was greatly rewarded, for the Scene was something most magnificent—The Grotto, bridge Villas Marques formed a most enchanting coup d'oeil.

Crowds of spectators had come within the ropes. Music was heard in every part and of every kind and really the sensations, which this same inspired was something quite sublime. The Pandeans, Savoyards and Morris dancers greatly enlivened the spot. The band was in the middle of the water and indeed I was thunderstruck with surprise finding everything so totally surpassing my greatest expectations. I was surprised to find among the crowd, General Poulett and John, I spoke to them for some time, then lost sight of them, but I sent

Lord George to search them and then we walked completely round with them. John looked beautiful, and I got him in the grotto, to his utter astonishment, for every body turned round to see who he was. We remained in the grotto until the Prince got up from Supper when we took the round again and went home among the Shouts of the populace at two in the morning. The Knyvetts sung remarkably well in the grotto during supper and the fireworks succeeded very well indeed they were magnificent. I did really spend a most delightful evening, cet Arundell *etoit fort drole*. The gardens were crowded to near four o'clock, and every body seemed in high spirits. The Prince was delighted and I think the amusement was calculated to render him so. The Vases before the house were illuminated.

SATURDAY, 17TH AUGUST. After breakfast, Lady Mary, Miss, Mr., Mrs. Jerningham and I set out in Lady Temple's barouche for Wakefield lodge. We were followed by a great many, being in all 5 barouches, besides Cavaliers and the Princes' Landau. The road was crowded with spectators, and the Duchess of Grafton with three Lady Fitzroy's joined our party. The hounds were then turned out, and the Prince mounted his charger, and ils allerent a la chasse. The sport was nothing, but the scene was delicious and the grounds really lovely. At four o'clock, after being quite broiled in the Sun, we adjourned to the lodge, which is rather an ugly house, but delightfully situated, and commanding a true romantic prospect. All the Lady Fitzroy's both the Ducchess and Lady Euston's daughters are ugly, but very good humoured. We sat down to a cold dinner at half past four, qui fut assez bien servie, mais pas d'argenterie. Although it was Saturday, I eat meat, but pauvre Arundell quoiqu'il mourait de faim ne mangea qu'un peu de pain et fromage—he looked quite starved. I made Mr. Calcraft promise to ask the Prince to let us dance in the evening, which he did. After our repast we ladies walked out on the lawn and the Duchess of Bedford who is a most charming little woman made us laugh a great deal. Lady Henry Fitzroy's little girl was brought to be admired she is a nice child enough. At about eight we took our leave, and really our journey home was delicious, our barouche was followed by Cavaliers, on horseback, which consisted of Mr. Arundell, Lord George, Mr. Jerningham, Major Young, and Mr. Hervey. Lady Mary and I sung to the amusement of the spectators Ld. George played a thousand pranks, and he with Lord Ebrington had a match at *groussing*. We no sooner arrived than we all departed to make our toilet. We then adjourned in the Saloon, and I danced with Lord George and Mr. Arundell and at about twelve we sat down to a dinner supper, being by Everdino, I did not find it either long or tedious. We had glees and Lord Buckingham was taken ill and obliged to leave the table. Ldy. Mary sung Nanny very well, and pretended having heard what my neighbour told me which rendered me uneasy. He certainly is a drole de Corps, to make me his confidante, and I do sincerely pity him. After supper, Ldy. Mary contrived so well as to get most of my secrets out, and she is rather surprised at what I know on the subject.

MONDAY, 19TH AUGUST. The Prince and some of the party went to Insmore whilst others went out hunting, and Lady Mary drove me in the garden. Mair, and Mr. Jerningham and his wife, followed us in Ldy. Temple's. We overtook the huntsmen but did not see much of their sport. Before our drive, Lady Mary and I had taken a long *nap* on her bed. After dressing *very* smart, we went to dinner as usual by Everard who is quite charmant, he did not speak as much as usual, for Miss Berkeley was of the other side. The back part of the house was illuminated and looked quite beautiful, Major Bloomfield, Lady Mary and I went to see it from the Colonade. We began dancing at ten, as General Poulett was not come I begun with Major Bloomfield.

The Prince opened the ball with the Duchess of Bedford, and the Duke of Clarence and Lady Mary followed. I was surprised in turning round with a quizzical young man to find no more or less but Johnny metamorphosed in the oddest way with a *long pigtail.* I soon discovered Mary and sung, and to my joy the Papa was booted and could not dance. I thought the first dance intolerably long, we made a Second set and then it was very pleasant. We reposed sometime and John engaged me for the supper dance. I danced with Mr. Arundell in the second set composed of Six couples and enjoyed it much. We returned acquaintance with Miss Beaver who had often been at Irnham and he thinks her a very nice girl. We had a long conversation between the sets and I was so tired that I could not *foot* away with *éclat.* My dances with John were quite ridiculous—for in the middle of Sir Roger (which we danced snugly, in a corner of the room), Lord George armed with a pair of Scissors cut off my partners tail this caused great mirth among us, and we laughed for a long while. We went to supper at four, six tables were laid out in the Library, the Prince sat with his party in the Music room, and the Grenville room was likewise turned into a supper one. Covers were laid for 400, and all the county was present. The Miss Lowndes's were dressed very well and Robert made strong love to Miss Louren who in my opinion is far from pretty. John was quite odd during supper and reminded me of my fatal promise. We had great fun about it and I *refered* the *cause* to Mr. Jerningham. We did not sit long, and made a set for dancing reels, which was deemed a crime by Ldy. B. We returned to the dancing room and walked up and down for a considerable time and then sat upon the sopha until the Pouletts went, John promised to call on Saturday, and was je suis sure d'une humeur amoureuse. Lady Mary, Mr. Arundell, Major Talbot and I sat near the window laughing till past six, when exhausted with fatigue we retired to rest after having spent a most harmonious evening.

THURSDAY, 22ND. At twelve we went to draw with Mr. Nattes. I took a sketch passablement bien and Lord George told me he was going to Addington and I wrote a pencil note to Lucy which I gave Mr. Arundell to deliver to her. Lady Mary and I were the whole morning with Nattes and we sung to him whilst he drew. Mr. Arundell told me he met John at Buckingham and gave him my note. I teazed him for not sitting by me at dinner and we laughed a great deal. After dinner Lord Temple had a long conversation with Lady Mary and she cried. In the course of the evening she begged me to tell Mr. Arundell to meet us in the Portico tomorrow morning. I found a favourable opportunity to speak to him. He looked surprised.

FRIDAY, 23RD. I did not sleep well and got up very early. Went in Lady Mary's room before nine and found her dressing. Lady B. came in, in her night cap, looking half distracted and telling us she saw Arundell walking by himself and could not make out what rendered him so dull. We did not say much, but as soon as she was ready we got out and found Mr. Arundell in the library. He followed us to the Portico and we went down the steps which made him retreat, he however soon came to us, and the conversation which passed between them was most proper. Lady M. intreated him never to come back again, and explained matters so well, that he promised to go to morrow without fail. I think it luck there is no love between, as an explanation would have cost them very dear, instead of which they freely spoke their sentiments, and nothing not friendship ever subsisted between them. I was awkwardly situated and did not speak one word. We looked very dull at breakfast and Ldy. B. kept plaguing him to remain till next week but he seemed determined to go away. I hope nothing will prevail on him to stay after tomorrow. Ld. B. and I left them walking out together and at 11 we took our departure. I was truely distressed at leaving Lady Mary for she seemed quite sorry at losing me; I love her dearly and think she has acted most wisely on the subject of A. We stopped half an hour at Buckingham, and met John who says he will call to morrow just at the gate of Addington. We saw Lucy, Mr. Forster and Vera who had come to meet us and ask us to eat sandwiches which we refused. Mary continues wishing a great deal and Lucy begins. We got home by two and found all the Children well. Walked out after dinner, was rather dull.

Swanbourne, Saturday, 24th. At one John came according to promise, he had not been long here before Mr. and Mrs. and Miss LeMesurier came, I was quite vexed at their coming they asked us to dinner for Friday which we refused. John did not stay long and said very little indeed, he looked handsome mais *je ne l'aime plus l'amitié remplace mon amour.*

[Betsey on her return to Swanbourne found some letters from her husband:]

August 1st [1805] Cawsand Bay

My Dearest Love,

To you who know the perpetual hurry and the continued perplexities, that daily occur when a ship is but a few days in port, which are not *made* easier to a person like myself exceedingly anxious about his ship, I shall not apologize so much as I feel I am bound to do for the very shabby letters I have been in the habit of writing to you since I have been at Plymouth, I am now [nine at night] again settled on board my ship. The whole ships company paid a twelvemonths pay and everything as quiet as I could wish or expect, still my spirits are very low at the prospect of being separated for some months from all I love, and are so truly entitled to my best and dearest regards,—but in the present state of the country I am convinced I should not feel satisfied at remaining inactive on shore, and any appointment to a ship of this magnitude certainly ought to console me for all the importance it must naturally attach to me, of this I am fully assured that if we have the good fortune to meet the enemy I shall be much surprised if we do not gain credit, as I have every possible confidence in all about me,—I am very much afraid that you will not hear from me so frequently as we both wish, but do not let that diminish your custom of writing twice a week, I shall feel every possible anxiety until you are again confined, which I trust and hope in God will be attended with as favourable circumstances as the former ones, indeed I often consider how much our interests are interwoven with those of our little ones, and that it is only on the mutual support, they are to expect from us that they must ultimately succeed in the world,—I know so well the purity of every motive that governs you, not to be fully assured that you will persevere in the same line you have ever pursued, and this impression established in me makes my mind at ease with respect to my family concerns, I do declare to you that I have not had what I call a pleasant dinner on any one occasion since I have been here, that has given me pleasure beyond the moment, and the sight of little children has caused me on more occasions than one very sincere regret at being deprived of the society of my own, indeed I am glad to go again to sea, as there I am not tantalized, and the mind becomes habituated to the deprivation for which there is no remedy,—at this instant David is counting over my linen and making it all over to a lad whom I mean to putt into his place, I have not thought it worth my while to quarrel with him, but independent of his neglect in having lost so many of my things, his absolute want of attention, idleness and profligacy exceeds anything you can well imagine, you know how I hate new people about me, but as I plainly perceive that he is a worthless blackguard I have wished myself up to parting with him without much regret, my steward went on shore one day, and I found him dead drunk in the Street making a disturbance, this as you may well imagine does not make me very easy in my message, but I feel satisfied that no harm can possibly arise whilst the ship is at sea, or whilst I am on board, This fitting out has cost me some money, but I continue to think I shall be enabled to live upon my pay without any addition, indeed my present intention is to make it do tho' I think it is not worth the consideration making a want for a trifle,—I now acknowledge receipt of your affectionate letter of the 28th ult.—my band of music which I had flattered myself with the hopes of preferred staying on shore, so that I go without music and spare the expence of buying instruments which is not a trifle,—many thanks my Dearest Woman for the receipt for the toothache which I gave to Mrs. Loring who makes constant enquiries after you and Emma, I think Henley has managed uncommonly well about the horses, and I lament your new coach horse should be going blind, still you had better keep him as he will answer just as well for the carriage, at all events don't go to law about it as the expences will exceed what the value of another horse would be, I recollect Mr. and Mrs. Horston at Mrs. Prestons, she is a Gobba is she not?—I hope the poor little brats will recover before the autumn, I should be quite annoyed to hear the poor little things cough, and hoop,—

The Captain of the *St. Raphael* is an old acquaintance of mine, he is badly wounded and as that ship is in quarantine I have not had an opportunity of paying him a visit, I expect you will give me a regular journal of all the fine doings at Stowe, I shall be very inquisitive if you dont,—

Aug. 2nd. 1805.—I am now hoisting bullocks in and shall in all probability be off in a few hours,—God bless you my ever Dearest and best of women and believe me always

Your most affectionate husband,

T. F. FREMANTLE.

Neptune off Ushant 15th Aug. 1805.

Receiving your letters of the 4th and 8th, No. 12 and 13 has put me quite in good humour,—I hope you will get the letter I wrote you yesterday whilst you are at Stowe,—you did like a good officer in ordering the children to be kept in the weather as much as possible,—you do really surprise me much at what you mention, namely the likelihood of Lady B: increasing her family, how very strange,—many thanks for the information you give me about those who are expected at Stowe as also the news of Eugenia and her Colonel, what the Devil does that girl carry about her to captivate fools if the man is so, I would not have her marry a fool certainly, but as old Mrs. Mitchel used to say a bad husband is better than none, I have not heard a syllable from her and am dying to her letter which you say she has wrote, I have frequently heard of the man's family,—I thought the poor children would be delighted with my letters which you must have observed I took care to seal up secure that nobody might see what they contained,—I do give you very great credit indeed for having the wit and the courage to give a dinner to the Lovetts etc. I hope you took some of the old Madeira and the old port for my credit, indeed I am highly pleased at your keeping up that sort of respectability in the neighbourhood, which nobody understands better how to do than yourself, If my brother William will take Tom with him to Englefield Green, I think you will do right to let him go,—I just received a letter from poor Jackson who is gunner of the *Eugenia* sloop of war, I must endeavour to get him a better ship if I can—it is just night, since writing in the morning Lord Nelson with his whole Squadron has joined him, I put a boat in the water and was the only ship that had communication with him, Proby carried him all the newspapers I had and saw him for two minutes, he says Lord Nelson looked very ill and his message to me was that he was half dead, I fancy he must be not a little annoyed at his ill fortune in not meeting the enemy, we have now with us 36 or 37 sail of the Line, I conclude there will soon be a very large detachment sent off Ferrol and that we shall be one, and we are more complete than most of the other ships, it must be quite mortifying to all Lord Nelsons ships to be left here, when he is gone in,—with respect to Bazely's farm I must write to him, and also to Wyatt who must manage for me, indeed in all probability he may be able to arrange everything for me as well as I could do myself,—I am dying to hear about all that is going on at Stowe, how differently you must be passing your time to what we miserable wretches do, I have wrote to Lord Nelson to offer my services in any way, I hope his state of health will not deprive the country of his services, it is astonishing how much he is looked up to in all countries,—God bless you all.

Septr. 6th 1805 off Cadiz.

With a heart full of Affliction I sitt down at Night to communicate with you my Dearest Woman and best friend in whom I can confide even my Weaknesses,—since I wrote last we have been standing off and on without being offered the means of sending a letter even to the next Ship, our Admiral is an humble follower of Cornwallis, and I have not yet seen him or any body else, I am entirely confined on board and know no more what is going on than you do. We see the French and Spanish Fleets daily and what adds more to this cursed deprivation of Society is that the Weather has been remarkably fine and the Sea as smooth as in the Lake at Stow. I wish and hope either Lord Gardner or Lord Nelson will soon be here as I confess I do not bear patiently from Collingwood what I should do more with a man of better pretensions to such severity, under an Able, and a Man I could look up to, I should be as satisfied here as in the Channel, as good Weather alleviates in a certain degree the mortification of being deprived of our regular intercourse with our families and friends, but it is needless to complain and suffer I much fear there is no alternative left, I have no reason to complain of my Ship, which is in real perfect order, but my temper naturaly hasty is often put to the trial by my First Lieutenant, who has so long been in the habit of governing the Ship in his way, that he cannot bear the smallest contradiction, which in turn obliges me to follow up my own System without benefiting by his assistance and advice, this added to the influence he has got in the Ship obliges me to be very circumspect, and to take notice with a degree of Jealousy which would otherwise pass without comment but I shall tire you with my complaints which is very unfair in your present situation, independent of every other consideration we must endeavour to live and slave for the advantage of those poor little animals who naturaly look up to us for support and protection, and that consideration alone will I think enable me to bear up against all the disagrèments I daily encounter, it is now just a month since I heard from home, it appears an age.

God bless you all my Dearest and best of Women and

believe me ever
Your most affectionate
T.F.F.

SATURDAY, 7TH SEPTEMBER. Poor Doddy sett out in his gig soon after seven o'clock for Chalfont where Wm Fremantle sends for him—he was in very good spirits. I did not feel quite well this morning and had a visit at One from Lord Buckingham who called in his way from Liscombe where he dined yesterday—he had never been at Swanbourne before & liked the House very much. Mr. Delanos came to dinner but I could not sit down at table finding myself worse. I sent for Tookey and was safely delivered at twenty minutes after nine in the evening of a nice little girl.

HARRIET

SATURDAY, 7TH. It rained most shockingly, and poor Tom set off at seven o'clock appearing very merry and contented. Betsey felt a little uncomfortable all the morning and to our surprise Lord Buckingham called in his way back from Liscombe where he had been dining the day before. Mr. Delanos came for dinner, but Betsey was not able to sit it out, and afterwards her Misery began. We sent for Tookey who spent three hours with Mr. Delanos, and about nine I called him upstairs he was not there long, for Betsey was soon delivered of a nice little girl. I was quite happy when it was over. She really had an uncommon good time. I slept with Emma in the little room and had a very good night. I *do* not think much of a Lying in.

BETSEY

TUESDAY–WEDNESDAY 17TH, 18TH. I heard today from Mr. Morgan & Mrs. Wm Fremantle, giving me a most satisfactory & pleasing account of poor Tom—he went to school in tolerable spirits on Saturday but seemed much affected when his Uncle & Aunt left him, he however behaved remarkably well & Mr Morgan seems much pleased with him. It was an uncommon hot day & I came down stairs after my dinner but I felt extremely low & out of spirits all day thinking of the Boy, tho' Mr. Morgan assures me he was perfectly reconciled to school & his companions.

[Fremantle wrote again on the 1st:]

Off Cadiz 1st October 1805.

My Dearest Betsey,

I have seen and dined with Lord Nelson,—he shows me the same kindness and attention he has ever done. I had not been with him many minutes before he very handsomely told me, I should have my old place in the Line of battle, which is *his second*, this is exactly what is the most flattering to me in every point of view, he desired me to come to him whenever I chose, and to dine with him as often as I could make it convenient in short I am quite pleased with his manner towards me, he in the most friendly way delivered himself Harriets letter announcing your accouchement.—and now my Dearest Woman let me congratulate you on your recovery,—Harriets and your accounts have made me quite happy.—I must write Harriet a few lines to thank her for obeying my injunctions, I am quite happy to find you are strong enough to write your-self so soon.—I hope you will Christen the new one *Louisa*, I have taken quite a liking for that name, at all events let it be her first name.

We are all busy scraping our Ships sides to new paint them in the way Lord Nelson paints the *Victory*, this Ship is only a foot shorter than the *Victory* and appears much larger upon Deck. I cant help repeating how my mind is relieved at receiving all your letters, for I find I love you not a little my ever dearest Woman, kiss the newcomer for me, and tell Emma I shall give all the peepers when I come home to Louisa. Betsey Guggers Eyes I hope dont decrease in size, what is it that makes me think so much more of my Girls than my boys? Lord Nelson on presenting me with Harriet's letter asked me if I would have a Girl or a boy, I answd, the former, when he put the letter into my hand and told me to be satisfied, pray tell me if Bucky admired my pictures, and if he said mine was a good likeness, I am glad he dined at Liscombe as it will make them better Neighbours to us.—

Addio for to Night I shall leave room for a few words more,—The Signal is made for letters, I can only add that I am ever your most Affectionately and truly

THOS. FRAS. FREMANTLE.

11th Oct. I am just returned now, 8 o'clock from dining with Lord Nelson, who is so friendly to me that I have great pleasure and enjoyment in his society, we had many hours conversation, which relieved me for a time from the same dull occupation of my own ship,—I have today got my old Lieut. Green appointed to the ship, and my old first Lieutenant, who is rather sickly and will go home in the first ship in which there is a vacancy,—The *Prince of Wales* will sail tomorrow and I shall entrust this with all my other letters to Commissioner Otway who goes home in her,—Lord Nelson expects the French Fleet will come out, I confess I do not.

THURSDAY, 7TH NOV. I was much alarmed by *Nelly's ghastly* appearance immediately after breakfast, who came in to say Dudley had brought from Winslow the account that a most dreadful action had been fought off Cadiz, Nelson & several Captains killed, & twenty ships were taken. I really felt undescribable misery until the arrival of the Post, but was relieved from such a wretched state of anxious suspence by a Letter from Lord Garlies, who congratulated me on Fremantle's safety & the conspicuous share he had in the Victory gained on the 21st off Cadiz. He adds poor Nelson was no more, he lived to take the Spanish Admiral his opponent & to know he was victorious. In the midst of my delight to hear Fremantle had been preserved in this severe action, I could not help feeling greatly distressed for the Fate of poor *Nelson* whose loss is irreparable. The papers give an account of this grand victory, twenty ships have been captured but one had blown up in the action. In my way to Addington [*sic*] I met a Servant from Stowe with a most kind *mot* from Lord Buckingham & one from Lady Buckingham, he sent me the Gazettes in which I found the full detail of the action. Nelson's Fleet consisted of twenty seven ships, the French & Spaniards thirty three, came out of Cadiz the 19th & were over taken the 21st off Cape Trafalgar where the action was fought & appears to have been very severe. A violent gale of wind had obliged Admiral Collingwood to sink almost all the Prizes & he mentions in his last Letter the *Capt.* of the *Neptune* who had cleared & sunk the *Santissima Trinidada.* Capt. Duff & Cook were killed, & I fear the number of the killed & wounded will be very great when the returns are sent. How thankful I am Fremantle has once more escaped unhurt. The accounts greatly shook my nerves. I found on my return from Addington Lord Temple & Lord George, who had rode over from Aylesbury where they have been out with the Yoemanry—he brought me his Gazette & wished me joy of the good news in the most flattering &

friendly manner. How I long for a Letter from Fremantle, I am perfectly bewildered & can think & dream of nothing but the late Victory. Poor Nelson! had he survived, it would have been glorious indeed. Regret at his death is more severely felt than joy at the destruction of the Combined Fleets—ten ships only returned into Cadiz under the Command of Gravina.

EUGENIA

FRIDAY. 8TH. The King was deeply affected at hearing of Lord Nelson's death—few people I think would feel otherwise or would not throw a veil over his failings and weaknesses, which were overbalanced by many brilliant qualities—He has render'd eminent services to his Country, this is the 3rd decisive battle which he has won—It is evident that the enemy aimed at him, the shot which deprived him of life flew from the Shrouds of the *Santissima Trinidada*, and he was a conspicuous object not to be mistaken as he would wear all his orders and insignias—He fell immediately and survived only two Hours—his 1st. question was, how many ships had struck—He expressed a wish that he might have liv'd to see the end of the Victory—thank'd God for the success he had granted to the King's arms, and expired sending a farewell to all his brother Seamen—The last Signal he order'd to be made by Telegraph was to hope that every man would do his duty—It seems Lord Nelson had made up his mind to the loss of a Limb—and before he sail'd this last time he went to inspect a Coffin which was giv'n him by Captn. Hallowell, and was made out of the wood of *l'orient* (in the battle of the Nile) saying he should most probably want it—I suppose Ly. Hamilton is now in deep despair, and I think Ly.

Nelson must feel a great deal altho he behaved unkindly to her—They say Villeneuve is almost raving at finding himself a prisoner and his Squadron destroyed—famine, it seems drove them out of Cadiz—I do not envy the feelings of Sir Robert Calder who let this fleet escape him some time back—he has ask'd for a Court Martial—it may perhaps go hard with him.

SATURDAY, 30TH. Vienna has fall'n into the hands of the French, their successes are endless the Russians fly before them, and are a perfect scourge to the poor inhabitants who dread them almost as much as the enemy—

SUNDAY, 1ST DECEMBER. At last my Sister heard from Captn. Fremantle who sends a drawing of the Battle and we were all proud to see the *Santissima Trinidada* striking to him while he was warmly engaged at the same time with the *Bucentaure*—he gained great credit on that day, and I only wish Ld. Nelson was still alive to record it—Fremantle seems deeply to feel his loss—He had Adl. Villeneuve on board for two days and speaks of him as an amiable Man, mild and gentlemanlike, bearing an excellent character but greatly depressed and out of spirits—He had just sent him on board the *Euryalus* in which ship he is now arriv'd to England—Fremantle had still on board Villeneuve's état major, (who he says divert him greatly with their gasconnades) 450 Spanish prisoners and a Maltese Priest—a French Cook and a pug dog, are his prizes—The letter is written seven days after the Battle, during which time Fremantle had not time to breathe, busily employed (during a dreadful gale) in sinking or preserving prizes towing crippled ships and repairing his own misfortunes—He seems not to admire Ld. Collingwood particularly.

off Cadiz 28th Octr. 1805.

My ever Dearest and best of Women,—

If I know your heart, or your sentiments I think I may depend that you will be truly happy to hear that I am well after the very severe action we have had,— This last Week has been a scene of Anxiety and fatigue beyond any, I ever experienced but I trust in God that I have gained considerable credit, and that it will ultimately tend to the benefit of you and my dear little Children for when—alone I am now here,—I am at present towing the *Victory* and the Admiral has just made the signal for me to go with her to Gibraltar, which is a satisfactory proof to my mind that he is perfectly satisfied with Old *Neptune*, who behaves as well as I could wish, The loss of Nelson is a death blow to my future prospects here, he knew well how to appreciate Abilities and Zeal, and I am aware that I shall never cease to lament his loss whilst I live. We have ten Men killed and 37 Wounded, which is very trifling when compared to some other Ships, however we alone have certainly the whole credit of taking the *Santissima Trinidada*, who struck to *us alone*. Adml. Villeneuve was with me on board the *Neptune* over two days, I found him a very pleasant and Gentlemanlike man, the poor man was very low! Yesterday I put him on board the *Euryalus* with Admiral Collingwood, but I still have the pleasure of feeding and accomodating his Captain and his 2 Aid du Camps and his Adjutant General, who are true Frenchmen, but with whom I am much amused, I have also 450 poor Spaniards from the *Santissima Trinidada*, with a true Italian priest born at Malta,—I have found also an excellent French cook and a true Spanish pug dog—This fatigue and employment has entirely drove away the bile and if poor Nelson had not been among the slain I should be most completely satisfied, would you believe that Old Colingwood has now made the Signal for me to go off Cape Espartel instead of Gibralter, the poor man does not know his own mind 5 minutes together. I am afraid this brilliant Action will not put much money in my pocket, but I think much may arise out of it ultimately, I shall with this send you a copy of the Minutes kept by my old Lieut. Mr. Green, I hope with the Line of battle and the drawing you will be enabled to make it out, you may give the Ringers I think a Guinea on the occasion to save your credit to my brother William I send one also that you may show your plan over Buckinghamshire as much as you please,—My Cabin that was so elegant and neat is as dirty as a pig Stye and many parts of the bulk heads are thrown overboard, however I shall find amusement and indeed employment in having them fitted in some new way—These Frenchmen make me laugh at the gasconade as well as at their accounts of Buonaparte the Palais Royal Paris etc.—I hope you have ere this received my letter for Wyatt [the letter is torn here] The French Captain drinks your health regularly every day at dinner, The poor man is married and laments his lot, one of the younger ones is desperately in love with a lady at Cadiz and Frenchmanlike carries her picture in his pocket—

Ever your most affectionate husband

T.F.F.

Minutes kept on board H.M. Ship *Neptune* by Lieutenant Andrew Green Signal Officer, the 21st of Octr. 1805:—

Little wind at Wbs.

At day light discovered the Enemy's Fleet on the

Lee Beam keeping their wind on the Larboard Tack, consisting of 33 Sail of the Line Four frigates and two Briggs. The English Fleet 27 of the Line four Frigates and one Schooner and one Cutter.

A.M.

6.15. The Admiral made the Signal to form in two divisions.
6.30. To bear up for the Enemy.
6.32. To prepare for Battle.
6.40. To Steer East.
7.25. For the *Brittania Prince* and *Dreadnought* to take their Station as most convenient.
7.35. For the Captains of the Frigates to go on board the *Victory*.
9.45. Was haild by the *Victory* and desired not to keep quite so close.
10. The *Mars* Signal to lead the Larbd. Division.
10.50. Telegraph to *Royal Sovereign* from Lord Nelson. It is my intention to pass through the Enemy's line and prevent them getting into Cadiz.
11.40. Telegraph to the whole Fleet. *England expects every man will do his duty*.
11.46. Prepare to Anchor during the ensuing night.
11.50. *Temeraire* to take station astern of *Victory*. Captain Blackwood of the *Euryalus* came alongside and acquainted Captain Fremantle it was the Commander-in-Chiefs intention to cut through the Enemy's line about their 13 or 14 Ship, then to make sail on the Larbd. Tack for their Van.
11.55. Engage the Enemy quite close.
11.56. The Enemy open'd their fire on the *Royal Sovereign* and in a few minutes after on the *Victory*.

P.M.

12.5. The *Royal Sovereign* most nobly began to fire and passed through the Enemy's line under the stern of *Santa Ana*, a Spanish Ship on three Decks. On the smoke clearing away saw the *Royal Sovereign* closely engaged with the *Santa Ana*, and several of the Enemy's Ships firing into her, the *Tonnant* in her Rear with a two Deck Ship on board her.

12.10. The *Victory* open'd her fire and endeavouring to pass under the Stern of the French Admiral in the *Bucentaur*, the *Redoubtable*, closed so near the *Bucentaur*, to support his Commander-in-Chief, that the *Victory* was obliged to lay that Ship on board, when both Ships paid off before the wind. The *Temeraire* in following gallantly Lord Nelson's Ship, fell on the opposite side the *Redoubtable*, from the same cause and the *Intrepide* alongside the *Temeraire*, the four Ships lock'd in and on board each other, and their Sterns to us. We put the Ship's helm a Starboard and the *Neptune* passed between the *Victory* and *Bucentaur* with which Ship we were warmly engaged (The *Conquerors* Jib Boom nearly touching our tafferail) we passed on to the *Santissima Trinidada* whose stern was entirely exposed to our fire without her being able to return a single shot with effect. At 50 minutes past one observed her Main and Mizen Masts fall overboard, *gave three cheers*, she then paid off and brought us nearly on her lee Beam, in about a quarter of an hour more,

THE BATTLE OF TRAFALGAR: A NEWLY FOUND LIST OF SHIPS ENGAGED (ENEMY AND BRITISH)

LINE OF BATTLE

No.	Ships' names	Nation	Guns	Captains	Result and observations
1	*Pluton*	French	74	Mr. Cosmao	Cadiz. Quite new from Toulon.
2	*Monarca*	Spanish	74	El C.D.V.D. Leodoro Argumoso	Taken and on Shore.
3	*Fougueux*	French	74	Mr. Baudouin. Drowned	Taken and lost 15 only. Saved old Ship.
4	*Santa Ana*	Spanish	110	Aml. Don Alava. W.	Struck. Cadiz.
5	*Indomptable*	French	80	Mr. Hubert. Drowned	Lost in Port, with the *Bucentaur*'s men on bd.
6	*San Justo*	Spanish	74	El C.D.V. Don Miguel Gaston.	Cadiz.
7	*Intrepide*	French	64	Mr. Infernet. Killed.	Taken and burnt. Given to the French by the Spaniards.
8	*Redoubtable*	French	80	Mr. Lucas	Taken and sunk in the night of the 22nd. Lucas a man highly respected as a good officer.
9	*San Leandro*	Spanish	64	El C.D.V.D. Josef Quevedo	Cadiz.
10	*Neptune*	French	80	Mr. Maistral	Cadiz. —Two sister ships
11	*Bucentaure*	French	80	Aml. Villeneuve; Capn. Magendio	Taken and — new built at Toulost. — lon in 6 mths.
12	*Santis*[a] *Trinidad*	Spanish	130	Don Bantazan Ydalgo y Sisneroso	Taken and sunk.
13	*Heroe*	French	74	Mr. Poulain. Killed.	Cadiz. Tolerably repd. at Ferrol.
14	*San Augustin*	Spanish	74	El B. D. felippe de Cagegal	Gibraltar taken.

15	*Mont blanc*	French	74	Mr. la Villegriet	Meditern. Old.
16	*Asis*	Spanish	74	El C.D.V. Louis de Floris	Cadiz.
17	*Duguai-trouin*	French	74	Mr. Touffet	Meditern. Old and Bad.
18	*Formidable*	French	80	Alm. Dumanoir le Pelley; Captain Letellier	Meditern. Was in the action at Algeziras much broke and old.
19	*Rayo*	Spanish	80	El Brig. de Erequi Macdonel.	Lost coast.
20	*Scipion*	French	74	Mr. Berenger	Meditern. Good but a bad sailer.
21	*Neptuno*	Spanish	80	Antonio Valdez. W.	Cadiz.

CORPS DE RESERVE

No.	*Ships' names*	*Nation*	*Guns*	*Captains*	*Result and observations*
22	*San Juan*	Spanish	74	El B. D. Cosme Chioviuca	Cadiz.
23	*Berwick*	French	74	Mr. Camas	Taken and lost. Sails well and had been repaired at Toulon.
24	*Principe de Asturias*	Spanish	120	Aml. Don Gravina. W.	Cadiz.
25	*Achille*	French	74	Mr. Denieport	Burnt in the Action.
26	*San Yldefonso*	Spanish	74	El B. D. Josef Bargas	Taken.
27	*Argonaute*	French	74	Mr. Epron	Cadiz.
28	*Swiftsure*	French	74	Mr. Villemadrin	Taken. Leaky and not in good repair.
29	*Argonauta*	Spanish	74	P. Antonio Escano. W.	Taken and sunk. In tolerable good repair.
30	*Algeziras*	French	74	Mr. le Contre; Aml. Magon. Killed. Capn. Letourneur. Wounded.	Cadiz. New.

	Montanez . .	Spanish	74	El C.D.V. D. Fras. Alecedo. W.	Cadiz.
	Aigle . . .	French	74	Mr. Courrege. Killed .	Cadiz. New.
33	*Bahama* . .	Spanish	64	El B. D. Dionicio Galino .	Taken.

ENGLISH LINE OF BATTLE

No.	*Ships' names*	*Guns*	*Captains*
1	*Victory* . . .	110	Vice-Adml. Lord Nelson; Capn. T. M. Hardy.
2	*Temeraire* . . .	98	Captain E. Harvey.
3	*Neptune* . . .	98	,, T. F. Fremantle.
4	*Leviathan* . . .	74	,, H. W. Bayntum.
5	*Conqueror* . . .	74	,, Isrl. Pellew.
6	*Agamemnon* . .	64	,, Sir E. Berry, Bt.
7	*Ajax* . . .	80	The 1st Lieutenant.
8	*Orion* . . .	74	Captain E. Codrington.
9	*Minotaur* . . .	74	,, C. J. M. Mansfield.
10	*Spartiate* . . .	80	,, Sir Fras. Laforey, Bt.
11	*Royal Sovereign* . .	110	Vice-Adml. Collingwood; Capn. E. Rotheram.
12	*Mars* . . .	74	Captain G. Duff. Killed.
13	*Tonnant* . . .	80	,, C. Tyler. W.
14	*Belleisle* . . .	80	,, Hargwood.
15	*Bellerophon* . .	74	,, J. Cooke (1). Killed.
16	*Colossus* . . .	74	,, J. N. Morris. W.
17	*Achille* . . .	74	,, Rd. King.
18	*Polyphemus* . .	64	,, Robt. Redmell.

19	*Revenge* . . .	74	„ Robt. Moorson.
20	*Swiftsure* . . .	74	„ Wm. E. Rutherford.
21	*Defence* . . .	74	„ G. Hope.
22	*Africa* . . .	64	„ Digby
23	*Thunderer* . . .	74	The 1st Lieutenant.
24	*Defiance* . . .	74	Captain P. O. Durham.
	To take Stations when Most Convenient:		
25	*Britannia* . . .	110	Rear-Adml. Earl of Northesk; Capn. C. Bullin.
26	*Prince* . . .	98	Captain Gundall.
27	*Dreadnought* . .	98	„ Conn.

her Fore Mast fell over her Stern, and shortly after an Officer threw a Union Jack over her Starboard Quarter, haild the *Neptune* and said they had struck. The Van of the Enemy had now Wore and were crossing us apparently with an intent to support their Admirals, the *Conqueror* at this time passed over to windward to engage them, put our helm a port and fired successfully with six sail of the line that passed to windward, the remaining three going to leeward of all, observed the *Leviathan* and another Ship who had passed on closely engaged with two of the Enemy's Ships, who had bore up and soon after struck. The *Victory* and *Royal Sovereign*, keeping up a brisk fire on the Squadron passing to Windward, at about ½ past 4 the firing ceased on both sides when the Signal was made to haul to the Wind on the Larboard tack. A French Ship in the rear *L'Achille* was on fire and soon blew up of the 6 sail which passed to windward on the Starboard tack, 5 stood on to the Southward, one was taken, the remaining part of the Enemy's fleet to leeward consisting of 16 sail of which we supposed 3 or 4 to be Frigates, were apparently forming to support their disabled Ships and standing towards Cadiz. We at this time concluded that 14 of the Enemy's Ships were captured.

At 5 the Admiral made the Signal to come to the wind on the Starboard tack.

At Sun-set the Enemy's Squadron to leeward with their heads in shore.

The melancholy Account which we at this time received of the loss of our much beloved, honoured, and respected Commander-in-Chief threw a damp on our Spirits which we were by no means prepared for after so decisive a Victory.

HARRIET

SUNDAY, 1ST DECEMBER. At last Betsey received letters from il *Caro Sposo* and I was wisely employed in writing out the order of battle. John at last called and remained very long. I stole a dear little penknife he had. He is to come to morrow morning for Eugenia to try Frolic and Betsey asked him to dinner and to sleep here mais il a peur de venir.

TUESDAY, 10TH. It was a very fine frost. We dined at four and drest afterwards. It was about seven when we left this. We found the General, Miss Mac Lucy and Vera ready to receive us. Mary and John came in the latter was powdered and looking très beau. We set out from Addington at nine and Lucy Vera and I went in their carriage, Justina and Mary in our's. The Lowndes's and a Mrs. and Miss Browne were the only persons arrived. They soon all made their appearance. Capt. Watt was drest most finely in his regimentals and cuts a *great dash.* I danced the two first with the General. The next with John and Lucy made me with down the third although Capt. Watts engaged me. I danced the fourth dance with him and then went to Supper, he really is very Amiable and pleasant, told me a great deal about Macdonald, and I teazed him about the *Miss Forster's.* I sat two from Robert Lowndes, who made himself monstrous agreable, and I had the impudence to plague him about the Lowren's. He engaged me but I had already promised to dance with *Richard Coeur de Lion*, and finished the ball with *Bobby* by tripping down Sir Roger de Coverly. John asked me several times but I already had found partners, he flirted the whole night with Justina which did not excite my jealousy in the least. Mrs. Whitemore was looking very handsome, and two beauties graced the ball, two Miss *Thymes*, great awkward bold, brazen faced girls, who played a thousand *pranks* during supper and quite disgusted me. Les *Nymphes* de Winslow, were dressed real sights. Mrs. Partridge was looking interessante and the husband seemed particularly pleasant and danced with Justina. We were the last in the room and John, Justina Lucy and I went in our carriage we had great fun. I sat at the bottom of the chaise and they all abused me. It was seven before we got to Addington and sat up a little while. I did not once close my eyes Canary birds disturbing my sweet Slumbers and putting me in a rage. General Poulett is Stewart for the next ball, which is to be on the 1st of January. We had the Nursery.

BETSEY

SUNDAY, 22ND. Tom arrived at about six o'clock & I was much delighted to see him—he is grown exceedingly fat, and tall, his face is three times as big as it was, which is no embellishment, but he looks upon the whole very pretty, & is improved in every respect by his stay at School—his accounts are very entertaining & he appears to be perfectly comfortable & happy at Mr. Morgan's. He talked incessantly all the evening having much to relate—he went to the Princesses the day before yesterday. After a long debate we persuaded Eugenia to go to Stowe Tuesday the french Princes come on Thursday which will render the Xmas party very brilliant.

STOWE, TUESDAY, 24TH. Owing to some mistake the Post Horses ordered for Eugenia did not arrive, I went on therefore with Justine, Nelly & little Maria, and got in good time for dinner, Eugenia, Harriet, Tom & the maids only arrived in the evening. We found at Stowe, Lord & Lady Temple, the Pigots, Mrs. Nugent, Mr. T. Grenville, General Hervey, Major Moon & the Baron de Rolles—sat up & communed a la messe de minuit.

STOWE, WEDNESDAY, XMAS DAY, 25 DECR. 1805. We have Lord Grenville's rooms which are very comfortable. My Baby is found very pretty and Tom appears as great a favourite as ever. Lord Buckingham tells me Fremantle is not likely to return till late in the Spring his Ship having repaired at Gibraltar. The usual dinner for the Poor People to day.

HARRIET

STOWE, THURSDAY, 26TH. What I dreaded so much happened and I was closeted for an hour, avec Mde. La Marquisa. I was not sorry when I found myself once more at liberty. She talked very mildly, but I could not *help crying*. The Pouletts came for dinner. John has a powdered head and is a very fine Batchelor. We sung in the evening, and talked a great deal with Lucy. Il m'a l'air de mauvais humeur, et ne me parle point. Dr. Bridgewater and his dragon of a wife came. She seems un vrai diablesse and he a merry Sweeth. Major Moore is a very pleasant Man. He has several wounds opened at this moment and seems to suffer much.

BETSEY

STOWE, SATURDAY, 27TH DECEMBER. Lord & Lady Bridgewater comme des gens parvenus, set out in a coach & six with three outriders, they are immensely rich. Lady Temple was extremely ill, a violent Fever, which alarmed the whole Family, particularly Lord Temple who appeared wretchedly miserable about her. Mr. Grenville went this morning. Mary & Vera Poulett are more admired than Lucy, for whom I think George feels a *tender passion*, John is cruel to Harriet who feels *piqued* & is unhappy at his want of galantry.

EUGENIA

MONDAY, 30TH. We were all ready a great while for the reception of the French Princes before they arriv'd at last they came, and we all met them in the North Hall, which was lighted up as well as the Rotunda, at the four doors of which crimson curtains trimm'd with gold, were hung up—as soon as Monsieur, the Duc de Berry, the Duc d'Harcourt and Polignac appear'd, the Band (concealed) played God save the King—They immediately went to dress and did not keep us long—We din'd in the music room the side board was loaded with Plate which was set off by blue cloath trimm'd with gold and richly embroider'd with coats of arms—The Princes were very agreable, and we had Music in the evening—Le Duc de Berry and Polignac were en Extases—

Neptune Gibraltar 19th Novr. 1805.

My Dear Betsey,

Yesterday I received all your letters together up to No. 26—which is dated the 29th Octr. The gratification I felt you will easily imagine—eer this you must have received mine which I think must have been interesting, I assure you Mrs William Fremantle's and Mrs. Morgan's letter brought tears into my eyes, I could not bear the poor little boy's heart being full, but it has put your courage to the test a little, and you must by degrees accustom yourself to such deprivations—We just hear that Adml. Duckworth in the *Superb* with the *Powerful*, are arrived off Cadiz, this makes two more ships, and I think we must be in England eer long.—I have now little to worry or annoy me, but am rather anxious to hear how this brilliant Victory has been received in England,—to-day I am going to dine with the Commissioner and his Wife and to-morrow with the Governor who is Charles Fox's brother. The Squadron who ran away from us in the action are got into Rochefort, consequently we want less ships here and more at home. Eugenia's long letter with Justine's addition lays before me, and whenever I can get time to write an intelligent letter it shall be answered. I assure you I am quite happy at seeing your sisters go on so well, as to Eugenia her only hopes are in old Arundel, who would make a very good husband for her. I confess I should like my little *louse* to marry the young one, and you cannot notwithstanding all Lady B. can say do wrong in encouraging it —As to Miss Lovett and her inamorato I think it quite ridiculous, and both parties will be heartily tired of each other before the honeymoon is over. Mistress Tittler with a black Velour pelisse, tell her I desire she will not spoil it until I come home. I took out of the *Santissima Trinidada* a beautiful little pug dog that is now my companion, and at least always receives me with greetings, and congratulations in the poor animals way—Addio, my ever dearest woman, kiss all your Devils for me and believe me

most affly. yours,

T.F.F.

6th Decr. 1805.

My Dear Betsey,

As I have a famous opportunity of Writing all the nonsense I chuse, I shall write a billet doux every night and pack them up in Emma's box as I finish them—Yesterday at night we fell in and came up after three hours chase a brig from Cadiz laden with brandy. The poor wretch sailed only at 5 in the Evening and was on bd. *Neptune* by 9. I shall not get above 60 or 70 pounds for her, but that is something in these hard times—You are really a very good Girl in writing so often, I do assure you your letters are not thrown away, I read them over and over with pleasure, and would you believe that I was as great a fool as yourself when I read about poor Doddy's heart being so full the first night he was at school. What is there in Children that gets such entire possession of our hearts? I passed a tolerable pleasant time whilst I was at Gibraltar I made it my business to get acquainted with all the fashion of the place and in consequence dined on shore every day and went to a Conversatione, or rather land party in the evening. The only inconvenience I felt from this eating, was the punch after supper which always makes me suffer and still I am such a child I cannot resist the temptation when it comes in my way—Mrs Fyers and I are as great friends as possible, but I formed rather a friendship with a Mrs Jephson, who is the Wife of the Judge of the Admiralty Courts, she is young handsome and very amiable manners, and is in the way all Ladies desire to be who love their Lords. She has also three sisters handsomer than herself, but whose manners are not so engaging. The 2nd married to Col[l]. Kane of the 13th the 3rd only 16 going to be married to a very fine young fellow in the Engineers not 21.

The papa is Gen$^{l.}$ Smith with whom I got intimate—as to the Governor I saw a great deal of him but he is so lourde, and so selfish that I did not much covet his Society—Genl. Drummond the 2nd in Com$^{d.}$ is married to an Irish lady, who they say is low born. She professes great intimacy with my brothers and Mrs Taylor, be that as it will she was very attentive to me in all ways. She gives great parties. The poor woman has an *incurable Cancer* in her breast, which to avoid thinking of makes her live much in Society—

[Fremantle writes again on 31 December:]

. . . I do assure you I think of you and my poor little children all day and all night and my only comfort is in the consideration of the pleasure I shall feel at seeing you all again—

We begin to be a little impatient at not hearing from England, no news about our Lieutenants being promoted, or my encouragement held out. I think it is surprising.

I was not a little annoyed at reading in the Star newspaper of the 5th inst. a long panegyric of the *Neptune* and your humble Servant, this you will say need not give me offence; but it is likewise mentioned as if coming from this ship that the *Prince* and *Dreadnought* were very little in action, of course this will make us enemies in those Ships, and it is very ill judged in those who were so impudent as to put it in print.

I have banished my snuffbox and am now taking it out of a piece of paper, how angry you would be if you were here—my little dog is snoring in the Chair by me, and is a sort of companion. I have got a fine Copy of Verses, composed by the Laureat of the *Neptune*, tell Eugenia to be on her guard before she reads them, as they are truly laughable—Did I tell you that the fleet here have subscribed £3000 towards building a monument on Postdown hill to the memory of Lord Nelson, and that three Captains are named as a Committee to complete it, and that I am the senior Captain on that Committee, this you may publish, as I am a little proud at being so, and at having in the first instance proposed the measure, this however is entre nous as I have continued to give all the merit of it to Lord Collingwood, God bless you all my Dear Girl, give Guggin some good prayers for me, and Emma one slap on the face, ever yours

T.F.F.

bloody noses, I have wrote so much here I am obliged to put this in an envelope, my paper gets very short, and none to be got here.

CHAPTER 28

Eugenia

Friday, 24th [Jan.]. Mr. Pitt is no more he died yesterday at 4 o'Clock and his loss is a subject of universal and heartfelt regret—He died perfectly sensible, resigned, and with all proper sentiments of religion —It seems that his Stomach was quite destroyed from great application to business and the quantity of cordials he had taken to keep off the gout—Ld. Lowther is very much out of spirits he laments not only a great Man, but a particular friend—No one has a guess who is to come in, now, but all the ambitious and political heads are busy at work endeavouring to share the spoils, of this unambitious and disinterested Man, who died poor and in debt, while he held so many lucrative employments, which now tempt the avidity of several great persons. Henry Bankes arrived from Cambridge: He is looking well.

[As a result of Pitt's death the Grenvilles came in, and Grenville intended from the first that Fremantle should be a Lord of the Admiralty. But the Prince of Wales made 'most unreasonable demands' insisting on his 'paramount influence in the Administration,' and as a result of this 'persecution' on Prinny's part, Grenville wrote to his brother, Lord Buckingham, 'I must now put King into the Admiralty, though I had almost settled it so as to make room for Fremantle.']

Betsey

Sunday, 2 Feby. It rained all day & I finished Lady Mary Wortley's Letters, in the last from Venice she mentions our Aunts, whose Beauty she praises much. It is a great pity they did not make a better use of their charms and refused the many good offers they had in England to lead a single & miserable Life in Italy.

SATURDAY, 15TH FEBY. Emma's long expected Present at last arrived & with great eagerness did we examine the contents of the Box, in which we found a Work Basket, taken out of Spanish Brig, a *Meagre* Prize of the *Neptune's*, and in the Basket about a Dozen very interesting and amusing Letters, a Bottle of Otto de Rose for Emma, who expecting some finery was I think a little disappointed with this true Spanish contrived *Men's* Straw work. I was much delighted with my Letters and was taken up the greatest part of the evening reading them.

[On the 23rd Betsey received her first letter from Tom.]

Hampton April 22nd 1806.

Dear Mama,

I liked coming in the coach pretty well as we were not crowded there were only me and a man and a womman we did not talk at all. Mr. Morgan says he will come to you about Charles I hope he is quite well has he had any of those frites in the night. I shall come to you for the holidays some time in the middle of June but when I know the fixed day I will tell you. What did Mr. J. Butler give Charles and Emma Saturday. give my love to all

and Believe me allways
Your dutiful Son
T. FREMANTLE.

BETSEY

TUESDAY, 29TH APRIL. William Fremantle sent me two Tickets for Ld. Melville's Trial and called for me and Justine before ten o'clock. We were in the Royal Family's Box, in which the Dss. of York sat. The coup d'oueil was very grand, and the Procession of the Peers and Princes with their Bow to the Speaker and the Throne a magnificent sight—the awkwardness and graceless manner of some of the Peers truly ludicrous. Lord Melville appears dejected—Mr. Whitbread spoke for four hours and a half —We came away from Westminster Hall at three o'clock the string of Carriages reached St. James's Str. We walked to the Admiralty to meet ours—I went in the Evening to a party at Lady Lambert's where I met the Duke de Berri who shook hands with me tout a fait a l'Anglaise.

WEDNESDAY, 30TH APRIL. Mrs. Campbell went with us to the Rehearsal of the Opera Camilla. I liked the music extremely, the subject is taken from Mde. de Genlis's story of the Duchesse de C.—Il Signor Campbell mi pare fa l'amore a Eugenia—he asked leave to speak to-morrow to her at twelve—A proposal is of course expected. We went in the Evening to Mrs. Bankes to tell her of this adventure—On our return we left Justine and Harriet at a Ball at Mrs. Clarke's where all the *accoucheurs* doctors & Apothecaries of London were dancing comme des désespérés.

EUGENIA

WEDNESDAY, 30TH. Mr. Campbell went with us this morg. to the rehearsal of the new opera *Camilla* which I thought very fine—on our return he seemed much agitated and ask'd me at last to let him come and speak to me tomorrow morg—I cannot mistake his meaning—But I know him so little, that altho' what little I know *I like*, I am at a loss how to act—

He seems to like me, and is extremely clever and agreable—I have consulted my Sisters and Mrs. Bankes—they advise me to become better acquainted with him ere I determine—all this makes me feel very strange, and it makes my heart beat to think of tomorrow—

THURSDAY, 1ST MAY. Mr. Campbell came this morg at about two—we were left alone, and he then proposed to me, in the handsomest and most honorable manner, and with all the feeling of a Man who is sincere—That sort of agitation is strangely catching and I felt cruelly embarrassed at first, but at last, we grew bolder as our Conversation got into a better strain—He did not at all urge or press me for an answer and only ask'd leave to see me often and give him opportunity of winning my affections—which of course, I did not deny—He fairly stated his situation to me—He is at present totally dependent on his Father (who is very rich and fond of him): at his death an Estate of £1000 per annum is entailed upon him—He was brought up to the Law, but dislikes that profession and wishes to enter into the diplomatic Line for which he thinks he has talents which will ensure him success—He certainly has talents, his family is excellent, and I make no doubt that I shall very shortly think him worthy of my regard—Splendour, nor riches, is not what I seek—I am certain that I should be happy with a moderate income, with a Man of whom I have a good opinion, He is very well looking—and I should think about thirty—The Bankes' think I ought not to marry him, unless his Father allows him £1000 a year—but I think that I should be satisfied with less—

I went with Ly. Lowther to Grassini's Benefit—the opera of Fioravanti *Camilla* is I think charming, but too good for an English audience—

THURSDAY, 1ST MAY. A very handsome proposal made with much candour, honesty and tenderness—Eugenia seems already to like him excessively, he only asked leave to see her often that he may have an opportunity of winning her affections—But unfortunately he is only the second son, dependant on his father who has £25,000 a year—At his death he has an Estate of £1,000 a year entailed on him. The eldest Brother has married L^d^. Lorne's Sister. He wishes to quit the Law, to enter the Diplomatic line and has hopes of going Secretary of Legation to L^d^. Lauderdale to India—ce qu'il en sera je ne puis encore diviner—I received a Letter of Fremantle—still off Cadiz anxious to come home.

[Here it is.]

April 6th 1806.

If I had been at all prepared for the departure of my late First Lieutenant, who I hope you will have seen before you receive this I should have made up a packet like the one I sent home with Emma's work basket. I shall certainly send her diamonds the little hussy! her rage for them she has learnt from that Monster Eugenia who quite neglects me, I expect to hear of her from London, and desire her to tell me how you and Giustine behaved yourselves.—I forgot to tell you in my last of a miraculous escape I had at Gibralter walking one Sunday after Church with Captain Mundy of the *Hydra* just inside the Landpark gate, over the causeway, towards the neutral ground, conversing rather earnestly on some Naval topic. I heard a more than uncommon noise by a multitude of people behind me, which made me turn round, judge of my astonishment and horror at perceiving it was occasioned by an over droad [*sic*] Ox, quite frantic, which ran directly at me, one of its horns struck my right arm with great force, threw me down and the beast ran over me, after a short time it charged again whilst I was on the ground, and Captain Mundy who had got my hat, which was thrown some yards by the force of my fall, threw it at the animal and by that means turned him. I got up as you may imagine in as much haste as I could and ran into the gates, where the guard turned out (as is usual to Officers of my rank) and I was happy to *ensconce* myself behind the filibegs of the 78th Regt. with their bayonets fixed, the Ox followed me about a minute after—and galloped into the Town, alarming everybody and hurting one poor woman in the stomach very much, as you may imagine he was soon afterwards killed. Your humble Servant having rubbed the Sand off his Clothes went into Col. Tyers's where he got a glass of Madeira,—on going on board to dress I found my arm very black and very much Swelled with some of the Skin off where the point of the horn struck me, and my left side considerably bruised and bare but it did not in any way injure my appetite, or my Spirits, altho it might have been very serious, had not Captn. Mundy had presence of mind to throw my hat at him, this will not I think encourage you much, who are so much a coward where animals are in question,—I had quite forgot to mention it, I was so mortified to find that the letters I had written a month ago had been sent only the day before yesterday. I very much fear you will suppose I neglected your wants, indeed my Dearest Woman it is no fault of mine and I feel so satisfied with all you do,—how you would laugh to see me amused with my dog and Cat, my Monkey is so mischievous that the Sentinels never permit to enter the Cabin, the only time he

ever got in he contrived to break one of my Tureen covers which is a serious loss in this Country.

The want of attention on the part of the Admiral is certainly very annoying. I shall endeavour to get home if possible, for I am quite ashamed,—one of my Midshipmen who was with me on the *Ganges* on Copenhagen is made a Lieutenant into the *Neptune* in the room of the first Lt.—Young Badcock you know I got made a Lieutenant into the *Melpomene*, some months ago,—I have now only one remaining with me who has served his time, I hope to have an opportunity of recommending him before I leave the Mediterranean, all the Appointments here are sent out by the Admiralty board to the great annoyance of Lord Collingwood who has by his want of firmness and decision in the first instance lost the opportunity of providing for every one that was deserving.

BETSEY

FRIDAY, 2ND MAY. All four Sisters dined at Mrs. Wm. Fremantle, L[d]. and L[y]. Radnor and L[d]. and L[y]. Bulkeley, Mrs. Bouvery and the two Herveys—Rather pleasant. We went in the evening to Drago's Concert at Ly. Hertford's, a splendid House and a crowded, Excellent Assembly. The Prince of Wales recognised me and came up twice to speak to me. Eugenia sat with Campbell, and John remains faithful and true to Harriet.

MONDAY, 5TH MAY. We had intended going to the Play but finding ourselves disappointed of a Box we determined to stay at home and went out in the carriage early to ask a few friends to come to us in the evening. We succeeded in making up a snug party and on our return at two o'clock made preparations for a little dance. Our Impromptu Ball was composed of in all about thirty—Our dining room was just large enough for twelve couples. We supped at one, in the Drawing rooms—and I danced till three after Supper—Every body seemed much pleased and amused with our little Ball.

EUGENIA

TUESDAY, 6TH. Mr. Campbell and His Brother Walter call'd this morg. and we took a delightful long Walk with them in Kensington Gardens—I think it odd that Mr. Campbell did not say anything on a subject which wholly engrossed my thoughts—I cannot help feeling uneasy and unhappy, lest his Father should disapprove of the connection and the more I see of him, the more I like him—Justina and myself went to a Ball at Mrs. Blair's this evg. where I had got Mr. Campbell ask'd—I danc'd little, but was happy in talking to him the whole evg—He gave me to understand that he hoped in a few days to clear all my doubts they really become painful to me now, and I feel but too well that should his Father deny his approbation to our marriage, I never should know again what it is to be happy in this world.

BETSEY

TUESDAY, 6TH MAY. I went to see Turners picture of the battle of Trafalgar, it is confused and pleased me not.

April the 16th 1806.

If it was not for my poor little dog that I worry all day and who is so good that I allow him to sleep in my bed I should be more miserable than I am. I have read over again and again my friends letter and I cannot help thinking that he ought to do something for me. I have wrote to beg him to get me some civil naval situation in England, which will enable me to live with my family, I begin to feel that I am now 40 years of age, and that serving in a blockading Squadron will not answer my purpose in any way, in short I will not buffet about the Sea without better prospects, life is too short to pass it in that way it will be your business to say that I write out of Spirits and am very anxious to come home—Captain Hallowell—who is just come from Madeira has brought me two Casks of wine which will ruin me to pay for, but is so seldom opportunities come of getting such wine that I cant regret the temptation of taking them, I shall keep both for jolly Swanbourne, we drink Madeira as cheap as other people do Sherry,—how I long to see my little Doddy boy and Mrs. Tittler tell her I will give her a great many peeps for writing so well in your letter, Tom's letter from School is too formal, I prefer the Children's writing in their own way and their own nonsense.

EUGENIA

SUNDAY, 11TH. I prayed with all my soul to day at Church—at no period of my existence have I felt more how much I stand in need of that help—Betsey went to Hampstead to see Mrs. Cathcart who is very ill, and we went out in the barouche with Mrs. Jenkinson—I felt so unhappy—my present state of suspense, that I could stand it no longer, this evening, and wrote to C. to entreat if he has anything to tell me, that he will come tomorrow and say it at once—I went to the Lowthers, and to my surprize found they knew every thing—it made my heart ache to hear them *wish me joy* when perhaps there is sorrow in store for me I cannot make out how the world knows it already—I told them however that it was still very uncertain—We afterwards went to Ly. Kenmare's—it was one of her *good assemblies*, but the men insufferably stupid—

MONDAY, 12TH. I had a letter from C. this morg, which at once gratified me and made me miserable as it throws doubts on the issue of the event—nothing can be more honourable nor candid than his manner of acting towards me, and I am truly proud to be the object of that sort of affection which he expresses for me, as I shall never part with that Letter I shall refer myself to it now—I answered him nor could I disguise from him all I feel on the subject—He talks of the sacrifices I should make in marrying him, Heaven knows, that I love him too dearly to think anything a sacrifice which I should do for him—but it is natural that at his time of life he would not bear inactivity nor obscurity—He must therefore obtain a situation ere he marries me—Whatever may be my lot, I am certain that I never can be happy without him—T. Smith and Ld. Burghersh call'd here this morning to *wish me joy*, how painful that is—Mrs. Jenkinson invited herself to dinner, Captn. Athlone and C, we had ask'd before—He seemed in Spirits at having got rid of the *load* which oppress'd him, he little thinks that *I* now bear all the weight of it—He was all affection, kindness and tenderness to me, but if he does not get the appointment he wishes, I fear that I must never hope to be happy in this world. How different is the Love of a Woman to that of a Man!—There is nothing that I could not give up for him but he could not be happy on £ 1500 pr. annm leading an inactive life in Scotland—I love his pride, and admire his Spirit—but could not help spending the Night in tears—

BETSEY

THURSDAY, 15TH MAY. A long visit from our good old

friend Foley, who still looks at me with a tender Eye—He is much the same, rather *older* and dropsical. Called on Mrs. Lewis whose little Boy improves but is not a beauty. We went this Evening to Des Hayes Benefit. Capt. Arklom, Mrs. Campbell and John Poulett joined our party—Grassini sang better than usual in Zaira, and acted uncommonly well. The Divertissement of La Dansomane very comical, and the grand Ballet of Renaud and Armide has fine effect ending with a rain of fire—Des Hayes pas de deux with his wife quite beautiful—A long letter from Fremantle dated the 30th Apl. he has applied to L$^{d.}$ B. to ask to be sent home.

[This is all of the 'long letter' that can be found:]

Neptune off Cadiz 30th April 1806.

It is rather curious that I should have sent two of Lord Nelsons letters to my brother William before I got yours,—it might perhaps be worth mentioning that the first note he ever wrote with his left hand was to you.

I confess I am by no means satisfied with Bucky's behaviour to me; every person at all connected with him in the Naval Line has received some sort of benefit except myself, I am worried at the seeming want of attention.

Addio for I am tired and stupid

ever affect.

EUGENIA

FRIDAY, 23RD. Campbell call'd this morg—I thought he look'd annoyed that Ld. Burghersh should be here—The latter went with us to see West's picture of the battle of Trafalgar—I was disappointed in it —We paid a few Visits amongst others Mrs. Bankes —She advises me strongly to put an end to this in some way or other—but however her advice is more rational than the one Lady Lowther gave me the other day—

SATURDAY, 24TH. I saw Campbell only for a few minutes this morg—My Sister preaches to me, which does not heighten my Spirits—He was asked by Mrs. Bankes, but could not go with us—John Poulett went, we found the remnants of a dinner party, the Duchess of Gordon, the Chathams, Montagues, Thompsons, several more etc—We had some Music—and afterwards went to the Cornwalls we found their Concert nearly ending—Ld. Burghersh made strong Love to me, and wants to persuade me to give up Campbell—I sang tolerably well—

HARRIET

SATURDAY, 24TH. John came with us to look after some Masquerade dresses we fixed upon one for him which however I do not like at all. Justina, him and I sat in the parlour till four o'clock talking in so *sweet* and *delicious* a manner, that I cannot help wishing every Young Man of the present age to have as good *notions* and *principles* as John has, if he really acts according to his manner of thinking he must be a most worthy and good creature. We took him in the evening at Mrs. Bankess who had a large dinner party consisting of the Dsse of Gordon, Ld. and Ly. Chatham and others fashionables.

SUNDAY, 25TH. I spent all the morning with the Pouletts who did nothing but Sermonize us on the wickedness of this world. We did not get home till past three o'clock and I remained awake a long time having heard from Justina her conversation with John, in which I am much concerned and which made me very happy indeed. E viva, E viva.

SUNDAY, 25TH. I felt uncommonly melancholy all day —Campbell call'd for an instant—I was alone—but too much out of Spirits to enjoy any thing—Mr. Cornwall me faisait le galant—Campbell was acting *with prudence*—at supper he told me he never could bear the thoughts of seeing a beloved object less well off in the world than she ought to be—am I to look upon this as his definitive sentence—?—He certainly has not succeeded in what he wish'd, and my fate I fear will be very soon fatally decided—He cannot love me much if he can thus sacrifice me to a mistaken pride—I spent a sleepless night in tears—I never, never, have felt so unhappy!—to think that I love him so much, and he loves me so little! is insupportable to me—He could not bear to see me less rich than I ought to be—But if he has any feeling could he prefer to see me waste my life in wretchedness—?—He has loved other women before, and would have gone any lengths for them, but now he is too prudent and reasons too well for a man who really loves—I feel ashamed for thus giving way to grief, which nearly destroys me—if I could awaken my pride, I might yet conquer such a weakness—but there is no room in my heart, for pride or anger, it is too much fill'd with love and wretchedness—

WEDNESDAY, 28TH. I felt very angry with Campbell and am much tempted to believe that he does not care for me any more—He never call'd all the morning, nor did he meet us, as he had promised at Mrs. Bartolozzi's Concert—John Poulett went with us, and I was helped out by Wm. Jerningham who was very drunk—I disliked the whole very much, some part of the Music was good, but the company detestable and the heat insufferable—after that I went in another sort of crowd at Ly. Westmorlands' where I met Mrs. Bankes for my chaperon—It was a good assembly but too full—met many people I knew, and flirted with Ld. Burghersh out of spite—I saw an old flame of Mr. Campbell's, who look'd at me with the eyes of a *Lynx*—went to bed truly indignant against him—I thought he used me very unkindly—

[Meanwhile Betsey had two more letters from Fremantle:]

Off Cadiz 3rd May 1806.

The Ship is rolling so much I can hardly sitt at table, I shall therefor wish you a good Night so Addio *cara Bettina*, this is Saturday when Sailors think of their Sweethearts and Wives. Yesterday was a nasty drizzling day, and to day is not much better. I hope I have found out that our head is damaged I have wrote for a survey and if it is as bad as I think it is we must soon go home. Monday 7th May, it still blows a gale of wind and I am half sea sick. I am going to dinner and in order to make myself as comfortable as I can have got all the Old Stagers to be of my party our dinner Soup, brisket, two made dishes a Roast Turkey and ham,—but we dont live so every day mind you.—oh if I could but pop in on you all this evening instead of sulking here alone how happy I should be. Saturday 10th.—I have not been quite so well these two days a bad Cold and the Uvula of my throat down which is very unpleasant.—to day I have had a survey taken on the head of the Ship, which is torn and defective, the report on it says it cannot be repaired at Sea, I think it will occasion our return to England this Summer for I am heartily tired of such sleepy work. —13th. I have been dining to day with the Admiral where we had rather a comfortable sort of dinner taking it all together I am afraid he *feels* that I wish to quit the Station, which however true it may be, I am not desirous he should believe, his Secretary hinted I *thought* that if I made the proposal I might be Captain of the Fleet, of course I only answered that it did not become *me* so to do, but that I should not be justified in refusing so honourable a situation, but, I should like to know if he was authorized to sound me on the *subject*, time will develop every thing and I am neither very anxious or sanguine on the subject, it would certainly answer to me in point of pecuniary advantage altho I am well aware, I should lead the life of a dog, I cant be worse than I am, and shall not worry myself much on the subject. The times are so bad that it is difficult to say what is best to be done, could I get the appointment I have named, I should be so much occupied, and save so much, that I should be perfectly reconciled in staying a Year or two longer, but in a Ship without reaping any benefit I am by no means so,—I have in my usual way been ruminating in my easy chair these last three hours on this conversation, it is of such a nature that I dare not trust any person in the World with it but Yourself you will in course not open to any one, as after all I think it unlikely to take place, and I should not like such a report to be in circulation.—

I shall now go to bed, my poor little dog sleeps with me and is my friend and companion, my cat is quite tame and they appear quite friendly, eating out of the same plate and sleeping on the [the letter is torn here] God bless you all so good night—13th.—to day quite calm but we are such a distance from [here the letter is torn again] other Ships, I shall see nobody but my Officers,—

EUGENIA

FRIDAY, 30TH. I saw Campbell for a little while this morg—he seems to me to have something on his mind—Walter and Miss Campbell call'd. He gave Betsey some beautiful Indian stuff for a turban—at Night we first went to Ly. Cave's, who as usual press'd all she could out of us, and afterwards to Mrs. Thomson, who had Dragonetti's Concert—I was tolerably happy as I had a great deal of Campbell's company and conversation—he is amazingly clever and entertaining—Ly. Hereford likes him of all things and I see by her manner that she has found us out—Campbell brought me a picture of his this morg to look at—I wish that I could keep it for ever, but I shall return it tomorrow—

HARRIET

SATURDAY, 31ST. John called very early to see how I was, the boy looked rather dull and he took a *great dose* of Salts last night going to bed as he wanted to keep me company in my Misfortunes. I sent him to order his dress. John and I had a most interesting conversation. I promised him something in case he goes to Ireland which I shall fully keep to. I wish I was as sure of his remaining constant as I am of still loving him even after an absence of twenty years. Hang this Irish expedition it drives me mad. I went to bed happy and unhappy my thoughts too much engrossed tete parley to sleep.

SUNDAY, 1ST JUNE. Called upon the Pouletts and laughed much with them. John walked home with us. I was thanked most *cordially* in Porteur for what I promised last night. We walked in Kensington Gardens with Mr. Campbell Mr. Bough and John. It was very pleasant, the Sun not being out. Justina and I remained at home in the evening Mrs. Pepbe's party not promising us much pleasure. I wrote a note to John to ask for the size of his hat which he answered bien joliment.

[Betsey's life is dated by her precious letters:]

29th May 1806. To-day the wind is fresh, and I am most terribly bilious. The *Sophie* arrived from Gibraltar, hear that Adml. Villeneuve was assassinated on his way from Paris to his estate in Provence, so much for Bonaparte. We are in daily expectation of a convoy under the escort of the *Diana.* If laziness and Indolence constitute happiness, I am completely so. 31st May. I must now give you a little piece of advice for yourself as well as for Harriet, on the score of John Powlett, Altho' the boy is well disposed and good looking, and certainly a very adequate match for your sister, still you should be on your guard against giving any improper encouragement. I mean that if it does not take place, or that he should be flighty and off, which is very probable when he is older and knows more of the world, that an impression may not be made that will cause her uneasiness, or such as may go forward in the World. You will understand what I mean, and guard with your usual precaution against such a reverse, I dare say your Sisters will laugh, I don't care for that, and *Jenny* may pay me the £272 she owes me for all the good advice I have given her—if you attempt to send me a line of accounts, you will give me a fit of the bile, I have enough to do to take care of my own, which however are very regular. I have now answered all your letters, which came very opportunely,—I read in the Gibraltar Chronicle that Adml. Villeneuve was assassinated at Rennes on the 23rd of April, what a horrid Tyrant must Bonaparte be if he had anything to do with such a shocking murder. I have a note to-day from Lord Collingwood telling me that the Medals for the action of the 21st of Decr. are sent out to him. I confess I am very much of Lord Nelson's way of thinking, he declared he would never again wear a medal until he got one for Copenhagen— Young Hastings get Volumes by every opportunity, the boy is really good, his Mother put his letters to my address without an envelope, but as the part opposite the seal concluded with Your Affe. Mother it made no difference, as I did not read a Sylable, indeed if I had I conclude it contained much what Mothers write to their Children at that age.

T.F.F.

[Tom wrote to his mother too:]

Hampton May 28th 1806.

Dear Mama

I am quite recovered but not done taking draughts. I hope you are all well. The goods which you sent me were very good. Tell me how to direct to my Uncle William for he told me to write to him. I have had a great misfortune the lock of my writing box which was not a good one from the first is now quite spoilet. I shall be glad to see you when the Holidays come. give my love to all I remane ever your dutiful Son

THOMAS FREMANTLE

THURSDAY, 5TH JUNE. I was quite sorry to leave my poor Brats, and came away at eight o'clock with Harry, Nanny and Sally—arrived in Town at four —I find Eugenia very miserable, she has had an explanation with Mr. C—— who is gone out of Town—little hopes remain de *ce marriage*— Chilvers orders Harry to go to the Sea immediately —I went this Evening with Justine to Mrs. Thompson's Ball—very good, St. John Duckworth looked a great quiz—Ld. Burghersh handed us down to Supper and was very *amiable*.

HARRIET

FRIDAY, 6TH. Ldy. Temple's was very full and the temporary room extremely well managed. All London was assembled and most of the Prince's attended. I danced with a little *Dog* of a *Baron* who proved my companion for Supper. Ldy. B. got him me and I really could have strangled him. He stunk like a *pole cat*. The supper was a scrambling one but considering the number of people it was very well managed. I was to have danced with John but Eugenia was tired and we went home at five *John* came with us declaring it would be too stupid to remain when we left. I cannot say I was much amused. My partner was so horrible that I could have strangled him. I saw everybody I knew.

MONDAY, 9TH. The Pouletts called and I walked with them after dinner in the Mall. I was sorry to find they had *left John* quite *dead* drunk behaving infamously. I am quite vexed with him, for a drunkard in my opinion is the *worst* of all animals. I hope this was only thro' *accident* altho' I rather fear that he has indulged rather in *that way* lately. Mr. Campbell returned. I sat at the window all the evening the heat being suffocating. I went to bed not *at all* happy.

EUGENIA

MONDAY, 9TH. In the evening all the Cornwalls came but I went to Mrs. Jenkinson, she having sent me word that her husband and C. were returned—how it made my heart beat to hear that!—I went most anxious to know how C. would behave towards me —He came up to me in the most good humored manner and shook hands—ashamed and happy, I know not how I had the appearance of coldness—he reproached me with it—but we ended by making it up and being better friends than ever—he walked home with me and during the way give me every satisfactory explanation I or my friends could wish —I felt so happy that I could not sleep with joy—I am well determined he never shall have reason to complain of me again, altho' he says this is not the last quarrel we shall have together—I shall not be surprized, if he takes it into his head to be *the Master* when we marry—but I shall willingly yield to him, and shall not quarrel for that.

WEDNESDAY, 11TH. I began the morning with that puppy of a tooth drawer Mr. Waite—C. made me very happy by paying me a long visit this morning —I dined at Argyle House, and think Col. Campbell the most good humored Creature in the world—our party consisted of Mr. and Mrs. Jenkinson Mr. Hooke, Mr. Carter, and Ly. Elizabeth and Mr. Cole —couple peu aimable, elle est belle et mechante il est vilain, malpropre, et soufre sa honte avec beaucoup de philosophie—as soon as the desert was on the table, Miss Campbell Mr. Jenkinson, Campbell and myself set out for the Play: we had Ly. Hawkesbury's private box—*School for Scandal*, and *High Life below Stairs* formed our evening's entertainment; we then returned to Supper at Argyle House, and I came home very much satisfied with the manner in which I had spent the day—que je l'aime!—et il se plaint toujours de ma froideur—Mrs. Bankes is delighted we have made it up and yet—the naughty man has taken an aversion against her, which I seek in vain to eradicate.

BETSEY

GEORGE STREET, MONDAY, 16TH JUNE. A Grand Masquerade at Ly. de Spencer's this evening where we went a large party from our House, all the Jenkinsons, Campbells and Bankes—I went as Night, a very *quiet* character. It was excessively crowded and some very good and well supported characters. All the rooms were ornamented with flowers and the temporary room was like a grove, opening into the garden, which had a brilliant effect—the crowd going to supper was dreadfull.

EUGENIA

MONDAY, 16TH. Campbell and Walter breakfasted with us—We spent the morning in preparations for the Masquerade, and to my great delight C. was here almost the whole time—He met Mrs. Bankes and was civil to her—In the evening he appeared an excellent figure as a Lady in the heigth of the fashion—His brother Walter, was as a Morning Star and Betsey as Night (which made a Wit observe at the Masquerade, that, that was the longest day and shortest night he had ever seen) Harriet as an old woman dress'd young and having two daughters in John Poulett and George Bankes,—Justine was the Honble. Lucretia M'c Tab, a very good figure—Mr. Jenkinson handed her in a Domino, and Peter Joinket presented her in a Persian dress—I was dress'd as Sir Philip Sidney's Wife, I am told *handsomely and becomingly* William Bankes was my Sir Philip but I did not meet him 'till we got to the Masquerade,—Mrs. Jenkinson was a Beautiful Chinese, and Col. Campbell with his Sister in Dominos—Ly. L. De Spenser had erected a temporary room—the crowd was immense—in the number some very good maskes, and beautiful dresses—Campbell amused himself very much—but I saw little of him all the evening—I was almost killed by the crowd going up to Supper where eatables did not abound, the pressure on the Staircase being so great that the Servants could not carry up new provisions—Some men contrived however to get beastly drunk—We staid till five and Campbell with me got dreadfully mobbed at going out—I was upon the whole pretty well amused, but all the compliments I received *on my charms* did not make me amends for the loss of the company of the only person to whom I am anxious to please—however he told me that I look'd well too—I thought he was rather annoyed that I should have a *Sir Philip* altho' it was his own proposal that we should not go together—

TUESDAY, 17TH. Henry Bankes, John, Mrs. Jenkinson and Campbell call'd—He told me that the mob carried him all round the Square last night—he certainly was a most tempting figure for them to lay their hands upon him—in the course of the evening he met with several good adventures—the Duke of Cambridge, in the number made Love to him—

FRIDAY, 20TH. Call'd at Argyle House, when I scolded Campbell—he went with Mrs. Sidney last night—I have taken an aversion to the woman—He walked with us to Saunders where I saw his picture extremely like—He then sat some time with us here —I din'd at Argyle House where my Sisters joined us in the evening, we then all proceeded to Vauxhall it was a new thing to me and I believe that I should have enjoyed the Scene much had I not felt exceedingly ill the whole time, besides being *somewhat* jealous of Mrs. Sidney whom we met sometimes in our rounds—However Campbell is only in joke in what he says about her—but I love him so dearly and so truly that not for any instant could I even in thought prefer any body to him, I cannot therefore endure the idea that he should make Love to any other woman—I love him, almost to distraction—The fire works were fine—we staid some time after Supper, and saw a number of unhappy women, some of them half drunk exhibiting their *charms* and *graces* in dancing—to my surprize, some in the number, danced well—but upon the whole the sight is very disgusting—we met several people we knew—Daugh supp'd with us—

SATURDAY, 21ST. We drank tea with Mrs. Bankes—met George Jenkinson there—We afterwards went to Mrs. Jenkinson's where I had appointed Campbell to meet us, and there I experienced what I can hardly bear to think of now and what I hope he may never make me feel again—He had an air of triumph, and a sort of flow of *false spirits* like a person who is doing wrong, and knows it, and yet *cannot help* doing it—He was going to meet Mrs. S. at a Concert, and left me at cards notwithstanding the pressing entreaties of every one present—I alone did not dare say one word because I knew, *why* he was so anxious to go—but I felt so mortified, so hurt and so wretched, that the tears actually ran down my cheeks—but he did not see it, and went to gratify his vanity at the expense of my heart—Vanity is his prevailing fault and he cannot resist this abominable woman—I could not sleep and cryed all night—to be thus slighted by a Man whom I love with so much sincerity and tenderness and to be slighted for an unworthy object, who at best can only feel a whim for him, is too much for me to bear—it kills me—

MONDAY, 23RD. C. call'd this morning—he promises me never to see Mrs. S. again—& afterwards went to see Mr. Lambert, the *fat man* a most wonderful object of disgust.—

Thursday, 25th. I saw C. this morning—He does not seem in Spirits—Spent an insufferable dull evening at the Foleys where they made me Sing 'till I was exhausted—all the Fitzgeralds possible were there —in the number Pamela now Mrs. Pitcairn—she seems an affected little puss—

Friday, 26th. Campbell paid a short visit this morg.— I went to Lord Burghersh, with Betsey, who was greatly enjoying his own fiddling. I afterwards went to see sights with Ly. Lowther, Mary, and Charles Fane—The fat man, I thought more disgusting than before—The Panorama of Trafalgar is very good, and I saw a curious picture of all the mountains in the world grouped together to ascertain their respective weights—I dined at the Jenkinsons with Ld. Rancliffe and Campbell who at first was all attention and tenderness to me, and then all of a sudden without my being able to account for it, became dull and out of spirits—He would not go with me to the Bankes' (who gave a little dance for me) but met us there late, and neither danced with me nor spoke to me—Stung at his behaviour, I was determined to carry it off with a high hand, so that I seemed as happy as possible danced a great deal and flirted with every body—but I felt very uneasy and unhappy and could not make out what induced him to behave so to me—he seemed very unhappy himself, and when he came home in the carriage with us: I ask'd him, and he said *I* had behaved ill to him —Mrs. Bankes was looking very ill and seemed much displeased at Campbell's conduct—Henry is going to Sicily in a few days, he has an Ensign's Commission—I went to bed indescribably angry with Campbell—

Saturday, 27th. Campbell and Walter call'd here this morg—I spoke to the latter, who told me that I had made him miserable yesterday, by talking of my flirtations with others—He was besides out of spirits on account of the delay he experiences in his affairs —He seemed so agitated and so unhappy that I could not have felt angry another minute—He is to talk to Mr. Bankes to morrow—

Sunday, 28th. Campbell call'd before he went to Mr. Bankes who was gone out, Mrs. Bankes being ill yesterday forgot to tell him that Campbell was to go —I cannot describe the sort of anxiety and misery I am in—We call'd on Ly. Charlotte Campbell who treated us as relations and let us in—We then went to Mrs. Bankes who is looking very ill—walked in Kensington Gardens where Campbell joined us—he told me he had met Bankes—We spent the evening at Argyle House—when Campbell was in great spirits all love and affection—He is determined if Bankes approves of it to marry me immediately and carry me to his Father who he is very sure would be anything for me—all his family seem delighted at the prospect of the match, and I should have felt happy beyond measure if this *cruel information* did not damp my spirits—But I trust in God that every thing will be settled to my satisfaction with Bankes to morrow—poor Mrs. Jenkinson is out of spirits her baby being ill—Ly. Charlotte was very kind to me —She is a lovely creature—

Monday, 29th. I spent an agonizing morning in the midst of suspense and anxiety—Bankes call'd after his conference with Campbell, whom he persuaded to write to his Father to settle on him £700, per annum and to enable him to settle upon me and my children the Estate which it appears his Father is at liberty to sell during his Life time—Unless the

Father agrees to this Bankes advises me not to think of the match—Campbell afterwards call'd and seems full of hopes that his Father will agree—I could feel happy even in this suspense, did not that unhappy story haunt me—but so convinced am I that no blame can be attached to Campbell in it, that I long to talk to himself on the subject; only it is too delicate to mention—We dined at the Wm. Fremantles with the Cathcarts—spent the evening with Mrs. Jenkinson where we met all the Campbells—Robert was all affection to me and talks of nothing but our future prospects of happiness which he seems certain we shall enjoy—I was very near telling him every thing—

BETSEY

MONDAY, 30TH JUNE. I feel awkward and uncomfortable since the reports which prove unfavourable to Mr. C's character and know not what to do.

THURSDAY, 3RD JULY. Great worry and torments violent advice given, which Eugenia is determined not to follow, but it is thought wrong she should be so much with Mr. C before his Father's answer is arrived. I have determined to go out of Town next Sunday, and sent an excuse to a party on the Thames for to morrow which had been made on purpose for us, and given up since we declined going. The Mr. Campbells called for a moment in the evening and were very good humoured about it, but Robert much distressed at the thoughts of being parted for the present from Eugenia, who was in tears the whole night—I wish all may end well, but it is in a desperate way just now.

FRIDAY, 4TH JULY. We all went to Mrs. Bankes she fancies the Father's answer will not be favourable and that Eugenia will have an opportunity to break off. All the Campbell Family are certain the Father will do everything that has been asked of him in this case Eugenia is firmly resolved to marry *malgré* all her Friends injunctions against it. I cannot be brought to think so bad of the man as he has been by *some* people represented, but still would not promote the business, altho' I know that any endeavours to put it off would be perfectly useless. I am more anxious, teazed and distressed than any poor Creature ever was and should rejoice when I get out of Town.

[A letter from Fremantle seems to come from another planet—so far is he from all the worry and anxiety Betsey is going through.]

14th June 1806.

The weather to-day is delightful, close off Cadiz the water as smooth as the Thames and everybody as clean as I could wish, the ennui and want of occupation is not to be born, and I am tormented with bile, the only amusement I have is with my pug dog, who occasionally fights the Cat, and as often with the Monkey, it is really ridiculous to see him and the Monkey. I have within this day or two found out a conceited wretch of a french Negro, who with all the vanity and ignorance of one, professes to understand everything, to-morrow he is in my presence to give the Youngsters a lesson of dancing and fencing, they play the wretch such tricks, and make him do so many absurd things that it is quite impossible to keep one's countenance, is not this fine employment for a man of my time of life, and in my situation.

17th June. I have really nothing to write about but I am determined to persevere in my plan of saying something every day. I am much as I was yesterday, and uncomfortable—at 8 in the evening I assembled the Youngsters and Officers, and we had quite a famous ball.—18th. I have been staying upon Deck until 11 at night, seeing a performance between the french Negroe and an Italian, the latter worries the poor Negroe out of his Wits, but he is so good humoured, that it is impossible to affront him—I have been also to-day, playing a dozen games at drafts, with one of my poor Youngsters, who broke his leg about a month ago, he is now almost well, and has been confined in my cabin. You see to what straits I am drove for occupation. 19th. To-day I have been dining with Lord Collingwood which is little enough, the *Prince* has joined from Gibraltar where she has left all her stores, consequently she must go home. I think we shall have our chance yet by the autumn—I have lately left off drinking more than two glasses of wine and my bile is not so bad—I feel my complaint has more impression on the mind than the body—28th. Your giving a ball was delightfull, now the Ministry are changed Bankes is not afraid of coming to your house, which he certainly was the night before I left London. Between ourselves your good Sister's little head seems un peu tourné and I wish she could reason and communicate less in the stile of a Novelist, if I were to quote some of the passages in her letter to me some months hence she would I am sure be a little annoyed, that loving dearly after a fortnight's acquaintance and the Dear Man sounds so stupid to a fellow of 40 years of age, what think you my Tussy?—but keep this to yourself for your Life.

EUGENIA

FRIDAY, 3RD JULY. I call'd on Ly. C. Campbell, and

there met Robert, who had not slept all Night—He will do anything rather than give my Sister uneasiness, therefore he agrees not to come to this House any more—they all talked before me of our marriage as a settled thing—Jenkinson and Walter came to me and the latter, with that honest manner which no one can doubt gave me a most satisfactory account of the whole transaction—His family, he says, are obliged to me and will never rest 'till the whole is cleared up to the world and to my friends as it is to me—I enjoy with transport the thoughts of seeing him justified to all, and hope still to be happy—after that I had another conversation which damped my spirits—

SATURDAY, 4TH. Justine comes of age to day—Mrs. Wiseham, John Poulett and Hutchinson breakfasted here—We were distracted in the midst of packages, bills trades people, without naming the feelings of my heart—I call'd on Mrs. Jenkinson who at first told me she had a *sad story* to tell me and then refused to explain—Campbell was there he was left alone with me—expresst a doubt of our meeting again, and wept like a Child—that agony is not natural I am certain that he has something on his mind,—Walter call'd here—Ld. Rosslyn is to come to morrow and satisfy me about the story—Bankes is to meet him—I still hope for the best but I am almost distracted in my mind—a note from Robert to Justine, which I opened encreases my agony he has *a secret* and fears we may never meet again—But I trust God he will not forsake us—Whatever Robert may *have been*, I am sure he is now, an altered man, with as warm good and honest a heart as ever beat in a man's breast, sincerely attached to me—and that if I become his wife I shall enjoy the fruits of his reformation and never repent of my

Consort—Mrs. Bankes call'd and did not say much on the subject—Betsey allowed Robert to come before she went to the opera—He was a little more composed this evening and I endeavoured to comfort him—We met again at Mrs. Jenkinson's where I spent the evening—We played at Cards and tried to keep up our Spirits—Convinced as I am that R. is now trying to obtain satisfaction from Sir C. Douglas, I am too full of hopes as to the result and too anxious to see him justified in the eyes of the world not to bear his short abscence with fortitude—I hope and trust in God that we shall soon meet again never to part more—

SUNDAY, 5TH. I received this morg a packet of papers from Walter; with a written statement of the story signed by Lord Rosslyn and so compleately satisfactory to me, that I wrote to intreat the affair may go no farther and would not trouble Ld. Rosslyn to come as Bankes would not meet him—I however sent him the papers to see—whether they satisfied him or no, I know not, but whatever may be the opinion of the world and however numerous the reports against R. Campbell's character, I am fully convinced in my own mind that he has never done anything dishonorable, altho' by his own confession he has been guilty of many errors and follies—I should think that I acted very dishonorably now, towards him and his family were I to forsake him, I am therefore determined to marry him, even should all my friends think it proper to discard me on that account—all I wish now, is to hear no more advice or opinion on the subject as it only distracts my mind without altering my determination—We left Town at about 2 o'Clock, it was a wet day, and every thing tended to lower my spirits—The evening was better we arrived late after the Children were gone to bed—

BETSEY

SWANBOURNE, SUNDAY, 13TH JULY. The door Bell rang while we were at Breakfast and to our no small surprise the Mr. Campbells were announced. Robert was so delighted with his Father's answer which is all he could wish, that he came himself with Walter to bring Eugenia the good news, without seeing first Mr. Bankes as he had promised to do. I felt rather awkward and uncomfortable at their coming here, but as they had travelled all night and are going back to Town to morrow I could not do otherwise than offer them Beds for one Night. The Miss Lowndes and stupid Woodley called—Eugenia was delighted, and in the course of the day settled all her plans—Mr. R. Campbell is to see Mr. Bankes on his return to Town and to make every money arrangement with him. The Father promises to allow them £600 a year and to entail the estate on them and their *Heirs* hereafter. We shall go to Town next Monday week and the Wedding to be on *Tuesday*—John Poulett came this afternoon—it was Swanbourne Feast a bad one, and showery evening.

[On July 17 Mr. T. Grenville wrote to Lord Buckingham: 'I have almost persuaded Lord Grenville to take Fremantle instead of King and I believe Lord Grenville will write to you about it as an experiment that he will try. If Fremantle will set to work thoroughly he may do it well. I am inclined to think it best and that it will be tried. It is no small inducement, in addition that you will naturally wish it, and I now hope it will be done.'

On the same day Lord Grenville wrote to Lord Buckingham: 'I have taken the resolve today to send to Fremantle to offer him that he shall take King's situation upon an understanding that he takes it upon trial, and that he is not to be hurt if I should at any time hereafter be obliged to say to him frankly that I find it does not go on satisfactorily. This reserve I feel necessary because I cannot help doubting, when the novelty of the thing is once over, he will be able to bring his mind to so much unpleasant drudgery as the situation must necessarily require.' He was to be 'brought in' to Parliament either for St. Mawes, or for Enniskillen—actually, in the end, he was 'brought in' for Sandwich.]

Eugenia

George Street, Sunday, 17th. We heard Mass early in the morning, and I shall not attempt to describe all that passed in my mind and my heart while preparing to leave this place for London—it was a mixture of joy, and sober reflexion, happiness and fear —However by the time we had reached Uxbridge every other feeling had disappeared except that of delight at the thoughts of meeting Campbell—We arrived in George St. soon after eight and he came immediately—happy beyond measure to see him again I felt grieved to find that he is very much dissatisfied with the sort of settlement Bankes means to make—but he would not explain—I found a pretty little writing desk with the License in it and several presents—To my infinite surprise Mrs. Bankes call'd in the evg—she evidently wish'd to *sit out* Campbell but he was to cunning to allow that and she was at last obliged to depart—it is my opinion that she wanted to be ask'd to the wedding altho' a few days ago she absolutely refused appearing there and that Bankes refused giving me away —Mr. Jenkinson is to be my Papa, the Duke had intended it but he cannot put off his Father's mourning—Mr., Mrs. Jenkinson and Miss Campbell call'd in the evg—I feel quite happy and yet so odd—

MONDAY, 18TH. A strange thing is the eve of a wedding day—I began and ended with tradespeople and milliners, saw a priest, then Mrs. Erskine, my Lover almost the whole day, and all my Brothers and Sisters that are to be—I was at last quite exhausted —We dined at Argyle House—quite a family party —The Duke is looking better—became acquainted with his brother Ld. John, a little, ugly but very agreable man—after dinner, Campbell, Betsey and myself we slipped away to meet Bankes, Sheldon and a Lawyer in George St.—and there Robert showed me the temper of an angel, by signing without saying one word a settlement which I never should have signed had I known the contents.— When they were all gone he informed me of them, and they are so disgraceful, that I burst into tears— it made me unhappy for the whole evening and kept me awake at night—

TWICKENHAM, TUESDAY 22ND. This was a memorable day—the most interesting, in my whole Life—It made me feel very strange—I was afraid to reflect or to think least I should lose the courage which every Woman stands in need of on such an occasion —I was obliged to dress in a hurry to attend my little Catholic Priest who received my Confession, when that was over I found Robert and Walter already arrived—My dear Bridegroom was even perhaps more agitated than his Bride—We were instantly married by the Catholic Priest and no Woman ever pronounced her vows with a happier heart—Robert pronounced his with a firmness and at the same time a feeling which greatly affected me —We had but just time to breakfast, and then I had to dress for the second marriage—my *bridal array* consisted of a white satin under dress and a patent net over it, with a long veil—at about 12, the party was assembled, consisting, of Mr. and Mrs. Charteris, Mr. and Mrs. Jenkinson, Betsey Campbell, Col. Campbell, Walter, Mr. and Ly. Elizabeth Cole, Mr. Hooker, and Cte. de Beaujolois—my heart beat when we entered the church, nor could I go thro' the second ceremony without feeling even more affected—Miss Poole had been married a few hours before me, and I signed my name under hers with a steadier hand—I can never forget Jack's kindness to me before we left the vestry—We immediately went to Argyle House where we had a cold collation —Nothing can exceed the kindness I met with from every member of Robert's family—presents were pouring upon me, and Mr. de Beaujolois gave me a very handsome amethyst and diamond cross—at about four *the happy pair* set out for Ly. Elizabeth Cole's house at Twickenham—My Sisters seemed to feel a great deal when I left them—But they knew I was happy—

WEDNESDAY, 23RD. I experience nothing but attention and kindness and am truly happy—We drove to Hampton to see the Palace and the gardens—I walked till I was tired. We then returned to a late dinner—and went to our repose soon after—

The wedding over Betsey retired with relief to Swanbourne, where she found a letter from Fremantle awaiting her.

10TH, 11TH, 12TH. Much as usual. The *Ajax* is come from Gibraltar, and I am in expectation of going there, when I recollect that just this time *nine years ago*, I was there with a young girl of 18 for a wife, and all that has happened since; I do indeed think myself an old fellow, but as I have never for *one moment* had cause to repent, or be in the smallest degree dissatisfied with the connexion I then formed, so I consider the last years of the life I lived on shore, the happiest I ever passed, and I exist only in the hopes of enjoying it soon again. You may perceive Mrs. Tussy that I am not afraid of your being vain, or that your head will be turned, I have so much confidence in your sound sense, and good understanding that I can [be] satisfied that all my concerns are well conducted in your hands.

BETSEY

SWANBOURNE, TUESDAY, 29TH JULY. Spent the greatest part of the day in preparation for the arrival of Les Epoux. Decorated the rooms with Flowers and smartened little Swanbourne for this gay Occasion. They did not come till ten o'clock, the Bells rang all the Evening and half the night—Eugenia is not improved in her looks but appears a happy little creature—*et ils sont tres tendres*—

EUGENIA

SWANBOURNE, TUESDAY 29TH. We had several people to breakfast with us—I made a Will, with infinite joy—then had so many things to do, that it was past two o'Clock before we left Town—We departed as usual from Argyle House—soon after nine we reached Swanbourne in the midst of the ringing of bells and joyful shouts—I was most happy to see my Sisters altho' they *will* not treat me with *respect* —I went to kiss all the Children in their beds—poor Tom has a very bad cough—

EDGCOTT, SATURDAY, 9TH AUGUST. Went fishing with the gentlemen and spent a pleasant morning—Robert however, makes me uneasy by plunging every instant in the water and remaining with his

wet cloathes on—I fear it will hurt him, in time—
Had affectionate Letters from my Sisters—

Liverpool, Friday, 22nd August. The whole of the day was spent in viewing this town which is truly fine, and the docks which are reckoned famous—We went on board some Guinea-men and my heart revolted at the relation of the cruelties practised upon the wretched Negroes during their passage—The manner in which the Ship is arranged for their accommodation is sufficient to make one commiserate their sufferings, were not additional barbarities executed towards these unhappy wretches—Who has giv'n us the right thus to treat our fellow creatures?—God alone will show it on the great day when we are to account for our deeds—We were much disappointed in finding our things not yet arrived from Swanbourne—Robert was a little out of humor about it, and with some cause—yet—I saw him so for the first time—and I am so spoilt by his indulgence—that altho' he said nothing cross or unkind to me—I chose to cry for an hour about it, and felt ashamed of myself—he recovered his usual good temper even before I had recovered my Spirits I felt very tired with our long walks we however went to the Play—We afterwards supped and then embarked on board the Cutter—Sir John Reid accompanied us to the boat and promises to take care of our things.

Sunday, 24th. We had a dreadful Night, but this morning was something better—our stomachs were fortified and we were able to eat voraciously the dinner prepared by Robert and Walter—the night was again very stormy and the Sea rose Mountains high—However we made a great deal of way towards Islay—

Islay, Tuesday, 26th. I walked out with Robert this

morg—it was a delightful day only now and then interupted by partial showers—the View of the Sea, from the House is quite beautiful and this country altho' destitute of trees seems to lay claim to a high degree of picturesque beauty—I am diverted by the Sight of barefooted, and barelegg'd poor people who apparently enjoy themselves much thus unencumbered with too much attire—female beauty does not seem to abound, or at least they lose it early from the hard life they lead and the constant exposure of their complexions to the Sea and air—they wear no bonnets—We met a wedding all on foot, and bare legg'd, attended with bagpipes and flags—I am an object of curiosity to the inhabitants with whom Robert seems a great favourite—they crowd round us wishing us joy, and shake hands with him after kissing their own hand—they chiefly talk Gaelic, which I do not understand—

Monday, 15th. This day we at last put into execution the long meditated expedition to Jura, and left Islay House early in the coach—We breakfasted at Portascraig the view from the summit of the hill before you descend to the Village is quite beautiful—at 12 we got on board the Cutter our sail lasted nearly two hours, and was as usual, so uneasy as to make the Beaujolois, my maid and myself very sick—We were glad to get on Shore a truly wild country—far from the haunts of Man—a number of rocks make the navigation to it dangerous—The Count went to shoot deer but returned late without having killed or seen any—this disappointment however did not affect the spirits of the party and we were all very merry—

Tuesday, 16th. We all slept ill some complained of heat and some of cold—In the morning early M. de Beaujolois set out for the deer shooting which did not promise much amusement as the weather was showery—Robert for fear of spoiling the Count's sport, remained with us and the day was spent in fishing, scrambling amongst the rocks and picking oysters—the cutter struck against a clay bank, and it was some hours ere the flood helped her off again —Cte. Beaujolois returned late having had fine sport —he killed one doe, and wounded two—Robert and I retired to our bed very early after dinner the others sat up as usual—may the opportunities we give W and J—end as I and they could wish—they are both *stupid*, and I fear Love is more on her side than his——

THURSDAY, 18TH. Walter left us this morning he seemed very miserable to go, and we were all very sincerely sorry to part with him—many tears were shed on his account, and from what passed between him and Justine I begin to hope that he likes her and that every thing will end in time according to her wishes—I walked to meet Robert and Beaujolois on their return—I saw traces of the goodness of heart of the former after parting with his Brother— They had shocking weather and it was even hazardous their coming this morning—

BETSEY

THURSDAY, 18TH SEPTEMBER. I went with Emma to call on Miss Lord, who was sitting with her dirty Uncles, in a Room stinking of Tobacco—The poor girl must spend an unpleasant Life among such unpolished Beings. Letters from Islay, happier than ever, and Justine more in love than ever sans espoir *pauvre fille*! No crinoline en chemise.

EUGENIA

THURSDAY 9TH. We left Campbelltown early this

morning and were accompanied to the Cutter by a numerous Cortege—The Wind was fair, and we had a delightful sail to Skipness all the time following the windings of a lovely coast—It was near one when we landed on the spot which is to become our residence in time, and had I chosen for myself I could not have put together so many objects which please me so much as those by which I shall be surrounded here—The House is not in a good State and Robert talks of building another—Placed very near the Shore it faces the Island of Arran on one side, and on the other a most beautiful ruin of a Castle which was the original dwelling of the Campbell family—a little farther off the remains of a Catholic Chapel are now converted into a burying-ground for the family, and there my bones are to be laid—There is an exceeding pretty wood at the back of the House, and I think the situation so charming that I shall be quite delighted when we settle at Skipness—We were received on the shore by several of the Men who wish'd us joy and shook hands with us—one ugly old Man, told Robert I might be good but that I was very wee—The farmer's Wife who lives in the House gave us a dinner, and we departed after having gone all over the House which is certainly much out of repair but which I think might be made comfortable—Our *beaux* escorted us to the Shore and I gave them money—to drink our healths —They cheered us handsomely and I was weak enough to rejoice that the Man who had made the remark on me did not partake of my present—Oh! weakness of human Nature!—

FRIDAY, 10TH. We spent the Night at anchor at Lochgaer, and this morning landed to take possession of Traffard Campbell's home where we found a very good breakfast prepared for us—He has an excellent

House—We afterwards resumed our voyage, The banks on each side offered at every instant the most beautiful Views, a wooded Country old Castles and Country Seats—Towards evg we were becalmed and at last took to the boat—about an hour's rowing carried us safe on shore—We met with a very kind reception at the Castle—The Duke is considerably recovered—Ld. John looks very ill, Bonomi (the architect) quarrels with Traffard and is very entertaining—Mr. Brownlow North whispers softly—Ly. Augusta Clavering does the honneurs of the House very well—she has a lovely daughter and was once lovely herself—but she is now crooked, has a bad Husband and bad health—Mlle. La Chaulx the Governess is clever but talks a great deal—

Saturday, 11th. My eyes opened themselves this morg on the most beautiful views on every side, and were still more feasted when we drove out in the open carriage after breakfast—The Castle is a magnificent building in itself and has everything about it which can tend to make a place truly desirable and beautiful to the highest degree—The *ton* of the House is very pleasant because every one is left at liberty to do as they please—We dined very late, and shared the evg between Music and Cards—Ly. Augusta was once a good singer—

[From his school at Hampton Tom writes to Emma:]

Dear Emma,

I am sorry I could not write to you sooner. I hope you & Charles had a pleasant ride to Hoggerton & had a nice game with Mr. Howerd's children. I hope all Maids are well, Nurses, Emmy & Nanny, give my love to them all & believe me always your Dutiful Brother Thos. Fremantle give my love to Mama & tell her I will write to her soon.

THURSDAY, 9TH OCTOBER. I was happy to hear of the capture of four French Frigates by S. Samuel Hood who unfortunately lost his Arm—Delanos left us after Breakfast Another of my Cows was taken ill in the same way as the other two—I hope however the Beast will recover as the loss will be very heavy.

FRIDAY, 10TH OCTOBER. Lord Buckingham and Captn. Badcock called at one—the former told me in *Grand Secret* that Fremantle would be appointed one of the Lords of the Admiralty and have a seat in Parliament—this will be very comfortable and made me extremely happy, he likewise said the Atlas would sail on Tuesday to relieve him.

THURSDAY, 23RD OCTOBER. Harriet returned, there is an account of the Spanish Fleet having attempted to come out of Cadiz which I fear will detain Fremantle.

FRIDAY, 24TH OCTOBER. I have a horrid cold but the weather being fine I walked to Mursley to see an old Man who is a Hundred years old, his name is Peek, he married a few years ago a woman beyond seventy, who now takes care of him and of her own Mother who is past a Hundred, manages a small Dairy and does everything, the two Centurions have lived too long and are almost returned to Childhood.

SUNDAY, 26TH OCTOBER. Few joys can equal what I experienced on reading a Letter from Fremantle which he wrote at Sea in his way to Portsmouth where he wishes me to meet him. I soon got everything ready and set out with Harriet and Emma, I thought it more prudent to go the Sunbury road, where I might hear something of him in case he had arrived. I was so tired when I got to Mrs. Bishop's, for my Cold was so heavy that I was prevailed upon to stay the Night. I left an excuse for Ly. Charlotte in my way through Aylesbury, as I was to have gone to Hartwell to-morrow, and heard the House was so full that Walter with his two Friends, were obliged to have beds at Aylesbury.

Russell Place, Wednesday, 29th October. I could not pass Hampton without seeing my Boys. I found Charles the picture of health and much improved but Tom not as I could wish, he still looks delicate and his Eyes are weak. Mr. and Mrs. Morgan were out, but Mrs. Kearslick and the Maid gave a very satisfactory account of them. I called in Stanhope Street and hear from Mrs. W. Fremantle that Fremantle dined with them on Sunday in good health and spirits and was all anxiety about me—I received soon after my arrival in Russell Place, a letter from Sandwich and was more disappointed than ever at finding that as the Election is not till Monday he cannot return to Town till Monday Evening. I am really miserable at the thought that I shall not see him for so many days. Mr. and Mrs. Bishop are very kind to us in allowing me to have a Bed in Russell Place, as their House is whitewashing painting and new furnishing for the Spring. They wish me to go to Sunbury with them on Friday, which I shall do and return Monday to meet Fremantle. We went to the Butlers in the evening, the Family were all assembled and quite cheerfull—even the Old Woman is in better spirits than I expected. I heard a great deal of Fremantle who had spent the Evening on Sunday with them. I am quite jealous that they should have seen him before *me*. Played two rubbers at Casino which I won and music—Caroline Fountain in very good voice.

Monday, 3rd November. Fremantle writes me word that the Election is to day, but that as he must dine with the Electors to morrow he will not be able to return till Wednesday. Mr. Bishop was so kind as to bring Tom and Charles from School last night—Tom's eye is still very bad—Rain the whole day, it is miserably dismal here. Dined again in Charlotte Street.

EUGENIA

INVERESK, SATURDAY, 4TH. Sandy Grant, Mr. Campbell's man of business breakfasted with us—Several other people call'd in, and as it was a very fine day we walk'd towards the abbey leaving our carriages to follow us—We met the Duke in our way, to this ancient residence of the Scotch kings—it is a very fine old Palace, in which Monsieur used to live when he was in Scotland—there we call'd on the Cte. de Coigny, a very agreable Emigrant confined to his arm Chair with the gout; in him I found an old forgotten acquaintance and a great friend of Ml. de Rosenbergs he gave me one of her books—We then call'd on Rebourguil who showed us some rooms of the abbey and afterwards on Mrs. Campbell Carrie who has appartements there—She is an O.M.—but was chere amie to Ld. Frederic Campbell and scandal says she had a daughter by him—We then got into the carriage and proceeded to Mrs. Campbell Lochnells with whom we spent an hour and then went on to Inveresk—We found Mr. Charteris considerably better and his Wife quite well—he has Six fine Children—Mrs. Clinton is also here a Sister of Mrs. Charteris—Ld. Ellco dined with us I knew him at Vienna—or least he knew me, for I have forgot—

BETSEY

WEDNESDAY, 5TH NOVEMBER. I was agreeably surprised by Fremantle's arrival at seven o'clock this morning. He travelled all night, but seems not the worse for his fatigues and exertions at the Election. He went to the Admiralty after Breakfast and only returned to dinner. Mr. and Mrs. Bishop came to Town. I sent the Boys back to Hampton after they had seen their Father.

THURSDAY, 6TH NOVEMBER. Fremantle finds me grown very fat, he is, I think much the same in every respect. I walked with him after breakfast to look out for a House and took one No. 4 Sackville St. to which we removed at three o'clock. Mrs. Bishop called to take us to dine at Brompton Park. A very comfortable and elegant House a mile out of Town, where Mrs. Wm. Fremantle proposes to reside till the meeting of Parliament. Wm. Fremantle looked dreadfully ill when he came to dinner having had a fall with his Horses. Lionel Hervey is with them.

SACKVILLE STREET, FRIDAY, 7TH NOVEMBER. We are obliged to keep very early hours, breakfast at nine and Fremantle is at the Admiralty from ten till six every evening. I went with him to call on Ly. Neale, who is in the House we are to have at the Admiralty when they remove into Sir Phillip Stephens's. It is a most comfortable House and I wish we could soon get into it, but I fear it will be some weeks ere it is ready for us, as we have to furnish it.

SWANBOURNE, SUNDAY, 23RD NOVEMBER. I left Town at about nine o'clock with Fremantle and arrived at Swanbourne before six. Augusta and Louisa are grown fat and looking very well. He did not think the little Brat so pretty as I do—Augusta knew her Papa again. The Bells rang many peals, and we were very busy all the evening looking over papers, etc. etc.

SACKVILLE STREET, TUESDAY, 16TH DECEMBER. I have order'd the waggon to be in Town on Thursday morning and we hope to remove to the Admiralty on Friday.

ADMIRALTY, FRIDAY, 19TH DECEMBER. I was at the House all the morning and it begins to look tolerably comfortable—the Ships sofas and armchairs do not make at all a mean appearance in the Drawing rooms. I was made very wretched at the accounts which arrived yesterday of *l'Athenée* a 64 Ship having been lost in the Mediterranean, 349 men perished, and in the list of these unfortunate creatures is *Ensign Bankes* of the 35th. It can be no other than poor Harry Bankes who had taken his passage in that Ship from Gibraltar to join the regiment in Sicilly. I felt extremely shocked and distressed—Poor Mrs. Bankes was to be in Town for the meeting of Parliament yesterday, the idea of what they will experience on hearing the melancholy fate of their son really makes me perfectly wretched.

CHAPTER 29

THURSDAY, 12TH FEBRUARY. The Pouletts and Mrs. R. Butler came to see me dress for Court, my dress was only White Satin and patent lace drapery which looked very neat. Lady Temple called for me in her carriage, and as we drove through the Park into the inner courts of the Palace we got in without any difficulty. The crowd in the last drawing room just getting up to the Queen was very oppressive, but I went through the Ceremony of kissing the Queen's hand, and the whole business without any difficulty and much less awkwardness than I expected, and was home in little more than an hour. Fremantle was so overcome by the heat that he never arrived before the old Lady's presence.

[Next day Betsey goes to Ly. Salisbury's, where there was an excellent assembly.]

The Prince of Wales looked shockingly—I am sorry to see Lazard introduced, the Duke de Berri, Ld. Sefton and Ld. Cranley presided at the Lazard table.

[By early March the poor Fremantles realized that, after all their long patient waiting, their term of office would be short indeed.]

TUESDAY, 17TH MARCH. We fear that the change of Ministry is unavoidable—it is a pity Ld. Grenville proposed the Catholic Bill, since Pitt went out before on the same cause, and the King has ever been so decided during his Life not to grant it being against his Coronation Oath. Among these worries it was pleasant to get so friendly and approving a letter from Lord Collingwood.

WEDNESDAY, 18TH MARCH. Our residence here has been but short, arrangements are making for a new Ministry and I cannot help regretting, we have been at some expense in furnishing this House. I hope Fremantle will be appointed to a Yacht which will give him £500 a year and keep him on shore. I went with Harriet to Mrs. Bankes.

[Fremantle, Lord Grenville assures Lord Buckingham, 'will keep his yacht.'

'Fremantle has now quiet holidays,' Betsey observes on April 12th, 'and will in my opinion be much happier than when he was obliged to attend so closely to the Admiralty board. Captain Hope is to have our house and very good-humouredly allows us to remain as long as we wish in it which is a great accommodation to us.' Fremantle's brother William, however, did not take the change quite so philosophically. To Lord Buckingham he writes: 'You may easily imagine that this unexpected state of affairs has been a cruel and most unhappy break up to the society and intercourse and domestic enjoyment of my family. I lament it most seriously.']

FRIDAY, 24TH APRIL. Harriet is preparing for her Journey to Scotland, and is to travel with Col[l]. and Ly. Charlotte Campbell. Robt. is all impatience to get back to his little wife, and sends her presents every day in his Letters. We went this evening to Dragonetti's Concert at Ly. Hertford's, the heat was so excessive it was impossible to attend to the music, but we found it very pleasant in one of the adjoining rooms with the Pouletts. I asked the Duke de Berri to come to our little music on Monday next—The Prince of Wales was, as *usual*, at Ly. Hertford's and I enjoyed much seeing him divide his attentions between Mrs. Fitzherbert and the Ly. of the House. The former went away early, and left him to enjoy the society of this new flame, who certainly is a wonderful looking woman of her age.

FRIDAY, 1ST MAY. I am beginning to pay Bills, pack up, unfurnish our House and prepare for quitting this abode, where we have made but a short and ruinous residence. I dined at Ly. Wm. Russell's, who asked Emma to play with her little girl, and has really been extremely civil to me. The Duke of Argyle and a Mrs. Page alone were there and of course Ld. Wm. *quoiqu'il me parait un zero dans sa maison*—We had a very comfortable and pleasant dinner. The Pouletts called for me to chaperon them to Ly. Salisbury's where Drago's Concert was to-night, the rooms are ill calculated for music and it was so hot and crowded, I heard nothing but found the assembly very good and pleasant. The Prince of Wales came in for a short time but did not stay supper.

[Betsey departs into the country.]

UNDAY, 30TH AUGUST. I felt extremely uncomfortable all day but walked out and dined at table. Mr. Tookey was sent for in the evening and towards twelve o'clock I was happily delivered of another boy.

[Fremantle goes to Scotland in a Berwick smack, but the weather is disagreeable. 'Lady Charlotte was at prayers the whole night and they were obliged to put in at Yarmouth,' but on Sept. 25th Betsey writes: 'It was a great relief to me to hear of Fremantle's safe arrival They have had a ruinous and most tedious voyage.'

Lord Buckingham gives Gosfield to Louis XVIII and Eugenia has a son, 'an immense boy'. 1808 begins badly: 'I never spent a more uncomfortable New Years Day,' Betsey sadly notes. 'Still on the subject of Harriet, who certainly has behaved very foolishly but is so unhappy at what has happened that I trust the evil will be remedied. Fremantle rode over to see her.' Next day she 'hopes we shall be able to settle everything about Harriet, and that she will not marry Mr. J. Hamilton who certainly is by no means a desirable match altho a very good sort of man.' Alas, her affair with dear John Poulett ended miserably. He sent her a proposal by his sister, but she (we hope it was not Lucy) destroyed the letter, as she did not wish her brother to marry a Catholic. Years later, when he died, she on her deathbed, confessed her sin. Betsey's daughter, Emma, remembers her mother and Aunts Harriet and Justina sitting together at Swanbourne the tears pouring unchecked down their cheeks when they were told.

The annual visit to Stowe was particularly brilliant as the exiled French royalties, now established under Lord Buckingham's wing at Gosfield, were entertained as though the Revolution had been a regrettable incident occurring on one of God's afternoons out, of which it was unnecessary to take notice.]

Stowe

Saturday, 9th January. Found every body busily employed at Stowe preparing for the Grand Folk that are expected, we were lodged in the East wing, and very magnificently and conveniently, considering the Crowd there is to be. We were all full dress'd at three o'clock to receive the King, who had slept at Missenden, and arrived at four, with the Duc d'Angouleseme, Duc de Grammont, Chr. L. d'Amas and de Bouillet, the Prince de Condé, Duc de Bourbon, Duc d'Orleans, Duc and Dss. de Coigny, and

Cte. de la Chartres soon followed. The King is very corpulent and not unlike in figure and countenance to old Chaplin, Duc d'Angouleseme is much better looking than his Brother Berri, and has some resemblance to his father he is a little man extremely shy. The Royal Party after being received in the North Hall, went to dress, and we all remained in the state drawing room till dinner. A long Table in the Music room contained the whole party consisting of 44—the French Cook did not shine, and tho' he had the assistance of three more French cooks of his own choosing and that no expense was spared the dinner was neither good or bien choisi. Gunter was more successful in his Desert, Every thing else was very magnificent and princely. Ld. Buck^{m}. gave after dinner the Toast of the Royal and Illustrious House of Bourbons—Louis XVIII gave in his turn, in English, King George, and Prosperity to England—He knows the English language perfectly but pronounces it with a strong french accent. He eats immensely and seems to enjoy excellent health. He recollected having seen me at *Verona*, and hearing me play, which made him say I was *sa plus ancienne connaissance ici*. He is very prêvenant and has something obliging to say to everybody. There was dancing in the Evening, the King retired before supper, after a Rubber at Whist.

TUESDAY, 12TH JANUARY. The whole party met at breakfast in the Music room, we afterwards followed sa Majesté and all the Princes in their walk through the gardens, the day was fine and they admired them much—The King notwithstanding his size walks perfectly well, and takes in general a great deal of exercise. Mr. and Mrs. Loyd arrived this morning. Mr *D'Avary*/le premier ministre et Javrai, who seems dying of a decline/Cte. de la Bavière, came to dinner, Ly. Louisa Hervey, her two daughters, the Admiral and Ly. Temple, in the evening. We had music, but the King seemed to enjoy his rubber much more than our harmony. When he was settled at his Card Table, the young party danced.

THURSDAY, 14TH JANUARY. Louis XVIII having ordered wine and ale to be distributed to the Labourers who had planted the Oaks yesterday, they all passed before the House in their way to the Clumps, forming a ludicrous Procession, some with Spades, forks, or rakes, some driving wheelbarrows, and with other gardening implements, the Band playing before them, they marched into the Park where ministers had assembled, to drink the King's health, I walked to the spot with Ly. Buckingham, but was caught in a violent storm of rain. A little music again in the evening. Ly. Mary is in good voice and in great beauty. Ly. Buckingham does the honours so well that the King said, Mde. le Marquisa a tant de bontés pour moi que je pourrai croire être en France —he however told her that tho' he had great pleasure in paying her a visit here, he should have still more pleasure in receiving her in France. The toast at dinner was very good in these words—'The Lamp of Hospitality which burns in England and particularly here'—Harriet is still a trial.

TUESDAY, 12TH APRIL. I went with Harriet and Mrs. Bishop to try some Piano Forte at Broadwoods, where the sudden *entree* of Mr. J. Hamilton worried me considerably as he had more the appearance of a madman than a Gentleman, and certainly behaved most rudely to me. Harriet spoke very properly and we got away after having been much annoyed by his lamentations and entreaties for an interview and explanation, which has and shall be denied.

Stayed at home in the Evening, persecuted with Letters. But there is Balm in Gilead.

SATURDAY, 16TH APRIL. I am in great spirits at finding that my Maux de cours must have been fancyful.

[Fremantle writes from the Mediterranean:]

FRIDAY, 25TH APRIL. Felton Harvey was to be married yesterday to Miss Bacon, Sister to Jerome Buonaparte's Wife, Mrs. Patterson; I think Mrs. W. Fremantle must be greatly annoyed about it—she is a Roman Catholic. I took a walk and a drive along Murat's road, the day was most beautiful and the Bay looked quite magnificent, the Sea being of a very deep blue, the Town and hills as clear as possible and the distant Mountains of Calabria being topp'd with Snow—

[Poor Harry has lumps in his neck which are dealt with firmly.]

SATURDAY, 28TH MAY. Was out shopping all the morning to fitt out Harry for his Journey to Scotland, he is to go by sea to morrow with the Cook, who seems delighted at the Excursion. He is tolerably well excepting several Lumps in his neck, but I hope the sea air, and bathing will be of service to him. I chaperon'd the Pouletts to the Opera in a *high Box*, where I neither saw nor heard.

SUNDAY, 29TH MAY. I went myself to take poor little Harry to the wharf at Wapping, and went on board the Smack, it looked so dirty and comfortless that it required some courage to let the poor child sett out in such a vessel. He did not seem to care about it, nor was his Companion the Cook at all dismayed, but I shall be all anxiety to hear of his safe arrival.

STOWE

SUNDAY, 8TH OCTOBER. Lord Buckingham is a great deal better, and my Marito likewise recovering his good looks. The Cte. and Csse. de Damas came to dinner—she is a daughter of the dear Duc de Serent and seems a lively and clever little woman. Monsieur the Duc de Berri, Cte. Puisegun and Baron de Rolle arrived in the Evening from Hartwell. The rest of the party all come to morrow. Above thirty friends are expected, the Dinner is to be in the State Gallery, and preparing for Fifty.

MONDAY, 9TH OCTOBER. We all dressed ready by three oClock to receive the Royals. Le Roi with the Duc and Duchesse d'Angoulesme and Duc de Gramont arrived first. He is not quite so fat as when last I saw him. The Duchesse d'Angoulême has a most interesting countenance and is rather handsome, her manner very unaffected and pleasing. La Reine did not arrive for nearly an hour after in a heavy Berline with six Horses. I had heard so much of her Ugliness and deformed figure that I was not surprised in seeing a very hideous little Humpbacked woman, her Back really broken in two, her look, manner and dress very unlike a Queen, but she has an intelligent and clever Countenance. Her waiting lady, la Csse. de Narbonne is likewise Humpbacked, she is daughter to the Duc de Serant. The petite Duchesse de Serant is a dear little old woman, *un peu bossue* with a very pretty face, and great liveliness in her Eye. All the good people dressed and then assembled in the Library; we then went in to dinner, a long procession with the Band playing in the Saloon, the Table in the State Gallery looked very splendid and we sat in the following order:—

Capt. Fremantle

Cte. E. de Damas	22 Dishes on each side.	Mrs. Manule
Chevr. de la Rivière	Twice Twelve Removes.	Dr. O'Connor
Cte. de Rouille	4 Chandeliers in all 103 Candles in the Room.	Vte. d'Agout
Cte. de Damas		Mlle. de Choisi
Duc de Serent		Ld. Carlton
Mrs. Fremantle		Cte. de Rouille
Duc de Berri		Duc de Gramont
Dsse. d'Angoulesme		Csse. de Vaudreuil
Le Roi		Lord Buckingham
Lady Buckingham		Dsse. de Serrant
La Reine		Cte. Puisegun
Monsieur		Csse. E. de Damas
Lady Mary Grenville		Cte. de Vaudreuil
Duc d'Angoulesme		Mrs. Stapleton
Cte. de Narbourne		Mrs. Browne
Duc d'Havre		
Baron de Rolle		

Ld. George Grenville

We did not sit long at Table, and all returned into the Library to Coffee handed out in the same regular Order. The King and Monsieur played at Whist, the Dsse. d'Angoulesme sat to her work, and the Old Queen being fond of music I was made to play to her, and Lady Mary sang Duetts with the Duc de Berri. There was no regular Supper only the round Table in the middle of the Library and the Grand people retired early.

Tuesday, 9th October. The whole party with the exception of La Reine assembled at Breakfast in the State Drawing room. Her humpbacked Majesty made her appearance at eleven oClock, to attend Mass, with all the Poperies. At twelve different parties went out to see the Gardens, I walked with Mde. de Narbonne who is clever and pleasant. The Prince and Princesse de Condé and Mlle. d'Ortans, arrived to dinner, it is quite ridiculous to see so old a Bridal Couple, she still has the remains of having been a great Beauty. Lady Elizabeth Lee and Sr. George added to the numbers at dinner. The evening was spent much the same as yesterday. They are all so extremely pleasant and affable that it makes it much less formal.

SATURDAY, 13TH OCTOBER. I walked with Fremantle to Buckingham and found on our return the house thrown in great alarm and confusion, by a dreadful accident which happen'd to Mde. de Vaudreuil. She rode Lady Mary's horse and was thrown in the Park. She remained perfectly senseless and to all appearance a corpse for some hours and was brought home in that wretched State to her poor old Husband who was himself in Bed, under the Influence of une Indigestion. It was apprehended that her Skull was fractured and Grosvenor and the Chirurgien du Roi were sent for. They both arrived at twelve at night. Their report was more favourable than Grey's had been and they declared it only a heavy contusion. Her arm is much strained but not broken. She is to be kept perfectly quiet and the poor old Count who had done nothing but weep all day, was sent to Bed, being himself the picture of misery.

SWANBOURNE

MONDAY, 15TH OCTOBER. We left Stowe this morning and were happy to find ourselves quietly at home after spending so many days among fallen Royalty. Lord George came over to us one day this week and brought a favorable account of Mde. de Vaudreuil, but she still keeps her room.

SUNBURY

WEDNESDAY, 25TH OCTOBER. The Jubilee kept in honour of the King entering on the 50th year of his reign. It proved to be a most beautiful day, and all ranks of people could thoroughly enjoy themselves. Mrs. Bishop had a grand dinner, Lord and Ldy

Montfort, Sr. John and Lady Mawby, Genl. Stanwix, Lady and Miss Onslow. We all proceeded in the evening to the Hampton Court Ball, which was very numerously attended. The Duke of Clarence returned from Frogmore to preside at his Ball, and Chaperon Miss Fitz Clarence and two of his sons. The King's health was drank at supper, and much noise made. We did not get home till late.

[Stowe is still the centre of all their lives:]

STOWE

WEDNESDAY, 5TH OCTOBER. The Prince came to breakfast but Duke of Sussex only appeared later as he suffers much from an Asthma; he was taken so ill with it at dinner that it obliged him to go to his room and could not leave it all the Evening. The Prince makes himself extremely agreeable. We had music in the Evening, he admired Harriet's deep voice much. Ly. Mary sung extremely well.

FRIDAY, OCTOBER 7TH. The Prince always comes to breakfast and is so talkative that he keeps us sitting for two hours. The Duke of Sussex still keeps his room. Music again after dinner, the Prince joined in some English Glees and has a very fine Voice—*mais chante en Prince.*

Harriet goes off to Scotland and Fremantle to Portsmouth 'to see the monument to Lord Nelson which is now finished, having been erected under his direction.'

[And then from Swanbourne.]

TUESDAY, 29TH NOVEMBER. A long letter from Harriet to say she has accepted Hamilton's offer and would leave Fremantle to make all the necessary arrangements for her. I am not surprised, nor sorry. Heard at the same time from Mr. Hamilton to say he should come here, when convenient to receive him.

SATURDAY, 10TH DECEMBER. Hamilton arrived late,

tired and fagged to death, not en beaute but looking very happy, he has brought all the papers &c. &c.—and a very handsome *joint Cadeau* to us of a Silver Tea Urn. Mr. and Mrs. Biscoe dined with us but went away early. The Servants had a Ball, and the whole House in great Spirits, Harriet more ridiculous than ever.

MONDAY, 12TH DECEMBER. Mr. Clerkson the Chaplin from was here by Nine o'Clock and celebrated the Catholick Marriage Ceremony before breakfast in the School room, the Miss Pouletts came in time for it, Harriet looked modest for the first time in her Life, in a long french lace Veil and behaved very well. After breakfast we all adjourned to the Church in the Carriage, where Mr. Cathcart tied the second Knot, a great multitude was assembled to witness the gay wedding. On our return to the House, Harriet exchanged her Bridal apparel for her riding habit and at two o'Clock the new married Couple sett out in a new Chariot for Stoke Farm. The Horses were taken from the Carriage at the door, and they were drove by the *Swanbournians* all down the Village in the midst of great acclamations and huzzahing. Mr. Cathcart stayed to dine quietly with us, we were all exhausted and tired, but very glad every thing is over.

CHAPTER 30

TUESDAY, 25TH SEPTEMBER 1810. To my great joy I received a few lines from Fremantle dated the 10th off Cape Finisterre, he was still greatly out of Spirits, but he says Charles was delighted, had not been on board five minutes ere he was at the Mast Head, and that he climbs the Rigging as if he had been at Sea for years:

At sea near Cape Finisterre,
10th September.

My Barometer and Looking Glass are both broke by the neglect of my servant, altho I can do without both still I feel the utility and convenience of them.

THURSDAY, 11TH OCTOBER. I was greatly shocked to hear of the sudden death of Miss Ann Ongley while at dinner at Genl. Morgan's, the sting of a wasp, on her finger, brought on a fit of Laughing, in which she instantly died, she was stiff ere she could be carried to her room. She was an amiable young woman, and a particular favorite of all her brothers and sisters, poor Mrs. John Fremantle will have a great loss in her.

SUNDAY, 21ST OCTOBER. I continue to receive immense dispatches from Scotland about Justine's marriage, the Campbells approve and the Hamiltons disapprove—but the marriage will certainly take place.

WEDNESDAY, 24TH OCTOBER. I was made extremely uneasy on hearing from Mrs. Robt. Butler at Brighton, that my dear little Louisa has been ill since Friday night of fever and extreme Sickness at her Stomach, measles or Scarlet fever being apprehended, I found it impossible to think of going to her with my baby.

[Louisa dies, and Betsey, though sad, is resigned at the idea that she is now happy and free from pain, sin, or suffering.]

The dear little Angel expired at nine o'clock, on Monday morning the 29th Octr. She knew not Cole, on Saturday, and her agonies were great from that day to the moment of her death. My affliction almost overpowers me, at the loss of such a darling and lovely Child, but on account of my Baby I am obliged to exert myself in this severe trial. [Fremantle writes from the Mediterranean:]

Off Toulon.
October 30, 1810.

We are without a nail, a foot of plank or a fathom of Rope spare in case of accident—besides which our people want Clothing for this time of year. I have been obliged to write officialy to Cotton on the subject, and I am not without apprehension that the line I am pursueing will occasion him uneasiness, because to him as Commander-in-Chief much blame must attach for the Neglect and degradation into which the ship has fallen. As you may imagine I am very anxious to keep fair with all the world particularly with the Commander-in-Chief, but certainly not at the expense of my own reputation. What would I give to see you, Emma and Bibby for an hour tell Emma my pug dog improves daily but having given him a beating for doing his lawful occasions in my cabin, he dislikes coming out of the Servants berth; I will be more kind to him in future. I have been much employed today with my secretary drawing up a statement of my accounts for your information. You will perceive my exchequer is very low (keep Bill) but I am sure both you and I have made up our minds to be economical without neglecting the means of bringing up our children properly, there is nothing in the accounts that will accompany this that gives me real uneasiness. I am as idle and indolent as you please, I walk about my cabin, then write, then read, and whenever I have nothing else to think of take a pinch of snuff and this I am sorry to say happens much oftener than it ought.

November 18th 1810.
At Night.

My dearest and best of women,

How am I to begin a letter to you in answer to the very melancholy one I received two days ago, naming the death of our poor Louisa? The anxiety I feel about you, as well as distress of mind from our severe loss, has made me at times feel like poor Marianne in a state of stupor, this you will readily believe has not been alleviated by the death of Teresa, or the consideration of the impropriety of your sister's conduct. In short at no period of life have I ever received accounts from home so agonizing. I pity from my heart my poor sister Marianne. Your sisters make me mad; heavens! only consider the line of conduct they have severally pursued, ask yourself if ever girls have so completely thrown themselves away or have behaved in such a deceitful manner. I hardly know what term to apply to such people, and only praise God that they live so many miles from me, the Women are Mad and the men fools, and the less intercourse we have with people of that description the better. I recollect on Finlay being at Edinburgh a toady of Hamilton's, and if he was not a proper match for Justine why in God's name bring him into her Society? You have often thought me harsh and severe about your sisters, who has judged best now I beg? As to Hamilton borrowing £8,000 of Justine it is the dirtiest trick I ever heard, and he did not allow her to consult *me* who ought to have been consulted. I think so ill of the whole transaction, and that all of the parties to it have conducted themselves so improperly that individually I will not have anything to do or say with any of them, their system seems that of defaming each other. I beg you not to go to Scotland, nor to take Emma. Hamilton is a swindler and the only one who is harmless is the poor dog Finlay. Bankes is a wiser man than I am luckily, for Eugenia, who would otherwise by this time have been miserable.

I am on the most friendly terms with Cotton, Hood and Pittmore.

Mahon,
Sunday, December 9th,
1810.

I am afraid you will have thought me rather severe in what I wrote to you concerning Justine and Hamilton, but altho I might perhaps have softened my expression toward them, still I am of opinion that you would do wisely in not undertaking your journey to Scotland. Hutchinson seems to have been quite pleased with Campbell's and Eugenia's attention to him, and he says they live in *great style*.

Mahon,
February 28th, 1811.

My dearest Tussy,

On the 11th. I gave a most sumptuous ball to all the people here consisting of 330 or 400 people and we satt down to supper 250. Sir Samuel Hood on the 21st. did the same thing in the *Hibernia*, but having much more time, a larger ship and going to more expense certainly outdid me in many ways.

I have just received letters from Wynne and Martin at Palermo. Wynne talks of going to the Archipelago before he returns to England, and Sicily remains in exactly the same state as to politics.

Considering Hamilton's behaviour to Justine in all ways I am not a little surprized at his audacity in coming to Swanbourne.

Pray send me by the first conveyance through Alcott three pair of half boots from Mr. Hoby's in St. James Street also two Magnificent pairs of Epaulets for a Rear Admiral.

[Fremantle changed his ship shortly after this and hoisted his flag on the *Rodney* 74. He was to remain at Minorca for the protection of the island and writes again:]

March 26th, 1811.

I entreat you to impress on your girls the propriety of holding themselves like gentlewomen, this is the only subject on which I can possibly be ashamed of Emma and Augusta, and I daily see how much young women gain by manner. Pray make your servant clean my boots at least once a fortnight or else they will be dry rotten.

God almighty preserve you all and grant me a happy sight of you. Oh! the pleasures of superintending these people (carpenters etc.) and not having to pay the bill. I am a great officer here and certainly have more influence than any other individual. If ever man had real comfort and was made completely happy by marriage you have made me so.

EDINBURGH

SATURDAY, 1ST JUNE. We have all borne the journey surprisingly well and feel very little tired. Harriet's House is remarkably pretty and fitted up with great taste it has at the back a view of the Sea and coast of Fife, in front it looks into Gardens, and is very chearful and airy. Soon after breakfast my new beaufrère Mr. Finlay call'd bringing me a note from poor Justine who is not well enough to go out He is a very good looking Man, and seems bon Enfant mais pas elegant. We all walked to York Place to call on Justine, who I was happy to find grown fatter and looking better than I expected. She seems extremely comfortable in this House, she has lately purchased, it is large, and in an excellent situation fitted up very neat and comfortable but not at all extravagantly. I left Emma and Augusta to spend the day with Justine and walked to see a little of the Town, but it was so extremely windy that we could not go farther than Princes Street, and call'd to see some of Rayburn's paintings, the portrait he has done of Harriet I do not like, but some of his other Portraits are very finely painted. I am much delighted with the Situation of the Town of Edinburgh, the handsome appearance of the Houses and Streets, all the buildings being of White Stone, high, and the windows large, the Streets are very wide, and most of them command an extensive view of the Sea. We dined quietly at the Hamiltons and walked in the evening to St. Bernard's Well, which was very romantic and wild scenery, the walk being by the Side of a stream which runs with rapidity through Rocks, the banks are finely wooded, and it is so perfectly countrified that one could fancy oneself many miles from a Town.

Skipniss

Friday, 7th June. I left Heriot Row at eight oClock for Glasgow, where we arrived at three oClock, having travell'd very expeditiously considering Scotch posting, and a rough road through West Craigs and

Airdrie, not at all a pretty country. As we drove into the Town of Glasgow, Robert Campbell met us, and introduced us to his Sister, Mrs. David Hamilton who gave us an early dinner. I never saw my beau-frère look better, he is much fatter and growing more like his poor Brother Jack. At Mrs. Hamiltons we found his elder Sister Eliza, who is still a fine woman, they were uncommonly kind and civil to us, and the moment we had hurried down our dinner we continued our journey to Greenock, Robert went on with Johnny Dillon to order every thing for us, I was quite enchanted with the Drive from Paisley to Greenock, the road being by the side of the river Clyde the whole way, the view of Dumbarton Castle and of Ben Lomond in the distance, is magnificent, the evening lovely, and on our arrival at Park's Inn, we determined to embark for Skipniss after supper if the wind was fair. We walked a little about Greenock and along the Quay, there are now very few vessels here, but I was much struck and pleased with the appearance of this place. Dr. Cameron, Captns. Beatson and Dillon supped with us, immediately after we went on board the *Caledonia*, one of the Campbelltown packets which has been waiting for us since Thursday, it was a beautiful moonlight night and we sailed at twelve oClock, with a nice little breeze, I regretted its being night as I could see but little of the coast, I just perceived Bute, and ere we got to the Mouth of the Clyde, it began to be daylight, the wind freshened and we got on very rapidly between the islands of Arran and Bute towards the coast of Cantire. At a little after four we reached Skipniss point and Robert's barge came off for us—it was just beginning to blow very hard, the motion of the vessel had made most of the women passengers dreadfully sick, poor

Augusta was just giving symptoms of Sea Sickness, and I was very chilly and cold, having been upon deck all night, we were therefore not a little pleased when we got into the boat, which we found some difficulty in doing, the Sea being very high upon this shore, but we landed safe and sound. Poor little Eugenie had got up to come and meet us, she received us with as much joy and rapture as I felt in again meeting her and was delighted to find her looking the picture of health and happiness. She had prepared comfortable fires for us, which we thoroughly enjoyed, and after taking our breakfast and talking not a little, we went to Bed, but my head was too full of all I had seen and had yet to see to sleep, I soon therefore got up again and left the two Girls to recover from their fatigue. Eugenie brought me her three boys, who are very fine children. Walter is the image of his Father, George has more his Mother's Eyes, and look, and Johnny has fine black Eyes, but is rather pale having just been weaned. He will improve when he gets a colour, and is a tall and strong child. The day proved stormy and we could not get out, but we felt very happy and comfortable within and in the evening Eugenie sang with Mr. Dillon who is as pazzo pur la Musica as ever.

Skipniss

Sunday, 28th July. Robert remained with Justine and Miss Finlay at Skipniss, my two Girls, Eugenia and Zoe with little Walter embarked after breakfast on board our packet, which took us in little more than two hours to Ettric Bay, I walked to Kaimes and sent the carriage for Eugenia. I found Harriet and her Husband very comfortable in their Chateau agreeably surprised by our unexpected arrival. I was much pleased with the situation at Kaimes, as it is entirely surrounded by trees and really a very pretty place. Dillon is still here and two nephews of Hamilton's One the son of Danl. Hamilton, a very fine Boy who is dying to go to Sea.

WEDNESDAY, 31ST JULY. Hamilton being obliged to go to Edinbrugh, Harriet is to accompany us back to Skipniss where her Marito will join her next week. We waited all day and were looking out for the *Caledonia.* This vessel had been appointed to call for us this morning, but only made her appearance in Ettric Bay this evening and it was nine o'clock ere we got on board. It was blowing a strong Breeze, which encreased to a Storm by the time we approached Skipniss point and as it would have been impossible to land in the Bay, we were obliged to get into one of the herring boats, which we luckily met, and after much difficulty and alarm, it put us on shore on the rocks near Cullendroch. Our difficulties now encreased as it was pitch dark and no one could find their way to the Cottages, Eugenia in her situation, unable for much exertion and tired to death. Little Walter had suffered from Sea Sickness, and Robert was so nervous and unhappy about his wife and child that he had not power to speak or assist any one else. At last after scrambling among the rocks, and slipping and falling, we found a Cottage, and call'd up a man and his wife, who soon made up their fire jumped out of Bed and dress'd before us with no mauvaise honte or ceremony, gave us some milk, and got a Horse and a Car, for Eugenia and little Walter. She lay upon straw, and we all follow'd on foot, about three miles of rough highland road, at last we arrived at Skipniss at two in the morning. Justine little expected us. Such a stormy night and we felt most happy at having escaped our dangers and perils so well. Not many minutes after we had retired to our Beds, Finlay arrived, he had scrambled among the rocks in the same way we had done, and at last had laid down among them until day light, he came in an open boat from Greenock and must have landed nearly where we did.

SUNDAY, 4TH AUGUST. I was agreably surprised and waked up at four oClock this morng. by Tom walking into my bedroom. He came straight to Greenock, in the mail without taking any rest, and met at Greenock a Mr. Richie who took him to Wemyss Bay, where he was obliged to stay all Friday during the Gale of Wind, he came from Mr. Richie's in his sailing boat, and was becalmed all night. The Boy seems not at all tired, and delighted with his journey.

MONDAY, 5TH AUGUST. We are now a large and merry party, no less than 14 at dinner every day and shall certainly eat Eugenia's store room empty. There is already a famine for bread, and we are obliged to eat oatcake.

THURSDAY, 8TH AUGUST. The Abbé Gauthier is very pleasant and perfectly the gentleman in his manners, poor Cattanach is rough, and not brilliant, but has great merit for the fatigues and misery he must endure, in travelling on foot and in boats so great a distance, all the year round. My three Sisters and their Husbands are all comfortably together and rival each other in matrimonial felicity.

SATURDAY, 10TH AUGUST. I answered all my letters and wish I could get back to England immediately, as I am all impatience to see poor Charles. He was taken ill the 1st of June off Toulon, and as he has rather out grown his strength, and that the hot climate did not agree with him, the physicians advised his coming home. Fremantle writes from Port Mahon, and seemed quite unhappy to part with the Boy, who has behaved as well as possible, and was generally beloved.

KAIMES CASTLE

WEDNESDAY, 11TH SEPTEMBER. In our walk from Rothsay, where I had been with Robert and the children to sketch the Castle we met a funeral, this melancholy ceremony, is in the Highlands celebrated as a festival, the moment any person dies, even in the poorest Cottage, every relation, friend or neighbour that come to the house, are regaled with whiskey, and bread and cheese, on the day of the burial, all are invited to attend the funeral, they first partake of a *sumptuous* meal, and generally follow the corpse, half drunk and with unbecoming mirth, the one we met was of a publican's wife, sixty men at least follow'd it, all in mourning and respectable people. This savage custom of feasting at the death of a Highlander, obliges the poor to bury their dead almost immediately after the breath is out of the body. It is a most barbarous custom which ought not to be allowed to exist in a civilized nation.

THURSDAY, 12TH SEPTEMBER. All the Rothsay Gentry were invited to a Turtle feast, the limes failed for the Punch, but these good people made up for it in some other way, and all appeared after dinner with sparkling Eyes and unsteady Step they were obliged to dance reels and play at dumb Crambo.

INVERARY

WEDNESDAY, 18TH SEPTEMBER. We hired one of the Rothsay packets to take us to Inverary, and order'd it round to Ettric Bay, where we embarked this morning at nine oClock, Eugenia her husband Mlle. de Lestrade and myself, I left the children with Harriet during our visit. It was blowing rather hard when we embarked but the moment we entered Loch Find the breeze slackened and before evening it fell a perfect calm. We had taken provisions with us on board the *MacDonal*, cooked our dinner and made ourselves as comfortable as we could on board so dirty a Vessel. We had intended landing at Traffard Campbell's but being in hopes the breeze would spring up towards twelve oClock, we made up our mind to remaining in the Vessel, and contrived a bed for poor little Eugenia and sat almost all night upon deck, it was the finest clear night possible, the *Comet* more beautiful than anything I ever saw, and the noise of the herrings, which passed us in immense shoals, glittering in the Sea, like fire, with the multitude of herring Boats, who had thrown their nets, the whole formed a scene quite novel to me and very amusing. At day light we were in the finest part of Loch Fine and the sun rising behind the high Mountains which closed the horizon, threw a variety of light and Shade over the country around us, and nothing could be more beautiful that this coup d'oeil was. We went on shore for Milk and butter, bought fresh herrings for our breakfast, and as we approached to Inverary, we began our toilette which refreshed us much after the fatigue of having sat up the whole night. At One oClock we anchored just opposite Inverary Castle, we could not have had a more favourable day to see it to greater advantage. The Castle stands on a lawn, sloping to the Sea, commanding an extensive view of the Loch, surrounded by hills covered with finest wood, with high bleak mountains at the back. We landed beyond the bridge, close to the castle and walked to it. We just arrived as the whole party were assembled in the drawing-room. The Dutchess received Eugenia and her Marito very kindly and was very civil to us, we felt so uncomfortable after our Sea expedition and sleepless night that after having had some luncheon we went to Bed and got up again at dressing time for an 8 oClock dinner. The Dutchess is remarkably handsome, her five daughters are with her, all beautiful girls, the eldest is about seventeen. Ld. and Ly. Ponsonby, Ly. Augusta Miss Clavering and one of her Sons, Ld. John Campbell and Traffard Campbell are the only visitors here besides ourselves. The Duke of Argyle is all attention to his Dutchess and they appear perfectly happy—but their marriage has something so revolting and extraordinary in it, that I cannot believe she ever can feel perfectly happy. After so late a dinner there is regular supper at one oClock, but no one is obliged to sit up for it, and the evening passed away very pleasantly and quick. Eugenia is less fatigued than I expected.

FRIDAY, 20TH SEPTEMBER. I got up in time for a ten oClock breakfast, at which Ly. Augusta Clavering generally presides, she is deformed and has no remains of beauty, her daughter is a very handsome Girl with a look of her Aunt Ly. Charlotte Campbell. After breakfast I took a long walk in the Grounds, which are wild, and beautifully wooded. On our return after One oClock we found the Duke and Dss. at breakfast. At three oClock, hot joints and cold meat are brought in like a regular dinner and immediately afterwards the Barousche drives up to the door for those that wish to go out. We all went to a Lake about a mile and a half from the House to see the Salmon Net drawn, and immense numbers of very fine large Salmon were caught at every haul, but this not being the proper season for them, they were mostly thrown back. The dinner was at the usual late hour, and the evening therefore very short.

7TH. MONDAY, LOWTHER. We travelled a little more expeditiously to-day, but at Eulifisham we were obliged to take four Horses, for the first seven miles, being all Steep hills, as we approached Cumberland, every thing about the Country and Towns had an English appearance. We passed Gretna Green, a very neat village, the post boy pointed to the House of the famous blacksmith whose successor lives at another small House near the road. I intended sleeping at Penrith, we could not however get beds on account of the Assizes, and I found myself obliged to proceed on to Lowther, where we did not arrive till near two o'clock, every body being gone to Bed, we waited some time at the door, of this *huge* building which had more the appearance of a Citadel, by moonlight, than a Chateau du Campagne. At last the door was opened by a Maid and the Butler, who assured us our rooms were ready as we had been expected for Thursday. We got some tea, and went to Bed greatly tired with our long day's Journey.

8TH TUESDAY. Nothing could be more flattering than the reception I met from the Lonsdale family when I came in to breakfast. Ldy. Lonsdale show'd me through all the House, which is only half done, but will be most magnificent, altho' it has like every Gothic building of this magnitude, a Sómbre about it, and the outside of the building to *my taste* is too much crowded with turrets and parapets it stands in an extensive and very fine wood, I went to the top of the castle to see the mountains of Scotland, but the day was so clouded, that we could only see the wooded Grounds of Lowther, and from the famous terrace, we were equally disappointed in not being able to see the view, which is very extensive and considered one of the finest in England, I own that coming from Inverary, I could not admire it, as it appeared too tame and too flat. Ldy. Lonsdale after walking through the Garden, and making us take notice of some very ancient and fine fixtures at the back of the house, ordered the Barousche, to show us the Grounds, which are certainly very wild and fine, the Lowther burn which runs through them, being at this moment much swollen by the late rains, was in all its beauty, and then on some very wild and romantic Spots. The drive was not so agreable there being no regular road, and precipitous banks with four in hand, made it quite a source of danger, we were obliged to get out once, at the Quarry where all the stone the Castle is built with has been taken out, from it there is a fine view of the Place, Ly. L. who pointed to every remarkable spot, and made us admire the House in every point of View it was possible to see it, was in great terror of being over turned all the time and in terrible fidgets.

10TH THURSDAY, SWANBOURNE. The part of Yorkshire we passed in the morning is beautiful, so richly wooded, that it looks like a continued Garden, particularly about Harwood Castle, the face of the Country changed very much as we advanced towards Sheffield, there being in its neighbourhood nothing but Cast Iron works, the effect of those fires was particularly fine at Night, and it appeared as if we travelled through the regions of Plutus. From Chesterfield to Mansfield the road is a deep sand, and with four horses we had some difficulty in getting on, it was three o'clock when we left Mansfield after having refreshed ourselves with some tea, and just break of day when we arrived at Nottingham, there had been a Ball at the Inn, the House was still full of drunken and riotous rabble, who ran about the street in the most disorderly manner; we put up the blinds of the carriage while we were obliged to wait for the Horses, and at last to my great joy drove away from this horrible Town, at Leicester we had some Mutton chops, at eleven o'clock in the morning dress'd ourselves a little cleaner and went on without stopping to Stony Stratford, where we had some tea at a tidy little Inn, while I sent to the Town for Horses—It was very dark, and near twelve o'clock as we arrived at dear little Swanbourne, the children all in Bed looking beautiful, and poor Charles who had rode to-day from Stowe, was just gone to his Bed, having dispaired of our arrival. We made him get up and I was much delighted to see him, looking in good health and grown quite handsome.

[Every life, like even the best novels, has, and indeed, should have, its dull patches. Betsey, after she returned from her Scottish trip, settled down to a pleasantly uneventful round. This is illuminated by entries such as 'Even I danced merrily after supper'; 'Tom has altered his costume (at Eton) now he is in the 5th form, and looks very funny in a long coat, tight inexpressibles and Hessians'; 'We stayed on with Mr. Bankes, it toadying me and my brats.'

Many things happen, many people come and go, Lady Buckingham dies, then poor old Bucky, and his son succeeds, but 'has grown thinner, and lives upon Perigord pies'. The neighbours are news: 'Old Verney was struck by lightning the day we dined there, but was more frightened than hurt'. Lucy Poulett marries Lord Nugent, and the old general, after 'a lawsuit was decided in his favor went to tell old Lady Poulett of it, and was seized of a chill and spasm in his stomach, drank several glasses of hot brandy, but in a few hours died'.

There is family news too: Harriet has a daughter, Charles goes to sea and is taken prisoner by the

Yankees, but has only one month's captivity at New London after which he is exchanged. Fremantle is made a Baron by the Emperor of Austria and given the Order of Commander of the Cross of Maria Theresa, and poor Robert Campbell has a stroke.]

At Sea off Ancona,
August 15th, 1811.

If Emma does not hold herself like a gentlewoman I shall certainly send her to School. Poor old Bucky. Tell Mr. Doc I hope the Elms that were planted by his wall are doing well. I am anxious about my trees.

From different vessels we have something like accounts of Bonaparte's having advanced too far and being a prisoner with the Russians, it can't be true.

I have got a light blue silk Coat; there was no dark to be procured, and am quite a figure in it without a neckcloth. I am to command in Sicily and to leave the Adriatic Squadron.

Off Sardinia,
August 22nd, 1811.

Am off to Palermo where I must play second fiddle. My lot will be to keep on good terms with Lord and Lady William Bentinck: she is a very aimiable and domestic woman and I hope to profit by their hospitality. You may drink away my second oldest port wine, but there is one of the '28 which is the oldest and that I wish to be kept.

Palermo,
August 29, 1811.

Nothing can equal the insolence and despotism of Queen. She has confined 5 of the principal inhabitants in the solitary small islands in the neighbourhood. The poor King is too indolent to concern himself with public affairs. The only young man here is a Mr. Howard, a jolly Catholic and heir after his father to the Duke of Norfolk. Tell Lord George Greville that I shall be happy to see him here, there is great occasion for an Algernon Sidney.

DECEMBER 26TH. Lord Wm. arrived the 7th of this month, and contrary to my expectation everything remained perfectly quiet—during the month he had a conference with the Queen, who was very violent, this good lady seems determined to make every opposition to our demands, and is intriguing in every way to impede our progress. One day she appears to be desirous of accommodation but her mind is in such a state of irritation it is quite impossible to depend upon a word she says. The King is furious and will do no business, and I believe she and the King are on a perfect good understanding. None of the Neopolitan Ministers are dismissed, but an addition has been made of four counsellors of state quite inimical to us—this must bring the business to a crisis. The *Achille* is at Melazzo with the Transports and Troops, the *Herald* is to go to Tinpani and unless the Court give way we shall be obliged to use force, the Queen has neither money, or means to visit us and now is the time for settling the concerns of the Island. I hope for the best and my advice has always been for strong and firm measures. The Sicilians are certainly well disposed to the English and the hereditary prince sees the consequence of assistance; he has however very little influence with either his father or Mother.

[Betsey ends the year on a quiet note.]

27TH FRIDAY. I was most happy to hear of Eugenia's confinement that she has a Girl this time, after three Boys; it proves quite a treasure and she is as happy as possible.

[On the last day of 1811 she dockets a letter from Fremantle dated]

Palermo,
December 22nd, 1811.

I am every day with the Bentincks. Lady William Bentinck has had the kindness to study me, as well as to make allowances for my fits of bile, and tho she is by no means to be called handsome her manners and conversation are so agreeable that it is impossible to feel gene in her company. I am involved in politics, and my residence here I hope affords me the opportunity of being very useful to Lord William. I am on all occasions considered next the minister, for here they have a fool King and a mad Queen.

Palermo.
March 13th, 1812.

My Dearest Tussy,

On the score of politicks I have little to say nothing material having occurred since I wrote last, I believe everything is settled about a new Government, at the head of which Prince Belmonte will be placed having his and our friends as his coadjutors, still we have to contend against the Queen who continues to have too much influence over the mind of her son, and we must contrive some means to have her removed from Palermo.

With respect to myself I am quite well and comfortable, I have been guilty of a great piece of extravagance for which however I trust you will not blame me, I have purchased plate to the amount of a hundred and fifty pounds, I have for this a beautiful Tureen, and ladle, a silver plateau, with a handsome silver figure on it, two large dishes, four side dishes and 6 Beautifull salt sellers gilt with spoons, they belonged to the late Sir John Acton, and I got them for little more than the value of the Silver, consequently I can dispose of them for what I gave at any time—my etat major does not go on very brilliantly—but I have got a tolerable french cook out of a prize.

I have for these three days past under some anxiety having received an account of the escape of two line of battle ships and two frigates from Toulon. I am afraid they are gone to the Adriatic, if so they will play the Devil among our ships who are too much separated to act against them, two ships are however in search of them the *America* and *Achille*.

Yesterday we had a most superb dinner at the Prince Belmonte's, we satt down 27 to a circular table, which was covered with beautifull plate, indeed the whole was magnificent and remarkably well served—never did I witness such severe weather as we have had this year, luckily we have only lost one brig commanded by a Lieut^t. S. Edwd Pellew has wisely kept the fleet at Mahon.

I begin to be expecting Charles out, and I shall be very much disappointed if he does not bring me letters from all the family. Emma will I hope be very communicative—We have lately had no great gayities as it is lent, the same serious Opera of Joseppe is performed almost every night and I am not yet tired of the music which is quite beautiful. I continue to live as usual with the Bentincks, and the Lady I am as much attached to as ever, but I find him so cold in his manners, and he is so little inclined to meet my proposals on the subject of the Sicilian Marine that I am afraid we are training off, which I am sorry for, but you know me too well not to be aware that I cannot submit to become a Cypher in his hands. You say Arnfield is a very good boy and goes on very well. Frank is grown quite a man and is most attentive. I like my Captain much, and I have now Young Molesworth whom you may recollect quite a Youngster in the *Ganges* first Lieutenant, Hutchinson is sound. This is all the news I have to tell you, kiss a hundred times all your children for me, your description of Celia makes me most anxious to see her as well as the rest. God almighty preserve you my dearest and best of women believe me ever.

Most affectionately yours,

T. F. F.

Palermo.

6th April, 1812.

My Dear Betsey,

It is an age since I have written to you, having been absent from this place now five weeks—Our party consisted of Lady Wm. Bentinck, Mr. Fazakerly, Mr Howard, Mr Joinville, Mr Oben and Mr Miner; we went first to Griganti where we landed and saw all the magnificent temples which you have read so much of and of which you must have seen so many drawings. We were all very well pleased and our party was increased by the junction of Lord Wm. Bentinck, Genl. Campbell and Major St. Laurent—in 24 hours we arrived at Malta, and here again we were much delighted with the strength of the fortifications the magnificence of the houses, and the hospitality of the people—here we amused ourselves for a week, Lord William returned back to Palermo, in a brig, and we sailed for Tunis where we arrived in three days. We all went on shore there with our baggage and took up our abode at the Consuls. We visited Carthage, Utica, and in short everything worth seeing and lived four days at the Minister's house about ten miles in the country, we had parties almost every day and it was very pleasant indeed, the purport of my taking this trip you are aware was to get released the Sicilians Slaves as well as to arrange some affairs of our own, my first audience with the Bey was on the 3rd day after my arrival. I was attended by 50 Officers and Gentlemen from the Ships, and Lady Wm. with a pair of loose *pantaloons* and a Great Coat that reached low down was in the suite. We were graciously received, and took Coffee, but as this was merely a visit of Ceremony nothing material passed, the next day I went with the Consul when we began an affair, the Old Gentleman who has the Eyes of an hawk first disputed my powers, when you will easily imagine I drew up and referred him to the Prince Regent's as well as the Minister's letters, I then demanded peremptorily the liberation of all the Italians who were taken under the English flag, to which he told me he would answer the next day. I was a little angry with the dog and spoke *fluently* in Italian to him. After a great deal of Jaggling and much dirty negociation through the Consul, I contrived to carry all my points, so anchored here last night after a passage of 22 hours having 370 Slaves on board the *Milford*—in the morning of the day we sailed the Minister came on board with about 50 Turks, I gave him coffee and sweetmeats, manned ship and saluted him to his heart's content, he left 300 Sequins for the boat's crew, and was most superbly dressed indeed—One day Lady William was invited to go to the Harem to visit the Bey's Wives, here she was received in great gala, but of course the men were not admitted. My band full dressed mounted upon mules attended her Ladyship—the Bey and his Wives gave them (14 in number) 200 Guineas—

Whilst I was at Tunis I heard from Adml. Berkley about the Death of Lady Buckingham. You will readily believe how much I was shocked, and how much I have felt for poor Lord Buckingham, indeed it is at this moment I regret being absent from home, because I am persuaded I might have been assisting during all the poignance of his sufferings, I don't think I can muster courage to write to him, the same letter also tells me of our loss in Genl. Poulet, tho I did not very much like the man, still I know he had many very valuable qualities, and was a most affectionate and kind parent. I hope G.G. will persuade his father to let him marry, matters appear to me to have gone such a length, that his honour, even if his inclination did not prompt him, makes it quite necessary. I wish he would and settle at Addington—the Minister has presented me from the Bey with a magnificent gold snuff box, it is of french manufacture with a very large diamond on the middle, and may perhaps be worth two or three hundred guineas, Lady William had several presents made her, and she has given me a very handsome Shawl, which I shall send you by the first good opportunity that offers. I am rather in high spirits having so effectually succeeded in all my negociations, indeed nothing could be more gratifying than the sight when we anchored, the poor released Sicilians gaping at the town, many mothers brothers and sisters in boats alongside making such exclamations at the sight of their relatives who had been years in slavery, our pride and enjoyment at being the cause of their release, in short the whole was most animating and interesting. I am dreadfully behind hand with my papers, not having had an opportunity of writing with so much company on board, my menage is tolerably good. I have in my foremost cabin a round table which dines 12 or 8 upon occasion.

[Fremantle also sent home, marking it 'for your amusement' the *Bulletin of Political and Military information* drawn up by the Bey's private secretary describing the 'sejour de la division anglaise aux ordres de contre l'Admiral Fremantle [*sic*]'. 'Lady Bentinck,' this declares, 'accompanied the Admiral in the costume of a naval officer.' Nor does it describe Fremantle's triumph quite in the terms he uses: 'The Vice Admiral negotiated for the redemption of the Sicilians who were slaves in this country about four hundred and eighty people, but as the Bey asked three hundred Venetian sequins for each, he was unable to conclude the affair the same day. The Prince, however, promised to release, without any ransom whatever, the sixty-four slaves who had been taken in ships flying the British flag.'

The French version of 'to visit the Bey's wives' is 'to visit their Royal Highnesses, the Bey's Sisters and his wife.'

Fremantle, in stating he 'continued to carry all my points' omitted to state at what price the said points were carried. Each slave, including the 24 who had been promised gratis, cost 313 piastres and four Venetian sequins. One Bulletin also notes that on departure the Minister received a salvade of 21 guns and carried 80,000 piastres from the ship to complete the payment of the ransom. The Minister did not conceal the fact from the *Bulletin* 'that he was not as handsomely treated on board the ship "*Milford*" as he had been on board the French ship, the "*Scipio*" (Captain Vice Admiral Leipseigne) in 1807.']

TUNIS

15TH APRIL. The Consul came on board and dined, the meeting between him and his daughter very interesting—he had not seen her since she was a twelvemonth old.

16TH APRIL. Our whole party landed at the Goletta, Lady Wm. and I went up by land to Tunis. Weather very hot. Took up our abode at the Consuls.

22ND APRIL. Nothing can be pleasanter than our party. We walk talk and laugh, all the company smoke long pipes. Danced at night, tried to Valse, none of us could do the step.

25TH APRIL. Returned into town to our great annoyance. Not a comfortable sopha or chairs in the house.

30TH APRIL. Dined at the Spanish Consul's and afterwards had a dance, an Irish woman there, 15 years old as fat as Mrs. Jackson of Swanbourne. Gave the Spanish Consul a Watch.

PALERMO

11TH MAY. I am bored to death about Brisac who is abused by everybody—he don't call so often as he used to do.

12TH MAY. Mr. Graham resolves to marry Pauline, this match has been brought about by Lady Wm. Fazakerly and one or two more. Lamb was very droll about it.

13TH MAY. Dined with Prince Belmonte. 30 at dinner on a round table, Mr. and Mrs. Lester Warren are of the party.

23RD MAY. This day young Molesworth shot himself, everybody very much distressed about it. He left a very kind letter for me—I cannot account for this in any way.

29TH MAY. The Prince of Belmonte presented me with a magnificent snuff box worth £500 from—the Hereditary Prince.

At Sea and Malta

10th June. Dined at Lady Wm. Stayed there all the evening—it seems to be quite settled that the Sicilians are to have the British Constitution.

Sail

13th June. Dined at Lady Wm's then went to a ball on board the *Thames*, could hardly bring myself to take leave, went on bd. at 12, the Ship under way—made all sail and bid adieu to Palermo.

At Sea,
14th June, 1812.

My Dearest Betsey,

I sailed yesterday from Palermo on a voyage to the Adriatic, for the particulars of which I refer you to the *Cypher* that accompanies this. The weather has begun to be very warm, and I am not displeased to leave Sicily, altho I have certainly left many behind me to whom I am much attached—to Lady William Bentinck in particular I have the greatest obligations, and having now for over ten months lived so much under her roof I cannot but regret her society, I need not repeat that there never was formed a more amiable or interesting creature, indeed her manners and benevolence attract all descriptions of persons. I have sent to Malta to go home by the *Argo* 2 very large China Jars, and five beautifull smaller ones, with a bronze figure which I hope you will admire—by Captain Laurence of *Macisses* who left us a few days ago, I have also sent you a pacquet that I hope will be agreeable to you, it contains a large persian, and a Turkish shawl Gold and White shawl with six bottles of Otto of Roses for your Ladyship. There is also a long Turkish shawl which is to be cutt to any length you find necessary for the Girls, it will make four, there is also a little parcel for Mrs Emma and a bottle each of Otta of Roses for Lady Cave and Mrs Preston.

Don't be surprized if you have soon a visit from a friend of mine Mr Fazakerly. We have been living together near ten months and I have so high a regard for him and value his friendship so much that I am sure you will be as attentive to him as I could wish, he is very well informed and has travelled over all this Country as well as Turkey and Egypt, he has promised to make acquaintance with you all.—

15 June. Viva. We fall in with the Pacquet just off Macitarrio, and I find two nice letters from my Tussy of the 19th of April and 11th of May, this makes me quite comfortable before I go up the Adriatic, as they contain all I can wish, provided I know you and my children are well I shall be enabled to support myself and work for their advantage, but whenever that is not the case I know I shall fail, and be sick it may appear to you ungratefull, but I do assure you I feel myself at this moment very comfortable, and so you will think me when you read the cypher on other side this paper and that you consider also I have just received letters from home. My ship is in good order and I almost full manned, my captain and officers suit me, my menage is very tolerable, and my band are excellent, in short all I want is your society and that of my children. I have every prospect of success in my undertaking—I do not deny to you that I felt real sorrow at leaving my friends at Palermo, the hospitality and kindness of Lady William to me is beyond my praise, the length of time I have been living in such terms of friendship will fully account to you for my regrets, if ever you see that good woman you will admire the many aimiable qualities she possesses, but nothing is more apparent than the rectitude of her mind on every

point. I have perhaps greater obligations to her than others, because I am aware of my failings and that I can appreciate the goodness of that disposition which is perfect, and still makes allowances for others—recollect I have now been some hours in her company every day for ten months. We had a magnificent ball at Lord Wm.'s on the King's birthday, I covered an immense Terrace with Sails from the Ship, and on the inside Colours, it contained 600 people with comfort, here the company danced and they supped in the rooms, figure to yourself my dear Betsey your husband leading off in such a party with the Duchess of Orleans, Prince Leopold and Mad[lle.] followed and after the first dance we changed partners. I can't say I was much gratified at being *made* to dance, but there was no possibility of refusing with propriety. I sported my fine snuffbox, a plan of which I will send you, I am indeed rich in snuff boxes but have no good snuff left—Lady William has wrote to Captain Warren to desire Charles may be sent to her if a good opportunity of joining me does not offer from Malta when he returns. I shall leave it entirely with Warren to do what he thinks best for the boy, as he will be enabled to judge better of his physical force than I can pretend to do at a distance.

You may expect to find me a better correspondent in the Adriatic than you have found me at Palermo, the fact is it is a very Idle place, and I am happy at an opportunity of employing myself more to my own as well as to my Country's advantage—I think I have said all that is worth your knowing—if I had remained at Palermo for the feast of St. Rosalia I should have been obliged to have given a fête that would have cost me one hundred and fifty or two hundred pounds, it is better as it is, but I don't think

I shall improve my Society in point of *manners* at Lissa. Adieu, tell your Girls to hold up their heads and behave well until I come home, when I shall endeavour to keep them in good order—God bless you all. I have many thanks and Comps. to make to Mrs. Bankes, say all that is kind for me to the Painter, and tell the contents of your cypher to my Brother, Tom, I shall expect to see grown a Man, God bless you all again and believe me ever my Dearest Woman,

Your most affectionate husband,

THOS. F. F.

[During 1813 it is Fremantle's letters still that are news: Betsey's diary is only life.]

On board *Apollo*,
Curzola,
March 5th, 1813.

I am very much afraid you will have been under some anxiety, as the last letters that went from us were entrusted to a Captain Pettell who was taken by a French privateer and all the letters thrown overboard. The inhabitants of Curzola have asked for British protection, and I have given them a constitution.* They have agreed to build a fort and maintain a Company of troups and an armed vessel for their defence. The time is at length arrived when I feel myself fully warranted in asking to be removed and for leave to return to England.

*[He sent Betsey home a copy—from which some translated extracts are appended herewith:]

'Parliament considers that the English Constitution is the most apt to bring glory to the Crown and happiness to the State, and also the most in keeping with the laws and institutions of this kingdom, so that in order to second the beneficent suggestions of Your Majesty, it has passed a resolution, to which it begs your Majesty to assent, to the effect that the principles of this constitution should be adopted as stated in the following articles, with the omission of the articles on religion since this will have to be exclusively as it has been hitherto the Roman, Catholic and Apostolic.

'By a unanimous resolution Parliament has provided that legislative power is to be vested exclusively in Parliament. Enactments will, however, require the royal assent in or to have the force of law.

'The Judicature will remain distinct and independent from the executive and the legislative.

'Parliament will be composed of two houses—a house of representatives of the population and a house of peers. The clergy who now sit in both, must decide to sit in one only. Barons qua peers will have one vote only per head.

'Parliament hereby abolishes feudal tenure etc.

Milford,
Lissa,
June 8th, 1813.

I have lately been paying a visit to the Pasha of Scutari who made me a present of a fine arabian horse which I mean to bring home with me. The Pasha is 16, married eighteen months ago. He had completely the manners of a gentleman, tho he seemed diffident, as it was the first visit ever made him by one of my rank. The Plague is at Malta. This war in the Adriatic is a war of pots de chambres.

Milford,
Off Augusta,
August 8th, 1813.

My letters will be censored by the Admiralty so

I shall confine myself to general topics. I am not quite so fat as I was. I perspire most copiously.

Trieste,
November 16th, 1813.

We are blockading Venice by sea, and the Bocca di Cattaro. The Society here is not too bad. I shall come home when Venice falls. I am much older and thinner in appearance and my weight is 13 lbs. less than when I left England. I prefer talking Italian to English. Certainly the manners of this country are much more gay and sociable than those of good old England.

Trieste,
December 12th, 1813.

You will perhaps be surprized to hear that I am in constant correspondence with Mary Montalbano. She writes very sensibly and in the same hand as you did before I had the happiness of marrying you. She says all the troops pass Conegliano and that her family have suffered much from the French. She is living with her son. Everything now in this country is ours but Ragusa.

30TH MARCH. Called on several Ladies with Mrs. Lower, had coffee four times, pass my evening at the Boschi's where I stayed supper; very fine weather.

I have not been so annoyed since I left England as I have been this month, the imbecility of one person with the deceit of another makes me heartily tired of living in such Society. I hope all I have been doing at Curzola may be usefull to our cause, but everything in this Country will I am of opinion very much depend upon the line to be pursued by Austria. The Constitution I have formed for Curzola seems to answer all the purposes and I am much pleased with the reception I always get from the Inhabitants.

SEA

24TH APRIL. Killed an English sheep. Very bilious —took some medicine. Dr Nagle sick, above 160 people down with the influenza.

Milford,
Trieste,
March 6th, 1814.

Please God I shall sail tonight in the *Eagle* for England where I hope soon to meet all I hold dear in the world, for every place has been taken and nothing remains to be watched but Corfu and Vienne which do not so much depend upon Naval operations. I am in hopes to enjoy some years of quiet. Nothing could have been more unkind to me than the present Admiralty, but thank God I have no occasion for their assistance. I have been made Commander of the Order of Maria Theresa, which no other English officer except Lord Wellington has ever received. I am told that it also makes me and my heirs Counts of the Empire; so my little Countess hold up your head until I come to England and then you will be a good girl. I frequently look at some children here and endeavour to calculate the height of my own: it seems to me so unnatural to have a Child of 3½ years old that I have never seen. I cannot tell you how much I have and do feel for poor Marianne, I never had but one opinion of that boy, and be assured from me that much of the conduct of young people arises from their first impressions, altho I am by no means an advocate of severity towards children, I am persuaded that it is better than allowing them to do as they please, and the first ill effect generally is ingratitude and ill behaviour. I told you all about Mary Montalbano. I gave her in all about £80, but she worries me to lend her

800, but I know too much of that family to involve myself in any way. I am sure I have done honestly and even generously by her, and after all there is no end of such affairs in this country of Italy. I really have been too long out of England and honestly confess I do not think so much or so often of all I hold dear in England as when I first came out but let not this distress you my dearest Betsey. Lord Aberdeen wrote me on the 23rd February from Chatillon sur Seine to send me his Imperial Majesty's congratulation on the destruction of Cattaro.

[Whilst Fremantle prepares to return, events move fast and when the Allies enter Paris, Betsey sits down to write to 'Congratulate the Hartwell Family on the happy change which has taken place in France.' She is asked over, and, though she has 'A rheumatick pain in my head, I propose going over with Tom.' On the 13th, Wednesday, she writes:]

I arrived at Hartwell nearly an hour before dinner and was presented with my Son to his Most Christian Majesty, who is laid up with the Gout in his Great Chair, I afterwards paid a visit to all the Ladies in turn the Duchesse de Sedan Mde de Damas and Mdlle. de Cherin. Madame received us in the Salon before dinner and made me sit by her at table. A Multitude of people walked round us during dinner, the King was wheeled into the drawing room where we found him when we went in to Coffee, he then made us sit in a Circle round him, this was soon interrupted, by the arrival of two deputies from Bologne, who came to take their oath of Allegiance to Louis XVIII. I enjoyed the Scene very much and the accounts they gave of the State of France and of Buona Parte were very interesting. Soon after, Lord Morton arrived with a message from the Queen of England which he deliver'd in a long French Speech to the King. The Dsse. d'Angouleme is charming and seems wild with joy. I went to Lillis in the Evng. and found Mr. Hare and Mr. Hinks with the Nugents. The names of the two Deputies from Boulogne are the Cte. de Castilyas and Baron de Porde, men of very good address, and who wore magnificent uniforms.

[Fremantle at last returns:]

21st. Thursday.

I heard from Tom and his Father, that they would be here to-night, I was very ill indeed all day but towards Evng. got myself dressed after much pain and difficulty and sat in the Arm Chair by the fire, a perfect object with my right arm in a sling the Rheumatism being quite fix'd in my hand which is much Swell'd and I have quite lost the use of it. Towards nine o'clock my Marito arrived, and thank God appears in perfect health and Spirits, I had all the children with me, and Stephen fix'd his great Eyes on his Father and was very funny, Cicey is the one he most admired. I was too ill and nervous to enjoy the Scene, and was obliged to go to bed again immediately.

[Betsey read the remainder of Fremantle's diary as she recovered.]

22nd, Friday.

Kept my Bed very ill and with so much fever that Cowley gave me Calomel. Fremantle seems delighted with his children and his home, Ly. Nugent call'd. I am a sad object, and cannot move one Limb, it is cruelly distressing just at this moment which I have been expecting as the happiest in my Life.

[They go to town, to see the illuminations and Betsey meets Henri de Bombelles again. The two girls, Emma and Augusta, accompany their mother to breakfast at Temple Bar to 'see the Emperor of

Russia and all the great people go down the river to Woolwich'.

[Fremantle enters 'dined with my brother in my boots, went home early' and on Monday, March 20th, Betsey writes:]

Dined early after having hunted all the morng. after our dresses and a hairdresser who disappointed us at last. We met Ld. Hill riding who was surrounded by the Populace, and shook hands with them. I had to chaperone Fanny Wills and Fanny Fremantle to White's Fete. We went early and got in without the smallest difficulty, the court yard of Burlington House was most splendidly illuminated and had a beautiful Effect. The rooms were brilliant, and looked like a Fairy Palace. Great numbers of people were there when we came in, all the men in full dress Uniforms and the Ladies in plumes, and most rich dresses. The Emperor of Russia with the Duke of Oldenburgh, King of Prussia and all arrived at ten o'clock, I was close to them when they first walked round the Ball room and saw them very plain, they afterwards mix'd in the Crowd and Alexander danc'd the whole evening and flirted with his partners. When the Supper rooms were open'd the effect was quite beautiful, 2000 people set down without any inconvenience or confusion. I stayed till seven o'clock in the morng. and met almost every body I know in London, Fremantle got tired and went home an hour before us. Old Blucher is a delight!

[Yet in spite of these public rejoicings, the year ended sadly: Justina died, and Robert Campbell. 'No two people ever loved each other more or lived happier together than he and poor little Eugenia, she is in the family way, which makes me even more anxious about her.' Betsey writes compassionately.]

CHAPTER 31

[1815 opens with a sad disappointment: Fremantle is made a Knight Commander of the Bath, but 'the Order is quite altered and spoilt, by being divided into three classes. An endless list of new Knights, Fremantle dreadfully annoyed at being placed in the Second class. . . . On March 2nd we are settling our places for going abroad next April and propose staying two years.' But a week later Buonaparte lands at Frejus, and 'we remain at Addington croaking over the news, all our travels are now put an end to.' Fremantle is offered the Cape, or Guernsey and Jersey, or second in the Mediterranean. He accepts Guernsey and Jersey. He goes over first, and there are one or two amusing entries whilst Betsey waits to join him.]

13TH APRIL. SATURDAY. When I first got up this morning, I found the whole Village assembled in the Church yard, to see an old Gypsey woman who died suddenly last night in the lane, I walked to the Church where the Corpse of the wretched woman was laid, merely wrapped up in the blanket she slept in with her black hair all over her head and face, not at all disfigured, the women were just going to wash and dress out the corpse, in the church yd. the daughters and sons of the deceased formed a most interesting Groupe, really all in the most deep affliction. The poor woman had been telling fortunes till quite late last night, apparantly in perfect health, she was in her tent in the lane with her two daughters, complained of sickness in the night and died quite suddenly. After breakfast we all walked to the church, where the corpse was very tidily laid out, it must remain there until it is buried. The poor Gypseys continue in affliction and will not take food until their poor old mother is buried.

15TH APRIL. I am much interested about a poor young Irish woman, who was confined a few days ago and I fear will die in consequence of Turner's being drunk when he attended her.

[Early in June Betsey joins her husband in the islands.]

JUNE 25TH SUNDAY. The Mail brought the account of a grand Victory obtained by the Duke of Wellington, at Waterloo, after three days hard fighting. Buonaparte was compleatly defeated, his whole army dispursed, and near 200 pieces of cannon taken from him. The slaughter of Officers and men quite tremendous, my Husband was obliged to break to Ld. Ponsonby the death of his brother Gen. Ponsonby who was kill'd in the action. A large party of Captains to dinner.

1ST JULY SATURDAY. I was much amused with Mde. de Blesies, a Chouanne, who fought in La Vendee for the last twenty years and was shot through the thigh—she is now going on an expedition to France under the Duc d'Aumont, she is very clever and is writing the Life of the Georges. She assured us that thousands of women had fought with herself and that the wife of La Roche Jacquelin was quite a heroine. [The Fremantles waste no time in crossing to the continent on the 25th July.]

25TH TUESDAY ST. MALO. Our party assembled at Deals by eight o'clock to embark in the Barge which took us on board the *Curaçoa*. We had a fair Breeze, and the frigate was under weigh in an instant, the day was charming, the band played the whole morning upon deck, and just as we sat down to dinner at three o'clock, we were off St. Malo and obliged to wait some time for a Pilot to take us in, the Bay being cover'd with rocks, and the navigation between them very narrow and intricate. We however sailed in very prosperously., and saluted with 20 Guns, but only one, from a shabby battery was returned. When we left the Ship to go on Shore, the Yards were mann'd and both Ships cheer'd us, the walls of the Town, which surround it, were cover'd with people, and on our landing we found the Gate shut. After waiting above a quarter of an hour, the Commandant, a shabby dirty looking man with a wooden Leg, open'd the Gates and made an apology for having kept us waiting so long, the Streets were crowded with an immense multitude of people chiefly woman and children, who vociferated in our Ears, cries of Vive le Roi, and follow'd us to the Hotel des Voyageurs, two National Guards, without uniforms clear'd the way for us, there are no troops in the Town. It stands in a fine bay, entirely surrounded by the sea, excepting a causeway bridge which joints it to the Town of St. Servant at the opposite side of the Bay. The Streets are narrow, and dirty, our Hotel a miserable looking House, kept by Le Roy, whose wife and daughters are attentive and good humour'd and seemed anxious to make everything comfortable for us. My Husband all the Captains and Gentlemen went to call on the Governor, a cross, drunken wretch Le Baron d'Orat, a violent Buonapartist who was not very civil to them. We were told that the appearance of our Ships had greatly alarmed them as they expected 600 English troops were come to Garrison the Town and to levy contributions.

26TH WEDNESDAY. We walked about the Town, I went to several Shops, but found nothing cheap but Shoes.

We had an excellent dinner at four o'clock were much amused by the arrival of a Diligence, with a *Haystack* behind, and all the party was very merry and pleasant. After dinner, the weather being fine we went in the Bay to see Brillantois a Country House about five miles from the Town on the Dinant River, we were follow'd by the Band of the *Curaçoa* in another Boat, which played the whole time and on our landing while we waited for the Key of the Garden Gate, the young party, whose spirits are beyond any thing I ever saw, began to dance, on a Green bank and made us *old ones* join in merrily, excepting Ld. Ponsonby who had climbed the Rocks, and stood on an emminence admiring our picturesque appearance. We then walked all through the Garden of this Chateau quite in the old french style. The grounds and woods are remarkably pretty and command a fine view of the River which is a branch of the sea and about a quarter of a mile wide. The House is small and in a low Situation, it belongs to a Négociant, whose son was very civil to us, but is a violent Buonapartist and seems greatly dissatisfied at the Bourbon Government. He is like all the present race of french young men of this class, whose morals, manners, and irreligion are quite detestable and hateful. It is quite shocking to see the multitude of Boys and children begging about the Streets, brought up to idleness and Ignorance. Just as we reached the Town it began to pour, the Gates were just Shutting, and we had some difficulty in getting in. We all went to Tea, and the Gentlemen supped at l'Hotel de France, with Bonpan, who seems to be a useful personage to them, Luigi plays on the Guittar, amuses them in every way and has no objection to plenty of eating, drinking and smoaking.

27TH THURSDAY. DINANT. We were all up early and the party assembled in the Boats in time for the tide, with a fair wind and a lovely day. We sailed up the Rance follow'd by the Band which played as we pass'd the different Villages and Country Houses, where cries of Vive le Roi cheered us. The sail up this River is charming, the Banks and Scenery very much varied and wooded, and the Country rich. We could not get nearer than within three miles of Dinant, as it is only at Spring tides that there is water enough for Boats to get quite up to it. We therefore landed and all walked, the Boats crew carrying our Luggage, the Band following, in all a party of 50 people. Fearing we should alarm the Dinant people, Mr Scott and Capt. Stirling preceeded us, the former knowing the Mayor well, he went to prepare him for our arrival and we waited at the Spring of Mineral waters, which is in a pretty situation, about a mile from the Town, for their return and for a Horse for Fremantle to ride up the hill, the Town stands very high, and the view as one approaches it is very fine. Mr Scott on his return to us assured us the Mayor (who embraced him tenderly) was determined to receive us in great style, we therefore walked on in full confidence, with our Band playing and all the populace following us, but on nearing the Gate, the Soldiers commanded us to *halt* most surlily threatening to fire upon us if we did not immediately obey, and refused us admittance. Mr Scott argued and said the Mayor had promised to give orders at the Gates, the orders had not been received or they refused to attend to them. However after a little annoyance and difficulty we are allow'd to enter, and we went to the Hotel, in an airy Situation with a public walk before it. We were all too tired to move again before dinner, the little Mayor came to apologize for the rudeness of the Soldiers and promised us every protection. After a tolerable dinner not so good as Mde. Le Roy's performance, we walked to a ruined Castle near Lion's Convent which is also in ruins, nothing can be more delightful than the wood and Valley which leads to it, with the ruin at the bottom, some charming views and I could have wished to have made some stay here to explore all this beautiful Country, the Peasantry all cry Vive le Roi and seem well inclined but the inhabitants of the Town are a horrid Sett, and I do not believe it would be safe to remain in among them, they are expecting to be plunder'd by the Chouans. On our return to the Town the band played before our windows and the young people danced some Reels and Walzes. A few large Stones were thrown in at the windows and at the Band, luckily no one was hurt and we pretended not to perceive it.

28TH FRIDAY. ST. MALO. Our Pilot sent us word to hurry early to the Boats, on account of the tide falling so fast that they would get aground and be obliged to remain here a week, we therefore made great haste, settled with Mde. Thomas who was very civil, and invited us to come and drink the waters in August and walked back to the Boats, a Carriage took Ly. Ponsonby and the Girls, who *roared* the whole way, laughing at the odd vehicle Horses and driver, I admired the Scenery and quite regretted leaving such a pretty Country so soon, in spite of the incivility of the Inhabitants. We just reached the Boats in time and came down the river with the tide and a head wind, which made it more tedious than our sail of yesterday. Towards halfway we met another Man of War's Boat, with Capt. Baldwin, who had orders to bring us the Letters and to my great joy, I soon recognised Charles's *face* of happiness. This meeting made the remaining part of the way most pleasant, hearing all the news, and the accounts of Buonaparte's having reached Plymouth where he is not allowed to land but is to wait orders and it is believed that St. Helena is to be his destination. We arrived at St. Malo at three o'clock, strol'd about Shopping till dinner, hired a little man for a Cook who goes back to Jersey with us, and in the Evening we walk'd on the Ramparts. Next day they returned to Jersey, delighted with our jaunts but quite sorry to break up our pleasant party.

27TH AUGUST. SUNDAY. We are making our arrangements for leaving this the instant we have answers from the Admiralty and shall go in the *Wye* to St. Malo. The usual party to dinner, I went to the Parade. [They were never to return to England during Fremantle's life time.]

8TH FRIDAY. RENNES. We set out from St. Malo at seven o'clock, Fremantle, myself and the three Girls in the Barousche with four Horses and only one driver. Stephen with Wassall and Alain in the Cabriolet and found the road for the first Stage quite detestable and I expected the poor carriage to break down every minute. The Country is cover'd with Trees, and not unlike Jersey on a grand Scale. We found every thing perfectly quiet, there are a great number of Prussian troops at Rennes, but appear peacable and we were not even asked for our Passports. The Hotel des Voyageurs where we lodged very bad. On inquiring about the Route through Tours to Lyons, we find it is quite safe, and as it would take us 60 posts out of the way, going by Bourdeaux and Touloun, we determined to take the former Road, particularly as the South of France is not quite quiet.

9TH SATURDAY. LAVAL. We left Rennes at eight o'clock and were obliged to pay for an additional Horse, hitherto we had only been charged for 6 horses at 30 Sous each and for the two postillions the same which made the expence exactly 12 Lions a poste, a poste is 6 miles. We travell'd very quick to-day, the Horses are good, and it is surprising how they get on, *tackled* in the way they are, with slight ropes for reins and braces, which break every ten minutes. I went one stage in the Cabriolet the roads are very wide and excellent but we were much annoyed with the dust, there has been no rain for three months. This Country is all cover'd with wood, and the greatest profusion of Apples and pears I ever saw, the road is lined with fruit trees, and where ever we stop, quantities of excellent pears are given us for nothing. We arrived at Laval at four o'clock a distance of nine posts and a half. We went to the Louise, a bad Inn, and there being a fair in the Town and great many Prussians, all was uncomfortable, except the dinner which was excellent.

10TH SUNDAY. LA FLECHE. The Hostess at the Louisa very imposing and disagreable. We got off at nine o'clock, and again travelled without the smallest inconvenience and arrived early at La Flêche a very pretty town, 8 postes from Laval, we got very comfortably lodged at the Star, the people civil and *clean*. We walked before dinner to see the College, instituted by Henri IV. It is a very magnificent building. His heart is deposed in the Chapel. There are only 250 Boys now but the College establishment is for 600, it is kept up at the expense of Government and is a very fine institution. The town is very neat and pretty, with a nice walk by the river side. The Country about it is flat, well cultivated, but not so much wooded as Brittany. There is a

Regiment of Prussian Dragoons in La Flêche, all fine young men who volunteer'd, they seem perfectly well behaved, and the woman of the Inn remarked that they were much more civil than their *own* French troops had been.

13TH WEDNESDAY. As the French army occupy all this side on the Loire, and are disbanded at Bourges, by thousands every day, we were advised not to go that way to Lyons, as it might not be safe, but to take the road through Orleans which is on the right of the Loire, and the whole of that Country is occupied by allied troops. Last winter there were above 1500 English here. I went to see the Cathedral, which is a fine Gothic building and the Palace of the Archbishop—there is a handsome Tomb Stone restor'd since the King's return, and put up in the Cathedral, of two children of Charles IX. It stood in the church of St. Martin which was destroyed in the Revolution but this Tomb was concealed and preserv'd. There is another fine Church of St. Julien also destroyed the first year of the Revolution, which is now converted into Stabling for Horses, and where all the Diligences stand, we went to see it, and it is quite shocking to witness such wickedness. The inside is of perfect Gothic Architecture, fine vaulted arches, handsome pillars, now a filthy Stable. We attempted to walk on the Ramparts but it was so sultry and so little to be seen that we came home early. This is a fine Town but it appears dull, there are no public amusements and not a Good Master of any sort.

14TH THURSDAY. ORLEANS. We set out at 8 o'clock from Tours, and were asked for our Passport by the Prussian Commandant at St. Simphorien. The road almost the whole way to Blois, is by the side of the river Loire, about three miles from Tours. The Bank is elevated and pretty enough having several habitations in the rock and some neat Country Houses, but the opposite bank is flat, without trees only now and then a plantation of Poplars. We found the heat oppressive the posting very good and arrived at Blois so early that we came on intending to sleep at Beaujerny, there we found the Inn occupied by Bavarian Officers, and the Eveng. being much cooler and pleasanter for travelling than the middle of the day. We came on to Orleans, having travell'd to-day 14 Postes in less than 13 hours. The Country not at all pretty cover'd with vineyards, which don't give any Grapes this year, not a hill the whole way and only one rather pretty view, a large Chateau the opposite side of the Loire near Amboise.

15TH FRIDAY. We remained at Orleans to-day and have determined to go on to Paris. This is a tolerably fine old Town, with a handsome bridge over the Loire, and there appears to be good Shops. We went to see the Cathedral, the front of it is the most beautiful Gothic Architecture I ever saw, it is not quite finished and the entrance is alloted for keeping Straw and hay. We went into church while the *Salut* was going on et la prière de 40 heures, which is order'd in all the churches, for the present distress'd state of France. It was well attended and the Service done with great solemnity by the Bishop, the one named by Buonaparte but who has never been consecrated another one will probably be named by the King.

16TH SATURDAY. PARIS. We arrived at Paris at eight o'clock, and drove to several Hotels and all over the Town ere we could get Lodgings, we at last met with a very comfortable appartment at L'Hotel Nelson, Rue St. Augustin but are obliged to pay 20 Pounds a week for it.

17TH SUNDAY. I went at ten to the Church of Notre

Dame to high Mass and afterwards to call on the Danvers where we met John Fremantle, Albinia Felton, and Lionel Hervey, and John Wells. Fanny is looking very pretty but thin, they expect Uncle Billy next week with Mrs Fremantle and Eliza, this will make it very comfortable for us. We visited the Louvre this morning, where one is quite lost in the multitude of Chef d'oeuvres of Sculpture and painting. It is quite wonderful to see this Collection, the plunder of all Europe. It would take months to examine the pictures, some of them have been already removed by the Prussians and those belonging to Belgium are to be taken down to-morrow by order of the Duke of Wellington. We drove a great deal about the town and were in admiration at the magnificence of the public buildings, the Thuilleries, Bridges, etc., etc. We dined early and went to the Theatre Fideaux, in the English Ambassador's Box. The Danvers, John and Brinny joined us there. The french singing quite detestable, the Theatre is pretty, but the performance very *caricature*. The piece was Le Czar Prince and Richard Coeur de Lion.

18TH MONDAY. I went with the girls to see the French Monuments, all that were saved from the destruction of the Revolution have been removed and form a Museum. They are chiefly handsome monuments from St. Denis, that of Richelieu, Mazarin, and of the several Kings of France, in the garden the Tomb of Abelard and Eloisa is put up, it was brought here when the Paraclete was sold. We dined at the Hotel and went in the Eveng. to a party at Ly. Kennaird's where all the English soon assembled and a few French. Mr Danvers' Coachman was thrown off the Box in going thru and the Horses ran away, they were not hurt only much frightened. Two young Ladies brought up by Josephine, sung Italian delightfully. They are going to England to teach. Dancing and Cotillions were afterwards danced. The Duse Castiglione was there, wife to Mareshall Nugerau. She is a very handsome woman, ladylike in her manners and danced very well. The Duke of Wellington, and *Grassini* were there. He looks old, Grassini more vulgar in her manner than ever. I met also Charles Steward who is now a great personage and much alter'd in every way since we knew (him) at Ratisbon. The party was very pleasant we came home as they were at supper.

19TH TUESDAY. We went with the Danvers and a party to see the Catacombs, we had to descend fifty feet under Ground and walked at least a mile in subterranean passages where all the Skulls and dead bones collected from all the burying Grounds in Paris, are placed in regular order forming a Wall on each side and a most horrid and melancholy sight, almost the whole of the Town of Paris is excavated under Ground, these vaults are supported by thick walls, it was begun thirty years ago, towards the Center there is an alter where Mass is said once a year on All Souls day. There is a little fountain also where a few little fish are kept alive in these dark Regions of the dead, we carried little wax tapers to light the way, it felt cold and unpleasant. On our return to Fanny's hotel we found two or three frenchmen, among them young Monsr. de Stael, Mde. de Stael's son who speaks English perfectly well.

20TH WEDNESDAY. I call'd on Mrs Loyd and several English who are now here, then went to see the Invalids, a handsome building, where all the Invalided Soldiers and sailors are kept, in a superior style to what they are at Chatham and Greenwich, only 3200 are there now but in the beginning of the Revolution it contained 7000.

21ST THURSDAY. We went with the Danvers to see the Fountains erected by Buonaparte, that of Chateau d'eau is very pretty, the day of his Marriage with Marie Louise, it was fill'd with wine instead of water. We then went to see the model of the fontaine de l'Eléphant, which is to be placed on the spot where the Bastille stood, the Pedestal is begun and we were told is to be finished, the Elephant is so immense that a staircase is to be placed in one of its legs, to lead to the Castle on its back and to Rooms in the inside of its body, it is a sublime idea of old Bonny, and I wish it may be finished, we saw another building nearly accomplished, which was to be Le Magasin de l'Abondance to contain provisions of every kind of live stock to supply the Town of Paris for a Year. We then went over the Bridge of Austerlitz which is beautiful and then went to take a walk round the Palais Royal. The Shops are the most tempting I ever saw, but it is the scene of everything most depraved in Paris. Before the Revolution it was the Palace of the Duke of Orleans. At four o'clock we went to the Place Carousel to see the King drive out in his Carriage driven with eight horses, and follow'd by another the same, empty, he looked very well and happy. We then went into the Palace of the Thuileries which I thought beautiful, but it was so crowded that we hurried through it. In the evening we took the Girls to the Varieties. Mr Acton met us. Potheir's acting was excellent.

22ND FRIDAY. Emma went with her cousins to the Review near Montmartre where Ld. Wellington review'd 80000 men nearly all English. I went to the Louvre Gallery. A great number of fine pictures are gone and the walls are quite bare. I understand every thing is to be restored to its owner and even the Venetian bronze horses in front of the Car on the Carousel, are to be taken down in a few days. The Parisians are quite angry, and say the English are pillaging Paris. The Vcte. d'Agoult call'd upon us, he was particularly civil and is only just return'd from the Country. He advised Fremantle to go to the King to-morrow morng. on his return from Mass. My husband went to a dinner at the Duke of Wellington's at 2 o'clock to meet the Emperor of Austria to whom he was introduced. He return'd quite happy from his dinner, saw the King, the Dsse. d'Agoulésme and Monsieur who were all very gracious to him. I called on the Danvers and went to see the Palais de Luxembourg, where there are several fine pictures of Ruebens, it was the Palace of Marie de Medicis, and the pictures all relate to her life and Regency. There are also all the Seaports of France by Verney. We dined at the Hotel and went to the Theatre Francais where we were in extecies, at the Tartuffe the acting was excellent, and Mde. Mars quite perfect. The afterpiece was also very amusing and well acted. There is no Orchestra and no music between the acts.

23RD SATURDAY. Fremantle went to the Thuileries.

24TH SUNDAY. We went to Mass at St. Roi and at one o'clock at St. Cloud, where a fair was held, and the Gardens were crowded with people, boothes and every sort of Shows. We saw the Palace which is most magnificently furnished and were delighted at the waterworks, the fountains and jets d'Eau are quite beautiful, they only play on jours de fêtes. I am told those at Versailles are still finer. We were sorry to leave St. Cloud so early and only returned near seven to dine at the Danvers where we met a family party, the Wm. Fremantles, John Fremantles etc., etc. I went with them this Eveng. to the Duke of Wellington's where there was a very handsome Assembly, all English. Grassini sung a great deal. Sir Charles Steward inquired after my Sisters and was very civil.

28TH THURSDAY. DIJON. We again set out early and were much pleased with our route, the Country gets hilly and much prettier towards Val de Seize, which is in a deep valley, surrounded by wood and mountains. We passed a Croat Regiment, the women that follow'd it were perfect Gypsies and horrid looking creatures. We arrived early at Dijon, the Austrians have an encampment here of 120000 men and are to be review'd by the Emperor on his passage through here to Milan. There is a triumphal Arch at the entrance of the Town which was put up when Monsieur pass'd here last year.

29TH FRIDAY. DOLE. I walked out after breakfast, went to Mass and in our way back were detained above an hour by an immense number of Austrian troops which marched through the town. There were several Regiments of Cavalry, Hungarians, Bohemians, at least 12000 men. It was a beautiful sight. Fremantle spoke to the Archduke Maximilian who rode at the head of his Regiment, he was very gracious and asked him to remain here to-day but we found the carriages ready on our return to the Hotel, and went on to Dole—rather a miserable place near the Jura Mountains, the Sun very indifferent. We met an English Gentleman with his son, of whom my marito made enquiries respecting the road, and he proved to be an old School-fellow of his named Astley. There is excellent wine made near Dole, we saw all the peasants busy carrying the Grapes in large Carts and squeezing out the Juice. The women were very industrious throughout France, and appear to work as hard as the men.

The whole of this Country is much oppress'd by the multitudes of troops.

1st October. Sunday. Aux Rousses. We rose at day light as usual, and set out early in the hope of reaching Geneva, but towards the end of the Second Stage after ascending some long and dangerous mountains, the post boy discover'd that the front axle Tree of the Carriage was breaking. We were obliged to get out and walk above a mile in a thick fog to the post house at Rousses, the most miserable place I ever saw. It was burnt down and pillaged by the Austrians two months ago, and only a few wretched Houses remain, not a blacksmith in the place and we had no other resource but to remain in this vile place while the carriage was repair'd at Monz, where the fore wheels were sent to in a cart. Nothing can describe the filth of the Inn and the poverty of the place, two Austrian Engineers who are here taking plans of the Country gave us up their rooms, and with the help of a good fire, and Alains Cooking, we kept ourselves from starving. This place is on the summit of the Jura, quite in the clouds and the fog so intense we could not see anything. I went to Vespers, the church well attended, but a miserable place.

2nd Monday. Secheron near Geneva. I never spent so wretched a night, we had two beds made on the dirty floor, for myself and the girls, and the other two beds were occupied by the children and the Admiral. We were all kept awake by the *Fleas*, and by the noise of some Swiss Soldiers. Before day light we were all glad to get up, and were lucky in having a fine day, but not clear enough to walk to the highest part of Jura, call'd the Doss, from where there is a magnificent view over the Pays de Vaud, Monts St. Bernard, Mt. Gothard and Mont. Cenis and we found all was envellop'd in a cloud and therefor we missed our route which is through most picturesque Scenery, the woods are very fine chiefly of fir, mixed with forest trees and the whole *quite Swiss*. From La Vattay the road descends, and the first view of the Lake of Geneva and the surrounding mountains is very fine, at Grex we were plagued by an insolent post master who made us take six horses, the road is through a rich and beautiful valley, with a number of country Houses, vineyards and Orchards. We met Mr Barry who had been to see Voltaire's house which we pass'd. We did not go into the town of Geneva but remain'd at Secheron, a mile from it, where the inn is excellent, on the Lake. We were delighted to get into a clean house, Fremantle met Ld. Cunningham, who invited him to a party at Geneva this eveng. while Ly. C. offer'd to take me and Emma, but I was too tir'd to accept. Mr Barry and his friend a Mr Belsher dined with us. His Carriage broke down in the mountains the same as ours and another axle tree of an English carriage broke also. We had every thing very comfortable here, the House is full of English.

8TH SUNDAY. DOMO DOSSOLA. We were obliged to get up long before day light and set out at six for our long Journey over the Simplon. We began to ascend in the Town of Brigue and continued to mount for eight hours, the same horses go the six posts and back at Berisaal. The road from its width, smoothness and easy ascent is made perfectly safe, and guarded all the way by either strong railing or stone wall. In some places it is broken in and towards the top the precipices are tremendous. We had six horses to our Barousche and three to the Cabriolet. The Scenery is very fine. We eat some cold meat at Berisaal and walked some part of the way. We found the air cold as we got towards the top of the mountain which is always cover'd with snow. When we reached the 6th Refuge we were made to pay forty eight Lions, a tax lately imposed for the keeping up of the road, and we then descended for six miles and we reached the village of Simplon, where we changed horses, and kept on our descending until Iulle the first Italian town. The road down the Simplon is equally good, but the Scenery much more awful, and it must be extremely dangerous in winter and spring on account of the Avalanches. The mountains are on each side of this narrow defile, quite perpendicular. The road follows the river Iosa, which runs with violence, it is cut through the Granite rock, and the largest Gallery through which the route passed is 117 yards, it is under the village Gabbio. One of the bridges was blown up to prevent the passage of the Austrians, and a few iron bars put across to pass it now. It was dark before we reached Domo Dossola, which appears still surrounded by the Alps. The Duke of Bedford arrived about an hour after us with three mails and several servants.

11TH WEDNESDAY. MILAN. ALBERGO D'ITALIA. Fremantle went to Mr Mirabeau the Banker, and walked about in search of lodgings. He was delighted with the Opera last night. Mr Barry arrived in the evening, his carriage broke down again.

17TH TUESDAY. I had a visit this morning from Old Benincasa, my poor Aunt Csse. Rosenberg's *aerium ami*, he is till a fine looking man, 70 yrs. of age, but full of life and spirits, I had not met him since the Countess's death 24 yrs ago. I shall find him a very useful man in procuring masters etc. He is extremely clever, learned and continues to write for the press. We have been treating with Mde. Villa about her House in Porta Romana, and she has at last accepted of 100 Louis for the six months, which is rather dear, but eighty less than was asked at first. The Milanese impose dreadfully upon strangers.

[And so the wheel has come full circle, and Betsey is back in Italy again where first we met her, an Englishwoman Italianate. There is much of the waspish child in her still. Princess Meternich presents her and four other ladies to the Emperor. 'We five ladies rather alarmed the poor, dismal, silly-looking man who hummed a few civil speeches to us and then dismissed us.' 'Mrs Fitzherbert's flirtation with Lord Stuart shocks all the Italian ladies: the Duchess of Sagans is quite abandoned by him. She is much courted by all the Germans, and her having divorced 3 husbands is quite overlooked.'

[Betsey now takes her daughters to the same parties she went to as a girl, the same names occur again, it seems as though Bonaparte and the cursed french, the Revolution and the wars, had never existed. Was it for this, one wonders, the son of St. Louis ascended to heaven and Nelson died at Trafalgar? In order that pretty little Lady Fremantle might give the Miss Fremantles the same sort of good time that was enjoyed by the Miss Wynnes?]

Saturday 27th January. We dined at Prince Metternich's who gave his first gd. dinner to all the great people, he has been suffering with sore eyes—there were about 35 people, a grand set out and magnificent dinner, I sat by fat Diettrichstein and Trottmansdorf the grand Ecuyer, and found it pleasant enough, all the Gentlemen were in full dress, we went in the evening to a Ball at the Dsse. de Sagans, who was kind enough to invite me and the girls altho' I had not been introduced to her, it was the prettiest Ball and the pleasantest we have had yet, the company being select, all good dancers and scarcely any Italians. The Dsse. is really a very charming woman, and I only wish she had not divorced so many husbands. Mrs Fitzherbert was the only English not asked.

[Now the plague is at Naples instead of the Revolution, but the war to make the world safe for aristocracy ended as did the subsequent war to make the world safe for democracy, in a restoration of the status quo ante, with slight changes in personnel.

[The same intelligent interest is shown by Betsey in her thirties as in her teens: they visit a bronze factory.]

FLORENCE. SATURDAY 17TH FEBRUARY. The Marchese di Marignano call'd to take us to Manfredini's Bronze Manufactory, it is a very fine establishment and the gilding and work almost as good as at Paris, but unfortunately it will not be kept up, as it receives no support or encouragement from the Austrian Government. We saw a very beautiful clock which is made from the design of Guido's Aurora, the price is 22000 francs, the Emperor refused it, thinking it too dear, every article of jewellery is also made very neatly and the prices appeared to be moderate. We afterwards went to see Rafael's mosaics, the large picture of our Lord's Supper is nearly completed, and is the largest and finest mosaic work which has ever been attempted, it really is as beautiful as any painting, it will be finished in a year, and then this fine establishment is also at an end, the variety of mosaic ornaments is great and some are lovely. I went to the Opera this evening with Ctss. Crivelli, poor Bandiralli had his fine Manteau stolen out of our Ante-room while he was giving Emma her singing lesson, the two men servants were gone down and had left the door open. The robbing just now is dreadful, scarcely a night passes without some person being stabb'd, owing to the numbers of people out of employment and who are actually starving with their families.

FRIDAY 23RD FEBRUARY. Marchese Marignano call'd for us this morning at nine o'clock to take us to one of his farms, seven miles out of Town on the Pavia road to see the process of making the large Parmesan Cheeses. We walked all over this farm, which is one of the largest, about 124 cows, 30 large bullocks, 24 horses, I was much surprised to see the women and children of the Parish all collected in the Cow Houses, there they live entirely, and merely go to their homes to dinner and to sleep, the farther end of all these stables are allotted to them, there they sit, spin and rock their children who are lying in their wooden cradles, some *au maillot*, others quite naked, the poor brats are kept horribly dirty without caps on their heads, and the women themselves told me they never washed them now because the water was too cold, even gentlemen's children who are now generally sent out to nurse are kept in the winter, with the rest of the peasants, among the Cows, the heat is excessive, but I should think not at all unwholesome, this custom exists all over Lombardy—We went into the dairy which is not so nice as our English dairies and all the work is done by men, the butter is churned every day, and the milk is afterwards put into a large copper over a slow fire, with something to curd it until it becomes a hard substance, a man then lays over the Copper to place a cloth cover, it is then taken out, weighing 60 or 70 pounds, and put into tubs to salt, they are not good to eat under two years, one is made every day—We also saw the rice thrashed out, a great quantity and of the best quality is grown in this country which makes it unwholesome. Mr Marignano gave us an excellent breakfast and then drove us home.

SUNDAY, 25TH FEBRUARY. I call'd to see poor Benincasa who is dying of an indigestion he took at the fête de la Noblesse. He knew me but seems to suffer much and not likely to live till to-morrow. His son is not yet come, he is quite aware of his danger, and has received all the Sacraments, a Lady attends him who has been very attentive to him—he merely said Ah bonne Milady, je suis un Malheureux, qui souffre beaucoup que le bon Dieu vous benisse—I took a turn at the Corso after this melancholy visit it was very full, the Empress came in her carriage with her Mother at three o'clock.

[After twenty-five years, Betsey returns to Venice. 'I recollected it perfectly.' Mary Montalbano meets her again, with her son, who behaves very ill, she is just the same, only thinner. The Fremantles lead the same semi-highbrow life the Wynnes led: meet Canova, Pauline and Lucien Bonaparte. 'Prince Borghese's mother was a very clever woman and disliked intensely the Prince's marriage with Pauline. He never lived an instant happily with her and soon after his marriage complained to his mother whose answer was "Mon fils, quand on épouse 10,000 bayonettes on n'est pas couché sur des roses." Felton Hervey married Miss Bacon sister to Jerome Buonaparte's wife Mrs. Patterson.'

[In 1816 Fremantle was given the command in the Mediterranean, and with his family struck his flag in the *Rochfort*. Life on board amuses Betsey: they convey Metternich and his daughter; the Dukes of Kent and Devonshire wrote for favours or thanked for them.

[Life went on merrily until December 1819, when on Friday Nov. 5 the admiral writes 'Set a woman to work about my shirts.' That was his last entry. On Friday, December 17th, Betsey enters 'We all went to Lady A'Court's party, it was hot.' Two days later Fremantle was dead. On New Year's day 1820 Betsey writes a post scriptum to that death, the first event in her whole life that had caused her to miss writing daily in her journal.]

SUNDAY, 1ST JANUARY. Since the sudden, awful and most heavy loss I sustained I have been involved in too much sorrow and misery to attempt giving any account of an event so calamitous in its consequences, and for which I was so little prepared. A year which had begun with every prospect of happiness has ended with a misfortune which must weigh heavy upon us, but I must submit to the will of providence and bear my heavy affliction with christian fortitude. I shall give as short an account as possible of these distressing moments, they can never be obliterated from my mind and are too painful to look back to. On Saturday, 18th Decr. my dearest and ever to be deplored Husband, was perfectly well, took his usual drive, and seemed in very good spirits at dinner. He took his nap after dinner, and Emma having a bad cold stayed at home, and he said he should stay also. I went to Psse. Sablonowika with Augusta and Captn. Green, and when I came home before twelve o'clock, I found they had all gone to bed. Mr Munro sent to me at daylight to say the Admiral was not well, I immediately went to him and found him complaining very much of the pain and palpitation at his heart, which he was subject to, he had been sick, his servant sat up with him all night and he had drank a quantity of wine and water, above a bottle of white wine. I thought this had affected his head, for he talked in his sleep very incoherently and we sent for Dr. Reilly and also Dr.

Griffith. Mr Reilly bled him the moment he came, and this seemed to relieve his side and his breathing, but he remained in a state of stupour and perfectly insensible. Griffith came at eleven, bled him again and called in Dr Shortt everything which art could suggest was done, he was put in a hot bath of rum and salt water, had three blisters applied—but thus nothing could save him and he expired at ten o'clock without a groan or struggle—without a warning of his approaching end—and we are left to deplore his fate and the full weight of our Loss—I was not with him at the dreadful moment. I did not apprehend any immediate danger and the Doctors wished me out of the way—I scarcely know how I bore the blow, poor Charles was sent for and arrived in the night, his feelings can be easily conceived, he had left his father quite well on Saturday and found him a corpse on Sunday night. The kindness I have experienced from all my friends is beyond anything that can be said—as also Captn. Green and Mr Munro's exertions and friendly behaviour. The King who was much affected on hearing of this dreadful event, granted that the burial might take place with military honors—and Genl. Nugent came forward most handsomely on the occasion—the last duties were performed on Wedy. 22, attended by all the officers, almost all the English here, cavalry, and troops and the Neapolitan Marines and followed by fifty carriages, Duke of Leeds, Ld. Whitworth, Ld. Spencer, in short all the English were there and have shown the regard and respect they bore my departed Husband. Sir Wm. à Court sent an express to England, this will be a sad blow to Wm. Fremantle and poor Tom, who I fear will find himself in great difficulties at first, I do not know whether he has yet set out and I shall not be able to determine what to do until I hear from England, but probably I shall remain at Naples till the Summer. I have everything about me very comfortable and I cannot bear to move, I could not see anybody until Wednesday the 29th, when I had a visit from Ly. Lushington, and the following days I saw Ly. Alvanley, Ct. and Ctss. Nugent, the Dss of Leeds and Mrs Pellew—the weather has continued horrid, incessant rain and my poor Girls cannot even walk out, and look wretched.